Philosophies of Self

EXPANDING PHILOSOPHY OF RELIGION

Series Editors:
J. Aaron Simmons, Furman University, USA
Kevin Schilbrack, Appalachian State University, USA

A series dedicated to a global, diverse, cross-cultural, and comparative philosophy of religion, Expanding Philosophy of Religion encourages underrepresented voices and perspectives and looks beyond its traditional concerns rooted in classical theism, propositional belief, and privileged identities.

Titles in the series include:
Philosophical Hermeneutics and the Priority of Questions in Religions,
by Nathan Eric Dickman
Philosophies of Religion, by Timothy Knepper
Diversifying Philosophy of Religion, edited by Nathan R. B. Loewen and
Agnieszka Rostalska
Collective Intentionality and the Study of Religion, by Andrea Rota
Engaging Philosophies of Religion, by Gereon Kopf, Purushottama Bilimoria and
Nathan R. B. Loewen
Rethinking Religious Conversion, by Jack Williams
Philosophies of Liturgy, edited by J. Aaron Simmons, Bruce Ellis Benson
and Neal DeRoo
Art, Desire, and God, edited by Kevin G. Grove (Anthology Editor),
Christopher C. Rios (Anthology Editor), Taylor J. Nutter (Anthology Editor)
Art Making as Spiritual Practice, by Lexi Eikelbloom and David Newheiser
Rethinking Philosophy of Religion with Wittgenstein, by Thomas D. Carroll
Reimagining Philosophy of Religion, by Amber L. Griffioen
Material Spirituality, by Neal DeRoo

Philosophies of Self

A Cross-Cultural Introduction

Edited by Nathan R. B. Loewen
and Agnieszka Rostalska

BLOOMSBURY ACADEMIC
LONDON • NEW YORK • OXFORD • NEW DELHI • SYDNEY

BLOOMSBURY ACADEMIC
Bloomsbury Publishing Inc, 1359 Broadway, New York, NY 10018, USA
Bloomsbury Publishing Plc, 50 Bedford Square, London, WC1B 3DP, UK
Bloomsbury Publishing Ireland, 29 Earlsfort Terrace, Dublin 2, D02 AY28, Ireland

BLOOMSBURY, BLOOMSBURY ACADEMIC and the Diana logo are trademarks
of Bloomsbury Publishing Plc

First published in Great Britain 2026

Copyright © Nathan R. B. Loewen and Agnieszka Rostalska and Contributors 2026

Nathan R. B. Loewen and Agnieszka Rostalska and Contributors have asserted
their right under the Copyright, Designs and Patents Act, 1988, to be
identified as Authors of this work.

For legal purposes the Acknowledgements on p. xiv constitute an
extension of this copyright page.

Cover design by Louise Dugdale
Cover image © Space wind / Alamy Stock Photo

All rights reserved. No part of this publication may be: i) reproduced or transmitted in
any form, electronic or mechanical, including photocopying, recording or by means of
any information storage or retrieval system without prior permission in writing from the
publishers; or ii) used or reproduced in any way for the training, development or operation
of artificial intelligence (AI) technologies, including generative AI technologies. The rights
holders expressly reserve this publication from the text and data mining exception as per
Article 4(3) of the Digital Single Market Directive (EU) 2019/790.

Bloomsbury Publishing Plc does not have any control over, or responsibility for,
any third-party websites referred to or in this book. All internet addresses given in
this book were correct at the time of going to press. The author and publisher regret
any inconvenience caused if addresses have changed or sites have ceased to exist,
but can accept no responsibility for any such changes.

A catalogue record for this book is available from the British Library.

A catalog record for this book is available from the Library of Congress.

ISBN: HB: 978-1-3504-6366-0
PB: 978-1-3504-6367-7
ePDF: 978-1-3504-6368-4
eBook: 978-1-3504-6369-1

Typeset by RefineCatch Limited, Bungay, Suffolk
Printed and bound in Great Britain

For product safety related questions contact productsafety@bloomsbury.com.

To find out more about our authors and books visit www.bloomsbury.com
and sign up for our newsletters.

We dedicate this book to Purushottama Bilimoria, whose ongoing legacy includes generous gifts to us both. His scholarship is the original inspiration for ours. Purushottama, you have our profound thanks for your mentorship, collegiality, and friendship.

Contents

List of Illustrations x
Notes on Contributors xi
Acknowledgments xiv

Introduction   Nathan R. B. Loewen 1

1. **Udayana's Concept of the Self and Arguments for Its Existence and Persistence**   Agnieszka Rostalska 15
   1.1 *Ātman* 31
   1.2 Persistence 36

2. **The Making of the Person in Candomblé**
   José Eduardo Porcher 41
   2.1 *Ori* 55
   2.2 *Santo* 61
   2.3 *Assento* 66

3. **Self and Identity in Jainism**   Anil Mundra 71
   3.1 *Anekāntavāda* 82
   3.2 Identity 86
   3.3 Liberation 89

4. **Shinto: Indescribable Description of Self and Persistence**
   Maki Sato 93
   4.1 *Harae*: Purification of *Tsumi*, *Toga*, and *Kegare* 108
   4.2 *Kotodama*: Value-Neutrality and Multilayered-ness 114
   4.3 *Tama and* Dynamism: Unpredictable Spirit Freed from Human Consequences 120

5. **Selfhood in the Classical Confucian Tradition**
   Andrew Lambert 125

   5.1 Humaneness (*Ren* 仁) 143
   5.2 Ritual (*Li* 禮) 148
   5.3 Filial Conduct (*Xiao* 孝) 153

6. **Tshivenda, Self, and Persistence** *Mutshidzi Maraganedzha* 159

   6.1 *Murunzi* 176
   6.2 *Sialala* 179

7. **Embodying the Dao: Classical and Foundational Daoist Anthropological Views** *Louis Komjathy* 183

   7.1 Pneumatology 201
   7.2 *Shēn* 身 (Body/Self) 205
   7.3 Somatology 209

8. **The *Nguni* Conceptualization of *umina/ubumina* (the Self): Analyzing *Impilo*, *Umoya* and *Ukufa* through Isintuism** *Herbert Moyo* 215

   8.1 *Impilo* (Life) 227
   8.2 *Ukafa* (Death): A Cultural and Spiritual Perspective 230
   8.3 Umoya/Imimoya 233

9. **The Relative Self: Native American Conceptualizations of the Self** *Fritz Detwiler* 237

   9.1 *Hózhǫ and Hóchxǫ*: Walking in Beauty 252
   9.2 *Mitákuye Oyásiŋ* 257
   9.3 Tlingit: *at.oow* 262

10. **Iqbal and the Actualizing Self: Gift or Task?**
    Abraham H. Khan 267

    10.1 Immortality 280
    10.2 *'Ishq*/Love 284

11. **A Plural Conception of Self: Reading Jacques Derrida**
    Nathan R. B. Loewen 287
    11.1 Ipseity 301
    11.2 Secrecy 305
    11.3 Sovereignty 310

Epilogue: Comparative Philosophical Conclusions
    Tim D. Knepper 317

Index 329

Illustrations

Figures

4.1	Tsukumogami of the kitchenware	101
4.2	Oonusa on the left from Oomiwa Shrine in Nara	109
4.3	Spring water for *misogi*, Kifune shrine, Kyoto	110
4.4	Torii gate of the Oomiwa Shrine in Nara	111

Tables

7.1	The Five Phases with Associated Faculties	186

Notes on Contributors

Fritz Detwiler is retired from his position as Professor of Philosophy, Religion, and Leadership at Adrian College, USA. He researches Native American/First Nations philosophy, worldviews, and lifeways with particular emphasis on ontology and ethics. His publications include *Standing on the Premises of God: The Christian Right's Fight to Redefine America's Public Schools* (1999) and *Cosmology and Moral Community in the Lakota Sun Dance* (2022).

Abraham H. Khan is Professor in the Faculty of Divinity at Trinity College, of the Toronto School of Theology, associated with the graduate Department for the Study of Religion at the University of Toronto, Canada. He is the general editor of the *Toronto Journal of Theology* and convenor of the Kierkegaard Circle, as well as the author of "A Hint of Divine Rahmah in Iqbal's *'Ishq*,'" *Man in India* (2009), "Tagore and Kierkegaard as Resources for Political Theology," in Silas Morgan and Roberto Sirvent (eds.), *Kierkegaard and Political Theology* (2018), "Understanding (Forstand) in Kierkegaard's Religious Discourses," in Gerard Schreiber (ed.), *Interesse am Anderen* (2019), and with Sandra Dixon, "Christianity and Healing on Mental Health," in *Routledge International Handbook of Race, Ethnicity, and Culture in Mental Health*, ed. Roy Moodley and Eunjung Lee (2020).

Timothy D. Knepper is Professor of Philosophy at Drake University, USA, where he directs the Comparison Project. He is the author of *The Ends of Philosophy of Religion* (2013), *Negating Negation* (2014) and the pioneering *Philosophies of Religion: A Global and Critical Introduction* (2022). He is the editor of *Death and Dying: An Exercise in Comparative Philosophy of Religion* (2019) and *Miracles: An Exercise in Comparative Philosophy of Religion* (2022).

Louis Komjathy 康思奇 is Director, Chóngxuán 重玄 Chair, and Distinguished Scholar-in-Residence at Center for Daoist Studies 道學中心, USA. In addition to over forty academic articles and book chapters, he has published fourteen books to date, including *Dàodé jīng* 道德經: *A Contextual, Contemplative, and Annotated Bilingual Translation* (2023) and *Traces of a Daoist Immortal: Chén Tuán* 陳摶 *of the Western Marchmount* (2024).

Andrew Lambert is Associate Professor of Philosophy at City University of New York, College of Staten Island, USA. His research focuses on ethics and Chinese thought, particularly the relationship between personal attachment and conceptions of moral conduct. His publications include "Impartiality, Close Friendships and the Confucian Tradition" (2017) and "Confucian Ethics and Care: An Amicable Split?" in Mathew Foust and Sor-Hoon Tan (eds.), *Feminist Encounters with Confucius* (2016).

Nathan R. B. Loewen is Associate Professor in the Department of Religious Studies at the University of Alabama, USA. He has primary areas of research and publication: globalizing discourses within the philosophy of religion, analyzing the confluence between Religious Studies and Development Studies, and engaging a critical digital pedagogy. He co-edited with Agnieszka Rostalska the volume *Diversifying Philosophy of Religion: Critiques, Methods, and Case Studies* (2023) and with Gereon Kopf and Purushottama Bilimoria *Engaging Philosophies of Religion: Thinking across Boundaries* (2025). His is the author of *Beyond the Problem of Evil: Derrida and Anglophone Philosophy of Religion* (2018).

Mutshidzi Maraganedzha is Lecturer at the University of Kwa-Zulu Natal, South Africa. His research interests are in African philosophy and the philosophy of race. He is the author of "*A Normative Approach: Can We Eliminate Race?* 'The Function of "It" in Ifeanyi Menkiti's Normative Account of Personhood: A Response to Bernard Matolino" (2017) and co-author with Motsamai Molefe of "African Traditional Religion and Moral Philosophy" (2023).

Herbert Moyo is Associate Professor in the School of Religion, Philosophy and Classics at the University of Kwazulu-Natal, South Africa. His research as a comparative philosopher involves interests in demonstrating that, among the Nguni people of Southern Africa, "religion" is neither monotheistic nor a belief system. Moyo's publications include, "Isintuism the Mother of Communalism among the Nguni of Southern Africa," in Gereon Kopf, Purushottama Bilimoria and Nathan R. B. Loewen (eds.), *Engaging Philosophies of Religion* (2025).

Anil Mundra is Assistant Professor and Bhagwan Vimalnath Chair of Jain Studies and South Asian Religions in the Department of Religious Studies of the University of California, Santa Barbara, USA. His research focuses on how South Asian philosophers navigate religious diversity, especially in Sanskrit texts on the classical Jain theory of non-one-sidedness (*anekāntavāda*). He is the author of "Commonality and Difference: Jain Philosophical Approaches to Interreligious Studies," in *The Georgetown Companion to Interreligious Studies*, ed. Lucinda Allen Mosher (2022), "The Haribhadrasūri Philosophical Program," *Newsletter of the Centre of Jaina Studies at SOAS* (2024), and translated with introductory commentary an extract from

Haribhadrasūri's *Introduction to the Doctrine of Non-one-Sidedness*, in *Global Philosophy: A Sourcebook*, ed. Mohammed Rustom (2025).

José Eduardo Porcher is Senior Lecturer at the Federal University of Rio Grande do Sul, Brazil. He led the project *Expanding the Philosophy of Religion by Engaging with Afro-Brazilian Traditions* (2021–4), funded by the John Templeton Foundation, USA, and is the author of *Afro-Brazilian Religions* (2025).

Agnieszka Rostalska is an FWO Senior Postdoctoral Research Fellow at the Faculty of Arts and Philosophy of Ghent University, Belgium. She specializes in Indian and Cross-Cultural Philosophy, focusing on sociopolitical philosophy, epistemology, and philosophy of religion. In 2022, she was a co-PI in the project "Cross-cultural Conceptions of the Self: South Asia, Africa, and East Asia" awarded by the University of Birmingham, UK, and by the John Templeton Foundation, USA. She is President of the Logic and Religion Association, and an executive board member of the Society for Asian and Comparative Philosophy and the Global-Critical Philosophy of Religion Unit of the American Academy of Religion, USA. Rostalska co-edited with Nathan R. B. Loewen the volume *Diversifying Philosophy of Religion: Critiques, Methods and Case Studies* (2023).

Maki Sato has a PhD in Global Studies from the University of Tokyo, Japan. She is Van Bragt Fellow at the Nanzan Institute for Religion and Culture, Japan. Her research field is environmental philosophy, expanding her interest to the philosophy of religion to investigate the deeper layer regarding the relationship between humans and nature. She co-authored with Jonathan McKinney and Tony Chemero "Habit, Ontology, and Embodied Cognition Without Borders: James, Merleau-Ponty, and Nishida," in Fausto Caruana and Italo Testa (eds.), *Habits: Pragmatist Approaches from Cognitive Neuroscience to Social Science* (2021).

Acknowledgments

Our sincere thanks go first to this volume's contributors, who approached the project with open minds. They responded to a project plan that is at least one step removed from their wide-ranging, considerable expertise.

We chose to affiliate this volume with the idea of global-critical philosophy of religion (GCPR), which originated with Tim Knepper and Gereon Kopf. Their initiative led to the support of the American Academy of Religion for a five-year seminar as well as several grant-funded workshops. "GCPR" may be framed in terms of the ongoing conversations among dozens of scholars around the world about how to rejuvenate philosophy of religion. As with religious studies and philosophy, scholars in this subfield risk sustaining indefensible legacies of cultural imperialism without fundamentally diversifying its methodologies and topics. We hope that the program unit of the same title will be an ongoing feature of that Academy, and perhaps at other venues. We believe that GCPR is best thought of as a philosophical community of questioners.

We wish to acknowledge the support of several institutions that made this project possible. Many of us were involved in the 2022 project, "Cross-Cultural Conceptions of Self and Persistence," which was funded by a subaward from a grant provided by the John Templeton Foundation to the Global Philosophy of Religion Project (GPRP) at the University of Birmingham, UK. We thank Yujin Nagasawa for his leadership of the GPRP. The opinions expressed in this publication are those of the author(s) and do not necessarily reflect the views of the John Templeton Foundation or the GPRP. Administrative support to Nathan R. B. Loewen was provided by the Department of Religious Studies at the University of Alabama, USA. Ongoing technical support for the project website is provided by the Barefield College of Arts and Sciences at UA. Ghent University, Belgium, processed the subcontract that provided project support to Agnieszka Rostalska. In 2024, Sapienza University in Rome, Italy, provided the venue for several contributors to present drafts of their chapters at the XXV World Congress of Philosophy. We therefore acknowledge the duplicity of any claims that any scholarly work is solely the outcome of a named author.

Lastly, we acknowledge our indebtedness to everyone for the profound shortcomings of this volume. It is an experiment that was written in English. It is produced through Western institutions and corporate entities whose legacies very likely involve marginalization, at the very least, of several social groups and peoples from around the world through history and perhaps even the present. As Jacques Derrida's works regularly remind their readers, we can always know and do better.

Introduction

Nathan R. B. Loewen

Chapter Outline

Why Self?	1
Global Contents	2
A Critical Wager	11

Why Self?

Philosophy does work with concepts. Philosophical communities share the task of developing concepts through announcing, defining, and debating concepts. These communities share the commitment that ideas matter. Each community sustains their concepts through practices and methods that sharpen their conceptual distinctions and disambiguation. The distinction between person and self in English-language philosophy is just one example of a conceptual bifurcation practiced by one such philosophical community.

How might we investigate conceptualizations of "self" relative to communities from around the world? What philosophical approaches might enable cross-cultural analysis? These are open questions addressed by this volume, which introduces a variety of sources for learning about and evaluating philosophical conceptions of the self that are developed in relation to contexts from around the world. What is the nature of the self? Are monadic and/or possessive individual conceptions necessary for the concept? How might discussing "self" enable work across cultures? As such, this volume adds to scholarship that broadens philosophy of religion in terms of scope as well as critical reflexivity.[1] We hope this present volume builds on our previous effort, *Diversifying Philosophy of Religion* (2023). Beyond that subfield, philosophers who specialize on the topic will notice that the volume conspicuously side-steps most recent English-language scholarship on self. The chapters include discussions of Indian, Native American, South Asian Muslim, French post-structuralist, African/Venda, Jain, African/Candomblé, and Shinto traditions. The contents of this volume emerge from an online project in 2022 that involved eleven scholars located in just as many time zones across four continents. Support for the project was also circuitous. It was hosted by the University of Alabama with funding from the John Templeton Foundation distributed through the University of Birmingham. That project is part of an overall initiative that goes by "Global-Critical Philosophy of Religion."[2] We hope this book volume makes a substantive contribution to a future for philosophy of religion by presenting readers with cross-cultural philosophical investigations of self. We hope readers will find this volume useful to introduce sources of thought they might not encounter elsewhere.

Global Contents

The structure of the volume breaks with the orientalist, epistemic problematics of the "East–West" dichotomy by presenting chapter-length contributions that are each accompanied by short essays which elaborate upon key concepts in their respective chapters. These short essays situate the concepts' definition, philosophical significance, and historical context, based on the relevant works of key figures within cultural locations they appear. We decided to present the volume's contents without any sections or divisions. That decision emerged from concerns about unduly reproducing indefensible assumptions. The utility of section titles risks playing against the cross-cultural interests that brought the volume together in the first place. We want readers to make their own connections. They may opt to compare foundational ideas, track down the contributor's suggestions for further research, or, choose a combination of essays for an in-depth cross-cultural study. The volume's design therefore enables comparative inquiries into Self that do not assimilate their contents to an Enlightenment or Christian scheme. It emphasizes several underrepresented and relatively unknown paradigms developed within the intellectual histories of worldviews and voices of the representatives of traditions coming from South Asia, Africa, East Asia, and South America.

The opening chapter of this volume, by **Agnieszka Rostalska**, focuses on the thought of Udayana, who lived and wrote in South Asia during the tenth century CE. Like most of the figures mentioned in this volume, Udayana is likely unknown to many philosophical audiences. The ideas of Udayana will seem familiar, since his most prominent works make arguments for the existence of an all-knowing *God and for the existence of an individuated self. Rostalska uses an asterisk to note that

Udayana's proposals result in a *God that is not identical to the entity described by Abrahamic monotheisms or philosophical theism. That said, Rostalska's introduction of Udayana includes an interesting parallel with Thomas Aquinas. The work of Udayana forms an important, if not foundational, element of the Nyāya tradition of South Asian philosophy and present-day Naiyāyika philosophers.

The historical context for Udayana's works is the intense debates he conducted with philosophies of his time in South Asia. These included materialist, Jain, and Buddhist philosophers of the tenth to eleventh century CE. The focus of Udayana was on the logic of his interlocutors, where he argued for the actual, persistent existence of individual entities against those who argued that entities were either illusory or impermanent. For those interested in the various atheistic India philosophies, Rostalska's chapter outlines these competing views prior to Udayana's arguments.

Rostalska introduces us to Udayana's thought about of *ātman*, which is likely a familiar term to anyone who has read classical South Asian philosophy. Udayana employs *ātman* to develop an ontology of a self that is different from the senses, is the epistemic center of knowing, and is a continuously enduring substance. Rostalska outlines how Udayana makes these claims while also separating the self from any specific body. While Udayana did not originally propose the Nyāya conception of the self as a given, his arguments are the most rigorous defense of this inherited conception of self. From Udayana's perspective, his arguments decisively defeat both the Buddhists and materialists of his time. Rostalska explains how Udayana reverses the impact of Buddhist arguments about *karma*, and upends materialist claims about causation. Udayana's conception of *niḥśreyasa*, or the "ultimate state," is shown by Rostalska to explain the persistence of an essential self by virtue of an epistemic soteriology that releases the self from indeterminate cognition that is unique to his conception of *ātman*.

The objective of this volume is to introduce overlooked philosophies. The topic of self is secondary, since it is merely the occasion to gather experts into a single volume. Claims about necessary or essential topics, at least for this sub-field, have only worked to narrow its scope. **José Eduardo Porcher**'s chapter brings readers to the philosophical discussion of Candomblé. Porcher's chapter is suggestive of the fact that while many other humanist disciplines and fields conduct cultural studies on cultures such as Candomblé, philosophy generally does not and rarely offers an explanation or defense for the practice of overlooking philosophies from around the world. Rather than dwell at all on this point, we might assume that Porcher grants us the competency to work out the merits of his scholarship on our own. Porcher moves directly into explaining the social and historical context of Candomblé so that we might learn the relevant conception of self.

After introducing the historical circumstances of African slavery in South American colonial regimes, Porcher begins explaining the ontological categories that may be explained on the basis of Candomblé mythology. Attentive readers will understand how Porcher alternates the English terminology of "Supreme Being" and "deities" with terms from the languages of the myths and their teachings. Understanding the arrangement of supreme or divine beings enables Porcher to explain how individuals are conceived, where individuals are not limited to Western physicalism. He writes that "every person is governed by specific *orixás*," but this is nothing like soul, for example. The important understanding is that the so-called inanimate and the living are permeated by forces whose interplay and alignment is a matter to which humans should give their attention. Thus, the self is conceived as dynamic, and practices such as initiation and possession are important to negotiate spiritual energies such that the personality of the self emerges. Porcher's extensive descriptions are crucial for readers to understand the Candomblé conception of "self" as a ritually constructed space to house an entity characterized by multiplicity.

Readers wondering why Buddhist philosophies are not included in this volume would be well-served to read the entries from Komjathy, Lambert, Rostalska, and Mundra. As with the other three, **Anil Mundra**'s chapter on Haribhadrasūri provides some important historical context that helps situate the copious literature on Buddhist philosophy that pre-exists this volume. Mudra's chapter likewise makes an important connection to the similarly vast Western literature on the topics related to self that ranges from St. Augustine through the Enlightenment to contemporary philosophy, phenomenology, psychology, and cognitive science. Mundra begins with the challenge Haribhadrasūri's thought poses to conceptions of numerical identity as the basis for thinking self-sameness. That starting point is an important cue for understanding how important cross-cultural knowledge is for critical investigations of seemingly settled categories of thought. Mundra's chapter explains how Haribhadrasūri's formulation of non-one-sidedness presents important problems for thinking about identity in terms of multiple singularities.

Mundra surveys how Jain philosophers prefigured discussions about the relations of substances and qualities in Western, Enlightenment thought. He shows how debates among Jain philosophers are shown to helpfully parse the differences between Aristotle and Kant, drawing upon Haribhadra's works to criticize Sydney Shoemaker's much later problem of explaining how a qualitative identity might coalesce around an individual self with a personal identity. Mundra proposes one answer by investigating Jain philosophizing around Jain soteriology: How does individual liberation from karma work for entities that live multiple existences? A response comes via a critique of Buddhist philosophy and an emphasis on intentional awareness in the context of Jain ascetic practices.

Maki Sato's chapter enables readers to understand the philosophical resources of a tradition with which they may be familiar on the surface. Shinto (神道) ideas are popularized through various cultural media. The philosophical investigation of Shinto, however, is not common in Western literature. Sato's focuses this chapter on the concepts of tama (霊 or 魂), kami (神) and , kotodama (言霊) in order to explain how there is no persistent, same "self" in Shinto. The understanding of self that Sato derives from surveying Shinto is that of a neutral entity that responds to its environment. The practices of Shinto, then, are to mitigate impurities that would prevent proper relationships to the environment.

Sato's survey of Shinto is based on Shinto rituals and practices, which generate a particular collective sensibility among the practitioners. While acknowledging the connection to nationalist ideology after the Meiji period and the development of State Shinto (国家神道), Sato chooses to focus on both received and scholarly sources that emerge upon the separation of Shinto from the state enforced by the political outcomes of World War Two. Sato explains the idea that *tama* are divine spirits that may inhabit any entity, object or natural phenomenon. *Kami* name such instances of manifestation in substantial existence, which is ambivalent in terms of both morality and gender. *Kami* may cease without any necessary cause. The ambivalent neutrality of *Tama*, and correlatively of any *Kami*, is explained to be sympathetic to the Buddhist ideas that are often found within Shinto. Sato thereby explains the philosophy of Motoori Norinaga and Hirata Atsutane, who both predate the Meiji State Shinto. The sense of self that emerges from Sato's discussion is that Shinto ritual practices of venerating objects, showing respect for nature, and purifying the body are meant to both preserve and respect the dynamism of a world influenced by *tama* and *kami*. Beyond the important survey of Shinto conceptions of self related in the above, the final sections of Sato's chapter introduce new existential interpretations of Shinto thought.

"Self" is not necessarily a topic or problem for many philosophies. Many authors in this volume took up the challenge of discerning the topic in systems of thought. **Andrew Lambert** offers us a study of self in the canonical texts of early Confucian thought to offer insights into the nature of the self. Lambert, much like Moyo's chapter (see later), emphasizes the simple fact that there is no corresponding term for "self" in early Chinese texts. Lambert considers whether this fact is an outcome of the overarching context, where the concerns of Anglo-European and early Chinese philosophies do not directly map onto each other. If a definitive Confucian theory of self is impossible, then the cross-cultural upshot of Lambert's observations is not that "self" is somehow *there* despite Confucian thought. Nor is his point that there is no self at all in Confucian thought. Most readers already know we must be more sophisticated than this. The point is that "self" is not a natural kind, and also "natural" is not universal. Humans are often tempted to think that accretions of discussion around a topic somehow amounts to something being real. Scholars must always precaution themselves against this temptation.

Lambert identifies Herbert Fingarette's scholarship to be useful for exploring plausible grounds to theorize conceptions of self in Confucian philosophies. Fingarette's basic work on the topic helps us understand how early Chinese philosophy was not necessarily concerned with existential actualization of subjectivity. Lambert notes limitations in Fingarette's work that may be addressed by wider considerations of discussions about relationships and virtues in Confucian thought. These considerations also must be better informed, since Lambert finds they do not account for the Confucian emphasis on individual reflective capacities or the fact that it is individuals who willfully apply themselves towards the Confucian way (dao 道). Lambert explains the conception of emerging selfhood, which, reading the Confucian classic The Great Learning (Daxue 大學), a self by reflecting upon psychic and bodily relations with ever wider cosmic realms. The self is an emergent product of social and practical interactions. Lambert emphasizes how all of these findings are scholarly constructions that are easily recognized as influenced by interests in psychology, ideology, and patriarchy. Lambert's conclusion restates how any conception of self is always related to a larger framework of interests in social and political order.

Mutshidzi Maraganedzha provides important insights into the substance of debates among philosophers on the African continent. Continuing with one underlying point of this volume, these debates cannot be delinked from historical and contemporary national and global political interests. For those unfamiliar with these decades-long debates, Maraganedzha provides an excellent entry point into the general discussion points concerning these philosophers. The philosophical works explored in this chapter include a survey of important figures such as Ifeanyi Menkiti, Didier Kaphagawani, Kwasi Wiredu, Placide Tempels, John Mbiti, Polycarp Ikuenobe, and Bernard Matolino. Maraganedzha's objective for the chapter is to argue that while the concept of personhood is normative across many African philosophies, the normativity of that concept is not bounded exclusively by the concept of community. By exploring the term *Murunzi* according to the Venda culture, Maraganedzha shows there is a foundational metaphysical component to be understood about self in African philosophy.

Maraganedzha's chapter introduces readers to the variations of language and culture being drawn upon by previous scholarship on self in African thought. For example, the three theses on personhood by Didier Kaphagawani are presented in order to show that communitarianism already contains problematic counter-arguments related to identity. Maraganedzha develops these objections to support an argument that descriptive accounts of African personhood also require a metaphysical counterpart that would explain the persistence of self. He employs an explanation of Tshivenda culture to answer how persistence of self might be thought. If Venda language provides the ontological status of a person, then from a philosophical point of view there is an accompanying metaphysic. Maraganedzha moves from this point to develop a dualist conception of self based on the expression "*Murunzi,*" which is the particular "shadow" of the individual with Venda community. *Murunzi* is non-material and yet quasi-physical in being connected to the various realms of the Venda cosmos. Maraganedzha works out the problems of this quasi-physical status, where the linguistic limitations of the term must be accompanied by further context to show it as an attempt to understand the comprehensive nature of existence functioning in many African metaphysics. The upshot is to challenge the limitations of enforcing a strict disjunction between visible and non-visible as the fundamental definition of "physical." Maraganedzha's chapter therefore offers this methodological point in addition to a substantive introduction to self across various philosophers in contemporary scholarship.

Louis Komjathy provides an in-depth exploration of classical Daoism (350–c. 90 BCE), a body and world affirming perspective with an emphasis on energetics. Komjathy instructs readers in how to use English terms while suspending the temptation to assume Western meanings. Personhood is thought of in terms of an entity whose body is integral to the possibility of self. That is, Komjathy's chapter offers a conception of self that *a priori* rules out any soul/body dualism. Importantly in this regard, readers will not be misdirected by the introduction of the English term "soul" with reference to *hún* 魂 and *pò* 魄. Komjathy helpfully uses the English term "ghost" in his explanations. One has a heavenly aspect, and the other earthly. There is one more qualification, of course, to ensure English readers do not add a Christian referent to these various cognates: "heaven" is not a realm separated from earth by some ontology or soteriology. Heaven is always relating to earthly affairs. Komjathy's chapter thereby exemplifies the precautions required to undertaking a cross-cultural investigation of self.

Each perspective in the volume is situated within a larger cultural-historical milieu of debates and discourses that exceed most reader's expertise. Reading the volume is an exercise in fallibility and finitude. In the case of Komjathy's chapter, his scholarship marks out an innovative position in the context of contemporary scholarship on Daoism. These debates enable Komjathy to explain a critical awareness of the categories used in his chapter. For example, "theology" appears as a comparative category, and not the systematic presentation of what is ultimately real. Komjathy employs Daoist epistemology to make "theology" a comparative category, since the Dao/Way (reality) is only partly describable in discourse. From this perspective, contemplative practice is the path to knowing anything about classical Daoism. Others may use descriptors such as "mystical" or "apophatic" span the epistemic gaps, but Komjathy helps us realize they are inadequate for conceiving what might be meant by "person" or "self" in classical Daoist thought. A further example is Komjathy's explanations of heart-mind (*xīn* 心), which give expert notes about classical Chinese characters which include the *xīn* 心/忄 radical for thought, memory, emotions, disposition, intention, desire, will and aspiration. The Chinese characters depend both on their immediate context and the characters' formation depends upon a common radical. That is, Komjathy's explanation of "self" in classical Daoism is not a matter of the mind. Self is just as much a matter of the body. The epistemic paths to these insights are plural, where their realization involves the receptivity and subtle listening of Daoist contemplative practices.

The contribution by **Herbert Moyo** to this volume offers insights into his important scholarship on the philosophical insights to be learned from the Nguni culture of southern Africa. Moyo's chapter focuses on the term uMina/ubumina, which he translates to the term "self." As with most other authors in this volume, Moyo cautions readers against making a 1:1 correlation or comparison between uMina/ubumina and self. The path chosen by Moyo is to offer an understanding of "self" by analyzing the Nguni culture's praxis of *Impilo* (life), *ukufa* (death) and *Umoya* (Spirit). Moyo encapsulates that praxis with the term Isintuism, which he uses to name the shared understanding of the physical and abstract relationships that comprise everyday life amid Nguni communities. Readers of Moyo's chapter will be introduced to a wide variety of terms and ideas from the practices of everyday life. The chapter presents original findings that may be difficult to replicate or find elsewhere. Readers are therefore invited to learn about the Nguni philosophy of Isintuism.

Moyo's outline of self from the Nguni perspective begins with a discussion of the various cyclic patterns that establish the relationships within Nguni communities. These cycles animate realities that are in nature at once social, economic, environmental, and spiritual. The identity of a particular self is not something delineated solely by physical differences. Moyo offers a communitarian conception as the best way for a Anglo-European worldview to comprehend how identity and subjectivity are understood from the Nguni perspective. Moyo explains how the existence of the community is comprised of individuals, whose narratives intertwine the self amid others. Rather than some order of ontological priority, however, Moyo clearly underlines self and community as co-originary. His introduction to Nguni culture on this topic therefore shows how a metaphysics of the self may be organized on relationships that are without beginning or end.

Fritz Detwiler's contribution presents self as a moral entity. Detwiler's general survey of Native American thought offers a framework of moral reciprocity where conceptions of self are not limited to individual human beings. Beneficence and detriment are defined not through individual utility, but in terms of reciprocal community relationships of obligations and responsibility. The community of selves in this context involves not only human relationships, but the members of the ecological environment within which humans find themselves. As Detwiler describes it, the relations are with all alive things, where the status of "living" is a matter of connection to life-force. "Relationality," then, is the term Detwiler uses to summarize this worldview that sustains the conception of self in his chapter.

Detwiler's explanation of a general Native American conception of the world is based on scholarship regarding the varieties of perspectives of several social groups. The conception of personhood, according to Detwiler, seems to be widely held. The status of "living" is generated by relations and their proximity. An entity is more alive relative to another as a function of their connections with each other. The moral element of this relation is a function of understanding the reciprocity of one to others. These relationships, such as that of the relations of the earth and sky, may be observed for insights into other relationships that, for example, humans might have with each other, the earth, or the sky.

The latter part of Detwiler's chapter offers several conceptions of the world and self from specific Native American peoples: the Tlingit, Diné or Navajo, and Lakota. Detwiler's description of the Tlingit perspective illustrates the importance of reciprocity with ghosts, spirits, and ancestors. The Navajo or Diné perspective explains how gender informs relations as well as how shamans provide ways for creating balance and harmony within communities. The Lakota perspective explains the importance of the phrase "all my relations," which connects selves to a specific community.

Abraham H. Khan's chapter focuses on the thought of the poet–philosopher Muhammad Iqbal. While Iqbal's conception of *khudi* should not be taken as representative of Islamic conception of self in general, it is an indication that such a project produces generalizations of limited helpfulness. Khan's exploration of Iqbal is a concise illustration of how an idea as complex as "self" must always be historicized.

Khan's chapter is one of the best entry points in this volume for readers who wish to make connections with classical, Western ideas about self. He elucidates the thought of Muhammed Iqbal, whose Persian-language poetry directly engages ideas found in Enlightenment political and philosophical treatises. Khan's chapter outlines an argument that Iqbal's thought about selfhood is founded primarily upon readings of the Quran and South Asian Muslim intellectual history, which prefigure Iqbal's extensive engagement with British philosophers and his own studies at Cambridge University and the University of Munich.

Khan introduces us to Iqbal's poetic voice, which shows the importance of historical situatedness for the development of any conception of self. Iqbal's upbringing among Muslim social reformers and the privileges of education provided starting points for his unique perspectives. The context for Iqbal was to write poetry showing the vitality of a South Asian, Muslim self-identity by raising decolonial consciousness. Khan explains how Iqbal's poetry puts Quranic ideas in relation to twentieth-century politics such that the Muslim self can reflexively recognize its distinctiveness from the self presented by the European Enlightenment. Iqbal's experiences of British higher education produced several poetic works written in Persian, and Khan importantly notes that Iqbal never provided English translations of his works. We can see how this makes Khan's point, that the likely intention for Iqbal's poetry was to teach a specific conception of self to a particular, South Asian audience.

Khan's presentation of a highly individuated conception of self is therefore distinct from Western thought. Khan's explanation of *khudi*, Iqbal's term for self, is of a self-contained entity with three, interrelated axes of body, mind, and spirit. All three work together to existentially actualize the self through action among and with other humans. Iqbal's aim is to have individuals understand their selfhood as a passageway towards immortality. The realization of self-consciousness through Iqbal's poetry, as Khan explains it, is firstly realized by individuals. Iqbal's poetry mentally awakens subjectivity in relation to the ultimacy presented in the Quran such that the individual reader realizes their purpose in the world. Khan's chapter closes with a cross-cultural reflection that explains how Iqbal's emphasis on self-actualization is distinct from European philosophers such as Freud, Fichte, and Bradley. These distinctions are part of Khan's conclusion, too, where Khan suggests how learning about Iqbal's conception of self today might provide insights for humanity.

Much like Khan's chapter on Muhammed Iqbal, **Nathan R. B. Loewen**'s chapter focuses on the works of one philosopher: Jacques Derrida. The alignment of these two chapters continues in so far as the works of Derrida are also written with a specific relation to European philosophy. The commonalities quickly diverge, since Derrida did not write poetry in a non-European language with the aim of actualizing decolonial, Muslim subjectivity in twentieth-century South Asia. Nevertheless, Loewen's chapter does choose to focus on only three of Derrida's works because they present a specifically political conception of self.

Loewen presents a reading of Derrida that is consistent with Derrida's construal of philosophy as layer upon layer of readings. Each reading presents a novel interaction where no text is read in solitude. The practice of reading as an exercise in language requires the production of partial relations that likewise partially draw upon the breadth and depth of the reader's history of languages. The task of scholars is to clarify the relations among their readings to the fullest extent possible within whatever limits they have been given. In that sense, Loewen's chapter also presents readers with a general cross-cultural methodology within this volume. All the contributors offer scholarly readings within the limits of this present volume.

Derrida's historical situation in twentieth-century France makes Loewen's chapter perhaps the most direct engagement with European philosophies. Loewen explains how Derrida's thought may be informed by the facts of "Jacques Derrida" being interpellated by various French states as a Jew growing up in Algeria. At first Derrida is a subject of a French colony, then of the Vichy regime under Nazi control, and then as a citizen of France through to the end of the Cold War. Loewen's explanation of selected works in light of these events aims to show how the gravity of these major political shifts substantively informs Derrida's conception of self. The emphasis on language is taken by Loewen to be foundational for philosophical reflection. Just as there is no original "philosophy" from which all thought proceeds, so too is there no fundamental, basic "self." Loewen's decision to read Derrida's works historically proposes that the plurality of "self" has life-and-death consequences. He reads the upshot of Derrida's work as a reminder that whenever a political ideology aims to enforce only one option, language is always, already, reading otherwise in that very moment.

A Critical Wager

The wager of this volume is that nothing in the study of religion can be adequately separated from culture without entering absolute ineffability. Such passages into silence are often the outcome of scholarly decisions to sustain specific academic paradigms at all costs. Philosophy of religion has need of a global-critical future, since it is not a sub-field within the limits of philosophy alone. The experiment in this volume was to consider "self" as a category that might enable a broader scope of phenomena. The Epilogue, written by **Tim D. Knepper**, evaluates whether this volume has accomplished that outcome. One motivating principle for this book is that whatever projects philosophers of religion embark upon, they would do well to self-reflexively situate their work relative to specifiable interests at work in definable contexts. Many topics in classic and contemporary philosophy of religion are functional analogues to what Aragorn Eloff once called in passing "Trolley Land," a semantic space where philosophers typically mask the relevance of critical theory with uncanny efficiency. Philosophers of religion must consider how to teach future generations a reflexive, epistemic awareness that knowledge is always a site of overlapping magisteria. If "religion" has anything to do with culture, then philosophers of religion are in a good position to self-reflexively historicize their work. We hope the focus of this volume on category "self" may constructively facilitate that awareness.

A counterpoint to the claim that philosophy of religion must involve critical, cultural reflexivity may be inferred from Galen Strawson, whose works specializing on "self" have proved stimulating for recent debates among philosophers. Strawson's work is firmly situated in phenomenology and metaphysics, which are not philosophy of religion. "Self" is not a conventional category or topic elaborated by philosophers of religion. While Strawson does not overtly draw upon their sources, Buddhist philosophers nevertheless seem particularly engaged by him. Strawson's (2009: 2) counterpoint is that he delineates a scholarly sphere of philosophical investigation of self that purposely excludes folk or common understandings. Strawson emphasizes that philosophy is occupied with second-order analyses and conceptions of self. Thus, involving cultural perspectives is unnecessary. A philosophical conception of "self" may be developed by a philosopher, writes Strawson, whether or not selves do. Just as some philosophers do discuss "identity" in terms of identity relations (e.g., $S = H$) rather than identity politics, so too may they discuss "self" as a taxon within a conceptual system that does not relate to other possible frames of reference such as ordinary talk in public discourse. Strawson's (ibid., 21) point is that appeals to everyday public language is no way to solve philosophical problems. The argument may suggest that philosophers of religion should sustain their sub-field's narrow scope and not bother with culture.

We give Strawson pride of place for two reasons. There are many other philosophers writing in English about self, but their publications are far less provocative. Philosophers of religion, such as Terence Penelhum (1970), or Richard Swinburne (2019), frame their inquiries with terms familiar to Abrahamic religions and theism. Strawson's works challenge Western sensibilities, philosophical and otherwise, using their own terms and methods to propose a strictly naturalist conception of "self" perhaps only equaled by Jonardon Ganeri's (2012) proposals. Strawson's work produces a fairly airtight conception whose implications strongly argue against any "self" that persists across space and time. He shows various narrativist and endurantist conceptions face metaphysical problems that are difficult to solve without appeals to incorrigible commitments or fideism. The other reason is Strawson's strict exclusion of "everyday public language" begs us to ask which public and whose language? This volume is based on the fragile notion that there is scholarly benefit to considering terminologies and methodologies that emerge from non-English publics. Across histories and cultures, philosophers do set about developing and solving philosophical problems in a variety of social-historical contexts. They most certainly propose considerations that most certainly eschew the languages of everyday publics in modern, Western nation-states. Therefore, these philosophies are worth a look.

If the above claims ring truthful, however, we must acknowledge that the philosophies of other social-historical contexts simply don't include language and ideas relevant to the English term "self." The topic is a very historically and culturally specific outcome, and so whatever problems that might be related to self are not necessary for philosophizing. Since several chapters in this volume argue that self is simply not an issue for their philosophical contexts, the reasoning they marshal towards the issue may strike certain readers as not properly philosophical. We think this position is not only presumptive, it is irrational. We strongly caution against claiming there might be regions of semantic space, such as that of "self," left undiscovered or unexplained by the generations of humans who developed the thought systems elaborated in this volume. We do hope this volume's chapters provoke new questions and reconsiderations of received notions; but that is the challenge for us as readers. Our questions will be anachronistic and idiosyncratic. They will very likely lack merit across the expansive, prior history of others' philosophies. Therefore, the contents of this book are not at all novel relative to most of their historical contexts. They will likely be seen as *novelties* produced for audiences that were never previously identified or intended. Philosophy of religion in a globalized, twenty-first century is therefore at once relevantly actual to current circumstances but also completely irrelevant to the historical precedents both within and beyond the conventional, Anglo-European composition of the field. We think this matter of (ir)relevance forms a necessary risk for global-critical philosophy of religion. Without taking this risk, we wager that philosophy of religion may pass into silence at a far greater cost to humanistic inquiry in the twenty-first century.

Finally, after these bold proclamations, we want to note how this volume is the product of humans making connections with other humans. While we have not necessarily met in person, the contributions to this volume are the product of people choosing to exchange their ideas with each other. The relationships among us are widely varied, but the entire group shares a commitment that philosophy of religion broaden its scope of phenomena and method. We also share a commitment that human beings should have increased opportunities to make meaningful comparisons across the world's ideas. Our contributions to this volume present new phenomena for considerations which might otherwise take a great amount of research and risk significant misunderstandings. The chapters also propose methods that might be less prone to limit philosophical consideration to European conventions for concepts, debates, and procedures. Many chapters offer different methods for philosophizing that are no less rooted in long-standing conventions that may well overtly exclude European ones. We hope attentive readers will notice how these irregularities might be seen as productive counterfactuals that provide chances for robust reconsideration of accepted or tacit paths for philosophical reflection.

Notes

1. Ideally, we hope this might supplement classrooms and instructors learning from Tim Knepper's groundbreaking textbook, *Philosophies of Religion: A Global and Critical Introduction* (London: Bloomsbury, 2023).
2. "Global-Critical Philosophy of Religion" is an umbrella term referring to a diverse set of scholars in a variety of projects, such as books, seminars, workshops, and a program unit of that name at the American Academy of Religion, USA. Learn more at: www.globalcritical.as.ua.edu.

Bibliography

Ganeri, Jonardon. 2012. *The Self: Naturalism, Consciousness, and the First-Person Stance*. Oxford: Oxford University Press.

Knepper, Tim. 2023. *Philosophies of Religion: A Global and Critical Introduction*. London: Bloomsbury Academic.

Loewen, Nathan, and Agnieszka Rostalska. 2023. *Diversifying Philosophy of Religion: Critiques, Methods, and Case Studies*. London: Bloomsbury Academic.

Penelhum, Terence. 1970. *Survival and Disembodied Existence*. London: Routledge & Kegan Paul.

Strawson, Galen. 2009. *Selves: An Essay in Revisionary Metaphysics*. Oxford: Oxford University Press.

Swinburne, Richard. 1997. *The Evolution of the Soul*. Oxford: Oxford University Press.

Swinburne, Richard. 2019. *Are We Bodies or Souls?* Oxford: Oxford University Press.

1

Udayana's Concept of the Self and Arguments for Its Existence and Persistence

Agnieszka Rostalska

Chapter Outline

Introduction	15
Cross-Cultural Counterfactual Thought Experiment Involving Udayana	16
Introducing Udayana	17
The Context for the *Ātmatattvaviveka*	18
Nyāya's Rational *ātma*-logy—Conceptualization	19
Udayana's "Self-Awareness" of the Self	22
Self's Persistence	25
Conclusions	26
1.1 Ātman	31
1.2 Persistence	36

Introduction

This chapter constitutes an introduction to the concept of the self and arguments for its existence and persistence offered by the tenth-century Indian philosopher Udayana.[1] Theoretically and methodologically, it aims to develop cross-cultural philosophical inquiry into the concept of the "self" and related issues of its existence and persistence. The proposal breaks with the orientalist, epistemic problematics of the "East–West" dichotomy by focusing on "persistence." Likewise, the earlier version of this chapter was presented as a 'debate' around an exposition of the relatively unknown philosophical views of the tenth-century South Asian philosopher Udayana (rather than, say, a "Western European" figure or school); and further underwent online annotations, which served as an impulse for a public discussion between an engaged group of scholars,[2] specializing in less commonly taught philosophy.[3] The views of Udayana on the "self" presented further on served as a starting point for a cross-cultural counterfactual thought experiment engaging diverse global philosophical traditions.

Cross-Cultural Counterfactual Thought Experiment Involving Udayana

As a result of many years of academic research spent directing my focus towards the so-called Indian philosophical traditions (Hindu, Buddhist, Jain, materialist, etc.), I have chosen the Nyāya philosophical school as an example of rational theological enquiry. Nyāya is one of the major *darśana*s or schools of philosophical thought in India, essentially concerned with epistemology and logic. The term "nyāya" (which likely has etymological roots in "naya") signifies the skillful art of reasoning or methods ensuring fairness in argumentation and legitimate tactics. The example of Udayana is meaningful in this context as he is considered a "father" of the theistic refinements of this tradition—notably the author of two independent manuals: 1. *Nyāyakusumāñjali* (*An Offering of Flowers*), dedicated to the arguments for the existence of *God/ *Īśvara*, and 2. *Ātmatattvaviveka*, or: *Investigation of the Reality of the Self*, developing arguments for the existence of the self (*ātman*), which is the main text of this study.

I identify Udayana among the key innovative philosophical thinkers coming from India. His scholarship, dedicated to novel ideas of *self* and *God, is backed up by sharp arguments developed to defend these notions. In my view, Udayana's works are worth recognizing for study by philosophers of religion. The text of the *Ātmatattvaviveka* (ATV) is overlooked even by more narrow field specialists. There are yet to be studies of how Udayana's independent and novel treatise interacts with other Indian philosophical traditions or other philosophical traditions and key thinkers. Most scholars dedicated to the exposition of the Nyāya concept of *self* refer to the *sūtra*s and their commentaries (e.g., Chadha 2013). Notable previous interpretations of Udayana's works were done by Bimal Krishna Matilal (1994), Arindam Chakrabarti (1982), and Chakravarti Ram-Prasad (2001, 2017). Kisor K. Chakrabarti did a partial translation of this work and some commentary on it in his book *Classical Indian Philosophy of Mind: The Nyāya Dualist Tradition* (1999). Udayana is an example of how cosmopolitan, comparativist philosophers of religion may critically engage with others without defending any religious sect per se. The online debate, or cross-cultural counterfactual thought experiment performed on his innovative ideas, successfully engaged participants in cross-cultural dialogue and demonstrated that pursuing philosophical questions about *self* is possible as a genuinely global, comparative, and inclusive effort.

Introducing Udayana

The philosophical ideas of a particular thinker are always inseparable from their sociocultural and historical milieu. It is therefore important to ask: Who was Udayana? Which intellectual environment inspired his philosophical endeavors?

Udayana was born in a Hindu Brahmin family and lived in *c.* eleventh century in Mithilā,[4] near Dharbhaṅgā in today's state of Bihar, India (Amma, 1985: 3). His scholastic commentary *Nyāya-vārttika-tātparya-ṭīkā-pariśuddhi* ("Correctness of the Notes on the Meaning of the Gloss on the Commentary on *Nyāya*")—also known as *Pariśuddhi* or *Nibandha*—on Vācaspati Miśra's *Nyāyavārttikatātparyaṭīkā* suggests that he belonged to the lineage of early Nyāya (or *prācīna Nyāya*) tradition. As such, this text is a final voice in a series of the earliest or classical commentaries of the *Nyāyasūtra*s of Gautama (NS),[5] the primary treatise of the Nyāya tradition.

Udayana was also an innovator of the Nyāya tradition, as he is the one who synthesized the tradition of Nyāya with its "sister-school" Vaiśeṣika,[6] which gives a syncretic aspect to his texts. Some scholars credit him as the pioneer of a new Nyāya (or Navya-Nyāya) tradition, due to his intricate writing style and use of technical terminology.

Udayana's works are as deeply engaged with competing schools of thought as with peers in the Nyāya tradition, such as Bhāsarvajña (*c.* 860–920). Perhaps for this reason, Udayana's works are regularly commented upon as an authority by later Indian thinkers and present-day Naiyāyika philosophers. Some contemporary interpreters (i.e., Matilal 1977: 97) compared his mastery of logical argumentation with regard to the existence of "God" and "soul" with that of the thirteenth century, Italian Dominican Thomas Aquinas.[7] Udayana's scholastic style, which predates by a few centuries that of Aquinas, first presents objections (*pūrvapakṣa*) of the opponent (real or imaginary, at times reformulating standpoints so that they appear even stronger), confronts the objections (*uttarapakṣa*), and then endorses his own views.

Udayana engaged in both intellectual debates through his writings, and through debates in public (*vāda*). A story about his life reveals that when he won in a public debate with the Advaita dialectician Śrīhīra, the son of Śrīharṣa composed the text *Khaṇḍanakhaṇḍakhādya* ("The Sweets of Refutation") to avenge his father's defeat and public humiliation (Bhattacharyya 2010: 298). An example of Udayana's intellectual debating is his *Nyāyakusumāñjali* ("A Handful of Flowers of Logic"), which engaged atheistic Indian materialists (Cārvāka), Sāṃkhya and Mīmāṃsā philosophers, as well as Jain and Buddhist thinkers. His *Ātmatattvaviveka*, or the "Investigation of the Reality of the Self" also known as *Bauddhādhikkāra* ("Reproach to the Buddhists"), is meant to oppose four Buddhist schools, mainly: Sautrāntika, Vaibhāṣika, Yogācāra, and Mādhyamika, as well as early Advaita Vedāntins, and Materialists, among others. Overall, Udayana's focus in these debates is directed towards the Buddhist philosopher Jñānaśrīmitra,[8] a follower of Dharmakīrti's school. Thus, I think it is very appropriate to highlight Udayana's works among a diverse range of philosophical perspectives in a contemporary context.

According to some modern scholars, Udayana has, "demolished in final fashion the claims of the Buddhist logicians" (Bhattacharyya 2010: 298). Tachikawa writes that Udayana, "made the greatest contribution to driving the Buddhists out of India ... He may be said to have brought the conflict between the Buddhist logicians and Hindu logicians to an end ... Indian Mahāyāna Buddhism was subsequently unable to produce any scholar capable of refuting Udayana" (Tachikawa 1981: 8). A more moderate version of these claims is to recognize how Udayana's personage may be identified to provide scholars today with important evidence about the contents and history of Indian philosophy and logic.

The Context for the *Ātmatattvaviveka*

For the purposes of this chapter, I focus on Udayana's unique texts on the existence of self in the ATV. In terms of intellectual debate, the text's objective is to refute the Materialists and Buddhists theories of emergent *self* (materialism) as well as *no-self* and momentariness (Buddhism). The Materialists, as depicted by Udayana, argued that cognitions are qualities of the bodily organs, and that consciousness arises out of the bodily processes and is born when the body matures and dies when the body dies. Most Buddhists from the eleventh century argued that cognitions are only causally connected in a stream of awareness events, but do not reside in a substance called the self. For them, cognitions are not qualities but are produced by an association of bodily sense organs with preceding karmic dispositions. I am taking a departure from dwelling upon these polemical aspects of Udayana's thought. There are, of course, other ways to read the ATV. The primary aim of this chapter is to foreground the conception of "self" proposed by Udayana, and then make some remarks on his conception of "persistence."

It is useful to pause at this point to highlight Udayana's method of approaching different philosophical perspectives. Udayana's arguments constitute a fascinating polemics with other schools of thought; here, Udayana scholastically presents the opposing views—the doctrines opposed to the Nyāya's concept of the *self*—to refute the rivals and establish his own innovative interpretation of the traditional Nyāya postulations. He presents four distinct counterarguments which correspond to the views held by his opponents: (1) Momentariness theory [Buddhist, mainly Sautrāntika]; (2) Unreality of external objects, consciousness alone is real [Yogācāra Buddhist, "Idealist"]; (3) Non-difference between a quality and a qualified/quality possessor (or "quality" and "substance") [Buddhist and Advaita Vedāntin]; and (4) Non-perception (*anupalambha*) or non-experience of the self different from the body [Buddhist and Materialist] (Bhattacharyya 2010: 300; Amma 1985: 13). According to Udayana, "There are (these) views opposed to the reality of self, namely, that everything is of momentary duration, that there is nothing real apart from consciousness, that qualities and things endowed with them do not differ from each other and that the (so-called) self is never perceived (or observed)" (ATV 20, 5).[9] Before introducing Udayana's arguments in more detail, it will be useful to first define the related concepts that were brought out in their original context.

Nyāya's Rational *ātma*-logy—Conceptualization

The term for "self" across the Indian philosophical traditions engaged with by Udayana is "*ātman*." The concept of *ātman* has a long history on the Indian subcontinent, which is attested by the Upaniṣadic (*Upaniṣads*, composed *c.* 800–400 BCE) principal concern with the knowledge of the Self (*ātman*). Here, the term *ātman* generally signifies the immutable, undifferentiated, unconditioned, and autonomous principle of existence in human beings.[10] Liberation from rebirth (*mokṣa*) pertains to the realization, or direct perception of the self, *ātman*.

The issue of how the concept of the "self' is defined in the Nyāya tradition is directly linked to another question prevailing across all competing traditions in India, mainly: can the existence of "self" be known through the means of knowledge (*pramāṇa*s), such as perception, inferential reasoning, testimony? Moreover, if and how is the state of 'liberated consciousness' desirable by the self? Is it a happy or blissful state? These are the kinds of questions that guided the public and intellectual debates of Udayana and his peers.

To approach Udayana's conception of the self, first, I will briefly outline the prevailing Nyāya views on "self,"[11] which were the object of critique by and debate with mainly Materialist and Buddhist opponents. Their critiques predominantly motivated Udayana's response in the ATV. Udayana supposes his readers' prior knowledge of the concept of the self and the main Nyāya arguments for its existence and persistence; for convenience, I will briefly introduce them in the following paragraph. Afterwards, I will turn to Udayana's emphases and modifications. This will lead to examining Udayana's endorsement of the existence of permanent self (against the Buddhist "no-self" theory and "emergentism").

Nyāya thinkers admit the existence of infinitely many selves/souls (*ātman*), which are eternal, immaterial, and non-composite substances with characteristic qualities (e.g., cognition, pleasure, pain, or desire). The selves are singular and different in all organisms.[12] They experience when associated with 'body vehicles' composed of homogeneous atoms of a particular material substance. Before the connection with the mind (*manas*), an individual self is not conscious. In other words, the self must be embodied in order to experience awareness and cognitions (NS 3.1.18–26).

The Nyāya tradition may be briefly summarized to attribute three main characteristics of the self:

- First, the self is distinct from the mind and the senses, which enables it to recognize its own activity. However, the instance of 'mind' here is not an active or cognitive faculty but solely a passive internal organ, which neither thinks nor acts. It serves as an instrument for the self to experience (pleasure, pain, desire, aversion, merit, demerit, etc.) and cognize. Cognition is here a property of the self, since the self is a locus of awareness, and not a cluster of physical elements or non-sentient intermediaries. The self owns its qualities: cognitions, dispositions, memories, feelings, and actions. The self is therefore not pure consciousness, as Materialists or Idealists would claim, but is a highly individuated self with a personality.
- Second, the self is the substratum of knowing (*jñānādhikaraṇam-ātmā*).[13] The self is not conscious by nature, it is an inherent cause of consciousness or knowledge. One of the favorite examples used by Nyāya philosophers to illustrate their position, originally appearing in the context of causation, is the cloth and the yarn it is made of. In Nyāya terms, the yarn is an "inherent cause" (*samavāyi kāraṇa*) of the cloth, but that does not mean that the yarn is cloth by nature. Likewise, the self is an inherent cause of consciousness without being conscious by nature; that is, it is not always and necessarily conscious.[14] Knowledge is an adventitious attribute of the self, through the connection with a living body, consciousness emerges, but not as a necessary feature, but as an accidental feature.
- Third, because the self is a continuous spiritual substance, it retains its identity through the events of one lifetime and from one lifetime to another. Moreover, the Nyāya thinkers would argue that the self endures beyond death. Their argument is as follows: "Because, immediately being born, an infant has the experience of joy, fear and sorrow [and this] as a result of the "lingering of the memory" (*smṛti-anubandha*) of the past experiences" (Gangopadhyaya, trans. vol. 3, 1972: 33). The commentator Pakṣilasvāmin Vātsyāyana in the *Nyāya-bhāṣya* (NBh) explains

that the recollection of one's past experiences produces the experiences which are indicated by emotions. The underlying assumption here is that of rebirth, since how does the newborn know how to emotionally respond? Or, why does a newborn immediately try to reach out to the mother's chest for nourishment? According to this tradition, the answer is that these reactions are linked to memories. They are the results of previous experiences. The continuity of self stretches into the past, and consequently is projected into the future. This gives the self two fundamental forms of identity, that is to say, the identity of knowing: one and the same self apprehends cognitions. And, the identity of action: one self inherits the karmic fruits of action and suffers or enjoys them.

The Nyāya tradition considered the existence of the self as a given long before Udayana's involvement in their debates.[15] The self is listed in the NS 1.1.9 as one of the objects of knowledge, *prameya*s. It is discussed in that text as the topic of inquiry, as something yet to be determined. The Naiyāyikas do not support this conclusion, first and foremost, on the basis of testimony of sacred text, like the Vedas, nor on the reliable utterance of some source provided by an authoritative speaker (for instance, a sage (*ṛṣi*) or another noble person). They leave space for the possibility of learning about the 'self' through testimony. Among all accepted means of knowledge, the self's (*ātman*) existence is postulated with the use of inferential proofs, that is to say, through the process of inference (*anumāna*).[16] The self, however, cannot be perceived directly. What this means is that the self is something known based on experienced inner states. The following *sūtra* states that the self (*ātman*) is an object of inference based on "marks": desire, aversion, effort, pleasure, pain, and knowledge (NS 1.1.10). Udayana's broader intellectual context, therefore, included a predilection to conceptualize "self" as physically imperceptible, that is, only known by its inferential marks.[17]

Perhaps the above makes it all the more remarkable that the Nyāya tradition insists that a clear understanding of the true nature of the self is a condition for final liberation (*mokṣa*). According to Nyāya, *mokṣa*, or liberation from rebirth, or *apavarga*, the final liberation or beatitude, is the soteriological aim of all philosophical endeavors. In the emancipated state, the self is disembodied, and retains only its formal qualities (like oneness, separateness from other selves, etc.). Freedom from pain, or suffering (*duḥkha*), is brought about through the removal of all blemishes (attitudes and inclinations) and termination of activity. The self is released from the cycle of rebirth, yet it does not endure in the state of bliss, or eternal happiness (Chakrabarti 1983: 174–5) and persists without further cognitive states (Ram-Prasad 2001: 85–91).[18]

Udayana's writings do not fundamentally challenge the positions above. Instead, Udayana's writings can be seen to bolster these claims, with arguments about how 'self' (*ātman*) is directly apprehended through internal perception. His innovation, in the ATV, is that the self can indeed be an object of direct cognition.

Udayana's "Self-Awareness" of the Self

Amid the debates with the Materialists and the Buddhists of the time, Udayana's objective is to remove the grounds by which these intellectual peers were able to redirect the conventional Nyāya arguments in service of their own positions. In the case of the Buddhist philosophers, the Nyāya claim that the existence of a permanent self (*ātman*), that is to say, a quality possessor, may be inferred, was turned into an argument for no-self/*anātman*.

It seems that Udayana was not convinced by the dismissal provided by the Vaiśeṣika philosophers,[19] who argued that the self's non-perception is no evidence for the self's non-existence, since this non-perception is due to the self's subtlety (*saukṣmya*). Udayana also observed that, "[t]he self is not regarded by the Buddhist as cognizable or perceptible" (ATM, 343). To only double down on imperceptibility, as did the Vaiśeṣika, was simply not adequate. Following Vācaspati Miśra's interpretation of the possibility of knowing the self—through perception, he considers an argument (ATM, ibid.) about the non-apprehension of the self, which Chakrabarti paraphrases formally as:

> Whatever is not cognized is nonexistent.
> The self is not cognized.
> Therefore, the self is nonexistent.
>
> (Chakrabarti 1999: 268)

Udayana considers two cases of non-apprehension: either that the self is not apprehended by anyone (universally) or by the individual (particular). The first scenario is, in his opinion, questionable, as there is a possibility that the self is perceived by some or all. In other words, non-apprehension may provide a basis for doubt, but it does not disprove the existence of the self. In the second case, the individual's non-apprehension "applies even to cognizable entities," which also does not disprove the existence of the self and its possibility of being perceived.

Udayana's objective was to determine how the self might be known despite granting that it cannot be experienced empirically. Unless a thing is perceived, it cannot be called perceptible. So if the self is perceptible, it cannot remain unperceived. But how might the self be perceived? Udayana's first innovation was to make an argument for indeterminate perception:

> But what is the proof for the existence of the self? Perception itself for sure. The awareness as "I" is a matter of experience for all living beings. Certainly this awareness cannot be unobjective or endowed with dubious objectivity as it is neither verbal nor subject to contradiction. It is also not generated by the middle term in an inference. Even a person who has no knowledge of any middle term has self-knowledge. Nor is it recollection as what is not experienced cannot be recollected. It is also not reasonable

to say that this awareness is an objectless cognition which is beginningless and is generated by a beginningless urge. This can be said of the common cognitions of blue, yellow etc. also. If self-awareness could be discredited on the ground that it is the product of some beginningless urge, how can any other cognition be credited as valid so that one could depend upon the cognitions of blue, yellow etc.?

(ATV, 344)

This paragraph represents his major argument for the existence of the self. Udayana points here that the indeterminate self-awareness, common to all living beings, is: non-verbal, incorrigible (not subjected to contradiction), not inferential, not recollection, not an objectless construction (non-objective construction, *vikalpa*).

Udayana introduces the idea of "indeterminate perception" in order to argue that the self is perceived much in the way that other categories of things are perceived. In Sanskrit, the basis for this claim is the concept of *nirvikalpaka*, "in the raw," where indeterminate perception grasps a qualifier of something prior to forming a robust conceptual deployment and organization of it and does not require a "mark" since its object is perceived directly. The other manner of perception is *savikalpaka*, or "determinate" cognition, where something may be much more immediately produced as a concept within a verbal propositional. Something indeterminately perceived is not ineffable or inscrutable. Self-awareness simply does not require language, while ordinary cognitions are subjected to language and assessment (Chakrabarti 1999: 271).

Udayana's argument is that living beings have an indeterminate perception about themselves. If the Buddhists admit that the objects of indeterminate perceptions are real, then they must concede that the self is such an object, too.

Udayana thereby argued that while there are erroneous perceptions of the self, that does not mean there is no self. Self is something as real as the color blue. It is not an "objectless cognition which is beginningless and is generated by a beginningless urge" (or, a subconscious impression, *vāsanā*, which is not generated by some previous perception). In other words, if we were to try to challenge the reality of self-awareness in this way, by reducing it to an object-less cognition generated by subconscious impressions, in a similar fashion, we would challenge the reality of the color blue.

The general idea of indeterminate perception is not difficult to understand. Udayana's argument invokes color as the basis of the claim. There can be a determinate perception of things that are "blue," but Udayana's analysis finds that a determinate perception of blue presupposes an indeterminate awareness of blue. Udayana then extends that claim to the self. There is an indeterminate perception of what is "self."

Udayana states further that: "Nor is self-cognition baseless or objectless because the self is not cognized by external senses. Even the cognition of intellect or consciousness would be baseless or objectless. If self-consciousness is the ground of reality of intellect then in the case of the self too the evidencing ground is the mental perception of the self" (ATM, 346). Dravid (ibid.) explains this passage as follows: "Just as consciousness is its own evidence, so the self is evidenced by mental and not external sensation. Not only the self, but even pleasure, pain, etc., are known to be real only through mental sensation."

Udayana's objection to the Buddhist's arguments about causation provides another insight into his conception of the self. The Buddhist claim was that there is no self because each moment of time is the product of an entirely different set of co-determining factors. While these factors might create the background for a succeeding state of affairs, that succeeding state's identity is utterly different. That is, while one state of affairs—either that of a so-called individual or even that of the entire world—might succeed one after the other, the Buddhists argued there is no grounds to claim these states of affairs belong to the identical, same individual or world. Udayana explains this as the theory of momentariness, which he argues is unable to explain how empirical consciousness is continuous. He appeals here to the Nyāya inferential proof for the self from recollection: "it is the definite ascertainment of the earlier and later cognitions being caused by the same agent" (ATM, 349). Chakrabarti explains this argument as follows: "the support or source or object (*ālambana*) of I-consciousness is permanent, because it is also the object of recognition" (Chakrabarti 1999: 275).[20] Udayana argues that if there are grounds to claim there is a continuity that connects moments, then there are grounds to claim there is something like a "self" that provides that continuity and identity, and bounds previous perception and latter recollection of the knowing agent. If perceptions and recollections did not belong to the same knower, then the teacher's cognition could be remembered by a student. According to Udayana, this is absurd.

Udayana zeroes in on the Buddhist's agreement about *karma*. He states that the theory of momentariness cannot sufficiently explain the law of *karma* (accumulation of merits and demerits), according to which it is one person who reaps the fruits of his/her activities.[21] For a previous state is succeeded by the next state, and there is a (split-second) gap between the preceding and succeeding states. Something must, according to Udayana, connect across these gaps. "It is the self with merit that by its contact with things brings about their movements" (ATV, 375). Furthermore, according to Udayana, the Buddhists of his time could not explain memory. In Udayana's view, the Nyāya conception of causality does not encounter these issues. The self is the inherent cause of our awareness of ourselves. It is the same self which both perceives and remembers (Bhattacharya 2010: 308).

Finally, Udayana points out that the attempts to reject the reality of the self would pose a difficulty for one's final release: "A non-self-aware person cannot be a redemption seeker" (ATV, 376). Without the "self-awareness" of the self, nothing can be desired or avoided, including one's own final release or liberation.

Self's Persistence

Although there is a double reference to "after-life" through the concepts of (1) *paraloka*, the other or future world, or plane/realm of existence) or (2) *svarga*, "heaven" or temporary plane where the selves which have not yet reached the state of *mokṣa*, final release or liberation, the theological considerations of "afterlife" are not the focus of the Nyāya tradition within which Udayana wrote the ATV.[22] Given the arguments about karma above, the notion of "after-life" would have to be accompanied by a conception of "pre-life." And as we have seen in the mentioned earlier 'newborn's inheritance' argument,[23] revoked by Udayana, to ensure present recollections of past experiences, there should be a continuous self—the agent of apprehension (*anubhava*), dispositions (*saṃskāra*), and recollection (Amma 1985: 146).

The correlative terms for "persistence" such as "beginningless" (*anādi*), and endless (*ananta*) in Nyāya philosophy, suggest that "persistence" is a well-suited concept to describe Udayana's ideas. Persistence is a term much better suited to cross-cultural thinking, too. Udayana's conception of the self draws upon the Nyāya terminology of *ātman*. And, as we saw above, it does involve the concept of karmic disposition. Udayana's decision to use the concept of karma was not merely to serve a role in his arguments against the Buddhists. Karma is related to how this idea of self persists.

There is extensive literature on the philosophical understandings of "karma" across various schools and thinkers of Indian philosophy.[24] From Udayana's perspective, the persistence of a self provides the grounds for discussions about *karma*. His position is that while the conceptual understanding of *karma* depends on the self, the conception of the self does not depend solely upon karma. Instead, *karma* is among those phenomena that provide justification of the self as *ātman*.

As noted earlier, Udayana conceives of the self within the Nyāya tradition as a continuous, spiritual substance. On the grounds that newborns do not learn joy, for example, they must retain this as a lingering memory of past experiences (see Gangopadhyaya, trans., vol. 3, 1972: 33). These recollections of emotions indicate the persistence of the self through past experiences. But these past experiences do not destroy "free will," since Udayana, like other Naiyāyikas, makes knowledge as that which mediates the possibility of freedom. "Why should the unconditioned self be contemplated? Because by means of continuous contemplation of it, release is attained" (ATV, ibid., 377). The self is capable of gaining sufficient knowledge for the release from pleasure and pain, which are the indicators of karmic retribution. Udayana asks, "what is the nature of the contemplation of self? It is discrimination. Discrimination from what? From the body, etc., which are other than the self" (ibid.). Thus, acts of cognition to discriminate the self from extraneous phenomena are the means to freely realize the persistence of the self.

Udayana's discussion of how the self can achieve the purest of ideas is based in Nyāya's singular unifying concept—*niḥśreyasa*—which results from reaching a state which amounts to attaining comprehensive knowledge (*tattvajñāna*) of all there is to know. *Niḥśreyasa*, more than knowledge of the self, is an all-encompassing knowledge state. This is not the same transcendental state that is underscored in the more "spiritually" aligned or theological systems—such as, in particular, *mokṣa*, or salvific liberation from embodied existence. *Niḥśreyasa* as such has no necessary connections with life hereafter (Potter 1977: 29–34). This knowledge amounts to nothing more nor less than the destruction of all *mithyajñāna*, false understandings.[25] The liberating aspect of the *niḥśreyasa* state is that no pleasures are transported across. Not even the positive pleasures of life, desire-driven satisfaction, from luxuries of appetite to sensual-sexual pleasures (Halbfass 1997: 155–156).

The introduction of *niḥśreyasa* is useful to show how Udayana understands the persistence of the self. The self can be released and continues to exist independently in a joyless unending free-time seamless horizon—and steeped in a deep-sleep state minus the dreams (*suṣuptasya svapnādarśane*; see NS 4.1.62, M. Gangopadhyaya, trans., pt. 4, 1973: 86). In this state, the self is atemporal (*nityatva*) and cannot be extinguished. And there is no merging with the other, no greater or smaller of which could be thought. Udayana's formulation of "release without transcendence" amounts to a unique model of liberation that explains the persistence of the self.[26] The release of the self from indeterminate cognition occurs not because of any mental state succeeding it but by means of time associated with the destruction of the self's destiny.

Conclusions

In this chapter, I identified Udayana as one among the key innovative philosophical thinkers coming from India. As a relatively overlooked source of philosophical arguments about self and persistence, I have proposed Udayana's works to be worth recognizing for study by philosophers of religion. While the historical context of the *Ātmatattvaviveka* is that of debates with Materialists and Buddhists, I have shown how Udayana's polemics may be read to present some positive formulations on his understanding of "self," "self-awareness," and "persistence." Udayana's use of "indeterminate perception" enabled his texts to conceptualize an idea of self that persists both prior to and after the state of existing as a human being. The objective of this present chapter is neither to analyze the philosophical merits of Udayana's argumentation nor recommend his approach as a means of doing "global-critical philosophy of religion." I hope that readers will gain new insights into how ancient texts overlooked by Western canons, particularly in the philosophy of religion, can be read to propose novel conceptions of self and persistence.

Notes

1. This chapter is an outcome of the project Cross-Cultural Conceptions of the Self: South Asia, Africa and East Asia held in 2022, which was generously supported from the John Templeton Foundation, awarded via the Global Philosophy of Religion Project (GPRP) at Birmingham University under the leadership of Yujin Nagasawa. To view all the grant outcomes, see: https://globalcritical.barefield.ua.edu/cross-cultural-conceptions-of-self-and-persistence/.
2. The participants in the grant project were: Nathan R. B. Loewen and Agnieszka Rostalska (the project leaders) and Herbert Moyo, Ayodeji Ogunnaike, Oludamini Ogunnaike, Anil Mudra, Marie-Hélène Gorisse, Yuko Ishihara, Louis Komjathy, and Maki Sato as participating scholars. This pioneering online cross-cultural debate is accessible at: https://globalcritical.barefield.ua.edu/uncategorized/debate-on-self-and-persistence/.
3. See Bryan W. Van Norden's introduction of the term in *Taking Back Philosophy* (2017).
4. On the dating of Udayana's life, see Chemparathy (1972: 19–20), Potter (1977: 523), Tachikawa (1981: 14–16), Amma (1985: 4).
5. The series goes as follows: *Nyāya-sūtra* by Akṣapāda Gautama (*c.* 100 CE) ⇨ *Nyāya-bhāṣya* by Pakṣilasvāmin Vātsyāyana (*c.* 450–500 CE) ⇨ *Nyāya-vārttika* by Uddyotakāra (*c.* 550–610 CE) ⇨ *Nyāya-vārttika-tātparya-ṭīkā* by Vācaspati Miśra (*c.* 900–980 CE) ⇨ *Nyāya-vārttika-tātparya-ṭīkā-pariśuddhi* by Udayana (see, for example, Matilal 1977: 76–100).
6. He has crafted an erudite commentary: *Kiraṇāvalī* ("Row of Light-Beams") on the first two chapters of Praśastapāda's *Padārthadharmasamgraha* ("A Compendium of the Characteristics of Categories," on substance, *dravya* and quality, *guṇa*), authored two short manuals, *Lakṣaṇāvalī* ("A Series of Definitions," on Vaiśeṣika categories and their subdivisions) and *Lakṣaṇamālā* ("Garland of Definitions," on categories in Nyāya and Vaiśeṣika), and *Nyāyapariśiṣṭa* or *(Pra)bodhasiddhi* ("Supplement to Nyāya-[sūtra]," a commentary on the last chapter of *Nyāyasūtra*s on debate, *vāda*).
7. Common conceptions of these terms among philosophers of religion must be suspended in order to begin understanding Udayana's texts.
8. Jñānaśrīmitra was one of the most important Buddhist philosophers in the tenth–eleventh centuries CE, the teacher of Ratnakīrti.
9. *tatra bādhakam bhavat kṣaṇabhaṅgo vā vāhyārtha-bhaṅgo vā guṇaguṇibhedabhaṅgo vā anupalambho veti.*
10. A concise survey on a development of the concept of *ātman* in Indian thought is compiled by Bilimoria (2016: 15–27).
11. For readers interested in the Hindu–Buddhist debates on this topic, see Kuznetsova, Ganeri, and Ram-Prasad (eds.) (2012).
12. The self is inferred as an individual agent of perception NBh 16.5–20: the marks of the self (NS1.1.10) involve a synthetic cognitive activity that presupposes a single knowing agent (*jñātṛ*).

13. This definition comes from *Tarkasaṃgraha* of Annambhaṭṭa.
14. Thanks to Anil Mundra for his valuable suggestion of this clarification.
15. Due to limited space, Nyāya inferential proofs of the self are not going to be dealt with. I recommend that the interested reader turns to the scholarship of: A. Chakrabarti, J. Taber, B. K. Matilal, Ch. Ram-Prasad, K. K. Chakrabarti, K. Kanō, R. Perrett, A. Watson, Dasti and Philips, D. Berger, and M. Chadha.
16. An early Nyāya commentator Pakṣilasvāmin Vātsyāyana states it this way: "Of these (*prameya*-s) the self cannot be known by perception. Is it then to be known only from verbal testimony? (*āpta-upadeśa*)?" The answer is in the negative. It is to be known by inference as well" (NBh 1.1.9, Chattopadhyaya and Gangopadhyaya trans., vol. 1, 1967: 72).
17. See the commentary of Vātsyāyana:

    the imperceptible probandum is known on the basis of the same nature of the [perceptible] probans as any other [of which the relation between the probans and the probandum is already known], just as, for instance, the soul [is inferred] from desire and so forth. Because desire and so forth are qualities. [It is already known that] qualities reside in a certain substance. [Therefore,] that which is the substratum of these [qualities] is the [self]." (NBh 18.3–5 ad NS 1.1.5, trans. Kanō 2001: 408).

18. This paragraph is recurrent from a book chapter "Nyāya Critical Thinking on Matters Small and Great: Exploring the Rational Paradigm" (co-authored with P. Bilimoria) in Kopf, Bilimoria, and Loewen (eds.), (2025).
19. *ātmatvābhisambandhād ātmā / tasya saukṣmyād apratyakṣatve sati, Padārthadharmasaṅgraha* (PDS) 6.4.
20. Nyāya's resort to the instance of memory and argument from recollection were examined by D. Berger (2012) and M. Chadha (2013).
21. The Jains level the same criticism against Buddhist doctrines, namely, that moral responsibility implies a continuing self.
22. Udayana himself uses both of these concepts only once in his ATV.
23. Newborn babies experience pleasure, pain, desire, aversion, effort, and previously acquired knowledge, and such knowledge cannot reside in new sense organs; reactions of a newborn to stimuli it does not yet have familiarity with in the present life must require memory, and memory is a quality of the self; a child's inclination toward her mother's breast is not like iron being pulled toward a magnet, because a child's reaction to her mother's breast varies, unlike the iron's reaction to the magnet; a child's reactions are thus based on previous dispositions.
24. See, for example, Burley (2016).
25. Gautama writes (NS 1.1.22), "Absolute freedom from the aforesaid (pain, wrong knowledge, attachment, etc.)."
26. Some of this paragraph is adapted from my chapter, "Nyāya Critical Thinking on Matters Small and Great: Exploring the Rational Paradigm" (co-authored with P. Bilimoria) in Kopf, Bilimoria, and Loewen (eds.) (2025).

Bibliography

Amma, Visweswari. 1985. *Udayana and His Philosophy*. Delhi: Nag Publishers.
Berger, Douglas L., 2012. "The Abode of Recognition: Memory and the Continuity of Selfhood in Classical Nyāya Thought." In *Hindu and Buddhist Ideas in Dialogue: Self and No-Self*. Farnham and Burlington: Ashgate, 115–128.
Bhattacharyya, Sibajiban. 2010. *Development of Nyāya Philosophy and Its Social Context*. History of Science, Philosophy and Culture in Indian Civilization. Vol. 3, pt. 3. New Delhi: Project of History of Indian Science, Philosophy, and Culture, Centre for Studies in Civilizations, 297–335.
Bilimoria, Purushottama. 2016. *Horizons of the Self in Hindu Thought*. 3rd ed. Delhi: D. K. Printworld.
Burley, Mikel. 2016. *Rebirth and the Stream of Life: A Philosophical Study of Reincarnation*. Karma and Ethics. London: Bloomsbury Academic.
Chadha, Monima. 2013. "The Self in Early Nyāya: A Minimal Conclusion." *Asian Philosophy*, 23 (1): 24–42.
Chakrabarti, Arindam. 1982. "Nyaya Proofs for the Existence of the Self." *Journal of Indian Philosophy*, 10 (3): 211–238.
Chakrabarti, Arindam. 1983. "Is Liberation (*mokṣa*) Pleasant?" *Philosophy East and West*, 33 (2): 167–182.
Chakrabarti, Arindam. 1992. "I Touch What I Saw." *Philosophy and Phenomenological Research,,* 52 (1): 103–116.
Chakrabarti, Kisor K. 1999. *Classical Indian Philosophy of Mind: The Nyāya Dualist Tradition*. Albany: SUNY Press.
Chakrabarti, Kisor K. 2015. "Atmatattvaviveka (Analysis of the Nature of the Self): An Annotated Translation." *Journal of Indian Philosophy and Religion*, 20: 164–179.
Chemparathy, George. 1972. *An Indian Rational Theology: Introduction to Udayana's Nyāyakusumāñjali*. Vienna: Brill, Gerold & Co; Delhi: Motilal Banarsidass.
Dasti, Matthew, and Stephen H. Phillips, trans. and ed. 2017. "Self." *The Nyāyasūtra: Selections with Early Commentaries*. Indianapolis and Cambridge: Hackett, 74–94.
Ganeri, Jonardon. 2012. *The Self. Naturalism, Consciousness, and the First-Person Stance*. Oxford: Oxford University Press.
Gautama. 1967–1976. *Nyāya Philosophy: Literal Translation of Gautama's Nyāya-sūtra and Vātsyāyana's Bhāṣya*. Ed. Debriprasad Chattopadhyaya and Mrinalkanti Gangopadhyaya. Calcutta: Indian Studies Past and Present.
Halbfass, Wilhelm. 1997. "Happiness, a Nyāya-Vaiśeṣika Perspective." In P. Bilimoria and J. N. Mohanty (eds.), *Relativism, Suffering and Beyond: Essays in Memory of Bimal K. Matilal*. Delhi: Oxford University Press, 150–163.
Krishna, Daya. 2004. *The Nyāyasūtras. A New Commentary of an Old Text*. Delhi: Sri Satguru Publications.
Kuznetsova, Irina, Chakravarthi Ram-Prasad, and Jonardon Ganeri, eds. 2012. *Hindu and Buddhist Ideas in Dialogue: Self and No-Self*. Dialogues in South Asian Traditions Series. Farnham and Burlington: Ashgate.

Kyō Kanō. 2001. "Pariśeṣā, Prasaṅga, and Kevalavyatirekin – The Logical Structure of the Proof of Ātman." *Journal of Indian Philosophy*, 29: 405–422.

Laine, Joy Elisabeth. 1990. "The Concept of Self in Nyaya-Vaisesika Philosophy." PhD thesis, The Open University.

Matilal, Bimal K. 1977. *Nyāya-Vaiśeṣika*. A History of Indian Literature. Vol. 6, ed. Jan Gonda, Wiesbaden: Otto Harrassowitz 1977.

Matilal, Bimal K. 1994. "The Perception of Self in Indian Tradition." In Roger T. Ames, Wimal Dissanayake, and Thomas P. Kasulis (eds.). *Self as Person in Asian Theory and Practice*. Albany: SUNY Press, 279–295.

Perrett, Roy W. 1985. "Dualistic and Nondualistic Problems of Immortality." *Philosophy East and West*, 35 (4): 333–350.

Potter, Karl H. 1977. *Encyclopedia of Indian Philosophies. Volume II: Indian Metaphysics and Epistemology: The Tradition of Nyāya-Vaiśeṣika Up to Gaṅgeśa*. Delhi: Motilal Banarsidass, 521–603.

Ram-Prasad, Chakravarthi. 2001. "Saving the Self? Classical Hindu Theories of Consciousness and Contemporary Physicalism." *Philosophy East and West* 51: 3, Eighth East–West Philosophers' Conference, 378–392.

Ram-Prasad, Chakravarthi. 2017. "A Phenomenological Reading of the Nyāya Critique of the No-Self view: Udayana and the Phenomenal Separateness of Self." In P. Bilimoria, Purushottama Bilimoria, with Amy Rayner (eds.), *History of Indian Philosophy*. Routledge History of World Philosophies. Abingdon and New York: Routledge, 204–213.

Rostalska, Agnieszka, and Purushottama Bilimoria. 2025. "Nyāya Rationalism and Critical Thinking on Matters Small and Great." In Gereon Kopf, Purushottama Bilimoria, and Nathan R. B. Loewen (eds.), *Engaging Philosophies of Religion: Thinking across Boundaries*. London: Bloomsbury, 121–137.

Tachikawa, Musashi. 1981. *The Structure of the World in Udayana's Realism: A Study of the Lakṣaṇāvalī and the Kiraṇāvalī*. Dordrecht: Reidel Publishing Company.

Udayana Ācārya. 1940. *Ātmatattvaviveka*. Ed. Dhuṇḍhirāja Śāstrī. Varanasi: Chowkhamba Sanskrit Series.

Udayana Ācārya. [1907–1939] 1986. *Ātmatattvaviveka*. With the commentaries of Śaṅkara Miśra, Bhagīratha Thakkura, and Raghunātha Tārkikaśiromaṇi. Ed. Mahamahopadhyaya Vindyesvariprasada Dvivendin and Pandit Lakshmana Sastri Dravida. Calcutta: The Asiatic Society.

Udayana Ācārya. 1987. *Ātmatattvaviveka*. Text, trans., and notes Chitrarekha V. Kher and Shiv Kumar. New Delhi: Eastern Book Linkers.

Udayana Ācārya. 1995. *Ātmatattvaviveka*. Trans, explanation, and analytical–critical survey N. S. Dravid. Shimla: Indian Institute of Advanced Studies.

Van Norden, Bryan W. 2017. *Taking Back Philosophy: A Multicultural Manifesto*. New York: Columbia University Press.

Watson, Alex. 2017. "Self or No-Self? The Ātman Debate in Classical Indian Philosophy." In Joerg Tuske (ed.), *Indian Epistemology and Metaphysics*. London: Bloomsbury, 293–317.

Ātman
Chapter 1.1

The idea of "self" or "soul" has a deep-rooted history in Indian tradition. In Chapter 1, I discussed Udayana's arguments for the existence and persistence of the self in his *Ātmatattvaviveka*. Therefore, in this key word entry, I will briefly introduce the most common term for "self" across Indian philosophical traditions, which was debated by Nyāya philosophers: "ātman." The highly popular and perhaps the earliest philosophical discussions of *ātman* can be traced back to the Upaniṣads (see Black 2007), where the *ātman*, or the individual self, is seen as identical with *Brahman*, or the universal, transcendent reality. This idea later became a central tenet of non-duality in Advaita Vedānta philosophy.[1] Key terms that refer to the self in philosophical discussions include *jīva*, *jīvātman*, and *puruṣa*.

Before exploring the concept of *ātman* in more detail, I will briefly consider these closely related concepts of 'self' defended by philosophers of the coexisting traditions, which helps clarify what Nyāya philosophers were either opposing or supporting. I will start with the very general note about the self's negation expressed in Buddhist conception of no-self *anātman*: most Buddhists contended that cognitions are causally linked only within a continuous flow of awareness events, rather than existing in a substance known as the self. They viewed cognitions not as qualities but as phenomena generated by the connection between bodily sense organs and prior karmic dispositions. The Buddhist claim was that there is no fixed substantial self because each moment arises from a different combination of factors. While these factors may serve as the background for the next state, that subsequent state is entirely distinct. In other words, even if one state—whether of an individual or the entire world—follows another, Buddhists argue there is no reason to say these states belong to the same person or entity in the world. For example, the dominant Mahayana perspective (occupied mainly with Nagarjuna's thought), stresses that all phenomena lack inherent existence and are interconnected, arising dependently. The ultimate reality is defined by emptiness or nothingness, *śūnyatā*, and transcends conceptual comprehension. *Nirvāṇa*, the liberated state, is not an object to be reached but a realization of the true nature of reality, where distinctions such as the cycle of suffering, *saṃsāra*, and *nirvāṇa* itself dissolve.[2]

The Indian materialists, also known as the Cārvāka or Lokāyata philosophy, held that everything in the universe undergoes change due to 'change' occurring on its own, *svabhāva*. Mainstream interpretations of Cārvāka assert that all objects exist according to their inherent "own-natures" or follow their fundamental natures. In modern terms, materialists would be considered emergentists. It's important to note that their views are primarily preserved in the writings of their contestants. One of the earliest such thinkers was the Jain doxographer Haribhadra Sūri (seventh century CE), who observed that for materialists, cognitions are qualities of the bodily organs (Murty trans., 1986). Consciousness emerges from physical processes and appears when the body matures, ceasing when the body dies. Just as the intoxicating properties come from wine ingredients, so does consciousness. The self (Haribhadra uses the term *puruṣa*) is simply a body endowed with consciousness. Furthermore, for materialists, there is no concept of liberation (*nirvāṇa*, as used by Buddhists), and death itself is seen as final liberation or beatitude (*āpavargaḥ*, as used by Nyāya thinkers), and there are no gods (*deva*).[3]

An overview of traditions centered on the concept of the self is incomplete without mentioning Jainism, one of the oldest enduring philosophico-religious traditions in India. Jain thinkers differentiate between beings that are *jīva*, representing the self or sentience, and *ajīva*, the non-sentient. According to Jain teachings, all living entities (*jīvas*) possess varying levels of consciousness, or *caitanya*. The universe is divided into two primary categories: living substances and non-living substances. The *jīva* represents the essence of life, while *ajīva* comprises everything non-living, such as matter, space, and other non-material entities. Grasping the nature of both *jīva* and *ajīva* is crucial in Jain philosophy, as it informs the journey toward liberation, here under the term *mokṣa*. Moreover, the Jain worldview is not anthropocentric. Every sentient being is a self and therefore has the right to *ahiṃsā*, non-harm or nonviolence. This means that to achieve liberation, Jains must avoid harming all possible beings. Karma is not just a simple cause-and-effect mechanism, but more of a polluting "stuff" or "matter" that sticks to the self like dirt. Every action or thought adds more karmic contamination, weighing the self down like ballast and pulling it into the cycle of rebirth and a worldly state suited to the level of moral contamination. To reach liberation, the self needs to be free from burdensome elements by preventing new karma through practicing non-injury to all creatures and by following strict physical asceticism.[4]

While the Jains believe that the self, *jīva*, is not a static entity due to its inherent capacity for consciousness, experience, and self-awareness, philosophers from the Sāṃkhya and Yoga traditions view the self as an inactive principle. Here, the self, under the term *puruṣa*, is pure dispassionate consciousness. The self is not a self-aware entity that possesses qualities or properties. It remains neutral, indifferent, unconditioned, unmoving, unresponsive, and powerless—without beginning or end, and eternally free. Additionally, the idea of a substantial self is just a "product" or transformation of another principle, which is "nature" or *prakṛti*, interacting with the immediate presence of *puruṣa*. *Puruṣa* influences material nature much like light enters a crystal (Bilimoria 2016: 31). In the liberating state, here called *kaivaya*, the self separates or detaches itself from the world and the cycle of suffering, *saṃsāra*, after recognizing its true, independent nature that is distinct from "nature" or *prakṛti*.[5]

This introduction leads us to the Nyāya concept of *ātman*, which generally represents the unchanging, undifferentiated, unconditioned, and autonomous principle of existence in human beings. Liberation from rebirth, or *mokṣa*, involves the realization of the self, *ātman*. The question of how the concept of the "self" is defined in the Nyāya tradition is directly connected to another widespread issue among all traditions in India, mainly: can the existence of "self" be known through the means of knowledge or *pramāṇa*s, such as perception, inference, and testimony, etc.? Also, if and how is the state of "liberated consciousness" something that the self desires? Is it a happy or blissful state?

Like most Indian philosophies that acknowledge the existence of a permanent self, the Nyāya tradition posits the existence of infinitely many selves/souls or *ātman*s, which are eternal, immaterial, and non-composite substances possessing characteristic qualities (e.g., cognition, pleasure, pain, or desire). These selves are singular and distinct in all organisms. *Ātman* is inferred as an individual agent of perception. Initially, the self is separate from the mind and senses, allowing it to observe its own activity. Here, the 'mind' or manas is not active but a passive organ that neither thinks nor acts, serving as a tool for the self to experience and understand. Cognition is a characteristic of *ātman*, which acts as an awareness center. The self has attributes like thoughts, tendencies, memories, feelings, and actions. Thus, *ātman* is not limited to consciousness, as some materialists or Buddhists claim, but is a unique individual self with personality.

Nyāya thinkers tended to conceptualize *ātman* as physically imperceptible, meaning it is only known through its inferential signs or marks. In other words, it is an object of inference based on its "marks": desire, aversion, effort, pleasure, pain, and knowledge (NS 1.1.10). These marks of the self involve a complex cognitive activity that assumes a single knowing agent. They experience while associated with "body vehicles" made up of homogeneous atoms of a specific material substance. Before the connection with the mind or *manas*, an individual self is not conscious. In other words, the self must be embodied to experience awareness and cognition. *Ātman* is the substratum of knowing, an innate cause of consciousness. Nyāya philosophers use the example of yarn and cloth: the yarn is an "inherent cause" of the cloth but is not cloth by nature. Similarly, *ātman* causes consciousness without being inherently conscious; consciousness is an accidental attribute that emerges through its connection with the body.

As a continuous spiritual substance, *ātman* maintains its identity within and across lifetimes. Nyāya thinkers argue that the self persists beyond death, pointing out that an infant immediately experiences joy, fear, and sorrow, which come from memories of past experiences that go beyond those formed in the womb. And these memories generate emotions. The key assumption is rebirth: how does the newborn respond emotionally? Reactions are linked to memories of previous experiences. The self's continuity extends into the past and future, giving it two core identities: the identity of knowing—perceiving cognitions—and that of action—inheritance of karmic fruits and pleasure or pain (Dasti 2014).

Finally, Nyāya thinkers also acknowledge the hierarchy of the selves by arguing for the existence of the highest self, *paramātman* or Īśvara / *God (see Rostalska and

Bilimoria 2025). *God is the just overseer of karmic fruits, the one who actuates the karma of individuals or lower selves. Vātsyāyana in *Nyāyabhāṣya* (NBh) 4.1.19 states that compared to regular selves, Īśvara differs in qualities because he is free of demerits, mistaken cognition, or delusion, and possesses perfect merit, knowledge, and yogic concentration (*samādhi*). "His merit (*dharma*), which conforms to his intention, activates the merit and demerit collected in each individual self as well as in gross elements such as earth" (Dasti and Phillips 2017: 118).

As their ultimate goal, the selves aim for the liberated state of consciousness. Most traditions of Indian philosophy assume the persistence of the self, or at least the traits of one's personhood, in agreement with the (relatively) axiomatic karmic theory, i.e., transmigration or rebirth. One aims to stop all accumulation of coextensive with the self unobservable karmic properties, that is to say, merits, demerits, and impressions (*bhāvanās*). Nyāya thinkers use a few Sanskrit terms for this ultimate goal of philosophy, which are *niḥśreyasa*, the highest good, and *apavarga*, the ultimate happiness or beatitude, along with liberation (*mokṣa*) from ignorance (*avidyā*) and suffering (*duḥkha*). I discuss these concepts in the next entry on permanence.

Notes

1. Due to limited space, I am skipping the discussion of *ātman* proposed by the Advaita Vedānta philosopher Śankara and refer to work of Chatterjee (1988), Bilimoria (2016), and Medhananda (2025).
2. There is a vast philosophical literature on the topic of no-Self *anātman* in Buddhism, see, for example, Flanagan (2011), Ganeri (2012, 2017), Siderits (2015), Westerhoff (2018), Thompson (2020), among others.
3. Ramkrishna Bhattacharya (2011) conducted extensive studies on the philosophy of Indian materialists.
4. Among the vast literature on Jain conception of self, see Bajželj (2024).
5. For excellent scholarship of the Sāṃkhya and Yoga account of self, and related concepts of *karma* and rebirth, see Chapple (1986) and Burley (2007).

References

Bajželj. Ana. 2024. "Selfhood, Persistence, and Immortality in Jaina Philosophy." *Religious Studies*, 60 (1): 1–23.

Bhattacharya, Ramkrishna. 2011. *Studies on The Cārvāka/Lokāyata*. London: Anthem Press.

Bilimoria, Purushottama. 2016. *Horizons of the Self in Hindu Thought*. 3rd ed. Delhi: D. K. Printworld.

Black, Brian. 2007. *The Character of the Self in Ancient India: Priests, Kings, and Women in the Early Upaniṣads.* Albany: SUNY Press.

Burley, Mikel. 2007. *Classical Sāṃkhya and Yoga: An Indian Metaphysics of Experience.* London: Routledge.

Chapple, Christopher K. 1986. *Karma and Creativity.* Albany: SUNY Press.

Chatterjee, D. 1988. "Karma and Liberation in Śankara's Advaita Vedanta." In S. S. Rama Rao Pappu (ed.), *Perspectives on Vedānta: Essays in Honor of Professor P. T. Raju.* Leiden: E. J. Brill, 158–169.

Dasti, Matthew. 2014. "Nyāya's Self as Agent and Knower." In M. R. Dasti and E. F. Bryant (eds.), *Free Will, Agency, and Selfhood in Indian Philosophy.* New York: Oxford University Press, 112–136.

Dasti, Matthew, and Stephen H. Phillips. 2017. *The Nyāyasūtra: Selections with Early Commentaries.* "Self." Indianapolis and Cambridge: Hackett, 74–94.

Flanagan, Owen. 2011. *The Bodhisattva's Brain. Buddhism Naturalized.* Cambridge: MIT Press.

Ganeri, Jonardon. 2006. *The Concealed Art of the Soul: Theories of Truth in Indian Ethics and Epistemology.* Oxford: Oxford University Press.

Ganeri, Jonardon. 2012. *The Self: Naturalism, Consciousness, and the First-Person Stance.* Oxford, Oxford University Press.

Ganeri, Jonardon. 2017. *Attention, Not Self.* Oxford: Oxford University Press.

Gautama. 1967–1976. *Nyāya Philosophy: Literal Translation of Gautama's Nyāya-sūtra and Vātsyāyana's Bhāṣya.* Ed. Debriprasad Chattopadhyaya and Mrinalkanti Gangopadhyaya. Calcutta: Indian Studies Past and Present.

Haribhadra. 1986. *Ṣaḍdarśanasamuccaya: A Compendium of Six Philosophies by Haribhadra.* With trans. and notes by K. S. Murty. Delhi: Eastern Book Linkers.

Kuznetsova, Irina, Chakravarthi Ram-Prasad, and Jonardon Ganeri, eds. 2012. *Hindu and Buddhist Ideas in Dialogue: Self and No-Self.* Dialogues in South Asian Traditions Series. Farnham and Burlington: Ashgate.

Medhananda, Swami. 2025. *Karma and Rebirth in Hinduism.* Cambridge Elements. Elements in Global Philosophy of Religion. Ed. Yujin Nagasawa. Cambridge: Cambridge University Press.

Rostalska, Agnieszka, and Purushottama Bilimoria. 2025. "Nyāya Rationalism and Critical Thinking on Matters Small and Great." In Gereon Kopf, Purushottama Bilimoria, and Nathan R. B. Loewen (eds.), *Engaging Philosophies of Religion: Thinking across Boundaries.* London: Bloomsbury, 121–137.

Siderits, Mark. 2015. *Personal Identity and Buddhist Philosophy. Empty Persons.* Second Edition. Abingdon, New York: Routledge.

Thompson, Evan. 2020. *Why I Am Not a Buddhist.* New Haven: Yale University Press.

Udayana Acārya. 1987. *Ātmatattvaviveka.* Text, trans., and notes Chitrarekha V. Kher and Shiv Kumar, New Delhi: Eastern Book Linkers.

Udayana Ācārya. 1995. *Ātmatattvaviveka.* Trans., explanation, and analytical–critical survey N. S. Dravid. Shimla: Indian Institute of Advanced Studies.

Westerhoff, Jan. 2018. *The Golden Age of Indian Buddhist Philosophy.* Oxford: Oxford University Press.

Persistence
Chapter 1.2

The Nyāya philosophers are primarily epistemologists and logicians who investigate the nature of knowledge and the ontological structure of what is known. They provide rational means for a systematic or analytical inquiry to explore what can be known and how knowledge can be justified. Interestingly, all of their theoretical pursuits are directed at the supreme goal, which is the state of unconditional freedom of one's permanent self (*ātman*). They encourage epistemological growth by connecting cognitive achievements to successful actions, which are "motivation to seek righteousness (*dharma*), wealth (*arha*), pleasure (*kāma*), and liberation (*mokṣa*), and to avoid what is opposed to them, proceeds through comprehension of knowledge sources and their objects" (*Nyāyabhāṣya*, later for short: NBh, 2.1.20).

The ideal of persistence of the (variously defined across Indian philosophical traditions) self, or at least the persistence of one's personal traits, has been and remains one of the central assumptions for most Indian philosophers (Potter 1991: 93–4[1]). For Nyāya thinkers, the Sanskrit philosophical concepts used to designate one's ultimate goal are *niḥśreyasa*, the highest good, and *apavarga*, the ultimate happiness or beatitude, along with the abovementioned liberation (*mokṣa*) from ignorance (*avidyā*) and suffering (*duḥkha*) (see Krishna 1984: 61–67; Dasti and Philips 2017: 8, 156–161; and Rostalska and Bilimoria 2025). More direct terms used by the Naiyāyikas, which correspond to the English "persistence," are *sthira* (used in compounds *sthira-ātman*, or persistent self, and *sthira-dharmin*, substrate or persistent property holder) as well as correlative terms that refer to the self, such as "beginningless" (*anādi*), and "endless" (*ananta*). As one can observe, Nyāya's idea of the self is based on the notion of *ātman* and includes the concept of karmic dispositions.

What leads one to *niḥśreyasa*, or the highest good? The knowledge of the 16 topics of inquiry in epistemology, metaphysics, and debate theory listed in the *Nyāyasūtra* (NS) of Gautama, headed by the *pramāṇa*s, or means of knowledge, and the *prameya*s, or object sets and subsets, which are truthfully cognizable (*prameyatva*). "Knowledge sources, objects of knowledge, doubt, motive, example, accepted position, inferential components, suppositional reasoning, certainty, debate for the truth, disputation, destructive debate, pseudo-provers, equivocation, misleading objections, and clinchers: from knowledge of these, there is attainment of the supreme good" (Dasti and Philips 2017: 9). Gautama (NS 1.1.9) enumerates twelve cognizable object of knowledge, namely: self (*ātman*), body, sense faculties, objects of the senses, cognition (*buddhi*), mind (*manas*, the "internal organ"), purposive action (*pravṛtti*), vice (*doṣa*), rebirth, fruit of action, suffering (*duḥkha*), and final beatitude (apavarga), which is attained through the investigation of the self and its differentiation from all these tropes (Dasti and Phillips 2017, 95–97). But one's intellectual inquiry must undeniably integrate ethics. Here, leading a virtuous life aligns with the moral principles that comprise the eightfold path of the *Yogasūtras*. Gautama explicitly mentions the *yama*s, or restraints and *niyama*s, or observances, as essential for self-purification (*ātma-saṃskāra*): "for the purpose of attaining *apavarga*, there should be self-purification by means of yogic restraints or precepts and observances and by psychological instruction and methods taught in yoga" NS 4.2.26 (Dasti and Phillips 2017, 168). The yogic precepts include non-violence, truthfulness, not stealing, sexual restraint, and non-possession (YS 2.30, Chapple 2008: 124), while the observances are purity, contentment, austerity, self-study, and dedication to Īśvara or *God (YS 2. 32, Chapple 2008: 125). The Nyāya thinkers regarded *dharma* as ethical virtues, mainly as obeying universal moral laws that apply to all (*sadharana dharma*). Vātsyāyana (NBh ad. 1.1.2) states that *dharma* and *adharma* depend on body, or speech, or mind: (1) body—*adharma*: violence, theft, and unlawful sexual indulgence; *dharma*: charity, succor of the distressed, and social service; (2) speech—*adharma*: lying, caustic talk/rudeness, calumny/fault-finding, and absurd talk/incoherence; *dharma*: veracity/truth, talking with good intention/benevolence, gentle talk, recitation of scriptures; and (3) mind—*adharma*: ill will/plotting against others, covetousness, and irreligious thinking; *dharma*: kindness, disinterestedness, and faith or piety (Gangopadhyaya (ed.), 28). Interestingly, Naiyāyikas also recommended cultivating yogic practices, that is to say, the techniques of meditation and understanding of the deep self, akin to being in a state of yogic trance (Dasti and Phillips 2017: 161).

What kind of a state is *niḥśreyasa*? Persistence of the self amounts to its release, where the self continues to exist independently of the body in a joyless, unending, free-time seamless horizon—and steeped in a deep-sleep state minus the dreams, see: NS 4.1.62, Gangopadhyaya (trans.) pt. 4, 1973: 86). In this state, the self is atemporal (*nityatva*) and cannot be extinguished. There is no merging with the other, no greater or smaller of which could be thought.[2] Udayana's formulation of "release without transcendence" amounts to a unique model of liberation that explains the persistence of the self. The release of the self from indeterminate cognition occurs not because of any mental state succeeding it but by means of time associated with the destruction of the self's destiny.

When the self achieves the purest of ideas, it reaches a state which amounts to attaining comprehensive knowledge (*tattvajñāna*) of all there is to know. *Niḥśreyasa*, more than knowledge of the self, is an all-encompassing knowledge state. This is not the same transcendental state that is emphasized in the more "spiritually" oriented theological systems—particularly, *mokṣa* or salvific liberation from the embodied state of existence. *Niḥśreyasa* as such has no necessary connections with life hereafter (Potter 1977: 29–34). This knowledge amounts to nothing more nor less than the destruction of all false understandings or *mithyajñāna*.[3] The liberating aspect of the *niḥśreyasa* state is that no pleasures are transported across. Not even the positive pleasures of life, desire-driven satisfaction, from luxuries of appetite to sensual-sexual pleasures (Halbfass 1997: 155–156). The state of *niḥśreyasa*, or the highest good, represents a unique understanding of liberation that does not necessarily involve transcendence or eternal happiness, thus providing a nuanced perspective on the self's persistence and its implications for ethical living.

Clearly understanding what the self truly is is key to achieving ultimate liberation (*mokṣa*). According to Nyāya, *mokṣa*—also known as liberation from rebirth, or *apavarga*—is the primary goal of all philosophical pursuits. In a state of liberation, the self is free from a physical body and retains only its core qualities, such as being one and separate from other selves. By eliminating all flaws, like attitudes and predispositions, and stopping activity, the self achieves freedom from pain and suffering (*ātyantika-duḥkha-vimukti*). Although the self is freed from the cycle of rebirth, it doesn't enter a state of eternal bliss or happiness (Chakrabarti 1983: 174–175). Instead, it continues to exist without further mental states (Ram-Prasad 2001: 85–91; Das 2020).

Theological discussions concerning the "afterlife" are merely referenced here and are not the primary subject. Although the concepts of *paraloka* (a realm beyond this world) and *svarga* (a transient realm for those who have not attained liberation) are related to the "afterlife," they are not the central focus within the Nyāya tradition. Nonetheless, the existence of a self provides a foundation for discussing karma. Udayana argues that, although the understanding of karma depends on the concept of the self, the idea of the self does not solely rely on karma. Instead, karma is one of the phenomena that support the concept of the self as ātman. The law of karma involves the accumulation of merits and demerits, where a person reaps the results of their actions. According to Nyāya, a previous state is followed by the next state, with a short gap in between, in which something must connect these states across the gap. Furthermore, Udayana highlights that, in line with Nyāya's views on causality, the self is the inherent cause of our awareness of ourselves. And like the Jains, Naiyāyikas also admit that moral responsibility requires a continuous self (see Bajželj 2024).

My interpretation relies on specific readings of the texts and may not cover all perspectives within the Nyāya tradition. Future research could delve into the implications of these findings for modern ethical debates and the ongoing relevance of Nyāya philosophy today. Ultimately, understanding how the concept of self persists is key to grasping the moral aspects of Nyāya philosophy. Further exploration of these themes, especially how ancient philosophical insights can inform current discussions on identity, morality, and the nature of knowledge, is essential to making philosophy of religion a truly global and diverse field.

Notes

1. See also Anil Mundra's keyword entry on *Liberation/mokṣa* in Chapter 3 in this volume.

2. Small bits of this and the next paragraph are adapted from the chapter co-authored with P. Bilimoria (2025).
3. Gautama writes (NS 1.1.22): "Absolute freedom from the aforesaid (pain, wrong knowledge, attachment, etc.)."

References

Amma, Visweswari. 1985. *Udayana and His Philosophy*. Delhi: Nag Publishers.
Bajželj, Ana. 2024. "Selfhood, Persistence, and Immortality in Jaina Philosophy." *Religious Studies*, 60: 21–43.
Bhattacharyya, Sibajiban. 2010. *Development of Nyāya Philosophy and Its Social Context*. History of Science, Philosophy and Culture in Indian Civilization. Vol. 3, pt. 3. New Delhi: Project of History of Indian Science, Philosophy, and Culture, Centre for Studies in Civilizations.
Bronkhorst, Johannes. 2000. *Karma and Teleology: A Problem and Its Solutions in Indian Philosophy*. Tokyo: International Institute for Buddhist Studies.
Bronkhorst, Johannes. 2011. *Karma*. Honolulu: University of Hawaii Press.
Chakrabarti, Arindam. 1983. "Is Liberation (*mokṣa*) pleasant?" *Philosophy East and West*, 33 (2): 167–182.
Chapple Christopher K. 2008. *Yoga and the Luminous: Patañjali's Spiritual Path to Freedom*. Albany: SUNY Press.
Das, Nilanjan. 2020. "Vātsyāyana's Guide to Liberation." *Journal of Indian Philosophy*, 48: 791–825.
Dasti, Matthew and Stephen H. Phillips. 2017. *The Nyāyasūtra: Selections with Early Commentaries*. "Self." Indianapolis and Cambridge: Hackett, 74–94.
Gautama. 1967–1976. *Nyāya Philosophy. Literal Translation of Gautama's Nyāya-sūtra and Vātsyāyana's Bhāṣya*. Ed. Debriprasad Chattopadhyaya and Mrinalkanti Gangopadhyaya. Calcutta: Indian Studies Past and Present.
Halbfass, Wilhelm. 1997. "Happiness, a Nyāya-Vaiśeṣika Perspective." In P. Bilimoria and J. N. Mohanty (eds.), *Relativism, Suffering and Beyond: Essays in Memory of Bimal K. Matilal*. Delhi: Oxford University Press, 150–163.
Krishna, Daya. 1984. "Indian Philosophy and Mokṣa: Revisiting an Old Controversy." *Journal of Indian Council of Philosophical Research*, 2 (2): 49–67.
Medhananda, Swami. 2025. *Karma and Rebirth in Hinduism*. Cambridge Elements. Elements in Global Philosophy of Religion. Ed. by Yujin Nagasawa. Cambridge: Cambridge University Press.
Potter, Karl H. 1977. *Encyclopedia of Indian Philosophies, Volume II: Indian Metaphysics and Epistemology: The Tradition of Nyāya-Vaiśeṣika up to Gaṅgeśa*. Delhi: Motilal Banarsidass, 521–603.
Potter, Karl. H. 1991 (1963). *Presuppositions of India's Philosophies*. Delhi: Motilal Banarsidass.
Ram-Prasad, Chakravarthi. 2001. "Saving the Self? Classical Hindu Theories of Consciousness and Contemporary Physicalism." *Philosophy East and West* 51: 3, Eighth East-West Philosophers' Conference, 378–392.

Rostalska, Agnieszka, and Purushottama Bilimoria. 2025. "Nyāya Rationalism and Critical Thinking on Matters Small and Great." In Gereon Kopf, Purushottama Bilimoria, and Nathan R. B. Loewen (eds.), *Engaging Philosophies of Religion: Thinking across Boundaries*. London: Bloomsbury, 121–137.

Udayana Ācārya. 1995. *Ātmatattvaviveka*. Trans., explanation, and analytical–critical survey N. S. Dravid. Shimla: Indian Institute of Advanced Studies.

2

The Making of the Person in Candomblé

José Eduardo Porcher

Chapter Outline

Introduction	41
Candomblé	42
Who is in One's Head	45
Making the Saint (and the Person)	47
Where the Saint Ends and the Self Begins	50
Conclusion	52
2.1 *Ori*	55
2.2 *Santo*	61
2.3 *Assento*	66

Introduction

The theme of personhood is an especially fruitful source of discussion when drawing from traditions that practice spirit possession, the temporary displacement of a person's conscious self by a more powerful, immaterial being during a state of trance. In Candomblé, however, possession is not merely spontaneous; it is progressively learned and controlled. Mediums develop lasting bonds with their governing entities, enabling these beings to periodically manifest in the earthly realm. Investigating the nature of these bonds is crucial to fully grasping this complex and nuanced conception of personhood. As J. Lorand Matory notes, "Spirit possession is the most dramatic public demonstration of the vessel-based Yorùbá-Atlantic model of the person (2018: 11)." This model is defined by the coexistence of opposing forces and reflects historical encounters within the trans-Atlantic zone. The Afro-Atlantic self is composite, fractal (Gell 1998), networked (Latour 1987), and a "crossroads of forces" (Matory 2018: 286).

In this chapter, I first introduce Candomblé, discussing its social and historical context, deities, and core practices—particularly possession and sacrifice—most of which have been overlooked by philosophy. I then explore the Yoruba-derived concept of the "head" (*ori*), a key to understanding Candomblé's view of the self, demonstrating how the person in this tradition includes a multiplicity of entities that are progressively "settled" in one's head. Next, I analyze the practices of settling deities in material objects in relation to the novice, with a focus on the key ritual of initiation, revealingly called "making" in Candomblé, and how these practices link possession to the construction of personhood. Finally, I offer reflections on how the relationship between deities and their human adepts uncovers a complex dynamic between multiplicity and individuality.

Because Candomblé and other African-derived religions in Brazil are orally transmitted and lack a centralized doctrinal authority or tradition of systematic theology, it is essential—not optional—to draw upon often overlooked sources in philosophy, such as oral literature, mythic narratives, and ethnographic studies. Additionally, as Afro-Brazilian traditions have been largely neglected in philosophical discourse, the most profound insights into their philosophically rich dimensions have been developed by cultural anthropologists, whose work I rely on extensively. As Melville Herskovits (1956: 165) aptly noted, "the supreme compensatory mechanism of the very structure of Candomblé lies in its flexibility. There is no rule without exception; on every occasion, situations alter the case." What follows, then, is an introductory, exploratory, and tentative investigation, and any conclusions drawn from it should avoid the trap of excessive generalization.

Candomblé

Between 1500 and the 1860s, over four million enslaved Africans were forcibly brought to Brazil. This staggering number represented nearly 40 percent of all those subjected to the transatlantic journey, a figure that exceeded those sent to the United States by more than tenfold (Bergad 2007). These individuals came from diverse African ethnic groups, particularly influencing Brazil's early capitals, Salvador and Rio de Janeiro. They brought with them their languages, deities, rituals, cuisine, dances, and music, which merged with the traditions of other enslaved peoples and with the Roman Catholicism introduced by Portuguese colonizers. This fusion of traditions led to the simultaneous emergence of various religious families, such as Candomblé in Bahia, Xangô in Pernambuco, Tambor de Mina in Maranhão, Batuque in Rio Grande do Sul, among others.

Two main ethnic groups were brought to Brazil during the transatlantic slave trade. The first, often called the Western "Sudanese," included the Yoruba (known as Nagô in Brazil), the Ewe and Fon (known as Jêje), and the Ashanti, from present-day Nigeria, Ghana, Benin, and Togo. They arrived mainly through Salvador and worked in northeastern sugar plantations between the seventeenth and nineteenth centuries. The second group, from the Bantu ethnolinguistic family, consisted of Angolans, Kasanje, and Mbangala from present-day Congo, Angola, and Mozambique. They entered via Rio de Janeiro and worked along the coast and inland, especially in Minas Gerais and Goiás. Each "nation" has striven to preserve its deities, rituals, songs, and ceremonial traditions, though there has been significant intermingling—so much so that many temples (*terreiros*) identify as Jêje-Nagô, for instance.

Candomblé ritual worship revolves around the invocation and celebration of African deities, primarily known as *orixás*, along with semi-divine ancestors (*eguns*) and powerful spirits.[1] These deities form a pantheon, believed to be created by or to have emerged from the Supreme Being, Olorum—also called Olodumare (Porcher, 2025b). This mode of worship underpins several religious traditions shaped by New World slavery, such as Cuban Lucumí (also known as Regla de Ocha or Santería), Haitian Vodou, and Dominican Vudú. Although there are no specific myths, shrines, or rituals dedicated to Candomblé's high god, the Supreme Being plays a key role in myths concerning the origins of existence and the creation of the earthly realm (*aiê*). Before creation, only the spiritual realm (*orum*) existed. Following Yoruba mythology, Candomblé divides this realm into two spheres: a higher one where the Supreme Being dwells, and a lower one, closely linked to the earthly realm, which is home to the *orixás* and ancestors.

Juana Elbein dos Santos ([1976] 2012: 59) provides us with one of the few mythic narratives about what happened even before the emergence of the *orixás*, the creation of the earthly world, and its definitive separation from the spiritual world. It is especially useful to help us understand the primacy of two *orixás*, Oxalá and Exu:

> [I]n the beginning, there was nothing but air; Ọlọ́run was an infinite mass of air; when it began to move slowly, to breathe, part of the air turned into a mass of water, originating the great Órìṣà-Funfun, òrìṣà of white. The air and water moved together and a part of themselves turned into mud. From this mud a bubble or mound emerged, the first matter to be given shape, a reddish and muddy rock. Ọlọ́run admired this shape and blew on the mound, breathing his breath and giving it life. This form, the first endowed with individual existence, a laterite rock, was Èṣù, or rather, the proto-Èṣù, Èṣù Yangí.
>
> (ibid., 61)[2]

When Olorum decides to create the earthly world, the Supreme Being calls on the "great *orixá*" Oxalá, the "Lord of the White Cloth" (a literal translation of the Yoruba

'Ọbàtálá'). Oxalá thus towers above all the other *orixás*, but as the creation stories of Candomblé Nagô also make clear, even he is powerless without Exu: many narratives about the creation of the *aiê* have Oxalá ignoring the duty to offer a sacrifice to Exu and later failing miserably (Prandi 2001: 503–506). Exu is the messenger between worlds and the owner of crossroads who Monique Augras ([1983] 2008: 91) describes as "the personification of the principle of transformation" and the first individual being created by the Supreme Being. "Exu eats first," goes the saying, underlining the important moral that one must appease Exu before setting out to do anything.

Candomblé teaches that every person is governed by specific *orixás*. The deities are associated with elements of nature believed to be loaded with the energy of those deities. Key female *orixás* include Oxum (associated with freshwater), Iemanjá (the sea), Iansã (also called Oiá, connected to wind), and Nanã (linked to mud). Among the prominent male deities are Ogum (war and iron), Xangô (thunder and quarries), Oxóssi (hunting and forests), and Omolu (also called Obaluaiê, connected to healing and infectious diseases). Many of these deities have historically been syncretized with Catholic saints, a practice popular in Brazil since colonial times. However, in recent decades, there has been a movement among Candomblé practitioners to "re-Africanize" their traditions by symbolically removing the white masks from their deities, and in many cases, fully eliminating Afro-Catholic syncretism from their practices.

The *orixás* are believed to be literally present during Candomblé ceremonies, manifesting through spirit possession (or "incorporation"). Mediums, who serve as vessels for these entities, form lasting connections with the *orixás* and, consequently, often experience profound transformations in their self-awareness and physical autonomy (Seligman 2014). During trance states, their normal self-awareness fades, and their bodies act without personal intent. It is common for mediums to later report no memory of the events during possession, though they understand their actions were guided by a consciousness distinct from their usual identity and intentions.

As we will see, the entity that "comes down" during possession is not viewed as an abstract being but as one of its many manifestations, existing solely in the embodied form of a specific individual (Segato 2005: 98). For example, when discussing the actions of an *orixá* during possession, people do not refer to the *orixá* in general terms but specify the *orixá* of a particular person: "Julio's Xangô did/said . . ." The deeply personal nature of each *orixá* is reflected in how they are perceived by their followers, with the *orixá* of each individual having a unique appearance and distinct physical traits (Schmidt 2016: 113).

The primary ritual practices of possession, sacrifice, and initiation in Candomblé are ways of managing and exchanging *axé*, the spiritual life force that permeates all of existence, from the inanimate to the living. Maintaining the balance of *axé* is crucial for individual well-being, and neglecting ritual obligations to honor the *orixás* depletes one's *axé*, leading to various difficulties. However, *axé* can be replenished, reflecting the reciprocal relationship between humans and *orixás*. Honoring the *orixás* is thus a fundamental duty. Blood sacrifice, central to Candomblé, involves offering animals to the *orixás*, as blood is considered the main vehicle of *axé* (Schmidt 2024). While the *orixás* do not physically consume the offerings, they absorb its *axé*.

Finally, alongside *axé*, *odu* is a fundamental component of the Candomblé worldview (Silva and Brumana 2016), symbolizing an individual's life path and destiny. At birth, a child's *odu* is revealed, and it is essential to align one's actions with this prescribed *odu* to avoid misfortune and attract good fortune. The influence of one's *odu* permeates all aspects of life, which are revealed through divination sessions. In Candomblé, divining one's destiny typically involves the "throwing" of sixteen cowries (*búzios*): the positioning of the cowries, whether facing up or down, allows a priestess or priest to consult the *orixás* on behalf of the community or for personal matters, "peeking behind the curtain of life," as it were (Flaksman 2016: 18). This practice also provides guidance to clients seeking solutions, regardless of their religious background. The specific *odu* revealed by the cowries is instrumental in determining an individual's "head" or "front" *orixá*, that is to say, their primary guardian and the one they should be "initiated in." Both humans and *orixás* share an *odu*—a common thread that symbolically engages with elements of the natural and social worlds, influencing personality traits, behaviors, physiognomy, and life events. Thus, *odu* functions as an abstract intersection with *axé*, serving as a pivotal element in Candomblé's spiritual framework.

Who is in One's Head

Candomblé presents a view of the human being as shaped by the interplay of various forces, each uniquely combined at different moments in the formation of the person. This balance, however, is dynamic and rarely sustained, except during possession trance, when the individual and their *orixá* become one. To understand the construction of personhood in Candomblé, it is essential to first examine the concept and composition of one's "head"—referred to interchangeably by the Portuguese word *cabeça* and the Yoruba *ori*. Marcio Goldman (1985: 36) investigates the structured notion of person in a Candomblé *terreiro*, the way in which it is constructed over time, as well as its connection with ecstatic trance. The members of the *terreiro* in question maintain that the spirit of the human being is always composed of:

- Seven *orixás*, including the "owner of the head" (*olori*, from the Yoruba "lord of the *ori*"), that is to say, the primary *orixá*, as well as six others ranked by importance (second, third, etc.). These seven *orixás* always include Oxalá, Exu, and Omolu, though their rank within a person's *ori* varies. The remaining four

will vary from person to person. Together the seven *orixás* form the *carrego de santo* (lit., "saint-load")
- An *erê*, which is a childlike "quality" of the *orixá* and its "interpreter." The *erê* conveys messages from the *orixás*, as the *orixás* themselves do not speak. *Erê* also refers to the unique aspect of the *orixá* that reflects a personal connection to the initiate.
- The *egum*, the soul of the dead that wanders the Earth. *Eguns*, unlike *orixás*, are disembodied spirits and thus inferior to them in essence. This *egum* is specifically an *egum de santo* (lit., "saint-*egum*"), which refers to a soul that has never incarnated but is regarded as the person's true soul (*eledá* or *emi*).[3]

These findings corroborate Roger Bastide's ([1958] 2000) observations from his study of the composition of initiates' heads nearly four decades prior. Bastide noted, "we have seen that the *orixá*, although individualized, is presented in mythology as a "complex"; that is, every *orixá* is linked to one (or several) Exu,[4] as well as an *erê*. . . . The psychic structure—*orixá*-Exu-*erê*—is also, in theory, a constant structure, a permanent element in the definition of the person" (Bastide [1958] 2000: 240). Later, Bastide adds, "The *orixás*, the Exus, and the *erês* exist outside of us, constituting the divine world, while at the same time they exist within us, forming part of our intimate structure. . . . The sacred is both transcendent and immanent" (ibid., 244).

It is precisely these components of the person that are responsible for the various forms of possession in Candomblé. While it cannot be strictly said that a person is possessed prior to initiation, it can be argued that they are influenced by phenomena associated with possession. Indeed, an important goal of initiation is taming the body, preparing it to receive the deity (Sansi 2009: 144). Initially, due to its lack of regulation, the *orixá*'s manifestation in possession can be intense, forceful, and uncontrolled. Thus, before initiation it is not uncommon for people to be possessed haphazardly. However, through the long process of initiation, the individual learns to incorporate and manage the presence of the *orixá* within their body. During initiation, the priestess or priest ritually "seats" or "settles" the primary *orixá* in the novice's head through sacrificial rites. Over time, the initiate will have their six other *orixás* successively seated in ceremonies known as *obrigações* (lit., "obligations"), which are held one, three, five, seven, fourteen, and twenty-one years after initiation.

The composition of what Goldman refers to as the "load" (*carrego*) of a person's *ori* is determined through the divination of cowrie shells. In the absence of evidence to the contrary, the *orixás* revealed through divination are considered present in the person's *ori*. However, many variations are possible, and the initial divination is always provisional. Until the moment the initiate is sequestered for initiation, it is impossible to know with certainty which *orixá* will be the true owner of their head. Often, it is during initiation that it is revealed that the initiate must care for more than one *orixá*. There is no fixed rule for such cases, though the most common practice is to initiate the person in their "front" *orixá* and settle the others afterward during successive obligations.

Goldman (1985: 39) observes that although every person is thought of as being born necessarily composed of these elements, their existence remains in a virtual state, until the moment when these elements are fixed by the rites of initiation and obligation. The progressive settling of the various spiritual entities corresponds precisely to this aspect, whereby the faithful cease to belong to, and depend on, abstract and general entities, like non-initiates, and begin to be *made up* of individualized and concrete beings—"their" *orixá*, "their" *Exu*, and so on.

Clara Flaksman (2016) relates Goldman's notion of *carrego* to the perhaps more widespread notion of *enredo de santo* where *enredo* literally means "storyline" (or "plot")—the word being derived from *rede*, meaning "net," "mesh," or "tangle." Flaksman thus aligns Bastide's ([1958] 2000) argument that a person is composed of their stories with Goldman's (1985) argument that a person is the sum of their entities: "The formation of the person takes place in the sum of the stories involving human and non-human beings – the *enredos* – that make up their life" (2016: 19).

To be "entangled" with certain entities means not only to be involved in a common storyline but to have relationships which can occur in countless ways, since an entanglement can consist of relationships between *orixás* themselves as well as between humans and, often, between humans and *orixás*: "These relationships occur on different planes of existence – which, in the case of the *orixás*, involves both the "general" *orixás*, the entities themselves, and the "individual" *orixás*, who owe their existence, with a few exceptions, to the *feitura* of some [initiate]" (Flaksman 2016: 14). The way such entanglements are organized and made official, so to speak, happens in initiation.

Making the Saint (and the Person)

In Candomblé, initiation is called *feitura* (lit., "making") and also revealingly referred to as *fazer o santo* (lit., "making the saint"). It encompasses the process of constructing the initiates in relation to the *orixás* they incorporate as well as the "other body" of these entities—the material representation of the deity, known as its *assento* (lit., "seat") or *assentamento* (lit., "settlement"). As Miriam Rabelo attests, "The making of the *orixá* in the head is accompanied – sometimes preceded – by the settling of the *orixá* in the *terreiro*" (2011: 23).

Typically, the shrine (*ibá*) features a dais adorned with various containers made of clay and porcelain or sometimes wood, each wrapped in cloth and concealed from public view. Within these pots lie the *fundamentos* (lit., "foundations"), the elements embodying the *orixás* of the initiates. Settlements can take various forms, with stones or pebbles (*otás*), which are supposed to be found, and iron tools (*ferramentas*), which are wrought by religious blacksmiths, being the most common (Marques 2023). Each *orixá* possesses specific elements: for instance, the seats of Oxum and Iemanjá are adorned with shells and stones found in bodies of water, representing their association with freshwater and the sea, respectively; they will also reflect their associated colors (yellow or gold for Oxum, white or silver for Iemanjá). Similarly, the stones associated with Xangô are regarded as having been cast to the earth as thunderbolts, symbolizing his domain as the deity of thunder (Sansi-Roca 2005: 142).

When the *orixá* is fixed on the head of a new initiate and settled on a stone or tool, from that moment onward, there will be a specific and unique object that serves as the material seat of the person's *orixá* throughout their life. As Rita Laura Segato (2005) notes, the language used to describe settlements highlights the crucial idea that, while each individual belongs to an *orixá*, they only embody a personal and unrepeatable instance of that *orixá*—referred to as the "saint" (*santo*). Furthermore, because practitioners equate the settlements with the *orixás* themselves, their influence over initiates is profound.

Initiates who witness the systematic association of various objects and substances with the manipulation of their head and body – and experience their treatment responding to similar gestures and attitudes – are inclined to perceive these objects as their "external organs" (Sansi-Roca 2005: 144) or more broadly, as their person "distributed" in the material environment (Gell 1998). The frequent correlation between object/body manipulations and possession trance further deepens the intimate connection between the *otá* or *ferramenta*, the *orixá*, and the initiate's body, blurring the ontological boundaries between these three categories of entities.

Arnaud Halloy (2013: 137) recounts a striking episode where, while cleaning up after an offering (*ebó*) at an altar, he mistakenly discarded the small *otá* of an initiate's Iemanjá, despite a half-joking warning from the priest not to "throw out the *otá* with the *ebó*." As an initiate later explained to him, and as he personally experienced, losing the *otá* of an initiate constitutes a serious spiritual crisis. Many stories emphasize the severe consequences of abandoning, mistreating, or destroying settlements and altars, including physical or mental illness, burns, mutilation, run-ins with authorities, or even sudden death.

The proper initiation, or *feitura*, usually spans three weeks, during which the novice is secluded in the *terreiro*, undergoing ritual baths and cleansings for purification and protection while also strengthening their *ori* through a meal offering (*bori*). Once the head is fortified, and after the extended seclusion to learn the secrets of the tradition deemed appropriate for a novice—such as songs, the use of leaves, and sacrificial rites—the main initiation ceremony begins, typically lasting two days.

The novice emerges for the priestess or priest to shave their head, combining sacrificed blood with elements rich in *axé* and adorning it with the motifs of the novice's *orixá* (Porcher 2025a: section 3). The bond between the novice's head and the settlement representing their *orixá* is solidified when both are bathed in the same blood. This act seals a sacred alliance among the initiate, the *orixá*, their sacred symbols, and the overseeing priestess or priest. Finally, the new initiate (*iaô*) exits seclusion and is publicly introduced in a celebration, where the *orixá*, fully adorned, takes possession of the initiate and performs its inaugural dance.

Although the settlement serves as the saint's enduring and concealed presence, it is the dancing body of the devotee that truly embodies the *orixá*, even if its presence is fleeting. As Roger Sansi-Roca (2005) observes, while in the settlement the saint is nourished, during celebrations, the incorporated saint takes on the role of the host; while the settlement conceals the saint, within the body of the initiate, sthe saint emerges publicly and triumphantly; while in the seat the saint remains fixed, in the human body the saint dances. Possession is thus the pivotal ingredient in initiation.

However, possession is not always a smooth process, and neither is the relationship between the initiate and their saint. As Augras relays, in the *terreiros* she studied in Rio de Janeiro, "certain *orixás* are experienced by their children in the mode of absolute alterity, imposed in spite of the will of the children [i.e., initiates]" (1986: 195). Furthermore, individuals frequently assert that possession occurs at the will of the deity to descend, rather than stemming from the initiate. Segato uses this kind of tension to talk about initiation as a process of accepting another within oneself which includes the negotiated relationship between the self and the saint:

> It is common for people to refuse responsibility for the saint's exuberant deeds or ways of expressing themselves during possession. Whether on the part of the protagonists themselves or those assisting the possession, the language used to refer to the phenomenon is intended to emphasize the disconnection or estrangement between a possessed person and the *orixá* that "descended" on them (I've never come across any confusing statements regarding who said or did something: an individual or their *orixá*). A very common example of the way in which the *orixás* apparently act in blatant contradiction to the wishes of their children is by making them, while possessed, hug people with whom they have quarreled. This is, among other things, an indicator of the boundary that separates the self from the saint.
>
> (Segato 2005: 100)

Thus, in addition to their complementarity, possession and sacrifice are also supplementary, in the sense that possession is in its own way also a form of sacrifice. As Goldman argues, in the vocabulary of initiation, the novice "dies" to be reborn as a "saint's horse" (*cavalo de santo*):

> [P]ossession seems to generate a real contact with the deities caused by the symbolic death of a "spirit" of their own. This is because it is the deities themselves who manifest themselves, and for this to be possible it is necessary that not the body, but that which animates it moves away, in a movement similar to that which occurs in death, thus giving way to the space in which the *orixá* will incarnate.
>
> (1985: 47)

It is evident that *feitura* goes beyond mere education in myths, songs, and prayers, although it does encompass those elements. From the sacrificial offerings to feed the novice's *ori*, through the settling the saint, and finally in the initial incorporation of the *orixá*, initiation at once makes the saint and the person. While the generic *orixá* exists in a dimension beyond human space and time, a person's *orixá*—their saint—is "born" at the moment of initiation, only attaining individuality when manifesting in a human being. Conversely, a human being is not born fully formed but is constructed through the prolonged initiation process.

Thus, through the act of possession, the *orixá* transitions into an individual entity, acquiring a distinct personality. This is why *orixás* are perceived both as natural forces and as distinct spiritual beings: these manifestations refer to different expressions of the *orixá*, namely, the generic, force-of-nature expression, and the individual, personal-saint expression. This gives us a way to distinguish between the *orixás* whose narratives are recounted in mythic narratives and those capable of manifesting within a human form and settling in material objects.

Where the Saint Ends and the Self Begins

Drawing on Bastide's ideas, Goldman proposes a "basic monism" within Candomblé insofar as the spiritual energy of *axé* permeates everything in the universe through a process of differentiation and individuation (2007: 116). *Axé* would thus exist in surplus within a "virtual" realm, actualized through ritual practice: each entity crystallizes or coalesces as a result of *axé*'s modulating flow, evolving from a general and homogeneous force into diversified and concrete manifestations. Thus, *axé* as a pervasive force traverses all aspects of existence in varied forms, and Goldman sees it as offering an alternative perspective on the creative process: rather than *ex-nihilo* creation or the conventional addition of elements, this process involves refining and actualizing preexisting potentialities, akin to the sculpting of raw material into form. Making should thus be thought of less as creation and more as a process of composition and individuation of a series of forces that already exist excessively in the world.

The process of making the saint appears to follow a similar logic, where the "birth" of the saint and their child does not adhere to a dualistic pattern—it is not as if something nonexistent suddenly comes into being. Echoing Goldman, Carmen Opipari (2009) applies a conceptual framework borrowed from Gilles Deleuze (1967), who distinguishes two uneven, dissimilar, and asymmetrical "halves" within anything: the virtual and the actual. The virtual is actualized through differentiation: "It is not opposed to the real but to the actual, as they are not the same thing" (2009:

182). She thus argues, like Goldman, that the process of making should be understood as the actualization of something already existing on a virtual level.

Both Opipari (2009: 196) and Flaksman (2016: 15) argue that actualization does not imply individualization, whereas Goldman suggests that "making the head or making the saint ... actually means the ritual production of *two* individualized entities from two generic substrates" (2017: 112). Thus, according to Goldman, a more or less undifferentiated individual becomes a structured person and a generic *orixá* is actualized into an individual saint: someone's Iansã, someone else's Omolu, and so on. These individualized *orixás* "possess their own names and characteristics, in the same way that people are re-baptized and transformed during their initiation" (2007: 112). On the other hand, Flaksman states that: "*feitura*, which concretizes the relationship between the saint and their child, is the cement that allows for the creation of the person-*orixá* amalgam" (Flaksman 2016: 27).

Note, however, that there is no inherent contradiction between Goldman's view on one side and Flaksman's and Opipari's on the other. What Flaksman states with her amalgamation thesis is that initiation does not result in two *undifferentiated* individualities, that of the saint and their child, and this is coherent with Goldman's view: even in their constructed individualities, the saint and their child are unified and "almost overlap" during possession:

> The deity is not, therefore, just an element external to the human being, intermittently united with the latter. The [*orixá*] is made within the human being and at the same time its own person is also made. This means that the [*orixá*]inhabits in a constitutive way what Bastide ... called the human being's 'inner castle'. Perhaps this explains the crucial importance of possession, the key ritual modality of Candomblé since, as Bastide also suggests, possession involves more than the enactment of a rite: it amounts to a 'lived-experience ritual'. It is in trance that all the dimensions of the system appear to come together to produce a particular synthesis of the experience of the cult: the worlds of the gods and humans converge; the Candomblé adept and his or her [*orixá*] almost overlap; the various components of the human being tend towards unification and equilibrium, raising humans to almost divine status.
>
> (Goldman 2007: 112)

In this way, Goldman, Flaksman, and Opipari all acknowledge the multiplicity of the person in Candomblé, emphasizing the various entities that constitute them—whether referred to as *carrego* or *enredo*. These entities are settled in the *terreiro*, inhabit the adept's head, and manifest during possession. Flaksman (2016: 16) also points out that both Goldman and Opipari reject the psychologized interpretation of trance, which is deeply rooted in the Christian model of the unified self, leaving no room for multiplicity or heterogeneity. Instead, they resort to the metaphor of the theater (e.g., Augras 1983; Wafer 1991). However, the theater Opipari refers to is not one of representation; rather, it is a space where the actor is not merely embodying a character but serving as a potential vehicle for fragments of multiple characters. In this context, actualization becomes both a "singularization" and a "personalization," representing the merging of elements into what Opipari (2009: 196) describes as an "inseparable adept-saint block."

Conclusion

In Candomblé, every person is incomplete by nature and is always being constructed. Before *feitura*, the *orixá* is a natural cosmic force, and not an individuality of any kind; the initiate, too, is seen as a multiplicity, which the *orixá* helps to build and not simply modify, or to which they are added once it is finished. This process underscores that both the *orixás* and their adepts undergo individualization while remaining inextricably linked, particularly during possession.

"She's more settled now," Flaksman (2016: 20) quotes a friend in reference to a newly made initiate, alluding to her hitherto fickle emotional balance. Saints are settled precisely to give a person stability, but this stability is never absolute. It is always ephemeral. In other words, the person is not exactly an "I" to which other things are added (as if the *ori*, were an initial fixed unit to which other factors would be added). On the contrary, the "I", in this case, is already an aggregate (Silva 2007: 224–205). Nothing is fixed, and the process of construction is continuous. The *ori* that exists is itself already a construction, a set of stories and relationships, or *enredos*, to which others are added.

The gradual settling of each of the initiate's *orixás* through ritual obligations is essential for their full realization as a person. Until this sought-after state is achieved—typically not until twenty-one years after initiation—the individual exists in a delicate balance, susceptible to disruption by any violation of ritual responsibilities. Thus, the initiation process does not signify the completion of the individual but rather marks the beginning of a long journey of self-making, but not undifferentiated individualization, emphasizing both the relational and dynamic nature of identity.

Notes

1. The deities are also referred to as *voduns* (from the Fon and Ewe languages) in Candomblé Jêje and *inquices* (from the Bantu *nkisi*) in Candomblé Angola—the two main nations of Candomblé along with Queto (Nagô). In this chapter, I will employ the Yoruba-derived terminology because of its predominant usage and for the sake of brevity and clarity.
2. All translations from Portuguese-language sources are my own.

3. Goldman used material from research conducted by Wagner Neves Rocha between 1978 and 1980 in an Angola terreiro located in Tribobó, near Niterói, Rio de Janeiro. Later, between 1982 and 1983, Goldman compared this data with information he collected himself in another Angola *terreiro* in Ilhéus, Bahia. Apart from a few differences, the same basic structure was observed.
4. This might sound confusing, but while there is only one, "generic" *orixá* called Exu, there are myriad individual instances or "qualities" of Exu and, for that matter, every other *orixá*. In the next section, on the "making" of the person (and also their *orixá*), we will delve further into the distinction between the generic and the individual *orixá*.

Bibliography

Augras, Monique. 1986. "Transe e construção de identidade no Candomblé." *Psicologia: Teoria e Pesquisa*, 2 (3): 191–200.

Augras, Monique. [1983] 2008. *O duplo e a metamorfose: A identidade mítica em comunidades Nagô*. Petrópolis: Vozes.

Bastide, Roger. [1958] 2000. *O Candomblé da Bahia: Rito Nagô*. São Paulo: Companhia das Letras.

Bergad, Laird W. 2007. *The Comparative Histories of Slavery in Brazil, Cuba, and the United States*. Cambridge: Cambridge University Press.

Deleuze, Gilles. 1967. "La méthode de dramatisation." *Bulletin de la Société Française de Philosophie*, 61 (3): 89–118.

Elbein dos Santos, Juana. [1976] 2012. *Os Nàgô e a morte: pàde, àsèsè e o culto ègun na Bahia*. Petrópolis: Vozes.

Flaksman, Clara. 2016. "Relações e narrativas: o enredo no Candomblé da Bahia." *Religião e Sociedade*, 36: 13–33.

Gell, Alfred. 1998. *Art and Agency: An Anthropological Theory*. Oxford: Clarendon Press.

Goldman, Marcio. 1985. "A construção ritual da pessoa: a possessão no Candomblé." *Religião e Sociedade*, 12: 22–54.

Goldman, Marcio. 2007. "How to Learn in an Afro-Brazilian Spirit Possession Religion: Ontology and Multiplicity in Candomblé." In David Berliner and Ramon Sarró (eds.), *Learning Religion: Anthropological Approaches*. New York: Berghahn Books, 103–119.

Halloy, Arnaud. 2013. "Objects, Bodies and Gods: A Cognitive Ethnography of an Ontological Dynamic in the Xangô Cult (Recife, Brazil)." In Diana Espirito Santo and Nico Tassi (eds.), *Making Spirits: Materiality and Transcendence in Contemporary Religions*. London: Bloomsbury, 133–158.

Herskovits, Melville J. 1956. "The Social Organization of the Afrobrazilian Candomble." *Phylon*, 17: 147–166.

Latour, Bruno. 1987. *Science in Action*. Cambridge: Harvard University Press.

Marques, Lucas. 2023. "On the Art of Forging Gods: Techniques, Forces and Materials in an Afro-Brazilian Religion." In Zainabu Jallo (ed.), *Material Culture in Transit: Theory and Practice*. London: Routledge, 185–200.

Matory, J. Lorand. 2018. *The Fetish Revisited: Marx, Freud, and the Gods Black People Make*. Durham: Duke University Press.

Opipari, Carmen. 2009. *O candomblé: imagens em movimento – São Paulo – Brasil*. São Paulo: Editora da Universidade de São Paulo.

Porcher, José Eduardo. 2025a. *Afro-Brazilian Religions*. Cambridge: Cambridge University Press.

Porcher, José Eduardo. 2025b. "The Mythic Narratives of Candomblé Nagô and What They Imply about Its Supreme Being." *Religious Studies*, 61 (2): 506–522.

Prandi, Reginaldo. 2001. *Mitologia dos Orixás*. São Paulo: Companhia das Letras.

Rabelo, Miriam C. M. 2011. "Estudar a religião a partir do corpo: algumas questões teórico-metodológicas." *Caderno CRH*, 24 (61): 15–28.

Sansi, Roger. 2009. "'Fazer o santo': dom, iniciação e historicidade nas religiões afro-brasileiras." *Análise Social*, 44 (1): 139–160.

Sansi-Roca, Roger. 2005. "The Hidden Life of Stones: Historicity, Materiality and the Value of Candomblé Objects in Bahia," *Journal of Material Culture*, 10 (2): 139–156.

Schmidt, Bettina E. 2016. *Spirits and Trance in Brazil: An Anthropology of Religious Experience*. London: Bloomsbury.

Schmidt, Bettina E. 2024. "*Axé* as the Cornerstone of Candomblé Philosophy and Its Significance for an Understanding of Well-Being (*bem estar*)." *Religious Studies*, 61 (2): 1–13.

Segato, Rita Laura. 2005. *Santos e Daimones*. Brasília: Editora Universidade de Brasília.

Seligman, Rebecca. 2014. *Possessing Spirits and Healing Selves: Embodiment and Transformation in an Afro-Brazilian Religion*. London: Palgrave Macmillan.

Silva, Vagner Gonçalves. 2007. "Entre a Gira de Fé e Jesus de Nazaré." In Vagner Gonçalves da Silva (ed.), *Intolerância Religiosa: impactos do neopentecostalismo no campo religioso afro-brasileiro*. São Paulo: Editora da Universidade de São Paulo, 191–260.

Silva, Vagner Gonçalves, and Fernando Giobellina Brumana. 2016. "Candomblé: Religion, World Vision and Experience." In Bettina E. Schmidt and Steven Engler (eds.), *Handbook of Contemporary Religions in Brazil*. Leiden: Brill, 170–185.

Wafer, Jim. 1991. *The Taste of Blood: Spirit Possession in Brazilian Candomblé*. Philadelphia: University of Pennsylvania Press.

Ori
Chapter 2.1

Conceptual Definition

Ori literally means "head" in Yoruba, a term that has been adopted into Brazilian Portuguese to carry complex spiritual and philosophical connotations in Afro-Brazilian religious contexts. While it can be used interchangeably with the Portuguese *cabeça* (lit., "head"), *ori* encompasses far more than the anatomical head. It represents a unique, individual divine principle that shapes and governs the fate, personality, and spiritual essence of each person. In Candomblé, *ori* is considered the inner, deified head, a divine force that must be honored, cultivated, and aligned with through rituals to ensure personal well-being and spiritual growth.

Historical Context

In Yoruba and Afro-Brazilian cosmology,[1] the creation of the earthly world, *aiê*, is attributed to the divine rivalry and cooperation between Odudua and Oxalá—also known as Obatalá—the "Lord of the White Cloth." According to Reginaldo Prandi's (2001: 503–506) account, Olorum—also known as Olodumare—the supreme deity, initially entrusted Oxalá with the task of creating the world, granting him the necessary powers and tools. However, Oxalá, relying solely on his own abilities, disregarded Orunmilá's advice to make offerings to Exu before beginning his mission. Observing this, Odudua sought Orunmilá's counsel and made the prescribed sacrifices, thus taking position to fulfill the divine task.

When Oxalá faltered, succumbing to intoxication and falling asleep on his journey, Odudua took up the mission. With the tools of creation in hand, he scattered the primordial elements over the ocean to form solid land, bringing *aiê* into existence. While Oxalá missed his chance to shape the physical world, Olodumare gave him a new responsibility: the creation of living beings. Thus, Oxalá molded humanity from clay, breathing life into each form with the aid of Olodumare. This myth not only illustrates the origins of the physical and human world but also underscores the foundational roles of Odudua and Oxalá within Yoruba and Afro-Brazilian religious thought. It sets the stage for understanding the concept of *ori*, as Oxalá's role in forming individual human beings extends to shaping their destiny and personhood. To this end, Prandi draws from Wande Abimbola's (1975) *Sixteen Great Poems of Ifá* to present the following rendition of the story of the molding of mortals' heads by Ajalá, the primordial potter:

> Odudua created the world,
> Obatalá created the human being.
> Obatalá made man out of mud,
> with a body, chest, belly, legs and feet.
> He shaped his back and shoulders, his arms and hands.
> He gave him bones, skin and muscles.
> He made the males with penises
> and females with vaginas,
> so that one could penetrate the other
> so that they could come together and reproduce.
> He gave the creature a heart, a liver and everything else inside it,
> including blood.
> Olodumare gave man breath
> and he lived.
> But Obatalá forgot to make the head
> and Olodumare ordered Ajalá to complete
> Oxalá's creative work.[2]
> So it is Ajalá who makes the heads of men and women.
> When someone is about to be born,
> they go to the house of the potter Ajalá, the maker of heads.
> Ajalá makes the heads out of clay and bakes them in the oven.
> If Ajalá is well, he makes good heads.
> If he's drunk, he makes badly cooked heads,
> overcooked, malformed.
> Everyone chooses their head to be born.
> Everyone chooses the *ori* they will have on Earth.
> There they choose a head for themselves.
> Everyone chooses their *ori*.
> You have to be smart to choose a good head.
> A bad head is a bad destiny,
> a good head is wealth, victory, prosperity,
> all that is good.
>
> (Prandi 2001: 470–1)

The story reflects the Yoruba belief that Ori, the deity of the head, is responsible for each person's destiny. This belief, preserved in contemporary Candomblé, underscores that Ori is the first deity to be honored, as it governs the fate of every individual.

Philosophical Significance

The *ori* has two dimensions: one physical and the other transcendental. The physical aspect governs thought and the senses, while the transcendental aspect houses ancestry and mystical identity, referred to as *eledá*—the individual *orixá* who can later transform into a *santo* through initiation (*feitura*) (Cruz 2003: 3). This division directly draws from a traditional Yoruba distinction between the *ori ode* (outer/physical head) and *ori inu* (inner/metaphysical head). In philosophical discourse, *ori* usually refers to the *ori inu*, which is seen as the most powerful spiritual force in a person's life, even more potent than other deities. Success in life depends on a positive relationship with one's *ori*, mediated through ritual. Knowing and nurturing one's *ori* is central to Yoruba life and spiritual practice. Strengthening both the physical and transcendental forms of the *ori* fortifies the individual. As Juana Elbein dos Santos explains, the *ori inu* is made up of an ethereal element called *ipori*, symbolically described as a mass shaped by Ajalá:

> Each *ori* is shaped in the *orum* and its progenitor mythical matter varies. The portion of "matter" extracted from the progenitor "matter-mass" with which each head is shaped constitutes the person's *ipori*. This concept is very important, because it establishes a series of relationships between the individual and their matter of mythical origin. It will determine the *orixá* . . . that the individual will have to worship; it will establish their possibilities and choices, and, above all, it will indicate their prohibitions . . . particularly with regard to food. The personal *ipori* has its material representation which, properly prepared and consecrated, receives offerings and is venerated.
>
> (Elbein dos Santos 1976: 235)

According to Márcio de Jagun, the *ipori* represents the energy that comes directly from one's ancestors. This energy is connected to one's head (*ori*), *eledá* (ancestral guide), and destiny (*odu*). The *ipori* is not an individualized entity but rather functions like a hereditary particle, leaving its mark on one's personality, life, health, and ultimately, destiny. It can be understood as a kind of "spiritual DNA" (Jagun 2015: 40).

Although offerings are primarily made to the *orixás*, the following excerpt from a Yoruba-derived Candomblé myth illustrates the practice of offering a sacrifice to one's own *ori*:

> There was a woman with many problems . . . She consulted the cowrie shells (*búzios*) to learn what to do. She was told to make an offering to her *ori*, her head. She was instructed to perform a *bori*, to feed her head. The woman was to offer two *obis* to her *ori*. She then took the two *obis* (Cola nuts) and made the offering.
>
> (Prandi, 2001: 481–482)

This narrative emphasizes the central importance of the *ori*. As Monique Augras (1983: 62) observes, "Even before offering a sacrifice to the deities, each person must make an offering to their own head." Therefore, before initiation, the ritual sacrifice known as *bori* takes place—literally an offering to the head (*ebó* + *ori*). The *bori* ritual symbolizes the formation of an alliance with the *orixá*, as it is through the *ori* that the *orixás* connect with their devotees. Offerings are made to both the individual's *ori* and their *orixá de cabeça* (literally, "head *orixá*"), with various foods placed on both the person's head and the *orixá*'s altar.

Miriam Rabelo (2011) observes that the remnants of the ritual are transformed into a settlement (*assentamento*) at the altar, establishing the *orixá*'s presence in a sacred vessel. Following this ritual, the initiate becomes part of the house's community as a novice and assumes responsibilities toward both the *orixá* and the religious community, even without full initiation. Positioned within the hierarchy led by the priestess or priest, the individual also participates in the regular ritual washing of the *orixá*'s settlement, which is discreetly kept in a chamber accessible only to the religious leaders.

Being the seat of one's own divinity, the *ori* is that part of the person which is responsible for possession in Candomblé and its various manifestations occur in virtue of the *ori*'s composition or "load" (*carrego*), which is often referred to as the "tangle" or "storyline" (*enredo*) in which one's life interweaves with those of the saints to which one's *ori* belongs. In successive rituals of initiation (*feitura*), one's saints are "seated" in one's *ori* and henceforth the initiate can, in a controlled manner, be possessed by those entities. As Carmen Opipari explains:

> The person's saint is the lord of the *ori*. Determining this saint consists of establishing its *enredo* [entanglement/storyline], its relationship with the other *orixás*. ... The saint's *enredo* can also be called the saint's *carrego* [load]: what they carry. . . . two saints of the same "quality" can have different *enredos*. . . . The idea of quality as differentiation (a surname) is, in reality, much more present, and it is in the relationship between the "quality" and the *enredo* that we will try to establish the nuances of these differentiations. In addition, the second and third saints of the *enredo* will also have their respective "quality". . . In the search for the "quality" of their saint, the person will try, for example, to find the clues in their own story, which can reiterate the accuracy of the *enredo*.
>
> Opipari (2009: 189–90)

In sum, the notion of *ori* offers a profound lens through which to view personhood, destiny, and self-realization in Afro-Brazilian religious thought. Unlike Western notions of an autonomous self that shapes its path through free will, *ori* reflects a view of identity as simultaneously given and cultivated. Each individual's *ori* is both a personal essence and a divine gift that encapsulates one's potential and limitations, positioning fate not as something imposed from without but as emerging from within. Through practices like the *bori* ritual, practitioners strengthen their *ori*, actively engaging in the cultivation of self and destiny. Thus, *ori* challenges rigid dichotomies between self and other, fate and choice, material and transcendental, suggesting instead a more fluid, relational conception of identity. This philosophical framework underscores the inherent dignity and responsibility of each person, as one's *ori* connects them not only to personal fate but also to the community and the divine, bridging the human and the sacred in a unique narrative of personhood.

Related Emic Terms

assentamento, bori, carrego, eledá, enredo, feitura, ipori, odu, olori, santo

Related Etic Terms

consciousness, fate, head, mind, personality, personhood, soul, spirit

Notes

1. Because Candomblé and its sources (Yoruba, Bantu, etc.) are primarily transmitted orally, the historical context sections of these entries will differ from others in this book. It is nearly impossible to determine exactly when or where these terms first emerged or to identify the individuals who coined them. However, a rich tradition of oral literature, along with subsequent anthropological work, illustrates how these terms are used and how they intersect with other key concepts. As a result, I will primarily draw on traditional mythic narratives (e.g., Prandi 2001) and ethnographic research (e.g., Elbein dos Santos 1976; Augras 1983) to show how these narratives and discourses put the terms into practice.
2. As with every Candomblé mythic narrative, there are alternative tellings, and an important one (Beniste 2006: 47–48) skips mention of Ajalá entirely and has Obatalá/Oxalá mishandling the task of shaping mortals' heads.

References

Abimbola, Wande. 1975. *Sixteen Great Poems of Ifá*. Lagos: UNESCO.
Augras, Monique. 1983. *O Duplo e a Metamorfose: A identidade Mítica em Comunidades Nagô*. Petrópolis: Vozes.
Beniste, José. 2006. *Mitos Yorubás: O Outro Lado do Conhecimento*. Rio de Janeiro: Bertrand Brasil.

Cruz, Robson Rogério. 2003. "O saber medicinal dos terreiros." In José Marmo da Silva (ed.), *Religiões Afro-Brasileiras e Saúde*. São Luís: Projeto Ató-Ire–Centro de Cultura Negra do Maranhão.

Elbein dos Santos, Juana. 1976. *Os Nàgô e a Morte: Pàde, Àsèsè e o Culto Ègun na Bahia*. Petrópolis: Vozes.

Jagun, Márcio de. 2015. *Orí: A Cabeça como Divindade - História, Cultura, Filosofia e Religiosidade Africana*. Rio de Janeiro: Litteris.

Opipari, Carmen. 2009. *O Candomblé: Imagens em Movimento – São Paulo – Brasil*. São Paulo: Editora da Universidade de São Paulo.

Prandi, Reginaldo. 2001. *Mitologia dos Orixás*. São Paulo: Companhia das Letras.

Rabelo, Miriam C. M. 2011. "Estudar a religião a partir do corpo: algumas questões teórico-metodológicas." *Caderno CRH*, 24 (61): 15–28.

Santo
Chapter 2.2

Conceptual Definition

Santo literally means "saint" in Portuguese. In Afro-Brazilian religious contexts, it is used to refer to the personal, individualized instance of a deity or *orixá* that is inextricably tied to an initiate, fixed in a material *assento* (seat) or *assentamento* (settlement). The *santo* cares for and must be cared for by the initiate and, most importantly, incorporates in the initiate during ritual possession trance.

The entity that "comes down" during possession and interacts with humans is not viewed as abstract but rather as one of its myriad manifestations, existing solely within the tangible embodiment of a specific individual. For instance, when discussing the actions of the *orixá* that has descended during possession, practitioners will never refer to the *orixá* in general terms; instead, they specify the *santo* associated with a particular person: "Julio's Xangô did/said . . ." This personal connection to each *orixá* becomes evident in how they are envisioned by their respective followers, with each person's saint possessing a distinctly unique visage and physical characteristics. Moreover, the degree of reverence shown to an incorporated *orixá* is closely tied to the hierarchical position held by the medium facilitating the incorporation.

Historical Context

Drawing on mostly Yoruba and Bantu sources, Candomblé teaches that every human being is governed by specific deities called *orixás*. Most *orixás* are associated with particular elements of nature, believed to possess and impart the energy of their corresponding deity. In Candomblé worship, key female deities include Oxum (associated with freshwater), Iemanjá (connected to the sea), Iansã (also known as Oiá, related to the wind), and Nanã (associated with mud). Among the main male deities are Ogum (the deity of war and iron), Xangô (linked with quarries and thunder), Oxóssi (associated with hunting and forests), and Obaluaiê (also known as Omulu, linked to healing and infectious diseases). Throughout mostly the nineteenth century, each of these deities was syncretized with particular Catholic saints, who have been the objects of popular devotion in Brazil since colonial times.

The prevailing narrative among practitioners asserts that Afro-Catholic syncretism in Afro-Brazilian religions arose as a response to the continuous discrimination and prohibition against enslaved Africans worshipping their own deities. As a result, for example, the *orixá* Oxóssi, often depicted with a bow and arrow, has been syncretized with Saint George in Bahia and Saint Sebastian in Rio de Janeiro. This syncretism is frequently likened to a mask, as enslaved Africans integrated Catholic saints into their religious practices to disguise their worship of African deities, thereby safeguarding their traditions. As Ayodeji Ogunnaike (2020) notes, recent decades have seen a movement among Candomblé practitioners to "re-Africanize" their traditions by symbolically removing the white masks from their deities and, in many cases, erasing any remaining traces of Afro-Catholic syncretism from their practice.

Philosophical Significance

In Candomblé, initiation—referred to as *feitura* (literally, "making") or *fazer o santo* (lit., "making the saint")—involves a process of constructing the initiate in relation to the *orixás* they incorporate, as well as the "other body" of these entities, represented by the seat (*assento*) or settlement (*assentamento*). Scholars like Monique Augras (1986), Rita Laura Segato (2005), and Marcio Goldman (2007) converge on the idea that *feitura* signifies the recreation of the orixá within a specific human body, transforming the *orixá* into an individual entity (the "saint"). Simultaneously, the initiates themselves are "made" since a person is not born fully formed but is constructed through the long process of initiation. This highlights how the initial possession not only shapes the initiate but also imbues the *orixá* with identity, as the *orixá* begins as an indistinct, generic entity and acquires its individuality through the initiate.

Thus, while the term "*orixá*" can perfectly well be used instead of "*santo*," the reverse is not always true. This is because the term *orixá* is usually reserved for the deity in its most transcendent form, while invisible or not "fixed" in an adept's head through the appropriate rites. As Ordep Serra explains,

> This being is at the side of every person, as a "guardian angel" before any religious initiation, [but] only those who have been initiated have a saint, and several people can belong to the same *orixá*, even so their saints will be different when they [are born in] the little chamber—as different as the consecrated heads of the "children."
>
> (Serra 1978: 59–60)

The creation of an individual *orixá* takes place when the saint is seated on the head of the new child and settled on a material object (typically a stone or iron tool). From that moment on and throughout life, there will be a specific and unique object that will literally be the person's saint. As Segato observes, the language used to refer to seats or settlements emphasizes the fundamental notion that, although each individual belongs to an *orixá*, they only embody a personal and unrepeatable instance of that *orixá*, that is to say, the saint:

> Thus, there are as many saints as there are people and, using the *orixá* Xangô here merely as an example, although many individuals are children of Xangô, in no case do two of them possess the same Xangô, not even if they share the same quality of that deity. Therefore, two children of Xangô Aganju[1] will still be two different Xangôs when possessed, and will have two different stones, each one being the particular Xangô seated for each of these children. Furthermore, if a mother or father-of-saint [i.e., priestess or priest] has five children of Xangô, they will keep in their holy room five different stones set as Xangôs, one for each of them.
>
> (Segato 2005: 96)

The same point about unrepeatability applies to the sitting of the *orixá* in the head, and consequently, to possession. Through possession, the *orixá* becomes an individual entity, acquiring gendered traits and a distinct personality. This transformation is crucial, as it demonstrates that "an undifferentiated individual ... becomes a structured person, and a generic *orixá*... is realized as an individual *orixá*" (Goldman 2007: 112). Thus, *orixás* are understood both as natural forces and as distinct spiritual beings, representing two different modes of expression: the generic, force-of-nature aspect, and the individual, personal-saint aspect. This distinction helps differentiate between *orixás* as they appear in myths and those capable of manifesting in human form and settling in material objects.

The relationship between the initiate and their saint is not always harmonious. Augras notes that in the *terreiros* she studied in Rio de Janeiro, "certain *orixás* are experienced by their children in the mode of absolute alterity, imposed despite the children's will" (Augras 1986: 195). Moreover, individuals often assert that possession occurs at the saint's discretion rather than originating from the initiate. Attempts to explore this matter further or to understand the nuanced boundary between what constitutes a "normal" state of consciousness and the state of possession are frequently viewed as intrusive or disrespectful.

Segato uses this tension to describe *feitura* as a process of accepting another within oneself, encompassing the negotiated relationship between the self and the saint. This raises questions about agency: it is common for people to distance themselves from the exuberant actions or expressions of the saint during possession. Whether from the possessed individuals themselves or those assisting them, the language employed to describe the phenomenon tends to emphasize the disconnection or estrangement between the possessed person and the *orixá* that "descended" upon them. A common illustration of how *orixás* seemingly act against the wishes of their children is when they compel possessed individuals to hug those with whom they have had conflicts. This behavior serves, among other things, as an indicator of the boundary separating the self from the saint (Segato 2005: 100).

Contrary to the zero-sum assumption that granting agency to objects or other-than-human persons diminishes it for humans, Candomblé challenges conventional Western notions by redistributing agency among individuals and objects in a fluid and contingent manner. Moving away from the idea of the self as the sole locus of control and meaning attribution, Candomblé affirms the agency of both humans and non-human entities. Acknowledging the agency of objects such as *ferramentas* and *otás* necessitates a reevaluation, while understanding the agency of incorporated spirits requires a broader reimagining rather than a simple relocation of agency, Goldman (2012) suggests that Candomblé blurs the line between the "made" and the "given" by fostering an ongoing dialogue between human agency and the spirits, deities, and objects involved. This reciprocal relationship between human and non-human agents not only deepens our understanding of agency but also transforms our own capacity for agency as theorists. It encourages us to approach subjects without preconceptions and to dynamically explore the multifaceted nature of agency.

Related Emic Terms

assento/assentamento, eledá, feitura, olori, ori, orixá

Related Etic Terms

daimon/genius, deity (lesser), guardian spirit, guiding spirit, tutelary deity

Notes

1. In Cuba and other countries of the Afro-Atlantic diaspora, Aganju is venerated as a distinct *orixá*. In Brazilian Candomblé, however, Aganju is a "quality" that embodies the aspect of Xangô associated with explosiveness and lack of control, symbolizing the personification of volcanoes.

References

Augras, Monique. 1986. "Transe e construção de identidade no Candomblé." *Psicologia: Teoria e Pesquisa*, 2 (3): 191–200.
Goldman, Marcio. 2007. "How to Learn in an Afro-Brazilian Spirit Possession Religion: Ontology and Multiplicity in Candomblé." In David Berliner and Ramon Sarró (eds.), *Learning Religion: Anthropological Approaches*. New York: Berghahn Books, 103–119.

Goldman, Marcio. 2012. "O dom e a iniciação revisitados: o dado e o feito em religiões de matriz africana no Brasil." *Mana*, 8 (2): 269–288.

Ogunnaike, Ayodeji. 2020. "What's Really Behind the Mask: A Reexamination of Syncretism in Brazilian Candomblé." *Journal of Africana Religions*, 8: 146–171.

Segato, Rita Laura. 2005. *Santos e Daimones*. Brasília: Editora Universidade de Brasília.

Serra, Ordep. 1978. "Na trilha das crianças: os erês num terreiro angola." MA thesis, Universidade de Brasília.

Assento
Chapter 2.3

Conceptual Definition

In Portuguese, *assento* literally means "seat," while *assentamento* translates to "settlement." In Afro-Brazilian religious contexts, these terms are often used interchangeably to describe the initiatory practice of fixing the *orixá* within a material object. The *orixás*—frequently referred to as "saints" (*santos*) in their individualized form—first manifest in their material seat or settlement and, following initiation, in the body of the initiate through possession. Though these manifestations are distinct, both are vital to establishing the relationship between the *orixá* and the initiate, a connection that ultimately shapes (or "makes") them both.

Settlements can take various forms, with stones or pebbles (*otás*), which are meant to be found, and iron tools (*ferramentas*), which are crafted by religious blacksmiths, being the most common. Each *orixá* is associated with specific elements: for example, the seats of Oxum and Iemanjá are adorned with shells and stones found in bodies of water, reflecting their connection to freshwater and the sea, respectively. These elements also represent their associated colors—yellow or gold for Oxum, and white or silver for Iemanjá. Similarly, the stones linked to Xangô are considered to have fallen to the earth as thunderbolts, symbolizing his domain as the deity of thunder.

Historical Context

In the last decade of the nineteenth century, Raymundo Nina Rodrigues, a foundational figure in Brazilian anthropology, observed a curious phenomenon: among the Black population of Bahia, everyday objects like stones and pieces of iron, once consecrated, were revered as deities. Rodrigues noted, "Any iron object can be revered as Ogum, provided it undergoes consecration" (1935: 43–44). This blending of deity and object led Rodrigues to coin the term "fetishist animism," describing a stage where deities took on anthropomorphic traits while still retaining the external forms of "primitive" fetishism (ibid., 173). The accusatory notion of fetishism—where material objects, seemingly chosen at random, became enchanted objects of devotion among so-called primitive peoples—derived from the Portuguese word *feitiço*, meaning charm or sorcery. It implied a perceived mental confusion, where the distinction between the realms of immanence and transcendence, the material and the spiritual, was supposedly unclear (Latour [1996] 2010).

A century later, this intriguing fusion of objects and deities continues to captivate scholars of Afro-Brazilian religions. While social, political, and economic dimensions are often prioritized, the ontological dynamics of Candomblé objects—how they not only represent but also merge with persons and deities—has garnered significant attention in recent anthropological scholarship. However, this topic remains largely unexplored by philosophers of religion (Porcher 2025).

Philosophical Significance

Upon first encountering the world of Candomblé, one is immediately struck by its diverse array of objects—necklaces, musical instruments, clay artifacts, straw, porcelain vessels, and others. Each of these items signifies a connection to a particular *orixá*, forming part of a complex system that organizes the cosmos. Within the vibrant material culture of Afro-Brazilian religions, the objects that left a lasting impression on Nina Rodrigues—leading him to believe that practitioners attributed supernatural powers to inanimate objects—were the stones and iron tools in which the *orixás* "sit" or "settle."

The meaning of the seats or settlements arises from the ongoing engagement that people maintain with them, existing and persisting solely through this interaction. They are not independent of their materiality or sensible qualities; rather, they are interwoven with these elements, forming a relationship between the bodies of the adepts and their material, sensible, and localized presence in the *terreiro*. Moreover, the hidden presence of the altars amplifies their potency, which becomes tangible during possession rituals—an experience reserved exclusively for the initiated, who are capable of being possessed:

> In the chamber of the saints, a story is woven, invisible to outsiders, but quite clear and palpable to those in the house. A story of relationships between the adept and their saint, between them and their brothers- and sisters-of-saint, between everyone – deities and humans – and the mother- or father-of-saint of the house. The construction of this story is closely linked to the way in which these sacred objects mobilize the body, soliciting care, demanding certain gestures and postures, inviting activity or passive contemplation.
>
> (Rabelo 2011: 24)

A long phenomenological tradition, which has influenced ecological psychology, recognizes that humans perceive their environment as offering opportunities for action, rather than merely receiving sense data. This involves perceiving the value-laden properties of things in the world. While James J. Gibson (1979) primarily discussed affordances in the physical world, religious rituals involve the perception of not only physical but also affective and social realities as opportunities for action. In other words, religious practices afford material, affective, and social experiences that enable participants to develop the ability to discern what they should and should not see, feel, and do—encompassing the full spectrum of religiously shaped perceptions, emotions, and actions.

This perspective allows us to discuss *religious affordances*—solicitations of an agent's abilities that command respect for the superempirical resources essential for successful practice, while also acting in accordance with the environment's sacred or profane features. Consequently, this framework helps us understand religious practices not merely as mechanical rituals but as pathways for shaping one's identity, training individuals to perceive the world as presenting opportunities for meaningful engagement and appropriate action.

If a philosophical framework for religious practices adopts this perspective, it will necessitate an examination of normative subjective experiences. Since ritual participants may not always articulate—or even possess the ability to articulate—these norms, and because reflexivity and reasoned explanation are not prerequisites for participating in a religious form of life, the challenge in studying embodied religious experiences lies not in their privacy or inaccessibility but in their tacit nature. To address this challenge, it is essential to employ attention, phenomenological description, and critical reflection to bring these experiences to the forefront of inquiry.

To this end, Arnaud Halloy (2013) provides a cognitive ethnography of the ontological dynamics of objects, bodies, and deities in Xangô, an Afro-Brazilian tradition that developed in the northeastern state of Pernambuco in ways similar to Candomblé. Halloy argues that initiation rituals involving "things" create cognitively and emotionally salient ontological hybrids. This is because participants view the introduction and manipulation of cultic objects as more than mere expression or representation. As the saying goes, "the *otá* is the *orixá*." Furthermore, practitioners commonly refer to the *otá* of their altar as "my *orixá*" and to those of other initiates as "Maria's Oxum," "my brother's Ogum," and so on. The physical characteristics of the stones, the ecological and mental circumstances surrounding their discovery, and the oracular procedures for their identification all contribute to their evocative potential (ibid., 146).

Halloy describes the process connecting objects, bodies, and *orixás* in settlement and initiation as a transformation where objects become *object-gods* and object-gods become *object-bodies*. This radical shift in perception occurs through what he terms "invert isomorphism," where living beings are treated as tools, and artifacts are regarded as living beings (ibid., 149). During the sacrificial ceremony that typically follows the ritual washing of the medium with a special decoction of freshly picked herbs, the sacrificial blood is poured onto the *otá* or *ferramenta* that comprises the altar before being applied to the head and shoulders of the initiate, who kneels facing the altar of their *orixá*. Participants handle the objects with the utmost care—not because they are fragile, but because they are imbued with a new divine nature, transforming their status from passive to potentially active. In contrast, sacrificial animals are treated as mere artifacts, perceived only in their physical form: their blood serves as the primary carrier of *axé*, and their organs are the main ingredients in offerings to the *orixás*.

In sum, Candomblé practices create an environment where objects are not merely representations but active participants in shaping religious experience. This environment, informed by the affordances of ritual objects, cultivates the adept's ability to perceive the world as inherently relational and spiritually imbued—where material elements invite respect, care, and participation. The *assento* or *assentamento* is thus not merely a static artifact but a central, formative element in the construction of personhood within Afro-Brazilian religions. Practitioners learn to inhabit a world that is not simply encountered but actively shaped by the interplay of material, spiritual, and social forces, all of which are intimately bound to the development of self and identity in the religious life of the *terreiro*.

Related Emic Terms

axé, feitura, ferramenta, ibá, otá, orixá, santo

Related Etic Terms

altar, emblem, fetish, idol, sanctuary, shrine, totem

References

Gibson, James J. 1979. *The Ecological Approach to Visual Perception*. Boston: Houghton Mifflin.

Halloy, Arnaud. 2013. "Objects, Bodies and Gods: A cognitive Ethnography of an Ontological Dynamic in the Xangô Cult (Recife, Brazil)." In Diana Espirito Santo and Nico Tassi (eds.), *Making Spirits: Materiality and Transcendence in Contemporary Religions*. London: Bloomsbury, 133–158.

Latour, Bruno. [1996] 2010. *On the Modern Cult of the Factish Gods*. Durham: Duke University Press.

Nina Rodrigues, Raymundo. 1935. *O Animismo Fetichista dos Negros Baianos*. Rio de Janeiro: Civilização Brasileira.

Porcher, José Eduardo. 2025. *Afro-Brazilian Religions*. Cambridge: Cambridge University Press.

Rabelo, Miriam C. M. 2011. "Estudar a religião a partir do corpo: algumas questões teórico-metodológicas." *Caderno CRH*, 24 (61): 15–28.

3

Self and Identity in Jainism

Anil Mundra

Chapter Outline

Self-Sameness and Numerical Identity	71
Qualitative Identity and Substance Metaphysics	72
Personal Identity and the Self	76
Jain Ontology and Jain Identity	79
3.1 *Anekāntavāda*	82
3.2 Identity	86
3.3 Liberation	89

Self-Sameness and Numerical Identity

Likely writing in the eighth century CE, the Jain philosopher-monk Haribhadrasūri encapsulates his central metaphysic of non-one-sidedness (see keyword *Anekāntavāda*) thus: "all things (*vastu*) are what they are because they are subject to both being themselves and not being other things" (1940: 31; 1947: 228). A crucial word for our purposes here is the Sanskrit *ātman*, reasonably translated as "self". What is a "self," anyway? Or, to put the question in terms closer to ordinary language and to Haribhadra's treatment: What is it for something to be itself?

The more recent Anglophone philosopher of identity Sydney Shoemaker gives a typical definition of "self-sameness" as "the relation each thing has to itself and to no other thing" (Shoemaker 2006: 40). But this extensional enumeration hardly casts much light on the matter—can we say any more about just what this unique relation to oneself is? Many have thought that we cannot: that the relation of identity is too fundamental to be further analyzed.

Be that as it may, there are various senses in which we use the English word "identity," and interrogating these in conversation with Jain ontology can help to build out a fuller notion of the self. The self-sameness that many contemporary metaphysicians, like Shoemaker, consider to be the "primary" or "strict" meaning of "identity" has been dubbed, more technically, "numerical identity." And the usual presumption about numerical identity is that it is intrinsically temporal: part of what self-sameness entails is for something to remain the same (in some crucial sense) over time. David Hume puts the presumption this way: "We cannot, in any propriety of speech, say, that an object is the same with itself, unless we mean, that the object existent at one time is the same with itself existent at another time ... Thus the principle of individuation is nothing but the invariableness and uninterruptedness of any object, thro' a suppos'd variation of time" (*A Treatise of Human Nature*, 1.4.2). Hume's statement is generally interpreted as claiming that temporal persistence is all that provides "informative judgments of identity," in Shoemaker's words (2006: 42). But he also points out that this reading of Hume itself flies in the face of common sense: there are everyday identity judgments that make no reference to time, such as the judgment that "the building with the imposing stone pillars in the front is the same as the one with the rusty fire escape in the rear" (ibid., 42).

The presumption of time's uniquely important role in designating a thing's numerical identity is not merely a product of aberrant readings of Hume, though. It is visible as far back as Aristotle's various iterations of his law of non-contradiction : for example, "it is impossible that a thing should simultaneously be white and be not-white" (*Prior Analytics* 51b29-52a4, quoted at Horn 1989: 17); and "it is impossible for contrary attributes to belong at the same time to the same subject" (*Metaphysics* 1005b26-28, trans. at 1933: 163). The sole qualifier of identity in these iterations is a temporal one. But Shoemaker's common-sense example gives the lie to Aristotle's articulation too, since the building with the white marble stone pillars in the front is the same as the one with the non-white rusty fire escape in the rear—the very same building is simultaneously white and not-white. To put it another way: Aristotle allows for a substance to possess contrary qualities at different times—indeed, this is a definition of substance for him (*Categories* V 3b25-4a10)—but why should time be the *only* parameter allowing for such contrary predications of a numerically identical thing? Shoemaker's example displays the need for a more fine-grained analysis of self-sameness.

Qualitative Identity and Substance Metaphysics

Haribhadra gives us this finer grain. In his formulation of non-one-sidedness, he names not only time (*kāla*) but also place (*kṣetra*), substance (*dravya*), and state (*bhāva*) as parameters allowing for contrary predications. Taking what is for him the most fundamental pair of contrary properties—existence (*sattva*) and non-existence—Haribhadra elaborates his identity-statement that "all things are what they are because they are subject to both being themselves and not being other things" in the following way: any real thing "is existent and nonexistent because it is existent in the form of its own time, place, substance, and state, and is nonexistent in the form of another's time, place, substance, and state" (1940: 36). For example, something like a clay pot can be not only existent now and non-existent later, but also existent here while simultaneously non-existent in other places, existent as earthen but simultaneously non-existent as water, and existent as black but simultaneously non-existent as red (ibid., 37).

These parametric qualifications of a thing as being itself and not being something else bring us to a second sense of identity, beyond the bare self-sameness of numerical identity qualified only temporally: this second sense is what we can call "qualitative identity," a sortal that places the individual possessing it into a class, and so in some way and to some extent constitutes that individual as the *kind* of individual it is. This is the more colloquial sense of "identity," which classifies an individual in a group with others of its own kind on the basis of some quality. This would seem to be a very different sense of "identity" from numerical self-sameness, which involves only an individual in itself with no reference to any other individuals or qualities beyond itself. One payoff of Haribhadra's analysis is that he connects these two apparently very disparate senses, allowing us to see how they hang together.

A strong split between "numerical identity" and "qualitative identity" is encouraged by a certain kind of substance metaphysics that is dominant in both Western and Indian philosophies, from Aristotle to the Vaiśeṣikas. These systems consider individual substances to be ontologically primary, and they subordinate qualities (*guṇas*) to the self-subsisting substance (*dravya*) that possesses them. Aristotle says in the *Metaphysics* (1028a10-15) that the primary sense of a thing's "being" is its "substance," while its qualities are what it is only secondarily: "Hence that which is primarily, not in a qualified sense but absolutely, will be substance" (1028a32; trans. 1933: 313).

But Jain philosophers in the tradition of Umāsvāti's *Tattvārthasūtra* and Siddhasena's *Sanmatitarka* (Prakrit: *Saṃmaïtakka*) resist this priority of substance to qualities (Murti 1955: 11). "Indeed," Haribhadra says, "substance and quality are not regarded as belonging to entirely different classes by the Jains, as they are by the Vaiśeṣikas, but rather [only] in some way; substance is not partless, but rather has a single-cum-multiple nature (*ekāneka-svabhāva*)." (1940: 362). A multiplicity of qualities is contained in a single substance—qualities and substance are different, but inasmuch as they are wrapped up with each other, they're not different (cf. Matilal 1977: 101; Tatia 1951: 231). This is, of course, the multiple singularity of *anekāntavāda*; and many of its foremost modern interpreters (Murti 1955: 10–11; Padmarajiah 1963; Matilal 1981: Chapter 8; Jaini 1979: 90–91; Balcerowicz 2017: 77–78) rightly recognize the centrality of this metaphysic to Jain philosophy as a whole. But just how could it make sense for substance and quality to be so thoroughly intertwined, and what might this mean for identity?

As we did with the notion of "identity," we can here distinguish two distinct but related senses of the term "*dravya*/substance" in both its Indian and Western acceptations: (1) a temporal/diachronic sense as that which subsists or persists over time amidst change; and (2) a synchronic sense as the substrate of qualities at any given moment. Observe that each of these senses of substance respectively points to each of the senses of identity that we have already scouted: (1) to say that a substance is what persists diachronically is to emphasize its *numerical* identity; while (2) to say that it is the substrate of qualities is to emphasize its *qualitative* identity, or rather identities. It so happens that virtually all substance-metaphysicians run these two senses together—people tacitly tend to take both of these as equally constitutive of the notion of substance, and Umāsvāti's *Tattvārthasūtra* is no exception (Matilal 1977: 101). Haribhadra is one of very few philosophers to my knowledge who attempts to explain why and how these two senses of substance hang together, as I shall explain shortly below.

Kant nicely articulates something very close to the Jain view when, in his *Critique of Pure Reason*, he posits that "in their relation to substance, [qualities] are not in fact subordinated to it, but are the manner of existence of the substance itself" (A414/B441). To see why this makes any more sense than the Aristotelian subordination of quality to substance, the Jain terminology of "mode" or "modification" (*paryāya*) is helpful. While some Jains do distinguish "modification" (*paryāya*) from "quality" (*guṇa*) and other categories such as "state" (*bhāva*) and "transformation" or "development" (*pariṇāma*), Siddhasena (Saṅghavi and Doshi 1939: 120–121) and the tradition following him, including Haribhadra (see Padmarajiah 1963, 259), apparently do not. Therefore, an argument for Siddhasena's view (*Sanmatitarka* 1.12) that substance and modification are mutually inextricable can be read as vouching for the mutual imbrication of substance and quality in general. Haribhadra provides this argument:

> A thing has the form of both substance and mode, because there is no grasping of either apart from each other and since it wouldn't make reasonable sense [for it to be otherwise]. And it doesn't make sense because of the impossibility of clay-substance devoid of the aspect of its upper and lower part and so on, or of what has the aspect of upper and lower part and so on devoid of clay-substance. Indeed, a sky-flower substance, which is empty of the form of blossoming and so on, doesn't exist; nor do non-substances have that blossoming and so on. Thus it is established that things have both forms mutually intermingled.
>
> (1940: 120–121)

The "sky-flower" is the classic Indian philosophical chimera. Haribhadra's point, then, is that anything imagined to have substance without modification is just that: an imaginary thing, a chimera, just like a sky-flower.

Haribhadra furthermore appeals to our perception of everything as both persisting and changing, which are basic characteristics of substance and modification respectively:

> [A thing] is impermanent (*anitya*) just because it is permanent (*nitya*), since it is permanent insofar as it has the character of substance and because modification is intrinsic to that. And it is permanent just because it's impermanent, since it is impermanent insofar as it has the character of modification and because substantiality is intrinsic to that. And this is because both aspects are established by experience, and due to the absence of each if differentiated [from each other] one-sidedly (*ekānta*), since they are not apprehended in that way.
>
> (1940: 119)

While the imbrication of substance with modification may be a more conceptual matter, Haribhadra appeals to empirical experience to display the imbrication of permanence with impermanence, since an unchangingly permanent thing would seem imaginable in a way that substance without modifications is not. However, concrete empirical things (as opposed to conceptual abstractions) are substances, and their persistence consists in their substantiality. But substance is always inevitably imbricated with modification; and modification is essentially changeability. So the permanence of any substantial thing must also be imbricated with the impermanence of its modifications. And this is indeed what we find upon inspection: that nothing in our experience persists without some change, nor can we identify any change without attributing it to some persisting thing that is its substrate. This confirms the applicability of Haribhadra's analysis of substance and modification to the empirical experience of permanence and impermanence. And, as we will shortly see, this permanence-cum-impermanence of things is what is of the utmost importance when it comes to one's self.

To arrive at the self, it is helpful to recur to the distinction between numerical and qualitative senses of the notion of identity. Now, though, having made this distinction, let us ask the question of what might be the connection between numerical and qualitative identity, which latter Shoemaker calls "traits":

> What makes a set of traits an identity is its being such that, normally, numerically different individuals have different sets of traits of this sort, and, normally, an individual retains the set of traits over time—where this means that numerical identity between an individual existing at a certain time and an individual at a later time goes, normally, with the individual having (more or less) the same set of traits at both times.
>
> (Shoemaker 2006: 41)

Shoemaker is saying that qualities qualify as an identity when they tend to track a particular individual. When this happens, we have a qualitative identity, and this qualitative identity tracks a numerically identical individual. But Shoemaker doesn't explain just why this confluence of numerical identity and qualitative identity might obtain. Why should a qualitative identity coalesce around an individual at all?

Personal Identity and the Self

Until now, we've been discussing individuals in the most general sense: particular entities of any kind, whether human or not, animate or not. In the most general ontological sense, we can talk (as we have been) about any thing of any sort "being itself"—any thing that we can individuate has a numerical identity in this sense. However, this is not what we usually mean when we say "a self"—this term usually refers to a *person*. Likewise, although the Sanskrit term *ātman* can serve as a mere reflexive pronoun to refer to anything "itself," its more philosophically pregnant sense points to the true identity of a person. This brings us beyond mere *numerical* and *qualitative* identity to the issue of *personal* identity.

All of the considerations that we have discussed until now apply to the special case of persons. Indeed, there are further considerations about specifically personal identity that strengthen the confluence of its numerical and qualitative aspects. Shoemaker observes that in the case of persons, "identity seems to matter in a way it doesn't matter in the case of other things" owing to our "desire to continue in existence with a life worth living" (2006: 44). But what anyone regards as a life worth living is determined at least in part by one's traits—in particular, one's "self-conception and structure of goals, tastes, and values," qualities that tend to be fairly stably connected with a numerically identical individual over time (ibid., 47).

To have the trait of being a Jain is, normatively, to venerate certain beings (viz., Jinas) as the exemplars of liberation effected by a certain program of ascesis (Cort 1998: 9; Babb 1996: 5). This program is predicated upon a doctrine of *karma* according to which one will reap the future consequences of one's actions (Bajželj 2024: 29). Clearly, it is irreducibly temporal and presupposes the numerical identity of the person traveling it; but insofar as it is a *Jain* program, it also presupposes a certain qualitative identity for this person.

Haribhadra thus elaborates his doctrine of personal identity in the course of discussing this program of seeking liberation. He advocates a particular kind of ascetic practice that is highly Jain in idiom: *bhāva-tapas*. The term *bhāva* is an important and evocative one in Jainism, which most basically means a "state of being"—as in the tetrad of parameters to qualify a thing's identity that we saw in the previous section—but often connotes a more specifically *spiritual* state, the state that (within the Jain dualism of body and soul) is most reflective of one's conscious self rather than extraneous material things. Haribhadra says that to undertake this "spiritual ascesis" is "truly a property of the self (*ātman*)" (1947: 219). That is to say that it is neither extraneous to oneself, nor simply reducible to one's conscious essence: this ascesis is a real further quality, a constitutive aspect of a temporally developing self, which structures the project of engaging in practices aiming diachronically at liberation. The Jain self must therefore be understood as an identity that is constitutively both numerical—persisting over time in order to achieve certain goals—and qualitative, taking certain goals and projects as its own.

This self must furthermore be understood as being truly subject to the qualitative conditions that motivate it to undertake this ascetic program of liberation from the same. But this means, Haribhadra says, that "liberation makes sense [only] insofar as suffering, disgust, and the knowledge and realization of the path and so on have a single locus in some way" (1947: 106). That is, it must be numerically the *same* self that is qualitatively identified as suffering at one point in its career and as liberated later. But the former negative qualities are contrary to the latter positive ones—so the persisting and changing self is again a prime instance of non-one-sidedness. Haribhadra thus concludes that "it is only for one who is an *anekāntavādin* about things—whose essences are beset by contrary properties—that there is establishment of all everyday transactions" (ibid.).

It is importantly revealing, however, that Haribhadra is finally most concerned with the "establishment of all *everyday transactions*," rather than the loftier conditions for the possibility of the transcendent goal of liberation. In fact, most of Haribhadra's arguments bearing on personal identity in the liberation chapter don't actually presume any sort of grand cosmic karmic moral frame, or even the practice of asceticism. Although the goal of liberation clearly sets a certain ultimate horizon for many of Haribhadra's arguments—as it does for many Indian philosophical arguments for the self in various schools (cf. Rostalska, Chapter 1 in this volume)—it turns out that most of them work quite well even without that transcendent end in play. Even if liberation looms as a transcendent ideal, most of the arguments actually trade on much more local elements of mundane action and experience. Most of Haribhadra's arguments—as is common for Jain philosophers—are in the first instance concerned that everyday phenomena of action and awareness should be intelligible as the phenomena that we experience them to be every day. This intelligibility, he says, requires a metaphysics of the self as both persisting and changing:

> It is only for a permanent-cum-impermanent individual that the enjoyment of the results of action done by oneself and the relation between grasper and grasped and so on make sense: it is due to its being *in some way* persisting that these phenomena [of the enjoyment of results and the grasping relation] occur as they do, which is established by experience.
>
> (1947: 106)

Haribhadra is talking here about two kinds of phenomena: (1) the volitional act of seeking certain results with one's action; and (2) the cognitive experience of simply being aware of an object.

These structures of action and experience clearly apply to contexts far wider than the ascetic quest for liberation. They have to do with a central fact of human mental life of any orientation: namely, *intentionality*, that is to say, object-directedness, in both its practical sense of the motivatedness of action and its cognitive sense of the contentfulness of experience.

It should be clear by now why intentional *action* requires a self that both persists and changes: it must persist enough to expect to see its action through to its results, and this process of action and result itself also involves change. But why does mere intentional *awareness*—cognitively grasping an experiential content—also require the experiencing self to both persist and change? Well, consider the usual alternative: in the Buddhist epistemology that is Haribhadra's primary foil—as well as in Anglophone philosophy of mind—there is the attempt to "advanc[e] essentially causal explanations of the contentful character of thought" (Arnold 2012: 236). The preeminent Buddhist philosopher Dharmakīrti, for example, posits that "to be graspable is just to be a cause, which is to be capable of delivering a cognitive image" (1938: 193). On this picture, the relation between grasper and grasped is just the relation between an effect and its cause—an object brutely causes the awareness of it—and there is no philosophical need to appeal to the intentional fact that a resultant cognition is *about* the causing object, having the object as its *content*, beyond the causal fact that the cognition followed from the object (perhaps through a chain of mediating causes, whether neurophysical or otherwise).

However, Dharmakīrti also famously holds to a metaphysic of momentariness, according to which nothing at all persists for more than an instant. Haribhadra now objects that a momentary object's "capability of delivering a cognitive image (*ākāra*) is quite uncertain, since one cannot ascertain that consciousness (*saṃvedana*) has the image of an object immediately past, insofar as one doesn't grasp that [which is past] because it is non-existent at that time" (1947: 126). A momentary object will have passed away by the time it causes a cognition; this means that the cognition does not grasp the object itself, since the object is no longer present once the cognition is. So there must be at least enough persistence of both the grasping consciousness and the grasped object for the two to overlap temporally. But the grasping consciousness and its grasped object must also change in tandem, or else the cognition will not reflect the object: except for an absolutely unchanging object—which no empirical objects are—awareness *of* that object must also change. Since awareness is an essential characteristic of the soul that is one's true self in Jainism, intentional awareness requires the self to both persist and change.

Haribhadra's arguments for the persistent self, in my reading, thus repose upon very general considerations of identity, action, and awareness that far outstrip the soteriology of liberation. This does not render the soteriological frame entirely otiose, however. The grand Jain scheme of the soul's career toward liberation is not only consistent with Haribhadra's intentional analysis: insofar as liberation remains the highest good in Jainism, it holds a consummately important position even in the context of the more sprawling structure of goals, tastes, and values that characterizes a person's identity. The philosopher Charles Taylor in his own narrative account of personal identity observes that "the one highest good has a special place. It is orientation to this which comes closest to defining my identity" (1989: 63). This is because, even if I consider there to be many goods worth pursuing in a good life, this is the one that ultimately (by definition) matters most. It is the highest good that very largely helps us to narrativize our lives, to make sense of our lives as continuous wholes, with a structure of goals, tastes and values. And so, while Haribhadra's intentional analysis secures local persistence of the self—by tethering the self to its objects of action and awareness from moment to moment—it is the highest good that gives a self unity over the course of its entire career toward an ultimate object. This ultimate object of Jain ascetic action is liberation; and the cognitive correlate of liberation is, in the Jain view, omniscience (see keyword Liberation). Non-Jains often find this insistence on omniscience puzzling: even if the highest good plausibly involves some sort of improvement in our gnoseological situation, why should it require total knowledge of absolutely everything as Jains claim? But reading Haribhadra's analyses of action and of awareness as two sides of a single intentional coin makes this more intelligible: if *karma* is the bane of action and awareness, the ultimate volitional horizon should be liberation and the ultimate cognitive horizon should be omniscience.

Considering Haribhadra's arguments in their most essential form, then—as concerning everyday phenomena of intentional action and awareness—they are meant to apply to any personal self whatsoever, establishing the persistent but dynamic identity of anyone who acts and cognizes. The sense of identity in play in his arguments is primarily numerical, although I have suggested that the nature of human action and cognition implicates some values and goals to motivate and structure the required intentionality, and these traits count as qualitative identities (the more so the more enduring they are). In any case, though, when considered in the heavily freighted frame of Jain soteriology, the self shedding its karmic baggage through certain ascetic practices aimed at liberation depicts a rather robust qualitative identity: namely, a Jain one. In this frame, the numerical and qualitative converge on the Jain path.

Jain Ontology and Jain Identity

John Cort has posited that "a distinction between self and other lies deep at the heart of Jain ontology" (1998: 12). Cort is discussing, in the first place, the conscious soul and the karmic material that is other than it. But it should be clear by now that this applies very well to the fundamental non-one-sided ontology that Haribhadra offers to individuate selves. As he says, "the determinacy (*pratiniyatatva*) of all real things is established insofar as they are characterized by both presence of self and absence of other (*sva-para-bhāvâbhāva-ubhaya-ātmakatā*). Otherwise it is not established, because there is the absurdity of a thing abandoning its essence (*svarūpa*), with its mutualistic character (*itarêtara-ātmakatva*)" (1947: 235), the mutually-determining oppositional imbrication of self and other—that is, the determination of a thing's identity in contradistinction to what is different from it.

However, Cort also means for this opposition to outstrip metaphysics altogether, applying as well to the sociology of the 'contested Jain identities of self and other' (1998: 1–14). While the connection between metaphysics and sociology he proposes is a metaphorical one, we have now seen grounds in Haribhadra's own methods to develop the analogy. His intentional analysis, set in the grand frame of the ascetic Jain path to liberation, designates Jain identity in contradistinction to other identities. Not only does this analysis secure the metaphysical persistence and change of an individual self, then; it arguably provides for "stability and adaptability" at the sociological level too, at which the small minorities of Jains in any given South Asian societies faced challenges of "survival and growth" (Qvarnström 1998: 35; see also Barbato 2017 and 2019). This sociological perspective adds a further layer of meaning to the notions of "self" and "persistence"—here is an identity that is not only numerical and qualitative but social as well.

Bibliography

Aristotle. 1933. *The Metaphysics*. Translated by G. Cyril Armstrong. Loeb Classical Library. London: W. Heinemann, Ltd; G. P. Putnam's Sons.

Aristotle. 2014. *Categories; On Interpretation; Prior Analytics*. Loeb Classical Library 325. Cambridge: Harvard University Press.

Arnold, Dan. 2012. *Brains, Buddhas, and Believing: The Problem of Intentionality in Classical Buddhist and Cognitive-Scientific Philosophy of Mind*. New York: Columbia University Press.

Babb, Lawrence A. 1996. *Absent Lord: Ascetics and Kings in a Jain Ritual Culture*. Comparative Studies in Religion and Society 8. Berkeley: University of California Press.

Bajželj, Ana. 2024. "Selfhood, Persistence, and Immortality in Jaina Philosophy." *Religious Studies*, 60 (S1): S21–43. doi.org/10.1017/S0034412523001051.

Balcerowicz, Piotr. 2017. "Jainism: Disambiguate the Ambiguous." In Joerg Tuske (ed.), *Indian Epistemology and Metaphysics*. London: Bloomsbury Academic, 75–100.

Barbato, Melanie. 2017. *Jain Approaches to Plurality: Identity as Dialogue*. Leiden and Boston: Rodopi Bv Editions.

Barbato, Melanie. 2019. "Anekāntavāda and Dialogic Identity Construction." *Religions*, 10 (12): 642. doi.org/10.3390/rel10120642.

Cort, John. 1998. "Introduction." In John E. Cort. (ed.), *Open Boundaries: Jain Communities and Cultures in Indian History*. Albany: SUNY Press, 1–14.

Dharmakīrti. 1938. *Pramāṇavārttikam*. Ed. Rāhula Sāṅkṛtyāyana. Patna: Bihar and Orissa Research Society.

Haribhadrasūri 1940. *Anekāntajayapatākā*. Vol. 1. Ed. Hiralal Rasikdas Kapadia. Gaekwad's Oriental Series 88. Baroda: Oriental institute.

Haribhadrasūri. 1947. *Anekāntajayapatākā*. Vol. 2. Ed. Hiralal Rasikdas Kapadia. Gaekwad's Oriental Series 105. Baroda: Oriental institute.

Horn, Laurence R. 1989. *A Natural History of Negation*. Chicago: University of Chicago Press.

Jaini, Padmanabh S. 1979. *The Jaina Path of Purification*. Berkeley: University of California Press.

Matilal, Bimal K. 1977. "Ontological Problems in Nyāya, Buddhism and Jainism a Comparative Analysis." *Journal of Indian Philosophy*, 5, (1–2): 91–105. doi.org/10.1007/BF02431706.

Matilal, Bimal Krishna. 1981. *The Central Philosophy of Jainism (Anekānta-Vāda)*. Ahmedabad: LD Institute of Indology.

Murti, T. R. V. 1955. *The Central Philosophy of Buddhism: A Study of the Mādhyamika System*. London: Unwin Paperbacks.

Padmarajiah, Y. J. 1963. *A Comparative Study of the Jaina Theories of Reality and Knowledge*. Bombay: Jain Sahitya Vikas Mandal.

Qvarnström, Olle. 1998. "Stability and Adaptability: A Jain Strategy for Survival and Growth." *Indo-Iranian Journal*, 41 (1): 33–55. doi.org/10.1023/A:1002939911725.

Shoemaker, Sydney. 2006. "Identity & Identities." *Daedalus*, 135 (4): 40–48.

Siddhasena Divākara. 1939. *Siddhasena Divākara's Sanmati Tarka: With a Critical Introduction and an Original Commentary*. Ed. Sukhlālji Saṅghavi and Bechardāsji Doshi. Pt. Shri Sukhalalji Granthamala 5. Bombay: Shri Jain Shwetambar Education Board.

Tatia, Nathmal. 1951. *Studies in Jaina Philosophy*. Sanmati Publication 6. Banaras: Jain Cultural Research Society.

Taylor, Charles. 1989. *Sources of the Self: The Making of the Modern Identity*. Cambridge: Harvard University Press.

Anekāntavāda
Chapter 3.1

Anekāntavāda (un-ake-AHN-tuh-VAH-duh), literally the "theory of non-one-sidedness" in Sanskrit, is a characteristically Jain metaphysical and semantic doctrine according to which any determinate real thing admits of contrary predications. All things are complex, possessing an irreducible multiplicity of aspects that cannot be distilled to some singular, simple essence. As will be elaborated below, the most important thing in question—perhaps the thing after which other things are modeled—is the self persisting over time.

There are a few fundamental properties on which theorists of non-one-sidedness tend to focus: all things are said to be both existent and nonexistent; both permanent and impermanent; both universal and particular; and both denotable and undenotable. The contradiction that would *prima facie* result from the predications of such contrary pairs is averted by parameterizing each term so that it and its negation are not applied in the same way: for example, a thing is existent at one time and place, and nonexistent at some other time and place. The resultant propositions issue neither in contradiction nor in equivocation on the terms under discussion: "existent" and "nonexistent" remain genuine contraries, and they are genuinely predicated of the same single thing, but the scope of their truthful application to that thing is now appropriately specified. *Anekāntavāda* is thus a way to disambiguate language and fully determine the objects of discourse. Philosophers of non-one-sidedness take exception to the sweeping claims of universal scope that religious doctrines tend to promote about the fundamental nature of reality. They point out the ways in which such absolutist propositions fly in the face of common sense and undermine themselves.

Arguably the most important and contested concept in South Asian philosophy and religions is the self (*ātman*). Proponents of non-one-sidedness point out that if one's true self is said to be absolutely eternal—as some philosophers posit—there would seem to be no way to account for its apparent change and (most importantly) progress toward its ultimate goal; while if it is said to be absolutely transient and always in flux, there would be no way to account for its continuation along such a progressive path. The self must thus be conceived as both permanent (qua substratum of change) and impermanent (in the progressive development of its states).

The first intimations of *anekāntavāda* are found in the oldest Jain scriptures written in Prakrit. The founding figure of all current Jain traditions, the Jina Mahāvīra, tells questioners that the soul is permanent insofar as it continues, but impermanent insofar as it takes different forms in successive incarnations. Mahāvīra sometimes prefaces each of such contrary pronouncements with the qualification "in some way" (*siyā* in the original Prakrit). This hedge makes it clear why contrary predications can apply to the same thing consistently: they apply in different ways, and so do not contradict each other. These ways of applying predicates are often systematized in terms of a canonical group of parameters (called *nikṣepa*s), such as place, time, substance, and state. While a predicate may be truly applied to an object at some values of these parameters, its contrary may be applied with equal truth at other values. In the scholastic period, this approach will come to be called *syādvāda*, the "in-some-way theory" (*syāt* being the Sanskrit equivalent of the hedge *siyā*).

The most authoritative Jain doctrinal handbook—the Sanskrit *That Which Is* (*Tattvārthasūtra*) of Umāsvāti/Umāsvāmi (5.29/30) around the middle of the first millennium CE—encapsulates the basic ontological insight of non-one-sidedness in its pronouncement that all existents are marked by arising, persistence, and passing away. It also broaches a new way of parameterizing propositions: viewpoints (*naya*), that is to say, contexts or methods through which propositions are to be interpreted. These viewpoints are said to complement the reliable means of awareness (*pramāṇa*) that are at the center of Indian epistemology. Siddhasena's *Introduction to Logic* (*Nyāyāvatāra*) elaborates this relationship by suggesting that these reliable means of awareness serve to remove ignorance, while viewpoints provide access to partial truths that do not exclude contrary alternative views of the many-sided reality; but these various one-sided viewpoints can together fully determine an object through the use of *syādvāda*. The *Essay on the Dialectic of Right Thinking* (*Sanmatitarkaprakaraṇa*, which may or may not be by the same Siddhasena) undertakes to systematize the various viewpoints, proclaiming each one correct in its own sphere and *only* there: non-one-sidedness thus demands that none of them be regarded as either absolutely right or absolutely wrong.

As scholastic Jain discourse develops in conversation with other religions in the lingua franca of Sanskrit in the latter half of the first millennium, *anekāntavāda* is increasingly applied to a range of philosophical dilemmas. Samantabhadra's *Investigation of Authorities* (*Āptamīmāṃsā*) formatively tackles not only existence vs. nonexistence and permanence vs. impermanence, but also unity vs. diversity, identity vs. difference (particularly between cause and effect, substance and property, etc.), reason vs. scripture, and even the crucial ethical and soteriological issues of violence vs. nonviolence and the status of knowledge and ignorance vis-à-vis bondage and liberation. Haribhadrasūri's *Victory-Flag of Non-One-Sidedness* (*Anekāntajayapatākā*) and the works of Akalaṅka set the terms for the ensuing tradition by integrating Samantabhadra's approach into the reigning idiom of Buddhist logic and metaphysics, turning *anekāntavāda* back against the Buddhist idealism that challenges the realism of rigoristic Jain asceticism.

By the time of Prabhācandra and the great polymath Hemacandra in the first half of the second millennium, both the *naya*s and *syādvāda* are accepted components of *anekāntavāda*. The *syādvāda*, moreover, is at this point standardly considered not only to involve both affirmation and negation but also a third operator of inexpressibility (*avaktavyatva/avācyatā*), which is sometimes explained as encoding a fusion (*per impossibile*) of affirmation and negation. Later thinkers elaborate the formula (mentioned briefly in Siddhasena and Samantabhadra) of conjoining these three operators in every mathematical combination, so that *syādvāda* is now considered to involve a sevenfold (*saptabhaṅgī*) predication of contraries. And the *nayavāda*, for its part, is increasingly depicted as mapping extant philosophical schools, such that each is seen as affording its own partial view of reality.

Modern scholars have interpreted *anekāntavāda* in sundry ways: from "non-absolutism" (Mookerjee) and "non-extremism" (Sanghvi) to "relativity" (Balcerowicz) and "synthesis" (Matilal) or "syncretism" (Ganeri). Matilal's influential reading rightly rejects Padmarajiah's "indetermination"—since, as we've seen, *anekāntavāda* is in fact all about the determination of things—and Thomas's idiosyncratic "non-unequivocality"—since equivocation, as I've argued, is not to the point of the theory. But Matilal's own interpretation of Jain epistemology as "non-radicalism" or especially "intellectual *ahiṃsā* [nonviolence]" (following Dhruva) and "toleration" (following Kapadia) are not much better (Cort): they are adaptations of the classical theory to modern problems and idioms for which they may or may not be very well suited, and they tend to lose track of important aspects of the theory in its classical contexts and uses. We might say, in good non-one-sided fashion, that each of these glosses is applicable to *anekāntavāda* in some way but fails to unambiguously capture the thing itself in its full determinacy.

References

Balcerowicz, Piotr. 2008. "Some Remarks on the Opening Sections in Jaina Epistemological Treatises." In W. Slaje (ed.), *Śāstrārambha: Inquiries into the Preamble in Sanskrit*. Abhandlungen Für Die Kunde Des Morgenlandes, Bd. 62. Wiesbaden: Harrassowitz Verlag, 25–81.

Cort, John E. 2000. "'Intellectual *Ahiṃsā*' Revisited: Jain Tolerance and Intolerance of Others." *Philosophy East and West*, 50 (3): 324–47.

Dhruva, A. B. 1933. "Introduction." In *Syādvādamañjarī of Malliṣeṇa with the Anyayoga-Vyavaccheda-Dvātriṃśikā of Hemacandra*. Bombay Sanskrit and Prakrit Series 83. (Bombay: Department of Public Instruction, xiii–cxxv.

Dixit, K. K. 1971. *Jaina Ontology*. Lālabhāī Dalapatabhāī Granthamālā 31. Ahmedabad: LD Institute of Indology.

Ganeri, Jonardon. 2001. "Rationality, Harmony, and Perspective." In *Philosophy in Classical India: The Proper Work of Reason*. New York: Routledge, 128–150.

Kapadia, H. R. 1940. "Introduction." In *Anekāntajayapatākā by Haribhadra Sūri, with His Own Commentary and Municandra Sūri's Supercommentary*. Gaekwad's Oriental Series 88/105. Baroda: Oriental Institute, ix–cxxviii.

Matilal, Bimal Krishna. 1981. *The Central Philosophy of Jainism (Anekānta-Vāda)*. Ahmedabad: LD Institute of Indology.

Mookerjee, Satkari. 1978. *The Jaina Philosophy of Non-absolutism: A Critical Study of Anekāntavāda*. 2nd ed. Delhi: Motilal Banarsidass.

Padmarajiah, Y. J. 1963. *A Comparative Study of the Jaina Theories of Reality and Knowledge*. Bombay: Jain Sahitya Vikas Mandal.

Sanghavi, Sukhlalji. 1961. "Anekāntavāda: The Principal Jaina Contribution to Logic." In *Advanced Studies in Indian Logic & Metaphysics*. Calcutta: R. K. Maitra; distributors: Firma K. L. Mukhopadhyay, 15–28.

Thomas, F. W. 1968. *The Flower-Spray of the Quodammodo Doctrine: Syād-Vāda-Mañjarī*. Delhi: Motilal Banarsidass.

Identity
Chapter 3.2

Most generally, identity is what any thing is. In South Asian philosophy of religion, a most pressing question has always been the question of personal identity: what a *person* really is. This is usually phrased as the problem of the nature of the self (*ātman*) in Sanskritic contexts. The earliest Vedic Upanishads are famous for their inquiries into the self and their various grand pronouncements on who and what we really are. They often tend to identify one's self with one's consciousness, not unlike some early modern Western philosophers, although unlike the latter they do not always equate consciousness with intellection and emotion. The Sāṃkhya philosophy is a radical instance of identifying the person (*puruṣa*) with consciousness as distinguished from all mental functions and even ego, which are placed along with material objects on the side of heterogeneous nature. The Jain philosophical tradition agrees that consciousness is an essential characteristic of the soul; but this may not exhaust the Jain view of the self.

One of the standard criteria of personal identity is the presupposition, shared amongst all Indian philosophers, that anything deserving to be called one's true identity must be in some way permanent. Something flitting in and out of existence can hardly be said to count as oneself. Hindu philosophers tend to follow this line of thought to the conclusion that one's true self (*ātman*) transcends all empirical vicissitudes. On the other hand, according to scholastic Buddhist metaphysics, there is no such transcendent entity: everything is in constant flux from moment to moment and there is nothing at all having a stable nature.

The Jains, as is their wont, countenance both the permanence and impermanence of identity without acquiescing in either one-sided view scouted above (cf. keyword *Anekāntavāda*). The most authoritative Jain handbook—the Sanskrit *That Which Is* (*Tattvārthasūtra*) of Umāsvāti/Umāsvāmi (5.29/30)—defines an entity as that which is subject to origination, persistence, and dissolution, thus giving equal place to the stability emphasized by Brahminical philosophers and the momentariness of Buddhists. As their philosophers of non-one-sidedness say, indeed, it is just this conjunction of contraries like permanence and impermanence that singles out any thing as the particular thing it is, persisting in its identity through its various states of empirical change.

These discussions clearly involve issues of ontological identification beyond just one's self. What makes something the thing that it is, in contradistinction to other things? Does it possess a stable nature (*svabhāva*) that defines it? If it does, what is the connection between tokens of a type (*sāmānya*) of things with the same nature? How to understand a thing's persistence through time, particularly if it is observed to change—is it the self-same thing after the change, or has the original thing passed out of existence to be replaced by something else?

These are questions that have vexed philosophers of various stripes. Many have doubted whether there can be any rigorous concept of identity generalizable across the various contexts in which it is customarily called upon, and whether it is even possible to stipulate the concept without either circularity or incoherence. Part of the problem is that there are at least two basic acceptations of the term: most contemporary metaphysicians prioritize what they call "numerical identity" or "self-sameness"—a thing's simply being itself—over what is currently the more colloquial sense that classifies an individual in a class with others of its own kind on the basis of some quality, such that an individual can be said to "have" an identity, or even have various identities. This disjunction between what we can call "numerical identity" and "qualitative identity" coheres with an Aristotelian metaphysic that tends to cleave self-subsisting substance from the attributes that it possesses.

Jain philosophers, however, resist the presumption of the priority of substance to quality. According to Siddhasena's classic *Essay on the Dialectic of Right Thinking* (*Sanmatitarkaprakaraṇa*), substance and the qualities that it possesses are equally real and inseparable. Haribhadra's *Victory-Flag of Non-One-Sidedness* (*Anekāntajayapatākā*) furthermore suggests that both are equally necessary for the constitution of a thing's identity. This is another way to see why all identities are non-one-sided for Jains. Substance is precisely that which persists amidst change, as well as that *in which* change is seen to occur—that is, it is both the substrate of change as well as the substratum of attributes, both the basis of numerical identity and of qualitative identity. These two ostensibly different senses of identity thus converge in *anekāntavāda*. The most basic claim of non-one-sidedness is that any real thing is what it is, and is not what it is not—a statement of the meaning of identity if ever there were one. What is at stake in this ostensibly trivial proposition is a certain view of the determinacy of identity: that to *be* is to exist *as* something—articulated in terms of attributes determined along various dimensions of predication—and *not* to exist as something else. To be self-identical, on this analysis, is to possess a certain configuration of qualitative identities—which is to say that a thing's numerical identity is picked out by its qualitative identities.

The distinction between self and other on which *anekāntavāda* relies is fundamental for Jain ontology. Scholars from Y. J. Padmarajiah (1963) to John Cort (1998) have seen that the kernel of Jain ontology is the relationship of self and other, identity and difference. When it comes to the identity of a person on the Jain path to liberation, the most important distinction at issue here is between their soul and what is adventitious to it. But Cort also means for this opposition to extend to the social identities of Jains in relation to non-Jains. The ontology of identity thus shades into the more sociological issues involved in the qualitative identities that are most commonly at stake in the discourses of religious studies, namely, religious identities.

A non-one-sided view of individuals is partially definitive of what it is to be Jain and not other than Jain. Johnson has explicated how contestation over Jain views of the soul challenge and maintain the asceticism that is part of Jain social identity, and has suggested that the metaphysics of non-one-sidedness can serve as a bulwark against radical views threatening to obviate the physical rituals that make Jains who they are. One-sided approaches tend to overemphasize certain kinds of praxis, such as purely gnoseological epiphanies, at the expense of more gradualistic negotiations between body and mind (cf. keyword Liberation). Part of the way that Jains assert and maintain their religious identity is thus by philosophizing about identity itself.

References

Barbato, Melanie. *Jain Approaches to Plurality: Identity as Dialogue*. Leiden and Boston: Rodopi Bv Editions, 2017.

Cort, John E. 1998. "Introduction." In *Open Boundaries: Jain Communities and Cultures in Indian History*. Ed. John E. Cort. Albany: SUNY Press, 1–14.

Ganeri, Jonardon. 2012. *Identity as Reasoned Choice: A South Asian Perspective on the Reach and Resources of Public and Practical Reason in Shaping Individual Identities*. New York: Continuum.

Johnson, W. J. 1995. *Harmless Souls: Karmic Bondage and Religious Change in Early Jainism with Special Reference to Umāsvāti and Kundakunda*. 1st ed. Lala Sunder Lal Jain Research Series, vol. 9. Delhi: Motilal Banarsidass Publishers.

Kapstein, Matthew T. 2001. *Reason's Traces: Identity and Interpretation in Indian & Tibetan Buddhist Thought*. Boston: Wisdom Publications.

Matilal, B. K. 1976. "A Note on the Jaina Concept of Substance." *Sambodhi*, 5 (2–3): 3–12.

Padmarajiah, Y. J. 1963. *A Comparative Study of the Jaina Theories of Reality and Knowledge*. Bombay: Jain Sahitya Vikas Mandal, 1963.

Liberation
Chapter 3.3

Freedom has been a central concern of philosophers in far-flung places and times, but takes very different shapes depending on the conditions from which one seeks to be free and the goods that one hopes to be free to attain. Although set in culturally-specific cosmological frameworks, the basic South Asian concept of liberation captures certain elements that should be acceptable to any theorist of freedom, namely: the conditions from which liberation is sought are characterized by limitation and suffering; the limitations in question are imposed upon our actions and their results; but our actions, with the help of knowledge, may transcend these conditions to attain ultimate satisfaction. Such a view of liberation can be placed in fruitful dialogue with accounts of the metaphysics and ethics of free will, the philosophy of intentional action, and political discourses of emancipation. There is also an argument to be made, as Karl Potter has done, that liberation is a basic concern around which Indian philosophy revolves.

In this context, liberation (designated by Sanskrit terms including *mokṣa* (MOKE-shuh), *mukti, nirvāṇa, kaivalya, apavarga*, and others) is release from the cycle of life and death fueled by *karma*, that is to say, actions and their results. A variety of South Asian philosophies that disagree on many other fundamental issues agree on this much: that since life intrinsically involves suffering—since birth necessarily brings in its train old age, sickness, and death—liberation from the same is the *summum bonum*. *Karma* not only fuels the cycle (*saṃsāra*) but is fueled by it, too. It is thus usually considered to require immense time and effort, not to mention great good fortune, to break the cycle and be released from the bondage (*bandha*) of suffering, ignorance, and finitude generally.

As far as we can tell from the Ṛg Veda—the oldest known South Asian liturgies—liberation did not much figure into the early Vedic religion, which focused instead on the concrete rewards of ritual in this world and the afterlife. In the middle of the first millennium BCE, however, a cyclic view of life appeared and endless births and deaths came to appear rather tiresome and painful. In the Upaniṣads are found some of the earliest mentions of *karma* as an ethically-charged determinant of one's worldly fate and the importance of transcending its bondage. In the canonical Buddhist diagnosis from around the same time, the source of this bondage and suffering is ultimately desire and its solution is detachment.

Beginning in the same period, the Jains—followers of the Jinas, who are literally "conquerers" of the afflictions of life—draw the contours of liberation into particularly sharp relief. From the earliest Jain scriptures, *karma* is a material substance that binds the spirit to the world, obstructing and distorting one's vision and knowledge in the process. Through moral and ascetic practices that quell the passions and minimize the negative impact of one's actions upon other sentient beings, the Jain path of purification seeks to expurgate *karma* and stop any further influx of it into the soul.

Thus one develops right vision, knowledge, and conduct, which consummate in omniscience (*kevala/kaivalya*), as described by the authoritative Jain handbook *That Which Is* (*Tattvārthasūtra*) of Umāsvāti/Umāsvāmi around the middle of the first millennium CE. Some benign *karma* may remain after the most deleterious kind is removed, allowing an omniscient master to remain embodied in the world and teach for a period. Ultimately, though, a soul that has attained such a level will be perfected (*siddha*), having transcended all *karmic* action and now experiencing its eternally pure nature of consciousness and bliss at the roof of the universe where it has arisen after jettisoning its *karmic* burden. Purged of adventitious baggage, the soul is now pure and thus essentially identical to every other perfected soul. It does not, however, lose its individuality as imagined in Vedantic monism or Buddhist idealism: it maintains its particular identity and differentiation according to place, time, state, and even shape, as well as various more arcane parameters.

Such temporary persistence of *karma* and ultimate retention of elements of individuality may seem to compromise the degree of transcendence offered by the Jain notion of liberation. But it serves the important function of maintaining the coherence and salience of the very notion of *karma* and the ascetic practices meant to eliminate it. These practices seem fruitless in the most gnoseological forms of Vedānta and Buddhism: if liberation solely requires dissociation from the gratuitous aspects of one's personality and the insight that one truly is not who one usually takes oneself to be, *karma* turns out to be an illusion and one can apparently dispense with the concrete ascetic practices that target it. Nathmal Tatia has reviewed Jain criticisms of other philosophical attempts to reconcile gnoseological liberation with the metaphysics of the soul and karma.

This tension between asceticism and a purely gnoseological approach to liberation is felt acutely in the eminent Jain philosopher Kundakunda during the period of Umāsvāmi. Many philosophers in the ensuing millennium wrestle with this tension and resolve it in their own ways; but it is not until the rather heterodox Adhyātma movement at the dawn of modernity that Jain thinkers inspired by Kundakunda boldly disclaim the importance of all external practices to favor the liberating power of inner faith. It is indeed not unusual for lay practitioners to support movements like the Jain Adhyātma favoring inner faith over external practice. W. J. Johnson has read Kundakunda's ambivalence between asceticism and gnoseology sociologically as a capitulation to the laity's need for opportunities to pursue liberation without having to go in for the full renunciation required of mendicant specialists. The very nature of renunciation is as contested as it is central to asceticism. Does renunciation require one to physically abandon possessions and sever family ties, as mainstream Jainism and other traditions emphasizing mendicancy have traditionally taught? Or does it only require letting go of psychological desires for the possessions and relationships that one maintains in practice? This goes to the crux of the issue of liberation vis-à-vis the self: does liberation mean utter isolation (*kaivalya*) from all that is not the self, or rather only an attitude of detachment (*vairāgya*) within oneself?

Amidst the many and deep disagreements about the precise nature of liberation and the proper path to it, there seems to be one chief point of agreement at the place where the question of liberation coincides with the question of the self: namely, that we are not truly who we often take ourselves to be. True self-knowledge is thus mutually imbricated with liberation from the limiting confines of the profane and insecure illusion of a needy, vulnerable self.

This inquiry into the self becomes an issue of its persistence because there is another widely-shared intuition that a chief source of vulnerability is transience. Buddhists often say that pervasive impermanence entails that there is no stable self, while trying to hold onto one leads to suffering. In this view, liberation would be the end of holding any illusion of a stable self. Hindu philosophers aim to circumvent these challenging conclusions by seeking what is permanent (*nitya*) amidst this impermanence, the essence of the self that remains beyond all change. Liberation would then be realization of this transcendent self. But such a self would seem radically non-empirical, hardly to be found in any possible experience. Jains respond to this dilemma by recognizing the self as both persistent and changing. Indeed, on the Jain analysis, change can only be recognized as change *of* what persists, while persistent continuity can only be recognized against a background of change, or at least the potential for change through the passage of time. Liberation is then not only identification with the permanent aspect of the self, but also knowledge of all changing phenomena—total omniscience (*kevala-jñāna*). Padmanabh Jaini has written the classic work on the purificatory path of asceticism seeking liberation, although—like much classical literature—it is surprisingly silent on the nature and experience of liberation itself.

References

Jaini, Padmanabh S. 1979. *The Jaina Path of Purification*. Berkeley: University of California Press.

Johnson, W. J. 1995. *Harmless Souls: Karmic Bondage and Religious Change in Early Jainism with Special Reference to Umāsvāti and Kundakunda*. 1st ed. Lala Sunder Lal Jain Research Series. Vol. 9. Delhi: Motilal Banarsidass Publishers, 1995.

Potter, Karl H. 1991. *Presuppositions of India's Philosophies*. Delhi: Motilal Banarsidass Publishers.

Tatia, Nathmal. 1951. *Studies in Jaina Philosophy*. Sanmati Publication 6. Banaras: Jain Cultural Research Society.

4

Shinto

Indescribable Description of Self and Persistence

Maki Sato

Chapter Outline

Introduction	93
Account of Shinto	94
Kami Living with Us: Freedom and Liberty of Personhood and Self-Discipline	96
Keywords and Summary	103
Tentative Conclusion: Shinto and a Perspective on Self	104
4.1 *Harae*: Purification of *Tsumi*, *Toga*, and *Kegare*	108
4.2 *Kotodama*: Value-Neutrality and Multilayered-ness	114
4.3 *Tama* and Dynamism: Unpredictable Spirit Freed from Human Consequences	120

Introduction

This chapter sheds light on self and persistence through the lens of Shinto (神道), a Japanese indigenous belief system that worships *kami* (神). *Kami* are believed to inhabit all things, including phenomena (such as thunder and rain), non-organic (such as rocks and landscapes), and organic (including, but not limited to, deceased human beings, insects, and animals). Thus, *kami* can be understood as a concentrated invisible energy in nature that occasionally shows itself in visible form. *Kami* has strong links with nature, seasons, and humans' relationship with each other. The concept of *tama* (霊 or 魂) is inseparable from *kami*.

Divine spirits, four kinds of *tama*, are invisible floating spirits and are external to all beings and phenomena of nature. When it finds an object where it can reside, *tama* concentrates and manifests itself as *kami*. In other words, *kami* are dense and excessively concentrated *tama* that exceeds the wisdom and knowledge of the human mind. Natural phenomena are complex in that they bring grace and blessings through cultivation, but on other occasions, they can bring disasters, such as earthquakes and typhoons. Therefore, the unique aspect of *kami* is that it is believed to have both good and evil aspects, depending on the efficacy of *tama*.

Due to the uniqueness of the Shinto belief system, this chapter briefly summarizes and introduces Shinto to readers who wish to become more familiar with it. In the following sections, I will discuss how the keywords *tama*, *kotodama* (言霊), and *misogi* (禊) illustrate the concepts of self and persistence from the perspective of the Shinto belief system. *Kami* illustrates embodiment, the unity between the mind and the body, and how the self can be understood through bodily existence. Conversely, *tama* highlights the self in resonance with the work of the mind, separable from the body. *Kotodama* delineates the value of the persistent self in terms of self as inherently neutral yet reactional. Meanwhile, *misogi*, the purification act of self, works to sustain the persistent self from *kegare* (穢, impurity). Lastly, this chapter concludes with tentative conclusions and discussions for further study.

Account of Shinto

Shinto has been considered an indigenous religion in Japan since ancient times, as it appears in *Kojiki* (712, 古事記) and *Nihonshoki* (720, 日本書紀). Standard descriptions of Shinto for Western audiences often pertain to preconceived notions about religion. Thus, Shinto is often described in a form that resonates with the shared notion of religion in the Western sphere. A summary of a standard description can be read as follows:

> Shinto is an animistic Japanese religion going back to preliterate times. The myths of creation and how the state was established were preserved in oral traditions until written down in the early eighth century in two chronicles, *Kojiki* and *Nihonshoki*. These chronicles narrate the beginning of the gods and goddesses (*kami*) and the process by which the islands of Japan (or by extension the whole world) came into being through their actions. The most important deity is the Sun Goddess, Amaterasu. She is considered the direct ancestor of the Japanese imperial family and gives the throne a religious foundation.
>
> (Kasulis 2004: 72)

Such descriptions are correct in some sense. However, as Kasulis points out, one has to be cautious that its descriptions are made with a touch of Western understanding of "religion," which has sacred texts and hierarchies among the celestial deities (as in Greco-Roman polytheism) that Shinto does not pertain (Kasulis 2004: 72–74).

First, concerning sacred texts, Shinto is not a "religion of the sacred text" but is based on rituals and practices, actions, and attitudes, and it is a lived and shared spirituality that guides people in their daily lives. *Kojiki* and *Nihonshoki* are texts that refer to ancient Shinto. What is written in the *Kojiki* and *Nihonshoki* are the myths of deities shared in Shinto belief that describe myths such as how deities made the islands of Japan: *kuni umi* (国生み). Moreover, both describe historical accounts of ancient emperors and empresses in direct lineage with the grand mythic narratives of *kuni umi* by *kami*. These mythic narratives of emperors as being in direct lineage with *kami* caused Shinto to face its dark ages, before and during the World War years (from the late nineteenth to the early twentieth century), when it was used as the state religion attached to the nationalist ideology after Meiji Restoration. However, *Kojiki* and *Nihonshoki* are repositories of ancient Japanese mythic narratives, which implies that the text is not considered sacral. Although there is no sacred text in Shinto, there are twenty-seven *norito* (祝詞) that are coined in Volume Sixth of the *Engishiki* (820, 延喜式) that are still used today as base texts for calling out to the deities during ceremonial rituals (Kokugakuin 1999: 555). Scholars working on hermeneutics thus study *norito* to investigate the lineage of Shinto and how Shinto originates differently from imported religions such as Buddhism.

Second, the notion of *kami*, which refers to the celestial gods and goddesses, has no clear hierarchy, as seen in Greco-Roman polytheism. Motoori Norinaga (1730–1801, 本居宣長), a scholar during the Edo period in *kokugaku* (a study on ancient Japanese thought and culture, 国学), claimed *Kojiki* as the oldest surviving Japanese text. Volume Three of his *Kojiki-den* (古事記伝, *Commentaries on Kojiki*, 1790–1822) explains the notion of *kami* as follows:

> the excelling wise beings that provoke awe are called *kami*. The word excel refers not only to what is noble or good but also to what is excessively terrible or doubtful, and so on. In other words, if something in the world is excellent and wise in whatever sense, it is *kami*.
>
> (Kokugakuin 1999: 37)[1]

Norinaga also points out that "*kami* include the various *kami* of heaven and earth, as in ancient writings, and the divine spirits (*tama*) in shrines (*yashiro*, 社) dedicated to them, as well as humans, animals, plants, trees, grass, sea, mountains, and any others that are awe-inspiring" (Kokugakuin 1999: 37).[2] This is why Shinto is thought to be polytheistic, pantheistic, and animistic. What is notable is that *kami* includes humans and animals, as well as nature as such. *Kami*, the vehicle to Shinto, is regarded as there exists 8 million *kami* (*yaorozu no kami*, 八百万の神). Nonetheless, the number implies its pantheistic aspect and is not explicit. Shinto currently has approximately 80,000 *jinja* (神社, *yashiro* of *kami*) shrines scattered across Japan, according to the Agency for General Cultural Affairs as of 2022.[3] *Kan'nushi* (神主) serves as a priest who presents offerings, food (*shinsen*, 神饌), and dances (*kagura*, 神楽) to *kami* during rituals and ceremonies. Avoiding uncleanness (*kegare*, 穢) and ensuring purity (*harae*, 祓) is the most crucial concept shared within the Shinto belief system. Therefore, *kan'nushi* or Shinto priests must constantly abstain from *kegare* (*kessai*, 潔斎).

Historians have various theories on when Shinto emerged, whether it originated in Japan or was brought from the continent via Korea and China. However, the common understanding is that Shinto began to appear well before 300 BCE to 300 CE when Japan, as an archipelago, received inhabitants from overseas (*toraijin*, 渡来人). With its long history from ancient times, Shinto is complex in that it evolved as Shinto through the merging of Japanese ancient religious views toward nature, encountering various religious ideas such as Taoism, Buddhism, Confucius in the seventh century, and Christianity in the seventeenth century. Buddhism came to Japan around 600 CE, and the worship of *kami* saw a complex fusion of religious beliefs in Japan called *shinbutsu-shūgō* or *honji-suijaku* (神仏習合, 本地垂迹, fusion of *Kami* and Buddha).[4] Recent scholarly studies reveal how Shinto refined its uniqueness throughout history while encountering other religious beliefs and philosophies, not limited to Buddhism, but to Confucianism and Christianity (Kokugakuin 1999; Ito 2012). Because of its long history, various views and ideologies in Shintoism often provide an impression of internal paradoxes and ambivalence, a product of the amalgamation of different religious belief systems.

As most Shinto scholars agree, the turning point for Shintoism happened during the Meiji Restoration until the end of the Second World War, when Shinto and the emperor system were being used as a crucial ideology for the modernization of Japan. Most Shinto rituals and belief systems were reformed based on Yoshida Shinto (吉田神道), among other sects, when the government changed Shinto into State Shinto (国家神道).[5] Citizens were encouraged to worship the emperor as the living *kami* (*arahitogami*, 現人神) under the State Shinto formed by the Meiji government. In short, State Shinto made the emperor perform both politics (*matsuri-goto*, 政) and festive events (*matsuri*, 祭). After World War Two, Shinto was officially separated from the state governance. Nowadays, in Japan, Shinto is more of a lifestyle than a religion (Kasulis 2004: 38–39). Its beliefs rooted deep in Japanese culture are unconscious and inseparable from one's everyday life.

Kami Living with Us: Freedom and Liberty of Personhood and Self-Discipline

In this section, we examine the concept of *kami* and its implications for personhood in Japanese culture. First, we look into the general idea of *kami* and how it can relate to self and personhood. Then, we focus on thought history centering on Mootori Norinaga and his *kokugaku* and how he revived the original concept of *kami* in Shinto. Last, from the argued perspective of *kami*, it draws on the implication of personhood and self from the standpoint of *kami*.

Conceptual *Kami* and Its Background: Mergeable, Syncretic, Yet Self-Disciplined

The Shinto belief system thinks highly of invisible *tama* (divine spirits) that float everywhere and descend on any non-organic and organic object, including human beings. People can recognize its divinity through visibility and awe when the *tama* descends. *Tama* with excessive power and divinity are occasionally personified, some with their own given name (e.g., Amaterasu Oomikami, 天照大神, the sun goddess). However, most *tama* are unnamed *tama* that show and prove their existence through particular objects or natural phenomena. When the spirit (*tama, mono, chi*) concentrates its power, humans can recognize it as goblins (*yōkai*, 妖怪) or phantoms (*mononoke*, もののけ).[6] Because of *tama*'s inherent invisibility and the flexibility of not possessing the substantial body for its proof of presence, *kami* is freed from ontic existentialism.

In other words, just like *tama*, *kami* are everywhere, and paradoxically, *kami* are nowhere because they do not require substantial existence. While ontic focuses on *what is*, ontological explores *how* and *why* things exist. Ontologically, the Shinto belief system implies *kami*'s existence, allowing us to argue and contemplate them. However, such belief does not require *kami* to be related to ontic existences that are visible to humans. This is because, as discussed above, *kami* is a manifestation of *tama* that could reside with any existing being in the world, including non-humans and non-living things. In short, *kami* is mergeable with anything and everything.

Such ambivalent existence enables *kami* to unite with nature per se (e.g., Mt.Fuji as Konohanasakuyahime, 木花之佐久夜毘売[7]), with posthumous humans (e.g., Sugawara no Michizane, 菅原道真, 845-903, known as Tenjin, 天神), and even with icons in other religions. In the case of fusion with other religions, *kami* unites with bodhisattvas (Bosatsu, 菩薩) of the Buddhist belief and with Hinduism deities, such as Saraswati as Benzaiten (弁財天) and Mahakala as Daikokten (大黒天). The unification between Shinto and Buddhism is called *honji-suijaku* theory, which was crystallized and sophisticated in the medieval era. The theory of *honji-suijaku* claims that *kami* is the temporary form of Buddha and bodhisattvas to save sentient beings. Therefore, the Buddha and the *kami* are fundamentally the same, and it was believed that the Buddha (*honchi*) manifested itself to *kami* (*suijaku*) to suit domestic realities (see n. 2).

Additionally, because of *kami*'s inherent characteristics that derive from nature, there is no intrinsic evil or good attached to the concept of *kami*. Evil has a chance to become good; and good to be evil. There is no statical evilness and goodness attached to the idea of *kami*. This flexibility in evil and good makes sense, seen from multiple aspects. Even if something good happens to A, that good may be good in relativizing that with B being inferior to A. Think about A being a bully and B being bullied by A. A might enjoy temporal prosperity with a sacrifice of B. In this case, what is happening for B is far from good, but a causal effect of A being evil. However, C, who is a follower and shares the tentative prosperity of A, may not see A as an evil bully but as a superstar who shares his/her prosperity with others. Good and evil, seen from this perspective, are relative based on which standpoint you are being involved in or observing the relationship. In short, evil and good is a value-driven judgment through relativization unless it relates to serious anti-societal crimes such as killing, stealing, and damaging.

For example, in the case of Sugawara no Michizane (菅原道真, 845-903), who is worshipped as *kami* in the Kita-no-tenmangu (北野天満宮) shrine, was first regarded as *aramitama* (raging fierce *tama*, 荒魂) or more of a *tatarigami* (cursing god, 祟り神), transforming himself into thunder and fire after his death. Michizane was a brilliant scholar, poet, and politician in the Heian (平安) period. He was even a master of Chinese literature and poetry, earning immense respect for his writings. Because of his excellence in intelligence, he climbed the political ladder to become a trusted advisor to the emperor. However, due to court rivalries and jealousy, he was falsely accused of plotting against the throne and was exiled to Dazaifu (大宰府) in Kyushu, where he died in despair. He was believed in the Heian period to have become a cursing *kami* to punish his political opponents posthumously. However, because of the rituals of praying for his *tama* to be in peace, he gradually became a *kami* for wisdom and literature and is still worshipped elsewhere in Japan.

Reflexive to such a notion of syncretic *kami* freed from ontic existence and the static dichotomic divide between good and evil requires humans to self-discipline themselves and stay honest based on one's decisions based on their free will. In other words, *kami* shows various aspects of oneself that depend on the situation in requesting truth and righteousness (*makoto*, 真). Therefore, in Shinto, it is not God or the deity that gives orders and rules to sustain morality in human society, but it is up to each individual to decide what is right or wrong. Thus, self-discipline is the required norm in Shinto. Moreover, there are no sacred texts, such as sutras, that humans or *kami* can refer to for righteous and justifiable judgment. Hence, Shinto is freed from static moral judgment.

However, such judgment is made based on ever-changing relationality according to the world in which we are situated, and all righteous judges are dependent on one's righteous work of the mind. In order to keep a clear and right mind, cleanliness and purity are required in everyday life. To such a degree, *misogi* (cleansing of the body, 禊) and *harae* (cleansing via rituals and spoken words, 祓) become essential. In the following sections, we will further look into the concept of *kami* and its unique way of being.

Concept of *Kami* and Self: In the Context of Intellectual History

The persistence of self through self-discipline and keeping the righteous mind (*makoto-no-kokoro*, 真の心) was first argued by Motoori Norinaga. By establishing *kokugaku*, he initially intended to quest for the authentic Japanese mind that existed before the influence of China (*kara-gokoro*, 漢意). Through careful reading of *Kojiki* and *Nihonshoki*, Norinaga gradually attempts to find a pure idea of Shinto in the classic Japanese text. Buddhism and Shinto saw unification and fusion from the early stages when Buddhism was imported. In contrast, the relationship between Confucianism and Shinto teachings remained ambiguous. A careful study of its relationship started in the early Edo period after neo-Confucianism was imported into Japan.

Before Norinaga, Confucian scholars like Fujiwara no Seika (1561–1619, 藤原惺窩), Hayashi Razan (1583–1657, 林羅山), and Yamazaki Ansai (1619–1682, 山崎闇斎) argued about the similarity between Confucius and Shinto (*juka-shinto*, 儒家神道), in order to eliminate the Buddhism influence. However, Norinaga's interest was to unearth pure Japaneseness before the influence of China. While Hayashi Razan argued in an essay, *Shintōdenju* (神道伝授), that "there is no other *kami* outside one's heart–mind (*kokoro*, 心)," Norinaga denied the moral *kami* (Tajiri 2011: 141–143). In his essay, *Kuzuhana* (くず花), Norinaga argues that there is an inherent limitation in humans' ability and wisdom (Karube 2018: 133–138). If Confucian scholars think *kami* resonates with the human mind or vice versa, such thinking shows the impudent egoism that humans retain equal wisdom and reason as *kami*. For Norinaga, *kami* is unknowable by all means, and *kami* works as the total others to humans. Indeed, in *Kojiki* and *Nihonshoki*, *kami* does not directly interfere with the human sphere. Norinaga claims that the world is filled with wonders and mysteries of *kami*. Thus, humans are surrounded by unexplainable phenomena that are beyond humans' wisdom and reason. Works of Norinaga were later succeeded by Hirata Atsutane (1776–1834, 平田篤胤), who elaborated and crystallized a base for State Shinto.

According to Norinaga, if something in the world is excellent and wise that naturally claims awe, it is *kami*. *Kami*, or the concentration of *tama*, represents natural phenomena due to their lack of a body. To interact with humans, *kami* embody sacred objects like swords or mirrors in *jinja* shrines and natural objects. *Kami* prefers settling in natural objects like mountains, trees, river streams, and waterfalls. In terms of the gender of *kami*, Norinaga applies the idea of Norinaga's master Kamo no Mabuchi (1697–1769, 賀茂真淵) in his essay titled *Kaikō* (1764, 歌意考), by contrasting the collections of *tanka* poems, *Man'yōshū* (万葉集) and *Kokinwakashū* (古今和歌集). According to Mabuchi, the ancient poems in *Man'yōshū* show *masuraoburi* (益荒男振り), the calm and bold expression characterized by powerful strength and assertiveness. On the other hand, a typical style in *Kokinwakashū* of the aristocratic Heian culture is more feminine and delicate, with grace and subtlety, showing elegance; *taoyameburi* (手弱女振り) (Tosa 1999: 29–30).

Through his careful study of *Kojiki* on *kami* in the text, Norinaga argued that although *kami* seemingly possess gender, their minds work more complexly to resonate with the given situation. For example, male *kami* in the profound loss of his deceased wife shows *taoyameburi*, the femineity, rather than *masuraoburi*, the masculinity. Therefore, Norinaga argues that although *kami* possess gender, their minds are more gender-free and neutral. Male *kami* can be feminine, and female *kami* can be masculine in their mindsets according to their given situation (Mori 1982: 53–55).

Norinaga's view on *kami*, which is gender-free and neutral, led him to elaborate further on his thoughts regarding evil and good. In his essay on Naobinotama (直毘霊, 1771), Norinaga addresses the problem of evil and good. Why does evil occur if the world is filled with *tama* and *kami*? *Naobi*, in Kojki and Nihonshoki, is depicted as a divine *tama* that rectifies wrongs and restores the balance between evil and good. It (verb. *naosu*) means "straightening" or "rectifying" and refers to correcting something abnormal, wrong, or distorted to restore the situation or personhood to its original normal state. This concept is often associated with purification and restoring order and harmony. It represents the ethical consciousness of Japan, emphasizing the importance of maintaining purity and order in both societal norms and personal conduct.

From the concept of *naobi*, Norinaga argues that *kami* should possess both evil and good aspects, which creates dynamism, movement, and force that constantly changes the situation (Mori 1982: 55–56). Norinaga also argues that the vitality of *naobi* is uncontrollable, and it is impossible for humans to understand the deep meaning behind their doings. Something that looks bad at once can give good in the long term or from a different aspect, and vice versa. For example, earthquakes and typhoons may destroy human habitats, but they may also work to rebalance the harmony between humans and nature. Just like the nitrogen cycle known in agricultural studies, which is crucial for plants to grow—lightning and rainfalls are essential factors to enhance its cycle. A thunderstorm for a family during a picnic might sound like a disaster, but seen from a nitrogen cycle perspective, in a longer term, it brings food for the family. In short, the concept of *naobi* connotes that humans cannot fully understand the consequences of the *kamis*' doings.

As argued, *kami* embodies itself in nature. Humans can also become *kami* posthumously worshipped as guardians. Some shrines, such as Kanda shrine (神田明神), worship Taira-no-Masakado, a Heian period warrior, as *kami* of battle; Sugawara-no-Michizane, a Heian period politician and a scholar, as *kami* of wisdom. Humans can become *kami* posthumously, freed and detached from this-worldliness (*sensei*, 潜

性 or latent), and be guardians for people of this-worldliness who are still suffering with their lives. In other words, the excellence in whatever ability humans have indicates that they are already guarded by divine spirits (*tama*), thus posthumously becoming *kami* and maintaining their lived personhood posthumously as *kami*.

The concepts of the spirits (*tama*) descending to objects and the descended object becoming *kami*-embodied-object (*shintai*, 神体) first appear in the *Kojiki* and *Nihonshoki*. In both *Kojiki* and *Nihonshoki*, it is written that Amaterasu (the Sun Goddess) gave her grandson, Niniginomikoto (the ancestor of the emperor, 瓊瓊杵尊), the mirror, sword, and stone jewel as the signifier of the spirituality when he descended on the earth. Although the episode is written in *Kojiki* and *Nihonshoki*, the word *kami*-embodied-object (*shintai*) appears only around the mid-Heian period. It first appears in the first Japanese dictionary, *Irohajiruishō* (1144–1165, 色葉字類抄), compiled by Tachibana Tadakane (橘忠兼). As explained above, the term used means an object where the *tama* descends, and the word *shintai* itself is not commonly used.[8] However, the *kami*-embodied-object concept is still widely accepted in the twenty-first century. The object where the spirit descends is called *yorishiro* (依代). For trees where the spirit descends becomes *shinboku* (神木). For rocks where the spirit descends, it is called *iwakura* (磐座) or *iwasaka* (磐境). Such a *kami*-embodied object (*shintai*) becomes the object for worshipping.

Although it would not be an object of worshipping as *shintai*, ancient objects used for decades are also *kamis'* favorite embodiment tool. These *kami* who reside with ancient objects are called *tsukumo-gami* (付喪神). Figure 4.1 is a scene from a scroll

Figure 4.1 Tsukumogami of the kitchenware.
Source: https://rmda.kulib.kyoto-u.ac.jp/item/rb00013599/explanation/otogi_05. Copyright: Kyoto University Library, 2001.

repainted in the Edo period on *tsukumo-gami*, initially made in the Muromachi period. *Tsukumo* is a homonym for the noun "ninety-nine (九十九)" and a verb "attached to an object (*tsuku*, 付く)." It has a double connotation in that it was believed that an ordinary object gains its *tama* once it is used over ninety-nine years (the number of the years is not explicit, but it implies long periods in general). Here, the angry kitchenware like a rice ladle, a whisk, a broom, a bamboo ladle, and a tea kettle who were treated badly by the humans have turned themselves into *tsukumo-gami* and are about to protest and retaliate against the humans who were using them without paying respect to them (Tsukumogami-emaki, Vol. 2).

Some readers may be familiar with the concept of *kami* in Shinto because of the Japanese *manga* pop culture. Spirited Away and Totoro, Miyazaki Hayao's film from Studio Ghibli, also features divine spirits in a modern style. The Japanese *anime* Pokémon features *kami* characters, such as *tochi-gami* (土地神) or *genius loci*, as Pokémon characters. Although appearing as animal-shaped monsters, Pokémon are spirits representing aspects of nature. Pokémon can generally evolve into more powerful versions of their original forms. For example, Pokémon, whose name is Eevee, represents *kami*'s relationship with nature. Eevee can evolve into various forms, each associated with a type. These types include natural elements like water, fire, or plants, signifying the plasticity of *tama*.

A scholar of Japanese intellectual history, Hiroo Sato, argues that the Japanese affection and passion for inventing new characters, called *yuru-kyara* (ゆるキャラ), that represent the characteristics of each prefecture, may derive from the internalized idea of *kami* (Sato 2021: 250–256). For example, providing a visual body to the prefecture as a prefectural character, such as *Kumamon* from Kumamoto prefecture and *Barysan* from Imabari, among others, leads to the idea of the *kami* of the particular land, similar to that of *genius loci*, gaining its visuality through concentration of *tama*.[9]

Kami and Personhood: Embodied Freedom

The concept of freedom is not explicitly written or explained in Shinto. Therefore, it is almost impossible to expressly identify how Shinto considers the idea of freedom. However, although discussion about freedom cannot be found in mainstream Shinto, paradoxically, the concept of *kami* embodies what it is to be freed. To be precise, *kami* itself is freed from (1) ontic object (the spirits can descent on anything, or it can appear itself through any natural phenomena), (2) sacred text (sacred texts do not exist in Shinto), thus freed from canon, the fixated and coined words. Furthermore, (3) the notion of gender, and (4) the divide between good and evil being vague and obscure. *Kami* can simultaneously be evil and good and have masculinity and femininity.

The idea of inner *kami* (*uchinaru kami*, 内なる神), which disciplines one's moral sense, emerged and was refined with the imported concept of Confucianism and

Christianity to Japan. In contrast, Buddhism's earlier influence polished somewhat an externality of conscience. For example, in the Heian period, people feared the Buddhist teaching of going to hell (*jigoku*, 地獄) after death. To avoid the suffering of this life and the life after death, people at that time needed detailed rules that could be followed, prepared by *onmyōji* (陰陽師, *onmyō* represents yin and yang, and *onmyōji* is a master who prepares the rule based on traditional Japanese esoteric cosmology), which was regarded as subordinate to Buddhism and Shinto belief. Thus, it was not about self-reflecting on one's conscience and daily doings; people weighed their importance more in resonating with Buddha's will through *onmyōdō* (*onmyō style*, 陰陽道).

On the contrary, since the notion of *kami* is freed from the sense of evil and good, *kami* may cause problems for humans (natural phenomena such as thunder, storms, and pandemics), especially when humans and *kami* are not in a harmonious relationship. *Kami* requires purity and honesty (*shojiki*, 正直). Therefore, in principle, humans are constantly required to question their daily life practices, which leads to developing a conscience, the ethical morality that disciplines oneself from within. This practice of self-discipline is the freedom of choice in what one is doing. One can do anything as long as one is willing to take the consequences of his/her doings. In this sense, in Shinto, as *kami* indicates, the persistent self exists only in resonance with relationships with other beings and the environment through self-discipline. For Shinto, morality is not given from the outside but from within through daily relationality with others. In short, one is free to do whatever one wants as a community member by virtue of a harmonious relationship with others.

Keywords and Summary

The keywords attached to this chapter are *tama*, *kotodama*, and *misogi*. This section briefly introduces ideas connected to each keyword as introductions.

Tama

In Shinto, *tama* are invisible divine spirits that manifest as *kami* when they inhabit objects, animals, or people, linking the spiritual and physical worlds. They are often found in natural elements, including trees and rocks, or in man-made objects, such as mirrors and swords. Unlike beliefs that classify entities as good or evil, *tama* embody both aspects. Their influence depends on their relationships and environment, bringing harmony or turmoil. This encourages balance and respect for the *tama*. Sacred sites such as shrines contain objects where *tama* reside, creating spaces where the spiritual and physical worlds converge. This promotes a deep connection with nature and emphasizes the sacredness of all elements, encouraging mindfulness and reverence.

Kotodama

Kotodama is the Japanese belief that words and sounds have spiritual energy that affects both the physical and spiritual realms. Speaking certain words with intention can have positive or negative effects. In everyday life, mindful speech is crucial, as kind words attract good fortune, while harmful words invite misfortune. This belief extends to writing and reading, giving texts a spiritual meaning. In Japanese arts such as poetry and theatre, the careful use of language evokes desired emotional and spiritual responses, underscoring the cultural appreciation of the power of words as vessels of spiritual energy.

Misogi

Misogi is a purification ritual rooted in Shinto spirituality. It promotes alignment with nature and spiritual energies and encourages mindfulness and introspection. It helps individuals release negative energies and prepare for new beginnings, integrating physical, mental, and spiritual well-being. People cleanse their bodies and minds by immersing themselves in natural water sources such as rivers, waterfalls, or the ocean, often at dawn. The ritual is both a physical and spiritual cleansing, connecting the individual to the divine. Historically associated with the deity Izanagi (伊弉諾尊), who performed a purification ritual upon his return from the underworld, *misogi* emphasizes the importance of purity and renewal.

Tentative Conclusion: Shinto and a Perspective on Self

This chapter investigates the perspective of self through crucial concepts of Shinto: *kami*, *tama*, *kotodama*, and *misogi*. All three concepts suggest that the essence of Shinto does not reside in persistence. Based on relationality, even the *kami* engage in "reactionary" acts toward other *kami*, humans, and the given environment. *Tama*, the spirit, has four characteristics (*aramitama*, 荒魂, *nigimitama*, 和魂, *sakimitama*, 幸魂, and *kushimitama*, 奇魂) that alter its nature in both good and evil forces, which can also be divided to enhance its unique character. *Kotodama*, which implies the vibration of sounds in resonance with words and incidents (a homonym of *koto*, 事 in Japanese), shows the multilayered idea of Shinto.

The three unique concepts of Shinto indicate that there is no solid self in Shinto. The idea of self only emerges through interactions with others and the world. Self always emerges in inter-reactional situations. In other words, the self is constantly being affected by and is affecting others, including nature and non-living things. Self is changing with others through constant interactions. The concepts of *kami*, *tama*, and *kotodama* symbolize relationality and flexibility that change through interactions with others. There is no persistent self, but the self is only realized through ever-changing relationality with others.

Are we persistent in our personhood? Is the notion of persistence self the creation of modernity to survive the complexity of modern relationality? Or do we recognize the "self" through the relativization of others? The notion of self of no-self in Shinto opens the question of whether the idea of persistent self is feasible. Living in society makes us play different roles on different occasions. I am a daughter to my parents, a sister to my sibling, an aunt, a niece, a friend, a professor, etcetera, etcetera, according to whom I interact. I know I adjust my personality slightly with the people I face. I am persistent, but my attitude and how I speak change when I teach the students and joke with my friends. Further discussion is needed to investigate in which layer of oneself can one find the persistent self freed from relationality and in what sense can religion secure the notion of persistence.

Notes

1. 可畏き物を迦微とは云なり、すぐれたるとは、尊きこと善きこと、功しきことなどの、優れたるのみを云に非ず、悪きもの奇しきものなども、よにすぐれて可畏きをば、神と云なり．
2. 凡て迦微とは、古の御典等に見えたる、天地の諸の神たちを始めて、其を祀れる社に坐ます御霊をも申し、又人はさらにも云わず、鳥獣木草のたぐい、海山など、其余何にまれ、尋常ならずすぐれたる徳のありて、可畏き物を迦微とは云なり．
3. www.bunka.go.jp/tokei_hakusho_shuppan/hakusho_nenjihokokusho/shukyo_nenkan/index.html (accessed September 30, 2024).
4. *Honji-suijaku* is a concept where *kami* are seen as manifestations of Buddhist deities, suggesting that the *kami* are earthly appearances of universal Buddhas. The earliest writings on *honji-suijaku* could be found in 825 (Kokugakuin 1999: 404). *Anti-honji-suijaku*, the reverse idea of *honji-suijaku*, appears around the fourteenth century. There, Buddhist deities are viewed as manifestations of *kami*, emphasizing the primacy of indigenous spirits over imported Buddhism.
5. The common understanding is that State Shinto started in 1870 when the *Proclamation of the Great Doctrine* (*Taikyō senpu*, 大教宣布) was issued in the name of Emperor Meiji. It declared Shinto (the "way of the *kami*") as the guiding principle of the state, and the concept of divinity was placed on the emperor.

6. Hayao Miyazaki animated movies, such as *Princess Mononoke* (1997) and *Spirited Away* (2001), feature goblins and phantoms as characters and are often related to the Shinto animistic view.
7. This *kanji* representation is used in *Kojiki*.
8. Japanese have various homonyms and the word *shintai* in normal context means "body, 身体."
9. *Kumamon* from Kumamoto prefecture: https://kumamon-land.jp/kumamon/; and *Barysan* from Imabari: www.barysan.net/.

Bibliography

Kamata, Touji (鎌田, 東二). [1951] 1999. *Basics Knowledge of Words Used in Shinto (神道用語の基礎知識)*. Tokyo: Kadokawa (角川書店).

Kamata, Touji (鎌田, 東二). [1951] 2017. *Intellectual History of Kotodama (言霊の思想)*. Tokyo: Seidosha (青土社).

Karube, Tadashi (苅部, 直). [1965] 2018. *30 Masterpieces of Japanese Intellectual History (日本思想史の名著30)*. Tokyo: Chikumashobo (筑摩書房).

Kasulis, Thomas P. [1948] 2004. *Shinto*. Honolulu: University of Hawai'i Press.

Kasulis, Thomas P. 2002. *Intimacy or Integrity: Philosophy and Cultural Difference: The 1998 Gilbert Ryle Lectures*. Honolulu: University of Hawai'i Press.

Kokugakuin University, Institute for Japanese Culture and Classics (國學院大學日本文化研究所). 1999. *An Encyclopedia of Shinto = Shintô Jiten (神道事典)*. Tokyo: Kobundo (弘文堂).

Mori, Mikisaburō (森, 三樹三郎). 1982. Motoori Norinaga and His view on Buddism (本居宣長と仏教). *Bukkyo University Departmental Bulletin Paper* (佛教大学佛教文化研究所年報). Vol. 1, 49–74.

Ōmori, Shōzō (大森, 荘蔵) et al. [1921] 2011. *Selected Works of Ōmori Shōzō* (大森荘蔵セレクション). Tokyo: Heibonsha (平凡社).

Sato, Hiroo (佐藤, 弘夫). [1953] 2021. *Japanese and Kami* (日本人と神). Tokyo: Kodansha (講談社).

Sato, Maki (佐藤麻貴). 2022. Around Sounds, Round-abouts of Sounds – The World of Tachi-araware Monism (音をめぐる、めぐる音ー立ち現われ一元論的音の世界). In 廖欽彬, 伊東貴之, 河合一樹, 山村奨共編著. Ed. Lin and T. Ito. 東アジアにおける哲学の生成と発展ー間文化の視点から *(Philosophical Arise and Its Development in East Asia – From the Perspective of Inter-cultural)*. 法政大学出版局 Tokyo: Hosei University Press, 598–615. www.h-up.com/books/isbn978-4-588-15123-1.html.

Tajiri, Yuichiro (田尻, 祐一郎). [1954] 2011. *Thought History of Edo* (江戸の思想史：人物・方法・連環). Tokyo: Chuokoronshinsha (中央公論新社).

Tosa, Hidesato (土佐, 秀里). 1999. Masuraoburi and Taoyameburi – Guidance for Waka (「ますらをぶり」と「たをやめぶり」ー古典和歌の指導のために). *The Japanese Literature and Language Education Society of Waseda University* (早稲

田大学国語教育研究). Vol. 19, 23–32. https://waseda.repo.nii.ac.jp/record/60570/files/WasedaDaigakuKokugoKyoikuKenkyu_19_4.pdf.

Tsukumogami-emaki. Vol. 2 (付喪神絵巻 2巻). https://rmda.kulib.kyoto-u.ac.jp/item/rb00013599. This particular copy was made in 1666 (寛文六年). According to the text, the Tsukumogami depicted in the Emaki became *kami* between *c.* 964. The original of the copy is said to have existed since the Muromachi period.

Harae
Purification of *Tsumi*, *Toga*, and *Kegare*
Chapter 4.1

The philosophy deeply rooted in Shinto is the idea of *jōmeishōchoku* (浄明正直)—a virtue comprising purity and clarity (*kiyoki*, or *jō*, 浄), brightness (*akaki*, or *mei*, 明), righteousness and justice (*tadashiki*, or *shō*, 正), and honesty (*naoki*, or *choku*, 直). Therefore, purification, that is, the *misogi* (禊) and *harae* (祓) of sin (*tsumi*, 罪), iniquity (*toga*, 咎, 科, or *ayamachi*, 過), and impurity (*kegare*, 穢れ), becomes essential for the Shinto rituals. In other words, the Shinto ritual and the idea rooted in *misogi* and *harae* come as a set with the concepts of *tsumi*, *toga*, and *kegare*.

The Concept of *Tsumi*, *Toga*, and *Kegare*

The Christian concept of original sin, which asserts that humans are born with inherent sin, has never existed in the Shinto belief system. Shinto differentiates wrongdoings into *tsumi* and *toga* without the notion of original sin. *Engishiki* (延喜式, 905), compiled during the Daigo Emperorship (醍醐, r. 897–930), categorizes *tsumi* into two types: *amatsutsumi* (天つ罪),[1] and *kunitsutsumi* (国つ罪). *Amatsutusmi* is defined as sins interfering with agriculture or those profane Shinto rituals and festivals. On the other hand, *kunitsutsumi* is defined as sins that interfere with the social order. In short, from the Shinto perspective, sins are immoral actions that provoke and lead to antisocial behaviors that go against the operation of the social community. *Toga* or *ayamachi* entails making mistakes. Thus, in the *Ootonohogai norito* (大殿祭祝詞) in *Engishiki*, *toga*, *ayamachi* is described as faults and errors that are corrected through "looking and listening again" (Kokugakuin University 1999: 392).[2]

Both *amatsutsumi* and *kunitsutsumi* are explicitly defined in *Engishiki*. *Amatsutusmi* is derived from the eight wrongdoings of Susanoo (son of Izanagi), which are written in *Kojiki*. Those wrongdoings include *ahanachi* (畔放), which obstructs paddy irrigation by breaking the shores of the rice paddies; *mizoume* (溝埋), which hinders irrigation by filling in the ditches built to draw water into the paddy fields; and *hinahachi* (樋放) that breaks down the drain pipes to the paddy fields. *Kunitsutsumi* primarily relates to antisocial sexual relations, which prohibits intercourse between parents and children and interspecies relationships that bring the *kegare* (impurity) of the bloodline. However, it also includes acts such as stealing, hurting, killing, and cursing, which are immoral actions in society.

Tsumi and *toga* are equated with *kegare*, that is, in a broader sense, impurity and defilement. *Kegare* is often explained in homonym as the state of qi-exhaustion (気枯れ) and qi-departure (気離れ), a state in which qi, which represents vital spiritual energy, has waned away. This state is abhorred as defilement. Therefore, *misogi* and *harae* are essential rituals for purifying oneself from such defilement. It is also believed that *tsumi*, *toga*, and *kegare* are not evils deeply rooted in human nature but could be purified by the purification ritual through *harae*. In this respect, as argued above, it differs from the original sin or vexation conception.

Harae: Purification and Cleansing

Shinto considers *tama* to be inherently neutral, and whether phenomena and objects turn good or evil depends on how humans treat *tama* with the attitude of *jōmeishōchoku*. However, this neutrality and the attitude of *jōmeishōchoku* are maintained through *harae* that sustains purity. *Harae* is a ritual performed to cleanse and purify *kegare*. It is usually conducted by sprinkling salt, chanting *norito*, and

Figure 4.2 Oonusa on the left from Oomiwa Shrine in Nara.

shaking *oonusa* (大麻, 大幣), which is made with silk, cotton, and, in later ages, paper. Shaking *oonusa* serves to exorcise (verb. *harau*) *kegare*. Generally, the *oonusa* is shaken from left to right and then to the left for the *kegare* to be removed from the person or an object that needs to be purified. *Yaku-barai* (厄払, to prevent misfortune), *Ooharae* (大祓, a large annual purification ceremony often performed around June), and various other purification rituals are performed within the *harae* (Figure 4.2).

Five seasonal festivals (*gosekku*, 五節供)— January 7, March 3, May 5, July 7, and November 9—are still performed in daily life as part of *harae* in Japanese culture. There are specific food menus that should be eaten on those days to *harau* (verb) the *kegare*. For example, on January 7, a porridge with seven spring herbs (*nanakusa gayu*); on March 3, a three-layered rice cake (*hishimochi*) or herb rice cake (*kusamochi*); and on May 5, *chimaki* rice cake are served to get rid of the inner *kegare* and to regain the qi. There are also rituals associated with those festivals. The most common ritual regarding *harae* is that of the March 3 ritual (*jōshi*, 上巳), which uses paper-made dolls as a *yorishiro* of the *kegare* and let loose the dolls into the water (*nagashibina*)— the festival is commonly known as *Hinamatsuri*.

Among *harae* rituals is *misogi*, a purification ritual deeply rooted in Shinto spirituality. It involves cleansing the body and mind through immersion in natural water sources like rivers, waterfalls, or the ocean. This ritual is often performed at dawn when participants immerse themselves in cold water to rid themselves of impurities and renew their spiritual energy. The process is considered a physical and spiritual cleansing, allowing individuals to connect with the divine and achieve a state of purity. *Misogi* is performed among Shinto followers, especially before important Shinto rituals and festivals (Figure 4.3).

Figure 4.3 Spring water for *misogi*, Kifune shrine, Kyoto.

Historically, *misogi* is linked to various Shinto myths and practices, with the original act of *misogi* found in the story of the deity Izanagi in the *Kojiki*. Izanagi and Izanami are the married deities who created the eight islands of Japan and the thirty-nine deities that govern the natural environment, including, but not limited to the sea, wind, trees, mountains, and fields. However, when Izanami gave birth to the fire deity (Kagutsuchi), she suffered severe burns and gradually began to lose her health. She died after giving birth to the deities of gold, earth, water, and trees. After burying her body, Izanagi missed Izanami and followed her spirit to the country of the Yomi (黄泉国, hades). Although Izanami asked Izanagi not to see her, Izanagi saw Izanami's decayed body, got frightened, and ran back to the country of the Ashiharanonakatsu (葦原中国).

After returning from the hades to the land of the living, Izanagi sought to wash away the filth of the hades at the seashore to cleanse himself of the impurities of the underworld. He removed his clothes and immersed himself in the seawater to purify his body. New deities were born from the clothes he took off, and more deities were born as Izanagi washed himself. Among the first deities who were born is Magatsuhi (禍津日).[3] Izanagi washed himself, and more deities were born. Finally, three of the most noble Shinto deities (三貴子) appeared when he washed his face. From Izanagi's left eye, Amaterasu, the sun-goddess, and from his right eye, the moon-goddess, Tsukuyomi, and from his nose, Susanoo, the god of the sea and storm, were born (Figure 4.4).

This act of purification is regarded as one of the foundational stories of Shinto, highlighting the significance of purity and renewal. *Misogi* remains a central ritual in Shinto shrines, performed to purify the mind and body before entering the shrine by washing hands and cleansing the mouth at the Torii gate. Shrines near the ocean or

Figure 4.4 Torii gate of the Oomiwa Shrine in Nara.

with a natural spring water source or waterfalls nearby have special rituals led by the priests on occasions such as festivals and New Year's Eve.

Turning Evil into Good: The Reversing Effect of *Harae*

The unique aspect of *harae* and the implication connoted in the act of *misogi-harae* are well depicted in the story of Izanagi in *Kojiki*. *Misogi*, as argued, is a version of *harae* that involves immersion in water. The uniqueness of the story of Izanagi lies in that after *misogi*, the countless deities were born from Izanagi's body. Because of the impurity of the hades, initially, the deities of the evil Magatsuhi were born. As each cleansing progresses, the deities of the sun, the moon, and the sea and storm are born. Finding an implication in the deities' birth order may be interesting. Still, here, I would like to focus on the effect of purifying the defilement on Izanagi. This is because the plasticity and flexibility embedded in the personhood idea of Shinto resonates well with the story of Izanagi.

When the defilements are purged and the qi is enriched, Izanagi regains the power to produce new deities one after another during the purification process. The process of rebirth involves qi that has been enriched by purifying the defilements, restoring them to a state where such pollution no longer attracts evil. Furthermore, Izanagi's story symbolically implies that *kegare*, once purified, may become a source of deity creation. This notion of *harae* and *misogi* as an impetus for transforming evil into good is embedded in Shinto mythology. In other words, defilements and pollution, which are sources of evil, can be purified and cleansed through *harae*. Moreover, evil can be neutralized through *harae* and *misogi* and become a source of something good. This idea resonates with the Shinto perspective on personhood, which holds that nothing is inherently bad or evil; if something is perceived as such, it is situational and can be cleansed and purified through a specific process of *harae*.

Notes

1. Shinobu Origuchi (折口信夫, 1887–1953) writes that *amatsutsumi* is not about heavenly *tsumi*. He argues that *tsumi* originates from the word *tsutsushimi* (verb. *tsutsushimu*, 慎む), which is about practicing modesty that turns into 障る (hindrance, verb. *sawaru*) in Section 14 of the essay *Oonamesai no hongi* (大嘗祭の本義) (天つ罪は、天上の罪ではない。本義は、五月の田植ゑ時の慎しみ、即、雨つゝみ（雨障·霖禁）である). www.aozora.gr.jp/cards/000933/

files/18411_27474.html. In old Japanese, *tsutsumu* (恙む) means "to have an adverse effect" (verb. *sashisawaru*, 差し障る), and from there, Origuchi argues that the idea of *tsumi* leads to the act that requires modesty.
2. 咎過あらむをば、見直し聞直して.
3. *Magakoto* (まがこと, 禍事) means something crooked and bad, therefore, the opposite of *nao* (直) that brings bad luck.

References

Kokugakuin University, Institute for Japanese Culture and Classics (國學院大學日本文化研究所). 1999. *An Encyclopedia of Shinto = Shintô Jiten* (神道事典). Tokyo: Kobundo (弘文堂).

Kotodama
Value-Neutrality and Multilayered-ness
Chapter 4.2

To further understand the volatile *tama* dependent on relationality with the environment and others, this section focuses on *kotodama* (言霊). *Kotodama* explicitly means *tama* (*dama*, spirit) of the *koto* (*kotoba*, words, 言葉), the *tama* of the spoken words. Every word is believed to possess its *tama*, and when the word is spoken, the *tama* of the word realizes itself into reality. In other words, spoken words have sacrality, incantational force, and the magical power of *tama*. When combined with words and voice, *tama* realizes the words in actuality. In *Kojiki*, there are numerous stories of *kami* reading *tanka* (short poems, 短歌) to show their pure emotions that describe what they see or want to see. These stories led Shinto to internalize the belief in spoken words, that words that possess *tama* – *kotodama* – and that the spoken words with *tama* attached can be linked with forces enabling changes and be realized in the real world.

Kotodama and its Historical Concept

The section dedicated to *tama* overviews the concept of *tama* as it is relational, that good and evil originate from whether the environment or the relation with the *tama* is pure, clean (*jō*, 浄), or not (*fujō*, 不浄). Shinto considers *tama* as inherently neutral, and whether the phenomena and the objects turn good or evil depends on how humans treat the *tama* with the attitude of *jōmeishōchoku* (浄明正直) virtue – purity and clarity (*kiyoki*, or *jō*); brightness (*akaki*, or *mei*); righteous and just (*tadashiki*, or *shō*); and honesty (*naoki*, or *choku*).

Because of the inherent value-neutrality and invisibility without bodies, *tama* can descend on spoken words, and its spiritual power is known as *kotodama*. *Kotodama* has been believed since around the seventh to eighth century Nara period, and the word *kotodama* appears in the *Man'yōshū* (万葉集), Japan's oldest anthology of short poetry. *Man'yōshū* literally means "Collection of ten thousand leaves (*yō*)." The word "leaves (*yō*)" connotes the word "*ha*," which transforms into "*koto-no-ha* (言の葉)," meaning "*kotoba* (言葉)," which means "word" in Japanese. The homonym of "*koto*" indicates both "incident (事)" and "word (言)." Therefore, the Japanese etymology of "*kotoba* (word)" indicates that words strongly relate to the phenomena.

In the *Kojiki* and *Nihonshoki*, several scenes describe trees and grasses (*kusaki*, 草木) asking questions *(koto-tou)* to *kami* – *kusaki-koto-tou* (草木言問) (Kamata 2017: 61–68). Unlike the Western concept of language, which is based on the Covenant with God and that the ability to speak language segregates humans and nature, the Japanese view allows nature to speak. Interestingly, various calamities happen when the trees and grasses start questioning because the vibrations and murmurs of their questions turn into sounds and noises. In other words, the vibrations and sounds of nature are regarded as voices of nature, questioning the status of the doings of *kami*. Therefore, in Shinto, the spoken words (or sounds and voices) and phenomena strongly resonate, leading to the concept of *kotodama*.

The word *kotodama* appears in three *tanka* poems, two from Kakimoto no Hitomaro (柿本野人麻呂) and one from Yamanoue no Okura (山上憶良) in *Man'yōshū*. All three poems describe Japan (the land of Yamato, 大和) as a country filled with *kotodama* that brings happiness and prosperity (Kamata 2017: 66). Below is the translation from the two most cited *tanka* poems read using the word *kotodama*:

> The land of Yamato, known as Shikishima, is a land where the *kotodama* brings forth help and prosperity. (Read by Kakimoto no Hitomaro, *Man'yōshū*, Vol. 13, 3254)[1]

> The land of Yamato, seen from the sky, is cherished by *kami*. A nation blessed by the sacred *kotodama* passed down and spoken of through generations.
> (Read by Yamanoue no Okura, *Man'yōshū*, Vol. 5, 894)[2]

Kamata points out that the *tanka* read by Kakimoto no Hitomaro uses the homonym *kanji* letter of "incident" for *koto* when using the word *kotodama*, indicating that in the eighth century, "incident" and "word" were essentially identical in old Japanese. Additionally, *kotoba* derives from *koto-no-ha*, the "word (incidents or things) of leaves," implying that ancient Japanese regarded nature as having its own say.

Since words may possess *tama*, *kotoage-seji* (言挙げせじ), which means "do not put into words," is one of the crucial rules for Shinto priests. Once the word is spoken, it can be realized whether it is good or bad. On the contrary, the word needs not to be spoken, but the attitude of *jōmeishōchoku* already represents the wish to be in harmony with *tama*, *kami*, and others. The Shinto priests are required to show their purified and peaceful minds by using their bodies in silence. Because noise and sounds in nature may not be understandable for humans, they may be the spoken word of *tama*. Therefore, the sounds of a *suzu*-bell (鈴), the sounds of leaves swaying in the gentle breeze, and the sounds of the running water symbolize the existence or arrival of *tama*. *Tama* is invisible, but one can suspect its existence through the vibration of *tama*, through the sound and noise of nature. In short, once the sound is in words, *tama* that resonates with words, *kotodama* is thought to have magical power and forces that bring *koto* (word and phenomena) into actuality.

2. Communicability with *Tama*: The Neutrality of Words and *Kotodama*

Words are used as a tool to communicate with *kami*. Because of the notion of *kotodama*, spirituality embedded in words is valued through spoken words. From humans to *tama* and *kami*, *norito* (祝詞) is spoken. *Norito*, words spoken towards divine spirits, can be either *yogoto* (寿詞), words of happiness; *haraenokotoba* (祓詞), for cleansing; or *juso* (呪詛), cursing words (Kokugakuin 1999: 554). From *tama* or *kami* to humans, *kuchiyose* (口寄せ) is performed to listen to what *tama* has to say through language via a person, often through *miko* (巫女, women who perform *takusen*, 託宣, revelation) (Kokugakuin 1999: 347). The words from *kami* are called *shinchoku* (entrusted words, 神勅). Among the three *shinchoku* described, the crucial *shinchoku* in the *Nihonshoki* is the *Tenjōmukyū* (天壌無窮) that Amaterasu, the sun goddess, said that Mizuhonokuni (瑞穂の国), Japan, will sustain itself as long as there is the heaven and the earth (Kokugakuin 1999: 391). In contrast to the Buddhist teaching claim of eschatology, Shinto believes in the prosperous continuity and eternity of life.

In *Kojiki*, a *kami* named Yagokoro-omoikane (八意思兼神, eight consciousness and thoughts) plays a role in subsuming all the thinking processes and consciousness of *kami-s* and consolidating them into words, representing the will of *kami-s* into words (Kamata [1951] 2017: 11). Yagokoro-omoikane appears in the famous story of Amaterasu, the Sun goddess, hiding behind the huge cave, ashamed of his younger brother, Susanoo's mischievous doings. When Amaterasu hid, the world became dark, and eight million *kami-s* became anxious and restless, and the noises they made out of anxiety caused chaos in the world. Yagokoro-omoikane was called to find *norito* (words) to convey the thoughts of *kami-s*, and his father, Takamimusumi (高御産巣日神), succeeded in bringing Amaterasu out through rituals, play, and dancing. The episode of Yagokoro-omoikane indicates that the concept of spoken words in Shinto is that the words are not for contracts but for well articulating the situation—how the situation is terrible and how much it has longed for the situation to be bettered. When the "how" is well-articulated and spoken with a pure mind (*naobi no kokoro*), the spoken words gain *tama* and become *kotodama*, which works to change the situation.

Kasulis points out that Japanese philosophy emphasizes not "what" questions that aim for integration but "how" questions that seek intimacy (Kasulis 2002). Such an attitude may be derived from the process of making *norito* from ancient times. In Shinto, the words are not as absolute and transcendental as the spoken words of God in Christianity but are relative and mundane. *Norito* describes the suffering situation and how the situation is hoped to change. Only with the *naobi* attitude does the word gain the magical *kushibi* power (*kushimitama*, the *tama* of wonders) that turns the value-free and neutral word into *kotodama*, which actualizes the spoken words in the real world. Words are value-free and neutral when not spoken; they only gain their *tama* with vibrations detected as sounds. *Kojiki* implies that the neutrality of a word changes and gains its embedded power once the word is spoken. The word realizes its meaning through the sounds and voices of the pure mind of the speaker, inviting the floating invisible *tama* to reside with the vibrating sound of the spoken word. In short, words gain their *kotodama* in certain conditions—in spoken words by *yorishiro* (an object including humans and nature) with a *naobi* attitude (*makoto no kokoro*, the real heart–mind) of honesty and truthfulness. Furthermore, in the Shinto belief system, when the spoken words gain *kotodama*, it can transform itself into realizing what has been said.

Kotodama: Relationality and Multilayered-ness

Japanese contemporary phenomenologist Ōmori Shōzō (1921–1997, 大森荘蔵) discusses the concept of *kotodama* from a phenomenological viewpoint (Ōmori 2011: 224–294). He argues that one can only realize his/her emotion through the phenomenological bodily sensation (Sato 2022). Referring to William James and Wilder Penfield, Ōmori argues that we understand that we are happy, frightened, or sad through our bodily reactions, but with causal relational description and narrative between bodily reaction and feeling (Ōmori 2011: 35–41). For example, when we are frightened, the body reacts first through the autonomic neuron system even before realizing we are frightened. Our blood pressure gets high; accordingly, the heartbeat rises, the sweats come out, and our body shakes.

Ōmori argues that the body reacts to the surrounding environment before the brain detects emotion and feelings. Unconscious bodily reactions will be analyzed in the brain system to narrate and explain what is going on to translate into words, and only then will one realize one's emotions and feelings associated with causality. It is not that we want to be frightened and be frightened, but the bodily reaction comes first. Referring to the notion of *kotodama*, Ōmori explains the relationship between body and mind that *koto* (incident) is consciously understood when it is given words (*kotoba*) for description. We realize we are happy only when we realize we are smiling. In a natural situation of deep content, he argues that it is not that we are happy and then we smile, but a smile comes first before the work of emotion.

In this line of explanation, Ōmori argues that we humans are not rational beings with emotions (*jō*, 情), but it might be vice versa. If the surrounding environment is the source of emotions, and we gain emotions affected by the surrounding emotional environment, it implies that the surrounding environment also has emotions (*ujō*, 有情). In his chain of logic, emotions derive from the surrounding environment, and we gain emotions when our unconsciousness resonates with them. In other words, for

Ōmori, solipsism will not evoke emotions or feelings, but we need "the other," including the natural environment, to realize that we are emotional beings with feelings.

The argument made by Ōmori, that "the incident (*koto*) evokes words (*koto[ba]*)," is not something unique to Ōmori. The Shinto belief in *kotodama* is the reversal structure to Ōmori argued, that it stresses that "the words evoke the incident." These notions imply that the concept of *kotodama* is multi-facet. Recalling the concept of *tama* and its characteristics as fundamentally relational with others, *kotodama* indicates the muti-layered-ness in its concept. In the following paragraphs, I would like to explain what I mean by multi-layered-ness in terms of sounds and relationality.

First, the multilayered in the sense of sound and noise. Attached to the first notion; second, by and by, the multilayered in the sense of relationality. These notions are equiprimordial (equally original or co-original; *gleichursprünglichkeit*). Let me explain further. For example, when we begin learning a foreign language, we only follow the phonetics of the spoken language without understanding what it means. Some sounds and noises may only sound like sounds and noises to one but could be understood as words by others. However, when we start to understand the meaning attached to the sound made, we understand that a particular combination of sounds has a tied meaning and realize that sounds are words. The meaningless "bar-bar" sound suddenly becomes meaningful words based on how far we train and study the foreign language.

The etymology of "barbarians" comes from the Greek word "bárbaros" to describe people who did not speak Greek. The onomatopoeic "bar-bar" represents the sound made by non-Greeks for the Greek people of ancient times. However, once the sound is interpreted into words, some sounds may be understood as orders or wishes to do something. When we understand the meaning, the orders and wishes are conveyed so that they can be actualized. Likewise, in the *kotodama* concept, the natural sounds—the sounds of the wind, thunder, running river, and birds chirping—that are a complete "bar-bar" to many humans may have attached meanings, and perhaps humans are not sophisticated enough to understand what is spoken in their language. The leaves of the words (*koto-no-ha*) need sounds and vibrations to be realized (*koto-wo-okosu*) by humans; however, whether the sounds are understandable depends on the ability of humans to listen. When the *koto-no-ha* gains the wonder of *tama*, it turns into *kotodama*, and those who understand the word, take action as to actualize (*koto*, 事) the spoken word (*koto*, 言).

Notes

1. 敷島の大和の国は言霊の幸はふ国ぞ真幸くありこそ.
2. 神代より言い傳て来らくそらみつ倭の国は皇神の厳しき国言霊の幸はふ国と語り継ぎ言い継かひけり.

References

Kamata, Touji (鎌田，東二). [1951] 2017. *Intellectual History of Kotodama (言霊の思想)*. Tokyo: Seidosha (青土社).

Kasulis, T. P. 2002. *Intimacy or Integrity: Philosophy and Cultural Difference: The 1998 Gilbert Ryle Lectures*. Honolulu: University of Hawaiʻi Press.

Kokugakuin University, Institute for Japanese Culture and Classics (國學院大學日本文化研究所). 1999. *An Encyclopedia of Shinto = Shintô Jiten (神道事典)*. Tokyo: Kobundo (弘文堂).

Ōmori, Shōzō (大森，荘蔵) et al. [1921] 2011. *Selected Works of Ōmori Shōzō (大森荘蔵セレクション)*. Tokyo: Heibonsha (平凡社).

Sato, Maki (佐藤麻貴). 2022. Around Sounds, Round-abouts of Sounds – The World of Tachi-araware Monism (音をめぐる、めぐる音－立ち現われ一元論的音の世界). In 廖欽彬，伊東貴之，河合一樹，山村奨共編著. Ed. Lin and T. Ito. 東アジアにおける哲学の生成と発展－間文化の視点から *(Philosophical Arise and Its Development in East Asia – From the Perspective of Inter-cultural)*. 法政大学出版局 Tokyo: Hosei University Press, 598–615. www.h-up.com/books/isbn978-4-588-15123-1.html.

Tama and Dynamism
Unpredictable Spirit Freed from Human Consequences
Chapter 4.3

This section highlights the concept of *tama*, which is a crucial concept in Shinto. It first defines the concept of *tama*, its relationship to natural phenomena and objects, and how it affects *kami* and humans. Second, it sheds light on four different kinds of *tama*. It explains how *tama* is independent of *kami* and their will, but dependent on the circumstances or situation in which the *tama* is situated. Because of the flexibility and dynamism of *tama* dependent on the situation, interdependency with the environment and others has become a crucial concept in understanding *tama*. Finally, it introduces some stories from *Kojiki* and *Nihonshoki* to further grasp the concept of *tama* concerning keeping purity and honesty, which is thought to be the basis for keeping and leading to harmony with others.

For readers to grasp the concept of *tama*, imagine the *tama* as an invisible force—much like the wind—you cannot see it directly, but you can feel its presence and see its effects on the world around you. You cannot see the wind itself, but you can feel it on your cheek and see the indirect force of wind through the waving ears of rice in the paddy field. *Tama* is just like the invisible wind, but though invisible, you can still feel its force when it is there.

Conceptual Definition of *Tama*

As argued above, Shinto believes that a pure divine spirit (*tama* or *mitama*) does not have its body. However, when *tama* concentrates and descends itself to an object, animal, or person, humans realize it as *kami*. Therefore, *tama*, which are invisible to humans, need to borrow or rely on objects where they can appear and communicate with humans. Usually, *tama* uses objects in nature as their object or place of descent (*yorishiro* or *mitamashiro*, 御霊代). At other times, *tama* may descend on human bodies or the living bodies of animals to reveal themselves. In the shrines, something like a mirror (*kagami*, 鏡), sword (*tsurugi*, 剣), jewel stone (*gyoku*, 玉), and column (*hashira*, 柱) are thought to be the objects where *tama* arrives and descents. Occasionally, a temporal shrine (*himorogi*, 神籬), set up with bamboo and tree branches, is made to call for the *tama* to descend. In nature, leaves, trees, waterfalls, mountains, capes, and rocks are believed to be where *tama* prefers to come down and settle (*yadoru*, 宿る). In other words, *tama* is not visible to humans but visualizes itself through the sacred objects and landscapes in nature. Since its inherent invisibility of *tama*, *kami* can be everywhere and be any being.

The concept of *tama* (divine or sacred spirit) includes *tama* with a given personhood (*jinkaku*, 人格). However, they are mostly considered *tama*, which derives from a motif of nature and natural phenomena (such as volcanic eruption), as can be read in the *Kojiki* and *Nihonshoki*. Shinto has a unique concept of *tama*: all *tama* have good and evil aspects. Therefore, there is no rigid dualism concept of good and evil in Shinto spiritualism (Kamata 1999: 77), which frees *tama* from the human concept of good and evil in humans' short-sightedness. No *tama* is pure good or pure evil. In other words, *tama* is freed from good and evil, dualistic or antagonistic frictions.

Accordingly, relationality with other *tama* and humans and where the *tama* is situated in the environment affect the mood of the *tama*. Likewise, though *kami* occasionally fight with each other, as read in *Kojiki* and *Nihonshoki*, this is not because of the inherent good or bad of *tama*. However, it is more of an emotional reaction based on the situation that they are thrown into. For example, *kami* gets angry, jealous, or irritated by other *kami*'s actions. Therefore, the *tama* of the *kami* is reactionary. Thus, from the human perspective, phenomena happen within the *tamas*' relationship of relationality with others, its generation (for example, the creation of the archipelago), and ever-changing dynamism happen because of the constant moving and changing process where the *tama* is situated.

In short, because of the inherent concept of invisibleness and its freedom from good and evil dualism, *tama* descents as a terror to humans in phenomena of natural disasters, such as earthquakes, pandemics, and famine. There will be fertility and prosperity when *tama* is peaceful and harmonious among themselves and with humans. Thus, the liberty of *tama* to embody themselves into objects and phenomena that are contingently regarded as good and evil to human society becomes the grounding reason for humans to feel awe, fear, and applause. Furthermore, a contingent and unpredictable mood of *tama* forces humans to continuously apprehend *tama*, which becomes vital for humans to keep in harmony with *tama*.

Tama and its Complexity

In Shinto, spirit (*rei*, 霊), a concentration of *tama* (or *kon*, 魂), is regarded to possess four different kinds of *tama*, such a concept known as one-soul-four-spirits (*ichirei-shikon*, 一霊四魂). To be precise, the *rei* has a personality based on which *tama* dominates the *rei*. This concept of *tama* includes the concept of personhood. One soul (*ichirei*) that is the base of the *rei* is named *naobi* (直霊 or 直毘). *Naobi* reflects and adjusts itself according to the relationship with other *tama* and the surrounding environment. Four *tama* that can affect the *rei* are *aramitama* (荒魂), *nigimitama* (和魂), *sakimitama* (幸魂), and *kushimitama* (奇魂). *Aramitama* is an outraging and fierce *tama* that brings positivity and aggressiveness. *Nigimitama* is a harmonious and calm *tama* that brings peace. *Sakimitama* is a wealthy and happy *tama* that brings happiness, and *kushimitama* is a *tama* that brings health and wonders. Depending on the environment and circumstances, a *rei* shows different facets of *kami*. Each *tama* has both aspects; if they are not harmonious, *tama* can show the opposite force of their power.

In *Nihonshoki*, there is a story of Oonamuchi (大穴牟遅神), talking with his *kushimitama* and *sakimitama* about his seeking reconciliation with his *tama*. As a result of the discussion, his *kushimitama* and *sakimitama* split from him, becoming the *kami* of the Oomiwa (大三輪) mountain, named Oomononushi (大物主神) (Kokugakuin 1999: 385). This story implies that even the *kami* cannot fully control *tama*. The characteristics of *tama* are relevant to how nature shows itself to humans. Natural phenomena are understood as their mood. In other words, *tama*'s moods affect natural phenomena. For example, when angry or irritated, *tama* can cause an earthquake or tsunami. Furthermore, crops become more prosperous when the *tama* is peaceful and happy. So, although *tama* is neither good nor evil, its influence on natural phenomena can positively or negatively impact human society. It passively and flexibly changes its character according to its given situation. No *tama* is either fully good or thoroughly evil. In Shinto belief, the common denominator among *kami*, nature, and humans is that they all possess *tama* (ibid., 376).

What is particular about *tama* is its non-dualistic nature. Unlike many belief systems that strictly categorize entities as good or evil, Shinto embraces the idea that *tama* embodies both aspects simultaneously. Moreover, as the concept of one-soul-four-spirits (*ichirei-shikon*) shows, *tama* possesses various characteristics. Because of this fluidity of characteristics, *tama* can change its personality according to where it is situated and how it has been treated. This is why the deities of Shinto, *kami*, can be kind, generous, forgiving, and good but may also get angry and do evil things, just like humans. If one treats others respectfully, respect will follow. If one feels deceived by others, then that person might retaliate by deceiving others. *Kami*, that is, the concentration of the force of tama, reflects this inherent nature of tama, but so do the humans. This fluidity of characteristics means that a *tama*'s influence—be it benevolent or malevolent—is shaped by its relationships and environment. It's not inherently good or bad; it is responsive and dynamic.

Tama and the Concept of Self and Persistence: Purity

The story of *Oonamuchi*, who had to discuss with his *kushimitama* and *sakimitama*, indicates that *tama* works as if it has its own will beside where it concentrated and descended. To let the *tama* calm down or regain its power, *matsuri* (rituals, 祭, 祀)

play a vital role in making that possible, called *tama-shizume* (鎮魂) or *tama-furi* (魂振). *Tama* is believed to regain its purity of *naobi*, the original characteristics of *tama*, and its power through *harae* (祓) and *misogi* (禊), the purification process of impurity (*kegare*, 穢). Because there is an episode in *Kojiki* and *Nihonshoki* of Izanagi (name of the *kami*, 伊弉諾尊) washing and taking a bath to cleanse the impurity, it is believed that *kegare* can be washed out by water and bathing (Kokugakuin 1999: 394). *Kami* and humans can commit sins (*tsumi*, 罪) and mistakes (*toga*, 咎) equally. To avoid such wrongdoings, to keep the purity of the *tama* is the most crucial concept in Shinto. Good and evil can be suspected through cleanliness and dirtiness; cleanliness indicates calmness and harmony, and dirtiness vice versa (ibid., 389). Therefore, in Shinto, cleanliness always resonates with purity and good.

To keep purity, *tama* must stay in the status of *naobi*, which indicates being regular, straight, sound, and honest. *Kami* and humans can commit sins when their *tama* is not in the *naobi* status. In other words, Shinto does not see *kami* or humans as inherently wrong with innate original sin. There also is a concept of *tsumi* (sin), which is wrongdoings that disrupt the norms and orders of society and need to be avoided, including antisocial behaviors such as robbery, killing, and interference with farming. Keeping in harmony with others is the most crucial attitude that both *kami* and humans have to follow. Because no view in Shinto sees original sin, all the sin is believed to be erased and removed through *harae* before any wrong happens. However, if any wrong happens, the one who committed wrongdoings should take the punishment (*batsu*, 罰) and will be kicked out of society for good.

For both *kami* and humans, keeping the purity of the *tama* becomes essential to flourish in their selfhood. Purity could be recognized through cleanliness, simplicity, discipline, honesty, and calmness. The unpredictability of *tama* could only be controlled through daily consciousness to maintain one's purity and the environment. Only through this consciousness can the self be persistent, and *tama* that descends on *kami* and humans will be controllable.

This perspective shifts the focus from labeling to understanding and harmony. Natural disasters like earthquakes or pandemics are seen not merely as random events but as expressions of *tama* in a state of unrest. Conversely, periods of prosperity and fertility reflect *tama* in harmony both among themselves and with humans. It underscores the importance of maintaining balance and respecting the spiritual forces entwined with the natural world. Additionally, the way *tama* interacts with objects and places adds another layer of depth. Ordinary items like mirrors, swords, or even natural elements like trees and waterfalls become sacred when infused with *tama*. It blurs the line between the mundane and the divine, suggesting that the sacred is all around us, waiting to be acknowledged. This resonates with the idea that divinity is immanent – present within the world rather than distant or transcendent. It invites a more holistic view of existence, where every element has the potential to be a vessel for the divine.

References

Kamata, Touji (鎌田, 東二). [1951] 1999. *Basics Knowledge of Words Used in Shinto (神道用語の基礎知識)*. Tokyo: Kadokawa (角川書店).

Kokugakuin University, Institute for Japanese Culture and Classics (國學院大學日本文化研究所). 1999. *An Encyclopedia of Shinto = Shintô Jiten (神道事典)*. Tokyo: Kobundo (弘文堂).

5

Selfhood in the Classical Confucian Tradition

Andrew Lambert

Chapter Outline

Introduction: Starting Clarifications	125
Theorizing the Confucian Self: The Risk of Imposing Western Assumptions	127
The Confucian Self as Roles and Relations	128
The Focus-Field Self	131
Other Confucian Selves: Avoiding Chinese Worldviews and Cultural Assumptions	134
Conclusion	136
5.1 Humaneness (*Ren* 仁)	143
5.2 Ritual (*Li* 禮)	148
5.3 Filial Conduct (*Xiao* 孝)	153

Introduction: Starting Clarifications

This chapter explores conceptions of selfhood rooted in early Confucian thought (roughly 1046–221 BCE), focusing primarily on the canonical texts the *Analects*, the *Mencius* and the *Xunzi*. While these texts do not explicitly and systematically tackle the problem of the self, they inform contemporary theories of Confucian selfhood derived from these texts. This chapter explores several such theories. These include presentations of the Confucian self as collectivist and self-sacrificing, as constituted by social norms and ritual practices, as roles and relationships, as a focus-field relational self, and as a self characterized by introspective awareness and reflective judgment. The chapter critically discusses these accounts, and in doing so highlights various aspects of selfhood addressed in classical Confucian thought: cosmological considerations, the body, emotions, tradition and history, social life, and roles and relationships. While the classical Confucian texts do not yield a single or unified notion of selfhood, they offer rich insight into various questions pertaining to the nature of the self.

A preliminary caution is needed when discussing the Confucian 'self'. As one contemporary sinologist notes, "In much of this scholarship [on early China], the English word 'self' is used in a general sense to refer primarily to Western notions, and it does not necessarily refer to any specific Chinese term" (Sommer 2012: 17). Early Chinese texts do not yield a simple equivalence between the English "self" and the corresponding Chinese term. "Self" often translates various Chinese terms, each with their own range of meanings. In addition, Anglophone terms around which specialized analysis and discussion have accrued, such as self, person, personal identity, the individual, and even (human) nature, are not consistently distinguished in the early Confucian texts, and even contemporary Confucian thinkers often treat them as a closely related cluster of ideas. In what follows, these themes will be discussed under the broad rubric of "self."[1]

The issue here is not merely linguistic or a translation difficulty. Theories of the self are often tied to particular intellectual traditions and their distinctive philosophical concerns and assumptions.[2] Such concerns might include: whether the soul exists, the relationship between mind and body, the nature of private inner life and its role as a foundation for knowledge; the nature of a rational capacity inherently worthy of respect; interest in individuals as the bearers of rights, as a safeguard against oppression or state power; the presence of a unique personal identity that persists over time; the nature of authenticity that prevails over social conditioning, or a subject that transcends baser human impulses; and an understanding of people as fundamentally motivated by personal projects and goals.

Such broader philosophical concerns typically underpin Western or Anglophone inquiries into selfhood, and these concerns sometimes motivate exploration of the Confucian tradition. This approach grants only a limited voice to the Confucian texts, however; they usually either confirm an existing view of the self or shed light on existing familiar problems of the self. This chapter attempts to let the texts speak for themselves. While the texts do not explicitly and systematically discuss the self as an independent topic, they contain various comments and insights relevant to an understanding of selfhood. Indeed, contemporary thinkers have woven together various textual "data points" to form theories of a Confucian self, to be explored below.

There is broad, but not uniform, agreement on the social and relational nature of the Confucian subject, and on the importance of personal cultivation to questions of personhood or selfhood. However, partly due to the terse and aphoristic nature of these early texts, the precise meaning and relations between terms and concepts in the texts evade simple definition. Further investigation thus requires caution. The following presents early Confucian ideas pertinent to Confucian conceptions of the self, and covers contemporary theorists who offer speculative accounts of that self, without aiming for a definitive statement of the Confucian self.

Theorizing the Confucian Self: The Risk of Imposing Western Assumptions

Historically, Western characterizations of traditional Chinese social life often highlighted a lack of individuality, a selflessness, or a contrast between individual and society in which the needs of society take precedence. For Hegel, for example, order in Chinese society is grounded in external social norms and sanctions, with little room for individual conscience and self-determination, "The laws of the state are partly civil ordinances, partly moral requirements" (Hegel 2001: 129).[3] Similarly, John Stuart Mill's conditional admiration for China was qualified by a fear that Chinese social and political order made "people all alike" governing their "thoughts and conduct by the same maxims and rules" (Mill 1991: 87).

Some contemporary accounts of traditional Chinese social thought also identify individuals willing to sacrifice their interests for the collective (Munro 1979), or note that an individual should fit into preordained roles, like a "cog" in an "efficient social machine" (Edwards 1986: 44), or that individualism conflicts with the demands of the traditional Chinese family (Yang 1959: 172). All imply a diminished individuality and a dualism of individual versus collective in which the individual is sacrificed when needed. Recent scholarship, however, rejects this characterization of classical Confucian thought. In what follows, we will explore a social and relational conception of Confucian selfhood, which draws more closely on views of the world found in early Chinese texts. This approach explores the processual and interdependent nature of the world and how this shapes the human subject.

Anglophone interest in Confucian thought and selfhood has revived in recent decades. One philosopher central to new Anglophone interpretations of it was Herbert Fingarette (1972). While questioning whether the self was an important category within Confucian thought, Fingarette nevertheless outlined possible features of a Confucian self in the *Analects*. He identified a familiar emphasis on an embodied first-person awareness and personal agency, "a self-observing and self-regulating individual, a self sharply distinct from Others" (133), whose will (*zhi* 志) and desires (*yu* 欲) were under the command of the individual. What was distinctively Confucian, however, is that the will should be determined by the Confucian way or *dao* (道), the

Confucian social code. Desires for personal profit, fame or sensual gratification were to be eliminated (134); and the will was shaped by ritualized practices which, when mastered, ordered social life and created a sacred ritual community.[4]

Significantly for Fingarette, in so far as it exists in Confucian thought, "the problem of the self" is not concerned with "actualizing" or realizing the self, understood as an individual perspective or distinctive personality. Fingarette's reflective and willful subject has "the task of becoming selfless" (129). Personal cultivation overcomes egoistical forces, and orientates a person towards the Confucian way.

Consequently, some argue that Fingarette's self wrongly denudes the early Confucian of meaningful individuality (Ames 1993), and so repeats earlier mischaracterizations of Confucian thought. A self that "shares in the pan-Asian ideal of selflessness" (Fingarette 1979: 137) echoes earlier accounts of generic individuals, prepared to sacrifice for the collective. The problem partly lay in Fingarette's understanding of the Confucian way as "a way without a crossroads" (1972: 18–36): the Confucian good life was rooted in mastery of ritualized and scripted social life with little awareness of practical dilemmas or the need for personal judgments of what was (yi義).[5] However, the early texts do recognize weighing difficult choices and breaking precedent when needed (Hall and Ames 1984).[6] Furthermore, the *Analects* is a portrait in sagehood that involves personality and distinctive character: Confucius ridicules students, chases Daoist hermits, taps old men with his cane, and is distraught at his favorite student's funeral (Eno 1990: 75). Confucius' followers, too, have notable personal traits that are important to Confucius' advice to them (*Analects* 11.22).

Some scholars, rejecting the fungible and selfless individual, identify a distinctive conception of self that is rooted in the cultural and historical milieu of early China. One such approach draws a contrast with conceptions of the self bound up with the history of the West, and claims that Western conceptions of individual and society are inappropriately imposed on the Chinese tradition, thereby obscuring authentically Confucian notions of self.

The Confucian Self as Roles and Relations

Henry Rosemont (1988, 2016) contrasts Confucian personhood with the dominant Western conception of a "rational, autonomous, rights-bearing individual" (2016: 49). The latter is found in canonical works by Descartes and Locke, as well as the American Declaration of Independence and the UN Declaration of Human Rights. Rosemont argues, however, that this abstract and putatively universal conception of the person is unrealistic. Human identity is tied to specific cultural communities, "each with its language, values, religious orientation, customs, traditions, and concomitant ideas of what it is to be a human being" (34). There are no "culturally independent human beings." The emphasis on rights, for example, emerged from a politically and economically dominant Northern European tradition, but is not easily integrated into the worldviews of other traditions. Accordingly, the conception of self that accompanies this putatively global value system is more parochial than typically recognized (38).

Setting aside questions about Rosemont's portrayal of a "Western" self, since it is primarily a foil for a Confucian account, his view aligns with the belief that self-conceptions are historically variable and culturally conditioned. This wider situating context provides "inescapable frameworks" (Taylor 1989) for understanding the self, and the relationship between the two can be investigated, using a kind of "philosophical archeology or genealogy" that recognizes the role of culture and history in conceptions of the self (Flanagan 2016: 225–252).[7]

For Rosemont, early Confucian personhood (selfhood and personhood are not sharply distinguished) is constituted by social and relational qualities. Self-understanding coheres around a web of relationships and social attachments, and the ritualized practices (*li* 禮) that sustain and extend them. This reflects the classical texts extensive discussions of familial and social relationships, and the foregrounding of interpersonal virtues, such as family reverence (*xiao* 孝) and shame (*chi* 耻). This relational approach is also expressed in the traditional Confucian doctrine of five socially basic relationships (*wulun* 五輪 or *wujiao* 五教), typically understood as: father-son, ruler-minister, husband-wife, older brother-younger brother and friend-friend.[8]

Here, the person is constituted by roles: "for the early Confucians there can be no me in isolation, to be considered abstractly: I am the totality of roles I live in relation to specific others," and "I am husband to my wife, father of our children, grandfather to their children; I am a brother, my friend's friend, my neighbor's neighbor ..." (Rosemont 2016: 52).

A role, however, is not merely a list of customary responsibilities or norms, which might suggest the problematic rigidity and passive subjectivity noted earlier. Nor is the content of a role determined, as in some modern medical practice, by Rawlsian reflective equilibrium in which reasonable and equal agents agree on which norms should govern a role. This would suggest the autonomous deliberative self with which Rosemont seeks a contrast. Instead, the content and normative implications of a role—especially roles pertaining to family life—are determined pragmatically and in situ; they emerge and evolve within everyday practice and via coordination with other roles. For example, marriage, and then a new family, reshape roles within the original biological family. Similarly, what is appropriate in a friendship depends partly on other roles. A bachelor friend might invite a recently widowed friend on a long cruise, but not while they were still a husband (53). This mutual influencing and shaping of roles structure Confucian personhood. Collectively, the roles "weave ... a unique pattern of personal identity, such that if some of my roles change, others will of necessity change also, *literally making me a different person*" (53, italics added). In sum, Rosemont believes this account reflects early Confucian social thought, and offers a corrective to dominant contemporary assumptions about personhood. The latter have resulted in social isolation, as well as divisive and irreconcilable claims of individual rights that have diminished the quality of communal life.

The claim that the Confucian self is emphatically relational faces difficulties, however. It involves a strong metaphysical claim that persons are entirely reducible to roles ("my roles change ... *literally making me a different person*"). But some aspects of the Confucian self are not directly reducible to role. Early Confucian thought contains a rich vocabulary for the deliberative, introspective and psychological aspects of the person. Reflective capacities partly define the Confucian exemplary person, and can be the locus of decisions to adjudicate among or act against certain roles, or to act for values or personal interests that do not readily fit with any role.[9]

A second, related problem derives from Rosemont's interpretive assumptions; specifically, what is most fundamental to the Confucian way. Rosemont believes that an early Confucian answer to the question "who am I?" would take the following form: "You are thus first, foremost, and most basically a son; you stand in a relationship to your parents that began at birth, has had a profound influence on your later development, has had a profound effect on their later lives as well, and it is a relationship that is diminished only in part at their death" (52).

What is *most* characteristic of the Confucian person, however, is not roles but a *commitment to follow the Confucian way* (*dao* 道). The *Analects* declares that one who learns of the way in the morning can die happy in the evening (4.8), and the way is more than roles and relationships. While roles and relationships can provide guidance, there is reason to doubt that they should be understood metaphysically, as solely constituting the self. There are other elements to the Confucian way and so to a person immersed in it. One element is learning (*xue* 學). This includes immersion in ritualized conduct and practical arts, such as archery and charioteering, while a music sensibility is repeatedly commended. Indeed, learning itself is an attitude or commitment, a quality of character, that is not directly reducible to roles. It includes a desire to learn from all ("Strolling in the company of just two other persons, I am bound to find a teacher" *Analects* 7.22). The Confucian emphasis on willful application or commitment (*zhi* 志) is another incongruent feature. The Confucian way involves an extended commitment ("The burden is heavy and the way is long," *Analects* 8.7), which suggests a certain situational or role transcending awareness and commitment. Similarly, Confucius' famous autobiographical declaration (2.4) lays out a self-contained vision of sculpting and polishing one's person (1.15), which results in unconstrained (non-role based) yet appropriate ways of behaving.[10]

The Focus-Field Self

A more plausible account of Confucian personhood might preserve the relational characteristics without reducing personal identity to roles. One such approach begins from the process cosmology found in early Chinese texts, such as the *Book of Changes* (*Yijing* 易經), treating it as integral to early Confucian thought (Ames 1993, 2021).[11] On this view, the cosmos consists of inter-related and mutually influencing dynamic and fluid *qi* 氣 forces—often articulated as interdependent dyadic *yin-yang* (陰陽) categories—which give rise to the events of the world. These interacting forces give rise not to natural kinds or essences, but to entities or phenomena that form and cohere through the dynamic balance of forces, yet which are also evolving. This fluid and changing world is seen in the changing seasons, shifts between night and day, the various human circulatory systems, and other natural phenomena.

Viewing the world in terms of correlative cosmology meant figuring out how to coordinate human concerns and social practices with the fluid natural world in which humans are embedded. There was little interest in understanding an underlying causal order, which also explains events in the world; rather, useful correlations and pairings that could guide action and benefit human life were sought, and these were provisionally institutionalized in customs and ritualized practice.[12]

This processual worldview also informs social and personal life. *Qi* spans the putative distinction between the mental and the physical, and between mind and body. A person's well-being, mental and physical, is partly dependent on the cultivation and flow of *qi*. In pre-Qin texts, for example, control of *qi* was sometimes linked to breathing exercises or to meditation techniques. Although the importance of *qi* theory in early Confucian thought is difficult to determine, it plays a role. The state of a person's vital energies affects a person's countenance and manner,[13] and *qi* affects the emotions (*Xunzi*, Chapter 1 2014: 7). The *Mencius* describes the possession of "flood-like qi" and uninhibited *qi* helps to sustain psychological functions such as willful determination; the psychological and *qi* thus stand in a symbiotic relationship (*Mencius* 2A2). Personhood is thus not the fulfillment of predetermined potential or a specific capacity, but rather emerges incrementally from the interaction of the myriad forces of the cosmos (*tian* 天). Persons are not bounded and discrete entities, but rather porous and relationally constituted.

Drawing on an earlier Chinese thinker, Tang Junyi, Roger Ames brings these themes together to identify a "focus-field" model of the person.[14] This model makes use of two classical Confucian terms, *De* 德 (focus) and *Dao* 道 (field). *De* 德 refers to the power, sway or influence of an individual, typically virtuous, on the surrounding world. Such influence is generated through personal cultivation and is attributed to exemplary Confucian figures in history. *Dao* 道, literally the Confucian way or path, here refers to the entire field of entities, histories and events within which that single person, that single focal point, exists. Through ongoing personal cultivation—

including mastery of ritual practice, reflection on conduct, literary learning that includes useful historical studies, and the transformative power of music, dance and song—a person becomes ever more capable of forming productive relationships with the elements within the field that makes up their existence. The cultivated person then exerts a shaping or guiding influence on those elements (including people, social events, and even kingdoms or states). Accordingly, Confucius is the "pole star" from which others take their bearing (*Analects* 2.1).

A guiding heuristic that illustrates this conception of emerging selfhood is found in the Confucian classic *The Great Learning* (*Daxue* 大學). The text offers the metaphor of ever wider circles or realms of personal effect or influence, beginning from within the individual and extending through ever larger social realms until such influence affects the whole world. The individual's influence is initially limited; arguably beginning in the introspection undertaken when alone (*du* 獨) and the work of cultivation is invisible outside the body. With time and application, the effects of the cultivated person spread outwardly, to the family, the clan or community and then to the state or nation. Ultimately, the outer limit of this field of things with which the single focal person engages is cosmological in nature; it extends to the entire cosmos and even into the future. The person or self forms a union with a cosmic whole, a process described as a completion of, or integration with, the myriad things of the cosmos (*Mencius* 7A4, 7A1). Reframing this insight within a concrete historical context, the exemplary lives of the sage rulers become models for the entire tradition.[15]

Crucially, the ideal of a person growing into and making the most of all elements in that personal field is available to all. Anyone can become a sage.[16] When many achieve this, overlapping networks of beneficial influence arise. This results in the mutual, and ongoing ordering of communal life, thereby realizing the Confucian ideal of harmony (*he* 和). This harmony is both dynamic and static, since the course of human interaction is open to change even though ordered patterns and customs emerge, persist and are institutionalized.

The focus-field approach also accords with Confucian discourse about the body. Several terms in early Confucian thought refer to the body, each picking out various characteristics.[17] One of these is the *ti* 體 body, which extends beyond the singular individual, and forms a larger whole to which the individual belongs in some sense and from which it gains identity. The Chinese character originally featured in plant-based vocabulary, indicating a root, from which various sapling emerge (Sommer 2012). In the case of roles, the *ti* (體) body means the "embodying" of the roles and relationships passed down through generations, constituting a tradition, and giving individual lives meaning and significance.[18]

In this account, the Confucian self is shaped by roles and relationships, and is a social and relational self. The emerging person is initially situated in the various relations of localized family life. The person develops by comparing and correlating conduct with those near at hand (*Analects* 6.20), putting oneself in the place of others (*shu* 恕) (15.24),

and committing to roles and ritualized conduct that reliably bring order to the innumerable small interactions of everyday social life. Persistent application in these interactions and roles is constitutive of power (*de*): learning to make the most of the cultural traditions and social practices in which the subject is located. On this view, the personal quality of de 德 is not translated not as virtue—which suggests idealized qualities of a generic individual—but as "relational virtuosity" (Ames 2021: 21), which acknowledges the idiosyncrasies and particularity of persons within such networks of attachment.

While this self is partly constituted by roles and received practice, the identity of the self is ultimately open-ended. This self evolves over time, ideally growing in influence in step with cultivation or learning, and eventually gaining a distinctive identity recognized publicly and commemorated historically. Exemplary Confucian sages are memorialized in the tradition, but each is different. In Ames' words, such a self is best considered not a human being but a "human becoming" (2021: 22).

This account of a Confucian self has several strengths. It interprets key texts plausibly, and a self that grows towards individuality avoids concerns about self-abnegation or selfless conformity. This account also faces challenges, however. One is a reluctance to address inner cognitive life in Confucian thought, and its consequences for a conception of self. This lacuna is partly due to the desire to avoid the importation of problematic dualisms centered on mind and body, which are alien to early Chinese thought. Of particular concern is the belief that there is first an inner cognitive event, such as a deliberative judgment, and then subsequent behaviors (Ames 2021: 68), which privileges mind over body. Some have argued (Eno 1990: 70), however, that the absence of discourse about inner conflict in early texts is due to literary norms and styles rather than their genuine absence or lack of practical importance. More importantly, what is at stake here is not simply the possibly wrongful assertion of dualisms in the text, or the disputed universality of the (typically Western) belief in explicit discursive rationality and argument. Rather, the neglect is concerning because of the features of Confucian texts that seem explicitly psychological and which are relevant to personal cultivation. Significant psychological states or experiences include reverence, delight, detestation, desire, shame, feelings of commiseration and alarm, and reflective introspective awareness.

The *Great Learning*, for example, certainly describes growth through social relations; however, this process arguably does not start from role, but from inward reflection. In articulating the metaphor of expanding circles of transformative influence, the text takes as much care to describe seemingly inner events as social relations and their effects on the wider community.[19] At the same time, however, highlighting the psychological in the texts need not imply the existence of a separate private inner world that demarcates the self. These experiences are compatible with a relational self, since those psychological states, introspective moments and motivations could be orientated towards and sensitive to others, rather than identified with private and autonomous acts of practical judgment. This is discussed further below, in David Wong's account of selfhood.

There is another problem with understanding Confucian selfhood as a particularistic self on a path towards communally-recognized individuality. This arguably understates the extent to which the self in the Confucian tradition is subject to multiple rules, duties and moral norms, whose enduring demands and static nature challenge claims that the Confucian tradition is primarily about highly particularistic "becomings." Commentators on the legacy of Confucian thought, particularly women, have worried whether Confucian social thought is conservative and drifts too easily into patriarchy, and whether later abstract presentations of the Confucian self and good life successfully mitigate gendered social hierarchies associated with the Confucian heritage (Nam-Soon Kang 2004; Lee 2021; Guisso 1981; Wolf 1994).

These reservations feed into a broader methodological question about the grounds for such a self. Within this East-West contrastive approach, the Western conception of the autonomous individual is described as an "ideology" (Ames 2021: 152, 164); but the claim that a small set of "uncommon assumptions" lie behind and explain the Confucian texts at a granular level might be regarded similarly, albeit as one with a claim to be grounded in the textual tradition. As Fingarette and others were influenced by a reductive notion of a selfless collectivist self, so perhaps this view relies on a broad notion of a processual world in which selves are events in a process cosmology (Ames 2021: 39–40).

As a result, this expansive approach is accused of not translating classical Confucian terms but rather employing terms infused with a degree of interpretation, such that they then fit into a unifying explanatory framework. For example, in this approach, *xing* 性—typically read as human nature or incipient tendencies—becomes "cultivating our human propensities" (Ames 2021: 21). However, this imports an ethical notion into the basic term. Subsequently, Xunzi's declaration that human nature is 'bad' (*renxinge* 人性恶) becomes harder to understand, if it means "cultivating our human propensities is bad." Consequently, some have called for a less theory-bound or "philosophical" reading of the early texts (Møllgaard 2005). In reply, perhaps all encounters with traditions as alien as ancient China must rely on interpretive frameworks and assumptions; and making these explicit is laudable. Ames argues that many Western sinologists are insufficiently aware of their metaphysical and philosophical assumptions when analyzing Confucian thought.

Other Confucian Selves: Avoiding Chinese Worldviews and Cultural Assumptions

Other contemporary philosophers agree that the Confucian self is relational, but explain "relational" without relying on a contentious underlying worldview or cultural assumptions. Some instead draw on contemporary empirical psychology. David Wong (2004), for example, explores a situationist account of the Confucian self: the dispositions of the self are often determined by context rather than an unencumbered "I." Action is not primarily determined by pre-existing and persistent desires or ends that direct choice, but rather "dispositions that are triggered by specific persons in specific social contexts" (Wong 2004: 422). Experiments in behavioral sciences, such as the Milgram and Stanford Prison experiments, illustrate how people are typically not the sole authors of their actions.[20] Furthermore, recognizing the relational nature of identity means that, arguably, Asian conceptions of identity better reflect reality. In a manner not sufficiently acknowledged by classical liberal individualism, people behave differently in different contexts. Kindness, for example, is not a character trait, either present or lacking, but is directed more towards loved ones, and less towards strangers. In the Confucian context, this means greater sensitivity to the nuance of different social roles and relationships.

This approach captures the importance of interpersonal comparison in texts like the *Analects*, and of openness to learning from others' example (*Analects* 6.30) as a means of personal cultivation. It also resonates with contemporary studies that suggest personal traits differ based on geography and cultural milieu, in contrast to the insistence on global character traits shared by all (Nisbett 2010; Flanagan 2016).

This situationally-sensitive relational self differs from the focus-field self model. The developmental endpoint of this self is marked by excellent practical judgment that actually transcends situations and distorting influences. In short, this mature self knows when to defy convention or resist the influence of others. While ordinary people are more susceptible to external cues, the exemplary person's judgment is consistent and authoritative. While Ames' mature relational self achieves a distinguished individuality that leaves its imprint on society and history, Wong's mature self features a situation-transcending ethical judgment (yi 義). This is a global trait, which constitutes a form of autonomy and qualifies the exemplary person as the "pole star" through which others find direction. Wong's account preserves insights into the relational aspects of Confucian thought, while maintaining that the Confucian exemplary person is characterized by practical wisdom. This avoids the more contested aspects of the focus-field self approach, including interpretive translations, and contested metaphysical assumptions.

Others have also highlighted the role of individual practical judgment in Confucian selfhood, characterizing it as reflective self-control undertaken by the mind (*xin* 心), which leads to personal "transformation" (Shun 2013). On this psychological reading, cultivation involves "overcoming the self" (*keji* 克己 *Analects* 12.1), whereby an incipient or natural state of "self-centeredness" is overcome. This "continuous self-reflective reshaping of oneself in adult life" (Shun 2013: 264) assumes a malleable self, but one transformed through inner reflection and effort. This reflection ensures the self is properly orientated towards Confucian ethical standards and other people, and inures it to the opinions of others, with shame understood not as a reaction to others but to any failure to uphold personal standards. Conversely, self-regard is derived from holding oneself to ethical standards to which the heart–mind commits, while the cultivated self has an intuitive or perception-like grasp of the right thing to do.

These two approaches make sense of important textual passages, which emphasize the role of rational self-control and reflection in a conception of self; Wong's account also incorporates the insight into relational sensitivity. Yet, these accounts face familiar challenges, which return us to our starting concern about imposing Western ideas on the texts. Their emphasis on mature practical judgment is a return to a familiar self, one that resembles the Aristotelian person of practical wisdom. In consequence, potentially distinctive but less-easily assimilated aspects of Confucian selfhood are overlooked or marginalized, such as the role of the family, embodied ritual practice and music.

Conclusion

This chapter examined recent attempts to articulate a Confucian notion of selfhood, while recognizing the lack of agreement about the precise nature of that self. Nevertheless, there is consensus that the ethical and social ideal of personal cultivation is central to Confucian selfhood. Metaphors of polishing a precious stone and agricultural metaphors of growth and reaching fruition abound, and allude to the refinement of incipient tendencies and cultural enrichment. Consequently, some features of the Confucian conception of self can be inferred, despite the absence of detail in the original texts. As an ideal, the Confucian self overcomes asocial impulses and comes to embody the social norms and ritual refinement of the Confucian way; it reflects on its treatment of others and corrects its course; it is affectively, bodily and rationally constituted—such that inner states can be read from external appearances; it exercises excellent ethical judgment, whether deliberative, intuitive or rooted in experience; it consists in a unique and exemplary individuality whose memorialization by others attests to the full development of personhood; and it is relationally constituted, perhaps to the point that a clearly bounded entity cannot be identified, and a firm distinction between self and other is not sought. A final heuristic is offered by Confucius himself, who describes the development arc of his life (*Analects* 2.4):

> From fifteen, my heart-and-mind was set upon learning; from thirty I took my stance; from forty I was no longer doubtful; from fifty I realized the propensities of the heavens (*tianming* 天命); from sixty my ear was attuned; from seventy I could give my heart-and-mind free rein without overstepping the boundaries.

Confucian thinking about the self might be further explored in several ways, but here just one insight can be noted, concerning the relationship between the self and political order. In early China, there is much overlap between the three realms of self, community (or clan) and the state. The Confucian person grows from incipient beginnings to become a virtuosic figure worthy of political authority. In contrast, Western liberal political thought has historically considered how to limit the power of the state to protect the individual. Liberal pluralistic social and political order is constructed upon belief in an inner private self that pursues its own projects. The classical Confucian tradition offers some perspective on this presumed relationship between self and political power. First, the Confucian self does not need protection from political authority; the cultivated self is the root of social and political order. Second, the early Confucian texts offer subtly different conceptions of the self, with different features prominent in different parts of the texts. This is perhaps why the appropriate form of a Confucian political modernity is contested, with candidates ranging from Confucian democracy (Kim 2018) to more authority-based meritocracy (Bell 2015). But if different conceptions of self are foregrounded at different times, and the understanding of self informs political thinking, this raises the question of which conceptions of self should be relied upon to inform dominant political and legal structures, including theories of punishment and justice. The early Confucians have no privileged answer to this question. The hope was that the presence of enough cultivated persons could transform communities and then the state, though this was highly optimistic. But their discourse should alert us to the dangers of prematurely hypostatizing one conception of self and using it to justify political structures.

Notes

1. On how the self has been portrayed in the Chinese tradition as a whole, up to contemporary times, see Elvin (1985) and Raphals (2009). Other studies of the self or personhood include Munro (1969), Tu (1985), Ames (1993), Ivanhoe (2000), Liu (2004), Shun and Wong (2004), Lai (2006), Rosemont (2015), and Li (2024). For an attempt to convert Confucian social thought directly into contemporary models of the self, see Hsü (1971).
2. Flanagan (2016) analyzes how different philosophical traditions have constructed selfhood; see especially Chapter 11. See also Li (2024).
3. See Hegel (2001: 126–128, 133–138).
4. See, for example, *Analects* passages 4.5, 4.14, 4.16, 8.13, 9.18. On the Confucian vision that shapes the will, see Fingarette (1972).
5. Robert Eno (1990: 69–78) also describes a self transformed by ritual practice, whereby the Confucians' investment in the earlier Zhou Dynasty's ritual code allowed little scope for change or dissent. In Eno's account, however, the benefits and hence the rationale for committing the self in this way, reside in the aesthetic and social goods of music, dancing and performance.
6. See, for example, *Analects* 4.10, *Mencius* 2A2.

7. In his global survey, Flanagan writes, "Homeric persons are dutiful beings with disciplined minds. The Daoist sage experiences himself or herself as like a butterfly... The selves of Russian peasants in Tolstoy's short stories are simple, unreflective, and devout. The selves of the pietistic Lutherans for whom Kant speaks are selves governed by severe consciences, stern superegos" (2016: 225–226).
8. For descriptions of the five relationships, see *Mencius* 3A4, Zhongyong (2001), Chapter 20, and the Lord Huan (6.2; p. 97) and Lord Wen (18.7; p. 573) sections of the *Zuozhuan* (2016). On the origins and evolution of the five foundational Confucian relationships, see Hsü (1971).
9. See the discussion below on Shun (2013) and deliberation, introspection and willful self-regulation. As noted by Fingarette, the texts recognize the separateness of oneself and others, and the cognitive and affective activities of the heart–mind (*xin* 心) might be as crucial to personal identity as role (e.g., *Mencius* 6A15). The presence of a golden rule-like standard in the *Analects* (5.12, 12.2, 15.24) also suggests a discrete reflective individual, and leads some to compare the humanity of Confucius to Kant (Froese 2008).
10. Other role-transcending aspects of the Confucian way are described in 4.15, 5.11, 7.1, 7.24
11. For accounts of correlative cosmology in early China, see Hall and Ames (1998), Granet ([1934] 2012), Keightley (1988), Lewis (1989), Li Ling (1991), Wang (2000), and Needham (1956).
12. One scholar describes correlative cosmology as "an orderly system of correspondence among various domains of reality in the universe, correlating categories of the human world, such as the human body, behavior, morality, the sociopolitical order, and historical changes, with categories of the cosmos, including time, space, the heavenly bodies, seasonal movement, and natural phenomena" (Wang 2000: 2).
13. The suggestion that a person's character, or at least their present inner state, can be read off their physical appearance is a common theme in early Confucian thought.
14. In later writing, Ames avoids the term "self" due to its reifying and essentializing implications (Ames and Rosemont 2014: 37–38), preferring "the focus-field conception of person" and "the focus-field narrative conception of human becomings" (Ames 2021: 360). Terminology aside, the processual entity described is equivalent.
15. The profound influence of cultural behemoths is exemplified by the sage rulers Yao, Shun and Yu. See, for example, *Analects* 8.19, 20.1; *Mencius* 3A1, 3A4, 4A2, and so on.
16. *Mencius* 6B2; Xunzi, Chapter 23 ([2014] 2015: 254–255).
17. On the body in early Chinese thought, see Sivin (1995), Ames (1984), Cheng (2002), Sommer (2008, 2012), and Shusterman (2015).
18. Other terms for body include: *qu* 軀, associated with the morally diminished bodies of petty people (*xiaoren* 小人) (Xunzi Chapters 1 and 4; *Mencius* 7B29); *xing* 形, an underlying structure or visible form; *gong* 躬, the body in ritual or ceremonial context; and *shen* 身, the cultured and public-facing body bearing social status (Sommer 2012).

19. The relevant passage reads: "Things being investigated, knowledge became complete. Their knowledge being complete, their thoughts were sincere. Their thoughts being sincere, their hearts were then rectified. Their hearts being rectified, their persons were cultivated. Their persons being cultivated, their families were regulated. Their families being regulated, their States were rightly governed. Their States being rightly governed, the entire world was at peace" (*Book of Rites* 1885: 677). The precise meaning of terms in the first half is open to debate, nevertheless, the terms appear to refer to some form of inner reflective or introspective undertakings.
20. Milgram (1974) and Haney et al. (1973).

Bibliography

Chinese primary Sources in Translation

Analects [*Lunyu* 論語] 1998. *The Analects of Confucius: A philosophical Translation*. Trans. R. Ames and H. Rosemont. New York: Ballantine Books.

Book of Changes [*Yijing* 易經] 1882. *The Sacred Books of China: The Texts of Confucianism – The Yi King*. Ed. and trans. J. Legge. Oxford: Clarendon.

Book of Rites [*Liji* 禮記] 1885. *The Sacred Books of China: The Texts of Confucianis*. Parts III–IV, *The Li Ki*. Ed. and trans. J. Legge. Oxford: Clarendon.

Great Learning [*Daxue* 大學] 2012. *Daxue and Zhongyong: Bilingual Edition*. Trans. I. Johnston and P. Wang. Hong Kong: Chinese University Press.

Mencius [*Mengzi* 孟子] 2009. Trans. I. Bloom. Cambridge: Cambridge University Press.

Wong, David. 2004. "Relational and Autonomous Selves." *Journal of Chinese Philosophy*, 31 (4): 419–432.

Xunzi [荀子] 2014. Xunzi: *A Completion Translation*. Trans. E. Hutton. Princeton: Princeton University Press.

Zhongyong [中庸] 2001. *Focusing the Familiar: A Translation and Philosophical Interpretation of the Zhongyong*. Trans. D. Hall and R. Ames. Honolulu: University of Hawaiʻi Press.

Zuozhuan [左傳] 2016. *Zuo Tradition / Zuozhuan: Commentary on the "Spring and Autumn Annals."* Trans. S. Durrant, W. Li, and D. Schaberg. Seattle: University of Washington Press.

Other References

Ames, R. T. 1984. "The Meaning of Body in Classical Chinese Thought." *International Philosophical Quarterly*, 24 (1): 39–54.

Ames, R. T. 1993. "The Focus-Field Self in Classical Confucianism." In T. Kasulis, R. Ames, and W. Dissanayake (eds.), *Self as Body in Asian Theory and Practice*. Albany: SUNY, 187–212.

Ames, Roger. 2021. *Human Becomings: Theorizing Persons for Confucian Role Ethics*. Albany: SUNY Press.

Ames, R. T., and H. Rosemont. 2014. "From Kupperman's Character Ethics to Confucian Role Ethics." In C. LI and P. Ni (eds.), *Moral Cultivation and Confucian Character: Engaging Joel J.Kupperman*. Albany: SUNY Press, 17–46.

Bell, D. A. 2015. *The China Model: Political Meritocracy and the Limits of Democracy*. Princeton: Princeton University Press.

Cheng, C. 2002. "On the Metaphysical Significance of Ti (Body-Embodiment) in Chinese Philosophy: Benti (Origin-Substance) and Ti-Yong (Substance and Function)." *Journal of Chinese Philosophy*, 29 (2): 145–161.

Dau-Lin, H. 1970. "The Myth of the 'Five Human Relations' of Confucius." *Monumenta Serica*, 29 (1): 27–37.

Edwards, R. R. 1986. "Civil and Social Rights: Theory and Practice in Chinese Law Today." In R. R. Edwards, L. Henkin, and A. J. Nathan (eds.), *Human Rights in Contemporary China*. New York: Columbia University Press, 41–76.

Elvin, M. 1985. "Between the Earth and Heaven: Conceptions of the Self in China." In M. Carrithers, S. Collins, and S. Lukes (eds.), *The Category of the Person: Anthropology, Philosophy, History*. Cambridge: Cambridge University Press, 156–189.

Eno, R. 1989. *The Confucian Creation of Heaven: Philosophy and the Defense of Ritual Mastery*. New York: SUNY Press.

Fei, X., G. G. Hamilton, and W. Zheng. 1992. *From the Soil: The Foundations of Chinese Society: A Translation of Fei Xiaotong's Xiangtu Zhongguo*. Berkeley: University of California Press.

Fingarette, H. 1972. *Confucius: The Secular as Sacred*. New York: Harper & Row.

Fingarette, H. 1979. "The Problem of the Self in the Analects." *Philosophy East and West*, 29 (2): 129–140.

Flanagan, O. 2016. *The Geography of Morals: Varieties of Moral Possibility*. Oxford: Oxford University Press.

Froese, K. 2008. "The Art of Becoming Human: Morality in Kant and Confucius." *Dao*, 7: 257–268.

Granet, M. [1934] 2012. *La Pensée Chinoise*. Paris: Albin Michel.

Guisso, R. W. 1981. "Thunder over the Lake: The Five Classics and the Perception of Woman in Early China." In R. W. L. Guisso and Stanley Johannesen (eds.), *Women in China: Current Directions in Historical Scholarship*. Youngstown: Philo Press, 47–61.

Hall, D. L. and R. T. Ames. 1984. "Getting It Right: On Saving Confucius from the Confucians." *Philosophy East and West*, 34 (1): 3–23.

Hall, D. L., and R. T. Ames. 1998. *Thinking from the Han-Self, Truth, and Transcendence in Chinese and Western Culture*. New York: SUNY Press.

Haney, C., C. Banks, and P. Zimbardo. 1973. "Interpersonal Dynamics in a Simulated Prison." *International Journal of Criminology & Penology*, 1 (1): 69–97.

Hegel, G. W. F. 2001. *Lectures on the Philosophy of World History*. Trans. J. Sibree. Ontario: Batoche Books.

Hsü, F. L. 1971. "Psychosocial Homeostasis and Jen: Conceptual Tools for Advancing Psychological Anthropology." *American Anthropologist*, 73 (1): 23–44.

Ivanhoe, Philip. 2000. *Confucian Moral Self Cultivation*. Indianapolis: Hackett Publishing.

Kasulis, T. P., R. T. Ames, and W. Dissanayake 1993. *Self as Body in Asian Theory and Practice*. New York: SUNY Press.

Keightley, D. N. 1988. "Shang Divination and Metaphysics." *Philosophy East and West*, 38 (4): 367–397.

Kim, S. 2018. *Democracy after Virtue: Toward Pragmatic Confucian* Democracy. New York: Oxford University Press.

Lai, Karyn. 2006. *Learning from Chinese Philosophies: Ethics of Independent and Contextualised Self*. Aldershot: Ashgate.

Lee, S. 2021. "Bracketing Women's Human Rights: A Feminist Critique of Contemporary Confucian Theories." PhD diss., City University of Hong Kong.

Lewis, M. E. 1989. *Sanctioned Violence in Early* China. New York: SUNY Press.

Li, Jin. 2024. *The Self in the West and East Asia: Being or Becoming*. London: Polity Press.

Li, Ling 李零. 1991. 試圖與中國古代的宇宙模式 ("Shitu yu Zhongguo gudai de yuzhou moshi"). *Jiuzhou Xuekan* (Chinese Culture Quarterly), 4 (1–2): 5–53, 49–76.

Liu, Y. 2004. "The Self and *Li* [Ritual] in Confucianism." *Journal of Chinese Philosophy*, 31 (3): 363–376.

Milgram, S. 1974. *Obedience to Authority*. New York: Haper & Row.

Mill, J. S. 1991. *On Liberty and Other Writings*. Cambridge: Cambridge University Press.

Munro, D. J. 1969. *The Concept of Man in Early China*. Stanford: Stanford University Press.

Munro, D. J. 1979. "The Shape of Chinese Values in the Eye of an American Philosopher." In R. Terrill (ed.), *The China Difference*. New York: Harper & Row, 39–56.

Møllgaard, E. 2005. "Eclipse of Reading: On the 'Philosophical Turn' in American Sinology." *Dao*, 4 (2): 321–340.

Nam-Soon Kang, K. P. 2004. "Confucian Familism and Its Social/Religious Embodiment in Christianity: Reconsidering the Family Discourse from a Feminist Perspective." *Asia Journal of Theology*, 18 (1): 168–189.

Needham, Joseph. 1956. *Science and Civilisation in* Chin, Volume 2: *History of Scientific Thought*. Cambridge: Cambridge University Press.

Nisbett, R. 2010. *The Geography of Thought: How Asians and Westerners Think Differently-and Why*. New York: Simon and Schuster.

Raphals, L. 2009. "Thirteen Ways of Looking at the Self in Early China." *History of Philosophy Quarterly*, 26 (4): 315–336.

Rosemont Jr, H. 1988. "Why Take Rights Seriously? A Confucian Critique." In Leroy S. Rouner (ed.), *Human Rights and the World's Religions*. Notre Dame: University of Notre Dame Press, 167–182.

Rosemont, H. 2015. *Against Individualism: A Confucian Rethinking of the Foundations of Morality, Politics, Family, and Religion*. Lanham: Lexington Books.

Rosemont Jr, H. 2016. "Rights-Bearing Individuals and Role-Bearing Persons." in R. Ames and H. Rosemont (eds.), *Confucian Role Ethics: A Moral Vision for the 21st Century*. Taiwan: National Taiwan University Press, 33–57.

Rosemont Jr, H., and R. T. Ames. 2016. *Confucian Role Ethics: A Moral Vision for the 21st Century?* Taiwan: National Taiwan University Press.

Shun, K. 2013. "Early Confucian Moral Psychology." In *Dao Companion to Classical Confucian Philosophy*. Dordrecht: Springer Dordrecht, 263–289.

Shun, K., and D. Wong. 2004. *Confucian Ethics: A Comparative Study of Self, Autonomy, and Community*. Cambridge: Cambridge University Press.

Shusterman, R. 2015. "Somaesthetics and Chinese Philosophy: Between Unity and Pragmatist Pluralism." *Frontiers of Philosophy in China*, 10 (2): 201–211.

Sivin, N. 1995. "State, Cosmos, and Body in the Last Three Centuries BC." *Harvard Journal of Asiatic Studies*, 55 (1): 5–37.

Sommer, D. 2008. "Boundaries of the 'Ti' Body." *Asia Major*, 21 (1): 293–324.

Sommer, D. 2012. "The Ji Self in Early Chinese Texts." In J. Dockstader, H. Moller, and G. Wohlfahrt (eds.), *Selfhood East and West: De-constructions of Identity*. Herzberg: Traugott Bautz, 17–45.

Taylor, C. 1989. *Sources of the Self: The Making of the Modern Identity*. Cambridge: Harvard University Press.

Tu, W. 1985. *Confucian Thought: Selfhood as Creative Transformation*. New York: SUNY Press.

Wang, A. 2000. *Cosmology and Political Culture in Early China*. Cambridge: Cambridge University Press.

Wolf, M. 1994. "Beyond the Patrilineal Self: Constructing Gender in China." In T. Kasulis, R. Ames, and W. Dissanayake (eds.), *Self as Body in Asian Theory and Practice*. Albany: SUNY, 251–267.

Yang, C. K. 1959. *Chinese Communist Society: The Family and the Village*. Cambridge: MIT Press.

Humaneness (*Ren* 仁)
Chapter 5.1

Ren 仁 is a foundational idea in classical Confucian thought; it appears throughout the *Analects*, and in the *Mencius* and the *Xunzi*, and is central to any Confucian account of self. The term is tied to the ideal of personal cultivation and the growth and refinement of a person's basic qualities or dispositions. Understood as a precondition of responsibility and authority, it also informs Confucian social and political thought.

Ren is sometimes understood as a single virtue or quality of character—such as benevolence or sympathetic response—and sometimes indicates a more general personal excellence. It can also describe a person who adheres to the Confucian social code or way, who treats people in accord with role and ritual, and who possesses practical wisdom, particularly among rulers. Evidently, concise definitions of the term are elusive, especially as its connotations evolve over time.

The variety of translations used testify to the term's capaciousness. These include benevolence, love, perfect virtue, goodness, consummate conduct, authoritative conduct, exemplary conduct, virtuosity in roles and relationships, co-humanity, manhood at its best, human-heartedness and humanity. The language chosen often reflects broader interpretive commitments employed in making sense of the classical Confucian texts. Such interpretive differences are partly due to the sparse language of the original texts, which invite the reader to contextualize content and possibly foreground one aspect of *ren*. For example, "benevolence" remains a popular translation, but arguably "psychologizes" the term, elevating the affective dimension but obscuring other aspects of *ren*. Similarly, "humanity" suggests a shared condition as members of the species, but arguably *ren* is an accomplishment, marked by the transformation of character or a life more generally. Some have preferred "goodness," on account on it being suitably vague, positive and open-ended. For convenience, "humaneness" will be used here.

The Chinese character for *ren* (仁) provides insight into its meaning. An early Chinese lexicon, the *Shuowen Jiezi*, notes that *ren* is composed of two characters, a person (*ren* 人) next to the number two (*er* 二). This graphic image of people in the plural suggests that ren is a relational quality or inheres among people, and hints at a conception of self that is social and relational. In the words of one contemporary philosopher on *ren*, "For Confucius, unless there are at least two human beings, there can be no human beings," (Fingarette 1983: 217) meaning that others are needed for a person to develop fully, that is to say, to become *ren*.

The History of the Term *Ren*

That *ren* is particularly important to early Confucian thought is evident from its limited appearances in pre-Confucian texts. It becomes a key term only in the *Analects*. *Ren* occasionally appears in Zhou Dynasty era bronzes and in some pre-Confucian texts, typically meaning largesse or virility, but is a relatively unimportant term. In early uses, in the *Book of Songs* (*Shijing*) for example, ren suggests martial virtue or is characteristic of the nobility; meaning "handsome and strong," it distinguishes nobility who take pride in manners and good breeding from the common people. Another early term that becomes important to the Confucians, *junzi* (nobleman; literally, "son of a ruler"), was also originally freighted with similar sociological and class-based meaning.

The emergence of *ren* as a key Confucian concept marks a historical shift in social thought in early China. In the *Analects*, *ren* no longer denotes a "nobleman" or good breeding, but is used as a moral term. It identifies the "noble man," a quality of character that can be attained by all people with due effort. The Confucian use of *ren* presents a new ethical vision, one in which all can commit to personal cultivation and, eventually, become *junzi* or exemplary people, although "the way (*dao*) is long and the burden is heavy" (*Analects* 8.7). Humaneness thus takes on an explicitly moral meaning, distinguishing a higher state of character and its salubrious social effects.

In the classical Confucian texts, humaneness is linked to other terms in Confucian social discourse as part of that ethical vision. However, the meaning of *ren* is difficult to pin down partly because the term is not clearly defined in the *Analects*. Confucius is asked several times about its meaning, and gives different answers each time. This persistent questioning by students is evidence that the term is indeed being used to articulate novel ideas or social practices and interlocutors are unsure of its meaning. The lack of textual precision has led commentators to offer several distinct interpretations of the meaning of *ren* in Confucian thought. Nevertheless, humanness is integral to the Confucian accounts of the self, and it is helpful to survey its usage in the classical texts, to illustrate the contours of Confucian personal cultivation.

Ren as Constitutive Personal Qualities

As a description of all-round personal excellence, *ren* encompasses various personal qualities that shape the self. At the general level, the "humane" person has achieved a balance between natural dispositions and impulses (*zhi* 質), on the one hand, and socialization and cultural refinements (*wen* 文). Word and deed are neither too wild or idiosyncratic, nor too constricted or contrived. Humaneness is also glossed as overcoming or disciplining oneself and returning to ritual (*Analects* 12.1)—ritual (*li* 禮) is instrumental in refining personal sensibility. A person, enriched by culture, becomes adept at the customs and shared social practices that constitute communal life, yet is also able to personalize such action, imbuing it with their own personality. This is one manifestation of Confucian harmony (*he* 和): conduct that integrates person, family and community while also expresses personal character and meaning.

Another personal attribute instrumental to this balance between natural dispositions and cultural refinement is a love of learning (*haoxue* 好學) (*Analects* 1.14, 5.15, 5.28, 6.3, 8.13, 11.7, 17.8, 19.5). Those who are *ren* are "broadly learned" (*boxue* 博學), able to draw on a knowledge of history, which includes historical exemplars and a rich storehouse of cultural and practical wisdom found in texts and the oral tradition. This leaning is contrasted with what might be regarded as isolated thought or reflection, possibly suggesting that private thought and speculative reflection are less useful than learning from daily life and the ideas, examples, and behaviors accumulated within the tradition.

Humaneness also involves a sense of responsibility towards speech and its consequences. Confucius warns against glibness (*Analects* 6.15), praises caution when speaking (1.14), prizes action above mere talk (advocating acting and achieving first and then speaking), and values trustworthiness or making good on one's word (*xin* 信) (17.6).

Ren is not merely inner virtue or dispositional in nature; it is also physical and embodied. The humane person is distinguished by posture and comportment, a kind of physical presence, as well as gestures and bodily communication. The early Confucian texts describe Confucius being visibly affected in several social situations: in sacred spaces or where reverence is called for, his countenance changes and his speech became breathless (10.4). Book ten of the *Analects* can be read as a study of the exemplary person's bearing in a range of social settings. Perhaps the careful study of exemplary models is important because, as the early texts warn, some folks appear humane but are merely keeping up appearances while pursuing reputation, honor or profit. Xunzi's description of the five hegemons or rulers who usurped the Zhou Dynasty's power is apt; they "relied on the appearance of being *ren*, but walked the path of obtaining profit."

The Relational Nature of *Ren*

Another feature of humaneness is the attention to relations with others. This discourse takes many forms in the classical texts. It includes being properly orientated towards people, often as defined by ritual propriety, and treating filial piety (*xiao* 孝) as a foundation of humaneness. The texts also promote concern for others' welfare, particularly when in positions of responsibility or power, the ability to draw out improvement or excellence from others (as Confucius was able to do with this students), and serving as a model or exemplar for others.

Contemporary discussions of Confucian ethics often identify a relational or social conception of the self in the texts. The *Analects* hints at a method for cultivating the self: "Humane (*ren*) persons establish others in seeking to establish themselves, and promote others in seeking to get there themselves. Correlating one's conduct with those near at hand can be said to be the method of becoming humane (*ren*)" (6.30). This theme is continued in other passages: "The exemplary person (*junzi*) helps to bring out the best in others, but does not help to bring out the worst." (12.16) This culminates in Confucius' socially-minded declaration that he would most like to "bring peace and contentment to the aged, to share relationships of trust and confidence with my friends, and to love and protect the young" (5.26).

As these passages make clear, *ren* partly entails care or concern for others (*ai* 爱). Perhaps the best known expression of *ren* as interpersonal concern or attachment is found in the *Mencius*. There, such concern acquires its most explicitly psychological form, as part of the Mencian theory of human nature. *Ren* is identified as one of the four innate sprouts or tendencies of human nature, and is characterized as the inability to bear the suffering of others (*ren* 忍). This is an incipient disposition and sensitivity possessed by all people. Sympathetic responsiveness to the difficulties of others will arise in all hearts and minds, as long as basic material needs are met. In the *Mencius*, *ren* is often translated as "benevolence."

The Political Implications of *Ren*

For the Confucians, humaneness (*ren*) is also necessary for legitimate political authority. The *Mencius* (1A7) describes how good rulership is rooted in the growth of this shared human moral sensibility. The strengthening of sympathetic response—along with other personal sensitivities, such as shame, a disposition to defer to others when appropriate, and an appropriate sense of what is right—makes a person fit to govern. The *Great Learning* (*Daxue*) outlines how sustained personal cultivation brings with it the gradual extension of a person's network of relationships and commitments, and an ever-increasing expansion of personal influence or moral sway (*de* 德). In the early Confucian texts, it is a widespread belief that the common people will emulate those in positions of authority and these people should be worthy models for others to emulate. (*Analects* 17.1, *Mencius* 1A7; *Xunzi* Chapter 10).

In conclusion, humaneness might be described as a cardinal virtue or a guiding ideal of early Confucian thought, indicating an achieved state of personal excellence that contributes to a harmonious community, but an idea which resists precise and final articulation. Accordingly, perhaps the best way to summarize *ren* is as follows: "*ren* is one's entire person: one's cultivated cognitive, aesthetic, moral, and religious sensibilities as they are expressed in one's ritualized roles and relationships" (Ames and Rosemont 1999: 49).

References

Ames, R. T., and H. J. Rosemont. 1999. *The Analects of Confucius: A Philosophical Translation*. New York: Ballantine Books.
Fingarette, H. 1983. "The Music of Humanity in the Conversations of Confucius." *Journal of Chinese Philosophy*, 10 (4): 331–356.

Ritual (*Li* 禮)
Chapter 5.2

Introduction: The Scope and Meaning of *Li* 禮:

The commitment to *li* 禮—"ritual" is a convenient though imperfect translation—was one of the distinguishing features of early Confucian thought. The Chinese term has religious, political and social connotations, and its meaning ranges from grand formal ceremony to small personal gestures and utterances. In classical Confucian thought, the term is bestowed with ethical or normative authority, which is not captured by the functional English term 'ritual.' There is some scholarly debate whether *li* or *ren* (仁 humaneness) is the most fundamental idea for understanding the *Analects*.

The Chinese character for *li* is composed of a ceremonial vessel on an altar stand (豊) next to a radical indicating petition or presentation (礻), and gives some hint of its origins in inscriptions referring to ancestral sacrifice, though the term is usually translated in various ways which reflects the breadth of its meaning. Aside from "ritual," common usages include "custom," "ceremony," "rites," or "(ritual) propriety", "morality," "ritualized conduct," and "etiquette."

Li, henceforth 'ritual,' initially referred to sacrifices to ancestors and deities, which served as a form of petition and established communication with spirits. Such sacrificial rituals were controlled by rulers and also served to legitimize their authority. The scope of ritual expanded beyond court life during the Zhou Dynasty, and came to describe a range of social practices and more secular and commonplace phenomena. These include formal ceremony, rites pertaining to natural and human life cycle (coming of age ceremonies, marriages and deaths), customary and moral norms, patterns of personal or interpersonal roles and relationships, a person's social demeanor and bearing, and even the practices and norms of social and political institutions. The effects of li thus span the political, the communal, the aesthetic, matters of personal style, and even symbolic gestures of everyday life. Ritual is also closely linked to music. According to the *Xunzi*, ritual makes distinctions while music unifies, and both are necessary for social harmony. Unsurprisingly, it is thus difficult to separate ritual from the dispositions, inclinations, and emotions that were integral to a ritualized form of life.

This range of application and relevance makes ritual an important idea in Confucian thought, and it features prominently in the *Analects*. For Confucius, ritual provides the foundations of social order, an approach that contrasts with attempts to order society using laws and punishment (*Analects* 2.3). This alternative to a legalistic social order involves the consummate performance of important rituals and ceremonies by figures of good character who carry social influence, the effects of which lead the common people to follow their examples and feel shame at any failures to uphold ritualistic practices and norms. Here, ritual is closely tied to the Confucian emphasis on personal exemplars.

Ritual also regulate the web of personal and social relationships that are the focus of early Confucian ethical thought, and which were later theorized as the five 'cardinal' relationships of Confucian society (*wulun* 五輪). Relations within the family and especially those between children and parents are subject to various injunctions such as, "when your parents are alive serve them with ritual" (*Analects* 2.5). Commentators have noted that a shared life conducted around specific familial roles is fundamental to the Confucian vision of the good life. Each role is governed by certain ritual expectations and precedents, while also, ideally, allowing for the personalization of each particular role or relationship.

More generally, ritual is central to Confucian project of personal cultivation: "The Master said, "I find inspiration by intoning the songs, I learn where to stand from observing ritual propriety (*li*), and I find completion in music" (*Analects* 8.8; see also 14.12, 16.13). Mastery of ritual is integral to the early Confucian ideal of *ren* (12.1, 12.2). Ritual is instrumental to conditioning or refining the self, and the concomitant transformation in personal conduct (9.11,12.1, 12.15).

Ritual serves to regulate emotion and conduct; in the Xunzi, ritual is an instrument that orders an otherwise chaotic set of human dispositions and desires. Humans are naturally attracted by fine flavors, sounds and sights, and by prospect of ease or comfort (Xunzi, Chapter 11), and these native impulses and dispositions are reshaped to produce conduct and behaviors that align with the *dao* (道) or social order. Music and ceremony, for example, can ensure that all participants feel the same appropriate emotion, and so contribute to the Confucian ideal of social harmony

Ritual assists in the cultivation and expression of appropriate emotions, particularly those most discussed in Confucian thought, such as grief, reverence, shame and delight or joy. Ritual moderates emotions that might otherwise be too intense—possibly violent and destructive—and amplifies emotions that might be initially too tepid—such as feelings for parents. Analects 8.2 reads, "Deference unmediated by ritual (*li* 禮) is tiresome; circumspection unmediated by ritual is timidity; bravery unmediated by ritual is rowdiness; candor unmediated by such propriety is rudeness." Ideally, ritual helps to establish the balance between a person's natural dispositions or impulses (*zhi* 質) and culture or proper form (*wen* 文) (6.18).

On the Confucian understanding, ritual is valuable not merely as accord with social obligation through formal and scripted action; ritual is valuable because it enables the expression of genuine feeling: "In referring time and again to ritual propriety (*li* 禮), how could I just be talking about jade and silk?" (*Analects* 17.11). If ritual is practiced perfunctorily, without any regard to the meaning of what is done, it becomes mere custom or ossified tradition. Similarly, since ritual often seeks to guide the expression of emotion, once the emotion dissipates then the need for ritual can diminish: "In aspiring to ritual propriety, it is better to be modest than extravagant; in mourning, it is better to express real grief than to worry over formal details"(3.4); "In mourning one does not go beyond the full expression of one's grief" (19.14). The Confucian texts warn against insincerity and simulation.

To master the rituals and practices of social life is to master a living "cultural grammar" (Li 2007). Once the basic norms of social life and their application are mastered, this permits a more stylized and personal interpretation of those norms and patterns of interaction. Such personalization and adaption of otherwise familiar norms and practices emphasizes the aesthetic dimension of ritual. The *junzi* or exemplary person is often described as pleasant or appealing, and this aesthetic quality forms part of his or her warrant to serve as exemplar or role model.

Various aspects of ritual practice are instrumental to becoming a public exemplar. Through personal investment in the performance of ceremonies and public rituals, people can see the personal qualities of the ruler, and so are moved to follow him (while the early texts contain little on the topic of gender, most of the public figures and exemplars discussed are male). The conduct of worthy people performing ritual can also induce direct emulation. When those in power perform ritualized acts of filial conduct, honoring parents or ancestors, then those "below," that is to say, the common people, are inspired to treat their own families with similar respect. Some have even suggested that the creation of shared public spectacle, in which members of different sections of society enjoy an awe-inspiring ceremony, involving music, dance and costume, serves to build social solidarity and loyalty to the ruler (Nylan 2001).

Contemporary Challenges

As with other tenets of Confucian social thought, the emphasis on ritual has sometimes been challenged by a critical contemporary sensibility. There is concern that looking to ritual to order the self and social life means undue weight on tradition, custom and precedent to decide matters, in place of reason, debate and individual discretion. A focal point for such interpretive disputes is the many portraits of Confucius' behavior in Book 10 of the Analects. On one reading, these passages offer a portrait in excessive fastidiousness and concern with the dogmatic minutiae of personal behavior, while another sees a study of a conscientious person deeply aware of their conduct and responsibilities, even when alone.

The texts themselves hint at the limits of ritual precedent and the scope for flexibility in conduct and social practice. The *Analects* (15.29) famously declares, ""It is the person who is able to broaden the way *(dao)*, not the way that broadens the person," and there are suggestions that rituals are not fixed but may evolve with the times (9.3) or that unusual cases or urgent need might overrule prevailing social and ritual norms (*Mencius* 4A17). Some have compared Confucian ritual practice to a musical score (Fingarette 1983); the musical notes are fixed but their expression involves personalization.

The texts recognize a general need for contextualized judgments of what is right or appropriate (*yi* 義) (Hall and Ames 1984), though the scope for such judgments in the early texts is disputed. Such flexibility in ritual practice is perhaps best understood within the context of the underlying social vision, which entails an obliging commitment to established patterns of social and personal interaction that have proven durable across time. The norms and practices that constitute ritualized life must be understood and mastered before variations are entertained, since they underpin mutual intelligibility among people, and are one foundation for the Confucian ideal of social harmony. Perhaps the strongest argument for this would not take a liberal individualist form, but would focus on the value of a shared social life, one comprised of a rich web of social meanings and shared pleasure, which might offset the costs of surrendering a more thorough-going individualism.

Modern Developments of Confucian Ritual

The idea that ritual plays a foundational role in the good society and the good life has led some modern thinkers back to Confucian ritual. Much has been written, for example, about how ritual practice helps with bereavement (Foust 2009; Olberding 2011; Chen 2012), since ritual allows people to structure and express grief in psychological helpful ways.

One influential construal of the significance of ritual viewed the mastery of it as a form of benign social power. While ritual has been neglected by Western philosophers, Confucius' great insight was recognizing the extent to which human conduct is structured by ritual, broadly construed as "the entire body of the mores, or more precisely . . . the authentic tradition and reasonable conventions of society" (Fingarette 1972: 7). Mastery of ritualized customs, norms and conventions was the basis for a person's effectiveness or potency (*de* 德) in the social world, and brought with it a "magical" power to induce the appropriate response in others. Such ritual mastery also gave expression to and brought to completion an important dimension of human nature. At its apex, ritual was central to a vision of the good society as an extended "sacred ceremony," participation in which constitutes a profound form of human fulfillment.

Another contemporary extrapolation of Confucian thought is the claim that the value of ritual lies in its creation of imaginary role-playing situations, described as "as if" or fictive worlds. This approach has roots in accounts of early Chinese ancestor worship, when a person—often a son—would play the role of the deceased in order to communicate with the living who performed the ancestral rite. In the contemporary context, the thought is that ritual engagement enables people to temporarily inhabit a different role or identity. Such 'pretending' enables participants to thereby gain greater insight into their enduring conventional and everyday roles and relationships, and make improvements accordingly (Puett 2008; 2016).

As opportunities increase for engagement between Chinese philosophy and the fields of sociology and anthropology, we might expect further insight into the Confucian commitment to ritualized forms of life.

References

Chen, B. 2012. "Coping with Death and Loss: Confucian Perspectives and the Use of Rituals." *Pastoral Psychology*, 61: 1037–1049.
Fingarette, H. 1972. *Confucius: The Secular as Sacred*. New York: Harper & Row.
Fingarette, H. 1983. "The Music of Humanity in the Conversations of Confucius." *Journal of Chinese Philosophy*, 10 (4), 331–356.
Foust, M. 2009. "Grief and Mourning in Confucius's Analects." *Journal of Chinese Philosophy*, 36 (2): 348–358.
Hall, D. L., and R. T. Ames. 1984. Getting It Right: On Saving Confucius from the Confucians." *Philosophy East and West*, 34 (1): 3–23.
Li, Chenyang. 2007. "Li as Cultural Grammar: On the Relation between Li and Ren in Confucius' 'Analects.'" *Philosophy East and West*, 57 (3): 311–329.
Nylan, M. 2001. "On the Politics of Pleasure." *Asia Major*, 14(1): 73–124.
Olberding, A. 2011. "I Know Not 'Seems': Grief for Parents in the *Analects*." In Amy Olberding and Philip J. Ivanhoe (eds.), *Mortality in Traditional Chinese Thought*. Albany: State University of New York Press, 153–176.
Puett. M. 2008. "Ritual and the Subjunctive." In Adam B. Seligman, Robert P. Weller, Michael J. Puett, and Bennett Simon (eds.), *Ritual and Its Consequences: An Essay on the Limits of Sincerity*. New York: Oxford University Press, 17–42.
Puett, M. 2016. *The Path: What Chinese Philosophers Can Teach Us About the Good Life*. New York: Simon & Schuster.

Filial Conduct (*Xiao* 孝)
Chapter 5.3

Xiao (孝) or filial conduct has been variously translated as filiality, family reverence, filial duty and filial piety. In general terms, filial conduct is a respectful or obliging attitude towards family and kin, which is most pronounced in the parent-child relationship. This is a lifelong relationship, not confined only to childhood. In so far as the filial subject is deeply concerned with family and kin relationships, *xiao* is suggestive of a social conception of self.

Key Features of *Xiao*

Xiao can be characterized in several ways. These include deference towards elders, awareness of how actions affect others, honoring the family name, reverence or deep feeling towards family, and intergenerational reverence. The character *xiao* first appears on bronze vessels in the later part of Shang Dynasty (1600 to 1050 BCE) or early Zhou Dynasty (1046–256 BCE). It features an old man above and being supported by a child, and signified sacrifices towards the deceased, whether fathers, relatives or an ancestral lineage (Holzman 1998; Hsiao 1978). *Xiao* likely initially expressed piety towards ancestors or deceased relatives.

The importance of the bond between children and parents in classical Confucian thought is expressed in various ways. A starting point is the traditional belief that the physical body is inherited from forebearers, and is to be returned intact. Amputation and branding were particularly shameful punishments in early China because they meant defilement of the inherited body. The *Analects* is replete with guidance for the relationship between parents and children, as well as the younger and elders within the community. This includes the demand to know the age of one's parents (*Analects* 4.21)—something which is a source of joy but also a source of concern as the years advance. Conversely, the texts also explain *xiao* by describing 'unfilial' forms of behavior (*Mencius* 4B30). These include an overly narrow focus on one's wife and children, indulging in sensual desires, and being quarrelsome and contentious—all of which can lead to the neglect of parents. The importance of filial piety at this time is further confirmed by the fact that even the Mohists—contemporary critics of classic Confucian values who promoted broad and impartial concern for others—did not reject it, but viewed it as a developmental step toward a more inclusive concern for others.

The care or concern for parents is elevated beyond the merely dutiful or practical by a closely related quality: reverence or respect (*jing* 敬). The *Analects* notes "Those today who are filial are considered so because they are able to provide for their parents. But even dogs and horses are given that much care. If you do not respect your parents, what is the difference?" (2.7) In short, *xiao* is a relationship marked by depth of feeling, such that demeanor is visibly affected, and a seriousness sometimes described as a family-centered religiosity. The demand for reverence complements another feature of Confucian moral psychology, namely a sensitivity to shame, and care not to bring disgrace to parents (*Analects* 11.5, 13.20). Such sensitivities ensure the appropriate parental funeral arrangements, mourning and then sacrifices to the departed.

The Political Dimension of *Xiao*

Xiao also shapes the understanding of the self in a political context, since it links the Confucian prioritizing of family with broader social and political responsibilities. Filial conduct frequently involves a demand for obedience, which begins in the family but expands with the extension of social roles and relations. The scope of this demand is disputed among contemporary scholars but, at a minimum, obedience requires the avoidance of conflict with parents. The *Analects* advises against acting contrary to parents' wishes (2.5), and endorses preserving a father's ways for three years after his death (1.11).

The social and political overtures of *xiao* also appear in its associations with the Confucian virtues of loyalty (*zhong* 忠) and fraternal deference (*di* 弟). Filial piety is a personal quality seemingly instrumental to social order and the absence of social disorder, the classic expression of which is *Analects* 1.2:

> It is a rare thing for someone who has a sense of filial piety (*xiao*) and fraternal deference (*di*) to have a taste for defying authority. And it is unheard of for those who have no taste for defying authority to be keen on initiating rebellion. Exemplary persons (junzi) concentrate their efforts on the root, for the root having taken hold, the way (*dao*) will grow therefrom. As for filial piety and fraternal deference, these are the root of humaneness (*ren* 仁).

The idea of an ordered state based on, and even analogous to, an ordered family became a powerful theme in later Confucian literature. According to the *Great Learning* (*Daxue*), to properly govern the state, it is necessary to first regulate the family, with social order radiating outwards from it. In addition, the ruler learns about rulership from within the family, while the sovereign should also be served with filial reverence and elders treated with fraternal deference.

From the later Han dynasty onwards, *xiao* is elevated as a value, such that there was some debate about whether it or *ren* (humaneness) was the more fundamental Confucian ideal. In the Han dynasty, the Confucian *Classic of Filial Piety* (*Xiaojing*), further codified the social and political importance of *xiao*. A person filial towards parents would be loyal to rulers, while learning deference to elder siblings led to obedience to superiors in official positions. The various accounts of filial devotion to parents popular from the Han onwards have led some commentators to compare the effects of *xiao* to those of religion in the Abrahamic tradition, especially the devotional zeal of Christian saints (Holzman 1998: 198).

Critics of filial piety see in it the roots of a troubling complicity and oppressive hierarchy. The *Analects* (13.18) discusses the case of a father stealing a sheep, and the son's appropriate response to such apparent wrongdoing. Confucius declares that being true or "upright" means "a father covers for his son and a son covers for the father," and some scholars take this as evidence that Confucian thought lacks a robust notion of impartial public interest. The moral hazards of filial devotion are also apparent from other schools of early Chinese thought. In the Daoist text, the *Zhuangzi*, merely consenting to everything parents do or say was flattery and unworthy of the virtuous, while the legalist text, the *Han Feizi* seeks explicitly to use obedience and devotion as a model for social control: the naturalness of the parent-child relationship is claimed for the ruler-subject relation, establishing the ruler as father to obedient children. This linkage of filial conduct and political authority was a target for China's reformers during the final years of the imperial dynastic system in the early twentieth century.

Defending *Xiao* as a Virtue

Whether or not filial devotion leads to a troubling political submissiveness and facilitates despotism and cronyism is disputed, however. Arguably, understanding of filial conduct in later history can be distinguished from the idealized ethical vision presented in the early texts, much as the variegated social history of Christianity can be separated form the moral prescriptions of the bible.

Being filial does not equate to mere compliance, since other values also guide the close but hierarchical relations central to Confucian familism and societal relations in general. One mode of conduct integral to filial conduct is remonstrance (*jian* 諫) (*Analects* 4.18, 19.10; *Mencius* 5A9, 5B9); when parents act badly, children should speak up. Indeed, several texts (*Xunzi*, the *Classic of Filial Piety*) are explicit that mere obedience is not sufficient for filial piety. A son is not filial if he simply follows the orders of a father, rather than considering the rationale behind those orders. Similarly, hierarchical Confucian relations are not based on power and domination but attention to reciprocal roles and responsibilities. Those in higher positions have a duty to consider the interests of the younger or more junior party.

In fact, the early texts hint at the nuanced moral psychology of *xiao*. Remonstrance can correct unwise parental decisions, but is conducted within limits; mutual demands for goodness diminish affection (*Mencius* 4A18, 4B30). Fathers do not typically instruct sons because attempts at correction and guidance can lead to resentment and estrangement. Similarly, not to feel and express resentment (*yuan* 怨) towards close relatives in cases of serious wrongdoing is a failure of intimacy and potentially unfilial (*Mencius* 6B3), while deference to outstanding personal character can trump obligations to kin (*Mencius* 5A4).

At the same time, some forms of hierarchy and de facto inequality, as well as differences in knowledge and experience—all of which might require deference and interactions that prima facie violate abstract notions of moral or personal equality— are regarded as instrumental to personal growth and the social good rather than regarded as oppressive or diminishing social and political agency.

A further reason not to construe *xiao* reductively, in terms of obedience and submission, is its connection to the central Confucian value of self-examination and moral vigilance. The mature Confucian person prizes reflection and self-awareness: "the exemplary person (*junzi*) seeks it in himself, the petty person seeks it others' (*Analects* 15.21); 'to fail oneself but attribute it to others—is this not devious!" (*Mencius* 4A4). A similar sense of personal responsibility is tied to filial conduct. The *Mencius* (4A20) notes that guarding over oneself is necessary to properly serve parents. Thus, *xiao* is closely tied to personal cultivation, and is a prerequisite for ethical social interaction with others, including parents, elders and those in positions of authority.

Intergenerational Transmission and Reverence

One final aspect of *xiao* underlines its social and ethical significance and addresses concerns about oppressive hierarchies. *Xiao* also expresses the importance of intergenerational transmission within a cultural tradition, nominally originating with the Zhou Dynasty that Confucius consistently praised. The *Doctrine of the Mean* defines *xiao* as: "being good at continuing the purposes of one's predecessors and at maintaining their ways." This echoes the *Analects*' twice-repeated call (1.11, 4.20) not to change a late father's ways for three years, arguably to better understand earlier generations. *Xiao* thus locates the human subject within a chain of beings that extends from the past into the future, with a person understood as one link in this extensive network of relationships and historical sensibilities. In classical Confucian thought, awareness of and due respect towards ancestors is an important moral sensibility.

Xiao intimates a provisional if defeasible deference among each generation to those who came before. Some commentators here identify a connection, both lexical and conceptual, between education (*jiao* 教) and filial conduct (*xiao* 孝). Being filial involves learning and absorbing. The texts often use accounts of historical figures and cultural heroes to convey the transformative power of education (e.g. *Doctrine of the Mean* 15-19).

Such intergenerational sensitivity has implications for personal identity. Rather than understanding a person as a discrete individual, driven to express private and inner forces in the style of J.S. Mill, a person is responsible for the reception of culture and values from previous generations, and the transmission of these—with appropriate modifications—to future generations. The content of social roles and relationships are similarly subject to intergenerational transmission. This is why one of the early characters for the world also means 'generations' (*shi* 世). Similarly, personal identity is here linked to membership of a larger extended community, much as the body (*ti* 體) in Chinese thought includes the sense of being one element of a large corpus.

Accordingly, deference is not necessarily owed to particular individuals who are privileged by established social hierarchies, such as fathers or rulers; rather, deference is owed to the weight of a cultural tradition to which one belongs and which, ideally, is embodied in the particular figures to whom specific acts of deference are made.

Filial conduct is thus a complex idea, and it serves as a tie that binds successive generations to each other, and facilitates an outlook in which kin and ancestors bear heavily upon emotion and conduct.

References

Holzman, D. 1998. "The Place of Filial Piety in Ancient China." *Journal of the American Oriental Society*, 118 (2): 185–199.

Hsiao, H. 1978. "A Preliminary Interpretation of the Origin of the Concept of *Hsiao* [*Xiao*] in the Shang Period." *Chinese Culture*, 19 (3): 5–20.

6

Tshivenda, Self, and Persistence

Mutshidzi Maraganedzha

Chapter Outline	
Introduction	159
Nature of Personhood in African Philosophy	161
Self and Persistence in the Tshivenda Culture	166
The Concept of Personhood in Venda Culture	168
Quasi-physicalism in Akan Thought	169
Conclusion	172
6.1 *Murunzi*	176
6.2 *Sialala*	179

Introduction

The question of personhood in African philosophy has been contentious for over four decades. In African philosophy, a question that was central to personhood is how community constitutes personhood. Ifeanyi Menkiti is a forerunner of the thinkers who have theorized about the concept of personhood in African philosophy. In his works like "Person and Community in Traditional African Thought" published in 1984 and "Person and Community—A Retrospective Statement" published in 2018. In both these installments, Menkiti contends that the community substantially informs personhood in African philosophy. This view creates a precedent that construes several misconceptions about the conception of personhood in African philosophy. Didier Kaphagawani,[1] on personhood, argues that there are three theses that expound the concept of personhood. Kaphagawani's project concentrates, "on the analysis of some conceptions of person propounded by philosophers in African philosophy, particularly those proffered as employing evidence from ... [sub-Saharan Africa]" (Kaphagawani 1998: 170). He identifies three thinkers as proponents of each of these theses. Placide Tempels's work on the Baluba's ontological system is identified as force thesis. Alexis Kagame's linguistic analysis of Kinyarwanda is identified as the shadow thesis, and John Mbiti's generalisation on African philosophy and religion is seen as the communalist thesis. Kaphagawani claims that he has limited his consideration to these three theses because they have a bearing on his Chewa culture; and Chewa language seems to have evidence both for and against these theses. Kaphagawani's analysis of the three theses is vital for understanding how personhood in African philosophy has been conceptualized in three theses. However, the analysis of the concept of personhood into three distinct theses is not universally accepted in the African philosophy canon. In light of this, Bernard Matolino (2016) states, in his reading of Kaphagawani's analysis of the concept of personhood, he only sees only two theses. One is normative and the other is ontological. In his words, Matolino states, "I seek to argue that there are two plausible ways of discussing the nature of personhood that generally best represent how the notion is understood on the continent" (ibid.).

In this chapter, after expounding the conceptions of personhood in African philosophy and its critics, I will point out that, contrary to popular belief, the concept of personhood in African philosophy is not exclusively normative. I argue that it must be noted that the concept admits to more than just a normative account of personhood. I object to the view that the African notion of personhood as only normative fosters a collective view in terms of the norms and encourages the *common good* (Menkiti 1984: 172). On this, Menkiti states that this is a state of a morally well-evolved human being, who by this estimation, is in harmony with both his species and the rest of nature; one who is in a social relationship with others and is promoting the common good. Thus, the conceptualization of personhood as a communal phenomenon that is acquired, "as one participates in communal life through the discharge of the various obligations defined by one's stations" is not wholly acceptable.[2] The idea that the community always takes precedence before the individual certainly diminishes the individual's autonomy and self-realization in the communitarian space. That said, this chapter will argue that the idea of personhood in the Venda culture admits to both normative and metaphysical notions of personhood. Simultaneously, this chapter will explore how the term *Murunzi*[3] embodies both normative and metaphysical significance in the communitarian space, where community and individual identities intersect. In this context, *Murunzi* serves as a lens through which to examine the complex relationships between community and personhood, shedding light on the rich and dynamic nature of Venda personhood.

Nature of Personhood in African Philosophy

I will open by alluding to the idea that there are two[4] possible ways of talking about the notion of personhood in African philosophy. Before we dive into the two possible approaches to understanding the concept of personhood, it is essential to explore the various categories that help define personhood in African philosophy. The concept of personhood invokes different interpretations and meanings from person to person and culture to culture. The sentiment of the previous statement is also captured in Kaphaganwani's analysis of the notion of personhood in African philosophy. The concept of personhood invokes different interpretations and meanings from person to person and culture to culture. As Kaphagawani's analysis of personhood in African philosophy aptly puts it, the meaning of personhood is far from uniform. Kaphagawani's analysis of personhood is insightful into how personhood is viewed in African philosophy. Although it is based on his Chiwa cultural outlook, it can be extended to African philosophy as a whole. In what follows, let us consider Kaphagawani's analysis of personhood to find out how he envisages the concept of personhood.

Kaphagawani proposes that there are three key theses that explain the concept of personhood. In his project, he aims to analyze certain conceptions of personhood presented by African philosophers, focusing on those that draw evidence from Central and Southern African cultures (Kaphagawani 1998: 170). Placide Tempels' work on the Baluba's ontological system is known as the force thesis. As Kaphagawani notes, Tempels was driven by a passion to uncover the Bantu difference. For Tempels, this difference lay in the Bantu notion of being. This led him to his famous characterization of Bantu reality in terms of force. His widely known conclusion states: "Force is not for them an accidental reality. Force is more than a necessary attribute of beings: Force is the nature of being, force is being, being is force" (Tempels 1959: 35). Kaphagawani presents a four-pronged critique of Tempels' argument for the prominence of force in his Bantu ontology. First, Kaphagawani argues that the thesis raises a question: since being is defined in terms of force, what does force mean in Bantu languages and thought? (1998: 171). Additionally, Tempels fails to provide a translation of the word in the Luba language, and the Chewa language lacks a word to match Tempels' use of force. Second, Kaphagawani argues that Tempels' use of the phrase "to die indeed" as an example of complete loss of force is a literal translation that lacks meaning. Third, Tempels' attempt to distinguish between human and person fails, as humans also possess the key qualities of persons, namely intelligence and will. Lastly, Tempels resorts to the Western distinction between humans and other entities, as his vital force relies on intelligence for its difference.

In light of the above, Matolino (2016: 8) suggests that a crucial issue worth noting is the shift from the concept of force to the term "the living *muntu*." He believes this transition is significant and should not be seen as a random change or mere swap of words. He thinks it is a deliberate statement about what it means to be a person among the Bantu. Tempels highlights that being a person is not just about having force, but about bringing that force to life. And the only way to bring it to life is through the relationships one has with their community. These relationships are where matters of personhood arise. The importance of these relationships stems from the metaphysical reality that the community has in an individual's sense of self. An individual has no other understanding of their identity and existence beyond being a communal person. This means the individual is under a strict metaphysical obligation to be in relationships with their surroundings to realize their personhood. At the heart of these relationships are the observance of communal rules and the attainment of moral worth, which transform one into a person. Tempels makes it clear that one's stature is determined by whether they have a role to play in the community or not (Tempels 1959: 67). Whether one has a role to play in society depends on the achievements one registers in relating to others. If one is successful and recognized as conducting themselves responsibly, they are considered to have an important role to play. Tempels (ibid.) notes that the Baluba categorizes personhood into those who have an important role (*muntu mukulumpe*), those of middling importance (*muntu mutupu*), and those who behave unworthily (*ke muntu po*). This distinction is based on the quality of relationships one has with one's fellow clan members. Dzobo supports this view, writing: "The person who has achieved a creative personality and productive life and is able to maintain a productive relationship with others is said to "have become a person" (*Ezu ame-Ewe; Oye onipa pa.-Akan*)" (Dzobo 1992: 131).

The second thesis, as outlined by Kaphagawani, is about communalism. While Kaphagawani's identification of this thesis and many of its associated claims align with his, some differences arise when it comes to its origins. Kaphagawani believes Tempels originated this thesis, but Mbiti popularized it. Although Mbiti indeed contributed to its widespread recognition, his version focuses on aspects of communalism that differ from Tempels' original idea. Mbiti's interpretation emphasizes how individual and communal fates are interconnected, as seen in his famous statement: "Whatever happens to the individual happens to the whole group, and whatever happens to the whole group happens to the individual. The individual can only say: 'I am because we are; and since we are, therefore I am.' This is a cardinal point of in the understanding of the African view of man [*sic*]" (Mbiti 1970: 141). This formulation highlights the reciprocal relationship between personal identity and community, central to the African view of personhood. Kaphagawani critiques this communalist perspective by questioning the validity of Mbiti's analogy with the Cartesian cogito. He argues that while a suppressed premise can make Descartes' argument valid, the same cannot be said for Mbiti's assertion. Moreover, Kaphagawani contends that this view risks undermining individuality by overemphasizing community. He asserts that acknowledging communality does not mean denying individuality; instead, it is crucial to balance these dimensions without favoring one over the other. Kaphagawani also critiques the epistemological superiority often attributed to elders within such frameworks. While elders may have greater epistemological authority due to experience, this does not imply an ontological distinction between elders and younger members of society. Additionally, he highlights that the elders' knowledge can become outdated due to changing circumstances, challenging the overemphasis on their epistemic primacy. This analysis emphasizes the need for a nuanced understanding of communalism that respects both communal and individual aspects of personhood.

The first two theses, as identified by Kaphagawani, lack the distinctiveness they claim to have, as they both fundamentally stress communal aspects of personhood. This overlap stems from Tempels' deliberate emphasis on relationality within his concept of individual force. According to Tempels, an individual is defined by their relationships—with God, the community, nature, or objects—and it is through these relationships that personhood is achieved. These relationships give an individual's force the status of personhood, highlighting the communal basis of his thesis. To further illustrate the communitarian nature of Tempels' position, one could outline the key features of any communitarian concept of personhood and evaluate how well Tempels' ideas align with these features. At the heart of communitarianism lies the prioritization of community in shaping individual identity. This often involves the community taking precedence over the individual, particularly in ethical expectations, where harmonious and productive relations with others define the individual's moral worth and, consequently, personhood. This line of thought aligns with Menkiti's assertion that personhood grows with the individual's mastery of normative responsibilities, which, when successfully fulfilled, render the individual "more of a person."

Another key aspect of communitarianism is the recognition of varying degrees of personhood, reflecting differences in individuals' moral standings. Personhood is thus dynamic and contingent, subject to the individual's adherence to normative processes. Communitarians acknowledge that not all individuals reach the highest state of moral development and personhood, underscoring the gradational nature of this concept. Tempels' thesis strongly resonates with these communitarian principles, emphasizing relationality and moral growth. While debates persist about whether his interpretation accurately represents African philosophical views on personhood, his thesis undoubtedly embodies communitarian sentiments. Kaphagawani (1998: 172) also supports this perspective, when he suggested that the communalist thesis has its roots in Tempels, although it has been elaborated and popularized by subsequent thinkers like John Mbiti, Ifeanyi Menkiti, and Kwame Gyekye. These later interpretations build upon Tempels' relational account, further developing the African communitarian concept of personhood.

The third and final thesis identified by Kaphagawani is presented by Alexis Kagame. Kaphagawani clarifies that Kagame has presented the "shadow doctrine" (ibid., 174). He explains the basis for understanding this thesis as a shadow thesis. According to Kaphagawani, Kagame believes that a human being is both a complete animal and an intelligent being. Humans are seen as complete because they possess a shadow, which is a vital principle of animality. Moreover, humans have intelligence because they are animated by a second vital principle, which is immortal. This second principle is where intelligent operations reside (ibid.). The faculty of intelligence allows humans to reflect, meditate, and compare past knowledge to create new ideas. Without this faculty, such a process would be impossible.

Another key feature that sets humans apart from animals is the possession of a heart. In many cultures, the heart is seen as equivalent to the will, and it integrates the inner person. Its main role is to harmonize the workings of intelligence. What sets the human heart apart from an animal's, like a pig's, is that it can control complex thinking, which is beyond an animal's capabilities. Kaphagawani supports Kagame's view by pointing out that in most Bantu cultures, especially among the Chewa, the heart represents an individual's personality. This personality is what sets one person apart from others, and it is used to distinguish one person from all others. Kaphagawani concludes that Kagame's analysis is correct, as it aligns with beliefs found in Central and Southern Africa. As he writes, "One advantage of Kagame's thesis, particularly regarding the significance of human personality, is that it moves towards resolving the problem of personal identity; for in Bantu languages and thought, an individual would be distinguished from another at least because of their personality and behaviour" (ibid.).

In other words, Kaphagawani's statement suggests that communitarianism is not the only way to understand personhood. Here, an individual's personality is unique and cannot be shared with their community. Instead, it sets them apart from the rest of the community. The community cannot share their personality, and they cannot participate in sharing others' personalities. Matolino (2016: 25) finds this point interesting for two reasons. First, if we consider personality to belong to the individual, then it defines them as distinct from social realities. We may also believe that personality is innate, as some people are born with certain traits, such as intemperance, and struggle to change them throughout their lives. Second, Kaphagawani views the communitarian notion as problematic, which is why he endorses Kagame's solution to address communitarianism's errors. According to Matolino (2016: 25), if we adopt Kaphagawani's terminology, focusing on personal identity, then communitarianism faces a problem: it fails to provide a coherent account of personhood. We could argue that the communitarian thesis neglects to address the core issue of identity.

The main point hinted at in the above paragraph is that there are two ways to interpret personhood in African philosophy, and the better approach is through two conceptions: normative and metaphysical. Polycarp Ikuenobe argues that there are only two conceptions of personhood in African philosophy, which he identifies as the metaphysical or descriptivist, and the normative. According to him, the normative conception is the most important. In his words, he states, "There are two plausible conceptions of personhood: metaphysical (descriptive) and normative. In the African view, the idea of a person has descriptive and normative dimensions" (Ikuenobe 2006: 51). Matolino concurs with the idea that there are two plausible ways to talk about personhood, but Matolino disagrees with Ikuenobe on two issues: naming the first category as descriptive and characterizing the second category as normative. Ikuenobe seems to get his cue from Kwasi Wiredu, who states that: "The Akan conception of a person has both descriptive and normative aspects that are directly relevant not only to the idea that there are human rights but also to the question of what those rights are" (Wiredu 1996: 157). Wiredu characterizes the relationship between these two concepts, saying, "Through the possession of an *okra*, *mogya*, and *sunsum*, a person is situated in a network of kinship relations that generate a system of rights and obligations" (ibid., 158). Here, we see a suggestion that kinship relations are important, and the so-called descriptive aspect enables a person to participate in the kinship system.

Wiredu explains the social structure of the Akan, showing how the matrilineal lineage extends into a clan and how the individual is expected to be a competent social being not only within the clan and lineage but also in the whole of humanity. "To the Akans, a human being is already social at conception, for the union of the blood principle and the personality principle defines a social identity" (ibid., 159). The reason a person is a social being beyond her clan is found in her possession of the *okra*, which is God's spark that links the individual with the rest of mankind. This possession creates obligations for the individual towards all of mankind. Ikuenobe contrasts the descriptive/metaphysical and communal notions, stating that: "By contrast, a descriptive or metaphysical conception of personhood seeks to analyze the ontological make-up of a person. It examines whether a person is material or immaterial, or whether a person is made up of one or two essential natures" (Ikuenobe 2006: 51). Like Wiredu, he emphasizes the importance of community in realizing personhood.

The problem with this account is its use of the word "descriptive" as an interchangeable category with metaphysics. Matolino thinks the use of the word descriptive and its interchange with metaphysics is misleading, leading thinkers to conclude that the communal is more important than the descriptive category. In philosophy, metaphysics is a more serious category than a mere exercise in describing entities. Metaphysics is concerned with the question of what entities exist and what nature of entities they are. Descriptivist accounts, on the other hand, do not investigate anything but merely narrate what is seen from a certain perspective. To say that one is a descriptive account and the other a metaphysical account is not to claim that both are engaged in the same exercise.

On the importance of community in the African understanding of personhood, Ikuenobe argues that, "The idea of community is also the logical and epistemic foundation of the normative conception of a person and the basis for a person's own view of self-identity and ways of doing things" (ibid., 53). Two important philosophical claims emerge from this understanding. The first claim is about logic and epistemology and how they relate to each other in arriving at this notion of personhood. The first claim seeks to rest communitarianism on logical grounds, providing philosophical cover for the notion from attacks or accusations of being illogical or violating fundamental laws of reasoning. The second claim is that this logical and epistemological notion of personhood extends to the domain of ethics. An individual who logically knows that her identity is communitarian either has to exhibit or ought to know that she must exhibit a moral outlook consistent with the communitarian ethic. Ikuenobe thinks this is the case because of the importance of community in all philosophical matters.

What this claim essentially amounts to is that all African reality, including philosophical truism, is grounded in the reality of the community. The community determines what reality is and what is to be perceived as important. All ideas and beliefs do not have any other origin besides the community. This means that anything that tends to exhibit non-communitarian features is regarded as false, as it is in contrast to communal reality. The communitarian notion is also invoked to show how traditional societies were structured, emphasizing principles of care and cooperation. This differs from being an ethic in that it becomes a sociological or economic description of how traditional societies were organized to cater for the material needs of all its members. It seeks to show that individualism was proscribed, and all social and economic activities by any individual always sought to find ways of promoting the good of all. From this realization, some thinkers—like Kenyatta (1979); Nkrumah (1963); Nyerere (1968b); and Senghor (1964)—have sought to extend this concept to the political realm by arguing for certain political philosophies that would be faithful to the traditional egalitarian tenet like that of African socialism.

Self and Persistence in the Tshivenda Culture

In the previous section, it has been articulated that the normative concept of personhood is not the only prevalent understanding to the question of what is a person in African philosophy. The answer to the question of what is a person in African philosophy occasions more than one response, as Kaphakawani has attempted to stipulate (even though that his stipulations are not entirely correct in Matolino's eyes). Some may be tempted to state that the question of what is a person in African philosophy can be accounted for in two distinct ways: one answer is the predominant one that of a normative, and the other is ontological. But the current section seeks to account to the question of self and persistence in the Tshivenda culture. Do the Venda people have any account to the question of a person and a person's persistence in their thought? This is a simple question has a simple answer, which is in the affirmative. Beyond that simple answer, I seek to offer a more complex way of unpacking the Venda thought around the question of personhood.

The idea of personhood from the Venda is not entirely difference from the Ngugi culture that it appeals to the famous aphorism "*Umunthu Ngumuthu ngabanthu*" (Molefe 2018: 352–367). In Motsamai Molefe's view that *ubuntu* and personhood is synonymous.[5] "*Muthu ndi muthu nga vhathu*," means a person is a person because of others. This aphorism forms a fundamental basis for how the Venda's conceive their being and how personhood is formulated. Being a person is different from being a human being. This should not necessarily be conceived as a state of confusion, as there is a clear differentiation based on the performance of an individual human to later attain personhood. But differently, we are all born as humans but over time we become persons.

The distinction to be understood about the Venda culture is that something fundamental seems to be doing the work in terms of accounting to the question of what is a person. Is *Murunzi*,[6] in the Venda culture, playing a role in the background accounting for the question of what is a person? *Murunzi* seems to have two properties about it, it is both normative and metaphysical in nature. This is visible when Venda makes this claim about a person, in most cases you will hear when they say "*Murunzi wa we utshe mutukhu*" This can be loosely translated to say "she/he is still young." In this context are they making a normative claim? I would certainly disagree with that observation; I can clearly contend that they are making a metaphysical claim about the individual person. In other instances, for example, you can hear them saying, "*Murunzi a u tsheho*," this can be translated to mean, "he is late, or he is dead." This then hints at the idea that *Murunzi* as a notion encapsulates "being" a person in the Venda ontology. From a philosophical point of view, what makes an entity to be is its true nature or being. In other words, philosophically, being is "that which is."

I hope my attempts are feasible, as it is impossible to define "being" in the strict sense a definition places the subject to be defined within the scope of a broader concept (its genus). But in order to define a being, one needs a more general concept within which being can be included; however, no such concept exists simply because "Being" encompasses all reality. Hence, instead of a strict definition, several descriptions of being has been given; being is "that which is," "that which exists," or "that which is real." In line with this line of thought, *Murunzi*—as a notion that encapsulate a person in the Venda culture—seems to form a central essence of the constituting a person in the

Venda culture. The sole reason for offering a cursory definition and understanding of the notion of *Murunzi* and its bearing on the essence of the person was motivated by the aim of the project. This section seeks to account for the question of what makes the same person over time. Put differently, is there anything that constitutes a person over time in the Venda culture? *Murunzi* is that characteristic that has the capacity to secure sameness over time. But not only does it have the capacity to secure sameness over time, but it also can be said to be the essence of a person.

The Concept of Personhood in Venda Culture

The philosophical ideas of any culture, including the Vendas, are deeply rooted in their language, beliefs, and practices. To delve deeper into the concept of personhood in Venda culture, examining their language, beliefs, and cultural practices is essential. The Venda language, for instance, offers valuable insights into their understanding of personhood. The expression *Murunzi*, which roughly translates to "shadow," holds significant normative and ontological implications. In Venda culture, *Murunzi* suggests that a human being consists of two distinct components: the physical body and the non-physical aspect, often associated with one's spirit. This belief is reminiscent of the ancient Greek concept of the soul, where the body and soul are seen as separate entities. Similarly, in Venda culture, the *Murunzi* is believed to be an integral part of a person's being, influencing their thoughts, actions, and destiny. The examination of the Venda language and beliefs provides a unique window into their understanding of personhood, highlighting the complexities and nuances of their philosophical ideas.

The concept of *Murunzi* is more multifaceted than a simple physical entity, contradicting the initial assumption that it refers solely to a dark shape on the ground. In the English language and culture, the term "shadow" is often perceived as a dark silhouette or outline that appears on the ground or a surface when something or someone blocks the light, such as a tree blocking sunlight or a person standing in front of a lamp.[7] However, in the Venda culture, the concept of "shadow" takes on a deeper, spiritual significance, encompassing a person's vitality, and through it, one can have ancestral connections. In this context, a person's *Murunzi* is believed to be their spiritual double, carrying their thoughts, emotions, and experiences. It is akin to a mirror reflection, but instead of reflecting physical appearance, it reveals one's inner self. This broader understanding of shadow challenges the Western notion of a shadow as a mere absence of light, instead presenting it as a complex, multidimensional entity that is intricately linked to a person's identity and being.

Quasi-physicalism in Akan Thought

The preceding position can be seen as a form of quasi-physicalism because it takes into account non-physical aspects of existence, such as spiritual, while still linking them to physical concepts. This is evident in the way *Murunzi* is portrayed in the preceding reflection on the concept of "shadow." Here, *Murunzi* is presented as a multifaceted entity that transcends the conventional physical understanding of a shadow. It incorporates spiritual, emotional, and ancestral dimensions, venturing beyond the physical boundaries of a shadow as a mere dark silhouette. This blending of the physical and non-physical realms resonates with quasi-physicalism, which acknowledges the existence of non-material aspects (spiritual or metaphysical) while maintaining a connection to the physical world (the shadow as a tangible phenomenon). The fusion of these realms embodies an integrated perspective on personhood, weaving together physical and non-physical aspects to form a cohesive and comprehensive whole.

Hasskei Mohammed Majeed is a suitable interlocutor for the position presented above. Although he does not directly address the question of Murunzi, in his work "A Critique of the Concept of Quasi-physicalism in Akan Philosophy" (2013), he attempts to show that the "*ōkra*" cannot be considered spiritual because it occupies a middle ground between the physical and spiritual realms, leaning towards the physical. Additionally, the "*ōkra*" is believed to accept offerings, can reveal itself to medicine men, and is accessed by them using physical or partially physical means. Finally, the "*ōkra*" is seen as a person's double. But Majeed's work critiques the quasi-physicalism position on understanding the concept of personhood in African philosophy.

Majeed, before his criticism of the Akan quasi-physicalism, laid out Kwasi Wiredu's quasi-physicalism. Wiredu makes reference to Hans Werner Debrunner's statement that the *ōkra* is a person's double, "conceived in his material image complete with a head, hands, legs, and all." But Debrunner's claim is a bit inaccurate. He seems to have been misled by the personal or rationalistic terms in which the *ōkra* is described to conclude that it has the same parts as the physical person. But this notion is completely absent in Akan language. It makes no sense to use phrases like "my *ōkra*'s leg," "my *ōkra*'s head"; or even say that "her *ōkra*'s chin is like this" or that "his *ōkra*'s hand has done that." Simply put, the *ōkra* has no such parts as claimed by Debrunner. It only makes sense to conceive of the *ōkra* as a person's double when it is interpreted as a spiritual aspect of an individual who has a particular physical shape. This is far from saying that the *ōkra* has that same shape. In cases where, as Wiredu suggests, the *ōkra* is "seen" by medicine men, there is still the question of whether the *ōkra* is "seen" in human form. While Wiredu seems to hold that this is the case, it is not quite clear whether the shape is the actual shape of the *ōkra* itself. Given the absence of expressions in the Akan idiom compartmentalizing the *ōkra*, it is not very likely whether Akan thinkers would consider any such shape, assuming the ōkra is indeed seen, to be its own shape. It is conceivable that it takes on the shape of the person it was known to inhabit just to identify its bearer easily.

In Majeed's view, Wiredu's quasi-physicalism is hindered by several challenges, primarily due to the intricate nature of personal identity, a concept that has puzzled philosophers for centuries. This complex idea poses a significant obstacle for anyone attempting to provide a comprehensive explanation of a person's identity, as it is akin to trying to grasp a handful of sand—the harder one squeezes, the more it slips through their fingers. To illustrate this, Wiredu's quasi-physicalism encounters its first obstacle when it acknowledges that certain entities, such as ōkra, do not conform to physical laws. This is problematic because quasi-physicalists regard physical laws as the ultimate authority on truth, much like a judge relies on evidence to make a verdict. In other words, if physical laws cannot fully explain ōkra, then the quasi-physicalist approach is incomplete, much like a puzzle with missing pieces. Furthermore, dualists, who propose the existence of both physical and spiritual realms, also face a dilemma. By admitting that the spiritual can be perceived physically, they create a conundrum: how can something non-physical be detected by physical means?

According to Majeed, "quasi-physicalist is a physicalist in disguise." Majeed claims that Wiredu's claim to allow for things that are not entirely subject to the laws of physics is misleading, much like a mirage in the desert that promises an oasis but delivers only sand. This claim initially seems as if it recognizes metaphysical realities that the Akan thinkers—like Wiredu and Kwame—see ōkra to fall within. However, in reality, what the quasi-physicalist means by something not being "entirely subject to the laws of science" is that it is something "which current laws of physics do not explain but might be proved by physics in future." There is every indication in the preceding quotation that the purported quasi-physical entities would not have been affirmed as real if they were not capable of becoming (known as) physical objects in future. So, given that all physicalists, quasi or not, already affirm the reality of physical objects, the quasi-physicalist becomes both today's physicalist and tomorrow's physicalist today. That is, he is a physicalist today who has the foresight of knowing what might become physical tomorrow, much like a farmer who plants seeds in anticipation of a harvest.

Majeed takes issue with quasi-physicalism, accusing its proponents of being "physicalists in disguise." However, this criticism oversimplifies the nuanced philosophical stance of quasi-physicalists. The core objective of quasi-physicalism is to develop a philosophical position that accommodates phenomena and entities that cannot be explained by strict physicalism. Moreover, it strives to provide a more inclusive understanding of reality by embracing not only entities within the physical realm but also those that transcend it. For instance, consider the concept of consciousness, which cannot be reduced to mere physical processes. Quasi-physicalists attempt to bridge the gap between the physical world and the unexplained phenomena that lie beyond. By acknowledging the complexities and ambiguities of reality, quasi-physicalism offers a more comprehensive approach to understanding the nature of existence. Majeed's dismissal of quasi-physicalism as disguised physicalism neglects the fundamental nuances that this philosophical stance seeks to address. It is essential to recognize the efforts of quasi-physicalists to reconcile the physical and non-physical aspects of reality, rather than being reductionists in their philosophical accounting for reality.

Let us delve deeper into Majeed's desert mirage analogy, examining its effectiveness in buttressing his case against quasi-physicalism. This analogy, where a traveller mistakenly perceives an oasis in the scorching desert, is meant to evoke a sense of dismissal toward quasi-physicalism. However, Majeed's comparison unfairly taints quasi-physicalism, insinuating that it is deceptive. But does quasi-physicalism truly deserve this label? A closer examination might reveal otherwise. Quasi-physicalism's primary objective is not to peddle false hopes about unexplained phenomena, but rather to remain open to future scientific breakthroughs that may shed light on these mysteries. This measured approach sets it apart from deceptive theories that make unfounded claims. In understanding quasi-physicalism's true nature, we can see that Majeed's analogy, in the case of the mirage, distorts reality, creating a misleading impression of this philosophical stance.

Majeed's critique rightly acknowledges that scientific inquiry often relies on future breakthroughs. However, it unfairly dismisses quasi-physicalism as speculative, failing to recognize that many scientific theories are temporary and subject to revision as new evidence emerges. quasi-physicalism is not merely a placeholder waiting for scientific validation, but rather a distinct approach that acknowledges the limitations of physicalist explanations and explores phenomena that fall beyond their scope. This distinction is crucial, as physicalism is often restricted to empirical evidence, whereas quasi-physicalism strives to integrate both physical and metaphysical dimensions into a cohesive philosophical position. By downplaying the philosophical potential of quasi-physicalism, as the criticism attempts, it will overlook how this perspective attempts to bridge current epistemological gaps and foster a more comprehensive understanding of reality. For example, quasi-physicalism might help reconcile the perceived disconnect between the natural world and human experiences, such as consciousness or spiritual encounters, which are often marginalized in purely physicalist accounts.

Now let us return to the considerations of the quasi-physicalism of *Murunzi*. The concept of *Murunzi* in Venda culture unfolds a captivating philosophical perspective on personhood, intricately weaving the physical and spiritual realms. Initially, *Murunzi*, translated as "shadow," may appear to refer to a purely physical phenomenon, a dark silhouette cast by the body when light is present. However, delving deeper, its profound normative and ontological significance comes to the fore. *Murunzi* encompasses more than the visible shadow; it embodies a profound, spiritual dimension of existence, connecting the individual to their inner self, ancestors, and broader metaphysical realities which represented the spiritual essence of an individual. This multifaceted understanding of *Murunzi* aligns closely with the philosophical stance of quasi-physicalism, which seeks to account for phenomena that straddle the boundaries of the physical and non-physical.

In Venda culture, *Murunzi* is understood as a dual aspect of personhood, comprising both the physical body and a non-physical, spiritual essence, much like the two sides of the same coin. This duality suggests that human existence cannot be reduced solely to material components, echoing the sentiments of Plato's mind–body dualism. *Murunzi* is not merely an absence of light or a physical outline; it is perceived as a spiritual double that mirrors an individual's inner self, reflecting thoughts, emotions, and experiences, forming an integral part of a person's identity and being. The *Murunzi* also serves as a vital link to ancestral connections, a role that further reinforces its spiritual significance. Through this lens, the *Murunzi* becomes a medium through which individuals interact with their ancestors, drawing guidance, protection, and a sense of belonging to the larger community, similar to the role of ancestors in many African cultures. This spiritual essence of *Murunzi* transcends the physical understanding of a shadow, embedding it within the metaphysical framework of Venda culture, where the fabric of reality is woven from both physical and spiritual threads. By examining the intricate complexities of *Murunzi*, we gain a deeper understanding of the Venda people's philosophical perspectives on personhood, highlighting the significance of considering both the physical and spiritual aspects of human existence.

So, all in all, it is evident that the Venda people's understanding of personhood goes beyond normative. The concept of *Murunzi*, upon closer examination, reveals a complex and multi-layered understanding of personhood that surpasses the surface-level questions of the normative considerations. Instead, it probes the fundamental aspects of human existence, merging the physical and metaphysical into an inseparable whole. By viewing personhood through the lens of *Murunzi*, the Venda perspective highlights that human existence cannot be reduced to mere normative considerations about actions, behaviour, or external communal judgments; it is deeply connected to the ontological aspects of being.

Conclusion

This chapter has critically examined the debate on personhood in African philosophy, focusing on the tension between normativist and ontological-oriented understandings. African normativists emphasize the importance of community norms in defining personhood, often prioritizing communal values over individual identity. However, this approach neglects the issue of self-persistence—how individuals maintain their identity and character over time. This chapter proposes an alternative framework that combines both communal and individual aspects of personhood by exploring the Venda cultural concept of *Murunzi*. The Venda perspective, with *Murunzi* at its core, provides a nuanced understanding of personhood that goes beyond the normative focus on communal obligations. Instead, it highlights the importance of an individual's ontological essence in sustaining self-persistence. This dual focus enriches African philosophical discourse by showing that personhood is not just a social achievement but also a deeply rooted ontological reality. The Venda worldview underscores the inseparability of the normative and ontological aspects of personhood through the lens of *Murunzi*. By exploring this concept further, it becomes clear that the Venda philosophy of personhood goes beyond normative considerations, delving into the ontological and existential questions of what it means to be human.

Notes

1. Kaphagawani (1998). It is worth noting that Didier Kaphagawani specifically is the only thinker in African philosophy who has explored African conceptions of personhood, focusing on the interplay between individuality and community. He critically engaged with the idea that African notions of the self are inherently relational, shaped by communal interactions and responsibilities.
2. Menkiti (1984: 176). I also expressed similar sentiments that personhood is attained through performance (Maraganedzha 2023).
3. The term *Murunzi* as a term used in Venda has both the normative and Metaphysical role in the ontology of the Venda. The term *Murunzi* is used in most cases to mean a shadow. But this is a direct translation that fails to capture the true meaning of the usage of the term when used (mostly) in the Venda language. I am certainly aware that the true essence of the meaning and nuances of the usage of terms in any language is more prevalent to those who are competent in the language. In this context, the usage of *Murunzi* means more than just a mere shadow, I specifically mean when it is used in conjunction with an individual. This is visible when Venda makes this claim about a person, in most cases you will hear when they say "*murunzi wa we utshe mutukhu*" This can be loosely translated to "she/he is still young."
4. There is no contestation over how personhood is categorized in African philosophy. Three thinkers and commentators on the debates in and around the concept of personhood concur that there are "two" broader categories of personhood in African philosophy. Ikuenobe's (2006) categorization of personhood into metaphysical and normative dimensions provides a comprehensive understanding of how individuals relate to themselves and their communities. This idea is also endorsed by Matolino (2016) and Molefe (2017). To further delineate this point, see Ikuenobe (2006), Molefe (2017), and Matolino (2016).

5. This view should not be taken as controversial as there is nothing entirely controversial about Molefe's view when he addresses the concept of *ubuntu* and personhood. In his opinion, expressed in his book, *African Philosophy of Personhood, Morality and Politics*, Molefe (2019) takes the talk of *ubuntu* to be the same as a talk of personhood. He is of the view that this is the case because at the heart of the idea of *ubuntu* is the idea of personhood. The idea of *ubuntu* is captured in terms of the maxim—a person is a *person* through other persons. The italicized word—person—refers to the normative idea of person salient in African philosophy. At the heart of *ubuntu* is the idea of a human being achieving personhood.
6. The term Murunzi as a term used in Venda has both the normative and Metaphysical role in the ontology of the Venda. The term Murunzi is used in most cases to mean a shadow. But this is a direct translation that fails to capture the true meaning of the usage of the term when used (mostly) in the Venda language. I am certainly aware that the true essence of the meaning and nuances of the usage of terms in any language is more prevalent to those who are competent in the language. In this context, the usage of Murunzi means more than just a mere shadow, I specifically mean when it is used in conjunction with an individual.
7. For instance, James George Frazer conveys a metaphysical understanding of the concept of a "shadow" when he describes how

> . . . we playfully chase the shadowy figure around newly cut lawns, trying to shake it off as it moves with us, stretches and shrinks, and then slips behind our back. Its ability to mimic us suggests that, as many cultures believe, it might be a mysterious and unfathomable part of ourselves, a magical extension of our soul. Despite our efforts, we know very little about this shape-shifting alter ego that avoids, yet is only visible in, bright sunlight. Its movements are not quite our own, and its intentions are beyond our understanding; it appears and disappears in ways we cannot always control. There is something unsettling about this vague and elusive being that follows us closely yet shrinks away when we try to touch it. (1929: 181–192)

Bibliography

Dzobo, N. K. 1992. "The Image of Man in Africa." In K. Wiredu and K. Gyekye (eds.), *Person and Community: Ghanaian Philosophical Studies I*. Washington, DC: Council for Research in Values and Philosophy, 123–135.

Frazer, James George. 1929. *The Golden Bough: A Study in Magic and Religion*. London: Macmillan.

Ikuenobe, Polycarp. 2006. "The Idea of Personhood in Chinua Achebe's Things Fall Apart." *Philosophia Africana*, 9: 117–131.

Kaphagawani, D. N. 1998. "African Conceptions of Personhood and Intellectual Identities." In P. H. Coetzee and A. P. J. Roux (eds.), *Philosophy from Africa: A Text with Readings*. Johannesburg: International Thomson Publishing Southern Africa (Pty) Ltd, 169–176.

Kenyatta, J. 1979. *Facing Mount Kenya: The Traditional Life of the Gikuyu*. London: Heinemann.

Majeed, Hasskei Mohammed. 2013. "A Critique of the Concept of Quasi-physicalism in Akan Philosophy." *African Studies Quarterly*, 14 (1–2): 23–33.

Maraganedzha, M. 2023. "'It' and Personhood in African Philosophy," *Arumaruka: Journal of Conversational Thinking*, 3 (1): 86–108.

Matolino, B. 2016. *Personhood in African Philosophy*. Pietermaritzburg: Cluster Publications.

Menkiti, Ifeanyi. 1979. "Person and Community in Traditional Thought." In Richard Wright (ed.), *African Philosophy: An Introduction*. 2nd ed. Lanham: University Press of America, 157–168.

Menkiti, I. A. 1984. "Person and Community in African Traditional Thought." In R. A. Wright (ed.), *African Philosophy: An Introduction*. Lanham: University Press of America, 171–181.

Menkiti, Ifeanyi. 2001. "Person and Community—A Retrospective Statement." *Filosofia Theoretica*, 7 (2): 162–167.

Molefe, M. 2017. "Individualism in African Moral Cultures." *Cultura*, 14 (2): 49–68.

Molefe, Motsamai. 2019. *African Philosophy of Personhood, Morality and Politics*. Cham: Palgrave Macmillan.

Nkrumah, K. 1963. *Africa Must Unite*. New York: Frederick A. Praeger.

Nkrumah, K. 1964. *Consciencism: Philosophy and Ideology for Decolonization and Development with Particular Reference to the African Revolution*. London: Heinemann.

Nyerere, J. K. 1968a. Uhuru na Ujama: *Freedom and Socialism: A Selection from Writings and Speeches*. Dar es Salaam: Oxford University Press.

Nyerere, J. K. 1968b. Ujamaa: *Essays On Socialism*. Dar es Salaam: Oxford University Press.

Senghor, L. S. 1964. *On African Socialism*. London: Paul Mall Press.

Wiredu, K. 1980. *Philosophy and an African Culture*. Cambridge: Cambridge University Press.

Murunzi
Chapter 6.1

The term *Murunzi* as a term used in Venda has both the normative and Metaphysical role in the ontology of the Venda. The term *Murunzi* is used in most cases to mean a shadow. But this is a direct translation that fails to capture the true meaning of the usage of the term when used (mostly) in the Venda language. I am certainly aware that the true essence of the meaning and nuances of the usage of terms in any language is more prevalent to those who are competent in the language. In this context, the usage of *Murunzi* means more than just a mere shadow, I specifically mean when it is used in conjunction with an individual. This is visible when Venda makes this claim about a person, in most cases you will hear when they say "*murunzi wa we utshe mutukhu*" This can be loosely translated to "she/he is still young."

In this context are the Venda making a normative claim? I would certainly disagree with that observation; I can clearly contend that they are making a metaphysical claim about the individual person. In other instances, for example, you can hear them saying "*murunzi a u tsheho*" this can be translated to mean "he is late, or he is dead." This then hints at the idea that *Murunzi* as a notion encapsulates 'being' a person in the Venda Ontology. From a philosophical point of view, what makes an entity to be what it is, is its true nature or being. In other words, philosophically, being is that which is. I hope my attempts are feasible, as it is impossible to define "being" in the strict sense a definition places the subject to be defined within the scope of a broader concept (its genus). But in order to define a being, one needs a more general concept within which being can be included; however, no such concept exists simply because encompasses all reality. Hence, instead of a strict definition, several descriptions of being has been given; being is 'that which is', 'that which exists', or 'that which is real'. In line with this line of thought, *Murunzi*—as a notion that encapsulate a person in the Venda culture—seems to form a central essence of the constituting a person in the Venda culture.

The sole reason for offering a cursory definition and understanding of the notion of *Murunzi* and its bearing on the essence of the person was motivated by the aim of the project. My primary chapter accounts for the question of what makes the same person over time. Put differently, is there anything that constitutes a person over time in the Venda culture? *Murunzi* is that characteristic that has the capacity to secure sameness over time. But not only does it have the capacity to secure sameness over time, but it also can be said to be the essence of a person.

In this entry, I will not be consumed by the normative aspects of a person as those aspects have been overly emphasized in the literature. In the literature the normative aspects of a person—in African literature—it has always been aligned with the moral theory of Ubuntu. I am certainly aware that Ubuntu is one of the core issues that formulates "being" in the Venda culture. But I wish to amplify the other metaphysical aspect of a person that is not well explored. As much as scholars have argued that the "self" can be meaningful by contributing to the well-being of others. In conclusion, as interesting as this might sound as it fosters the values of the community an individual person is also a person pushing the value of the common good.

Thevhula and Its Religious Connotation

Thevhula is conceived as the greatest sacrificial ritual that is performed by the Venda people. But one thing to note, although I have some serious reservations about this, it is conceived due to the reality that it is led by the royal family. It is not performed by commoners in public. It is performed secretively—or away from people's eyes—at the graves, where the ancestors lie buried. The whole group assembles, and a libation (*mpambo*) made of traditional beer (*mufhoho*) is poured out over the stone serving as a symbol of the departed ancestral spirits. The processes are done to inform the ancestors about a particular issue at hand, and in other instances for the person of worship.

The most criticized aspect of African rituals or even worship is the rituals performed for the living dead. Christians use their own term, worship, to define *Thevhula*. The translation is problematic as we do not know for sure how the words as meaning the same practice. This ritual or even similar ones has been recorded by academics as worshipping the ancestors (see Hammond-Tooke 1985 and Wanamaker 1997). Some scholars and other African sympathizers have argued that Africans do not worship ancestors, but they venerate them. The problem is that the word veneration is a synonym for worship. What is vital is that the living offer a service to ancestors in as much as the ancestors likewise offer a service to the living by protecting them from witches. The process is reciprocal. Ancestors are in the spiritual realm and therefore can offer a service to the living who are in the physical realm and therefore cannot operate in the spiritual realm. Ancestors then protect the living from spiritualities and bless the living. Similarly, the living dead cannot brew beer or slaughter for themselves in the physical realm. The living then offers a service to them by doing *Thevhula* in the physical sphere. The ritual is not performed by an ordinary person, it is performed by the traditional man (*maine*). Then *maine* will have to give a way forward with his bones.

Conclusion

Since time immemorial, *Thevhula* has been a ritual ceremony that the Venda people observed as ethnicity and within families. Now let us return to the reservation that I have alluded to above; I am of the view that *Thevhule* that just simply means shedding of blood cannot be reserved for the royal family only. As much as I do sympathize with the idea that it might be a useful word to describe the ceremony. But this word can easily be used even when other families are doing a similar ceremony. I am aware that those who are competent with the Venda language might disagree with my observations, but I am quite adamant about this reality.

References

Hammond-Tooke, W. David. 1985. "Who Worships Whom: Agnates and Ancestors among Nguni." *African Studies*, 44 (1): 47–64.

Wanamaker, Charles A. 1997. "Jesus the Ancestor: Reading the Story of Jesus from an African Christian Perspective." *Scriptura: Journal for Biblical, Theological and Contextual Hermeneutics*, 62: 281–298.

Sialala
Chapter 6.2

Sialala is simply captured as a way of life for the Venda people. In other words, *Sialala* is also conceived as a philosophy of life. *Sialala* refers to that which the Venda people have not lost over time even when civilization and globalization are interrupted. From this, what is visible is that there is an effect that had occurred on cultural and religious knowledge by colonialism and the persistence of globalization. Therefore, in several patches amongst the Venda people there are people who still practice (Venda) rituals—that gets to be implored and guided by the Venda cultural worldviews. In fact, in everyday life when one does things in accord with the traditional way, then it is said that such actions exhibit *Sialala*. This can be exhibited in the form of rituals, dressing, or even in the form of cultural music. The latter two in literature seem to take a bigger chunk. In other words, scholars who explore the Venda culture seem to be more interested in the unique dressing and Musical fibre of the Venda culture (Emberly 2013; Blacking 1971; 1973; 1995). In his, *How Musical is Man?*—this point is amplified when—John Blacking (1973: 6) contends that "Music plays a very important part in the life of the Venda of the Northern Transvaal, and even white settlers who suffer from the demented logic of readily admit that the Vendas are very musical people." This selective conception of the Venda people is questionable as it portrays a picture that their culture is more musically oriented.

Sialala is a normative Venda way of life. In a simple sense, *Sialala* is a continuously lived-out experience and practice of beliefs, customs, and culture. Similarly, any Venda-speaking person will endorse the sentiments that *Sialala* means a being, religio-cultural realities, worldviews/cosmology and etc. In other words, it is a life-lived experience through various rituals, observations, and behaviors that can be said to be tradition, culture, and religion.

The Venda people, unlike the majority of South Africans, originated in the Great Lakes region of Central Africa. They initially settled in the Soutpansberg Mountains. Venda culture is an unusual blend of several civilizations; it appears to have integrated elements of East African, Central African, Nguni, and Sotho traditions.[1] For example, the Venda people forbid pork consumption, a common prohibition along the East African coast. They also practice male circumcision, which is practiced by many Sotho but not by the majority of Nguni people. In the sixteenth century, the Venda language, TshiVenda or LuVenda, evolved as a unique dialect (Schoettler 1971).

Sialala and Muthu

The intersection of cultural values that I have alluded to above is also visible in the Venda conception of a person. According to Sialala "*Muthu ndi muthu nga vhathu*," which may be translated to mean, "a person is a person because of others." This aphorism forms a fundamental basis for how the Venda's conceive their being and how personhood is formulated. Being a person is different from being a human being. This should not necessarily be conceived as a state of confusion, as there is a clear differentiation based on the performance of an individual human to later attain personhood. But differently, we are all born as humans but over time we become persons. The African view of personhood conceives of it as some kind of moral achievement. To be called a person is to be morally recognized to be living a genuinely human life (Metz 2010). The moral agent achieves it relative to the quality of her performance. Menkiti (1984: 176) explains moral excellence or virtue that captures personhood in terms of "ethical maturity."

Sialala and, or as, "Religion"

Sialala—as captured above—ideally, everyday life must always be pleasing to the living and to the living dead. This is a way of life through actions, relationships, and words. It is this way of life that the Christian missionaries referred to as the African Traditional Religion (ATR) (Ushe 2018; Molefe 2022). African Traditional Religion refers to religious ideas, beliefs, and practices associated with indigenous people below the Sahara (Wiredu 1996). There is no word in the Venda culture that conceptually captures the meaning of religion, but the closest word is *Vhurereli*. *Urerela* can simply capture a form of worship that any other individual gets to engage in towards any deity. For purposes of simplification, I will refer to the practice of *Urerela* as religion loosely. It is worthwhile to note that ATR was invented by missionaries for Africans that had not yet converted to Christianity (Shaw, 1990). Rosalind Shaw (ibid., 341) has contended that "the term 'traditional' religions, adopted as a more positive and respectful relabelling of those religions categorized as 'primitive', emphasizes that such religions consist of that which is handed down from generation to generation as an integral part of life." I disagree with Shaw on the idea that the term traditional religion carries positive connotations. Right after her claim about the positive connotations of traditional religion, she argues that "it also, however, connotes that which is ancient, static, and pure, and thereby encourages an essentialist reading of these religious forms which denies them and their participants a history" (ibid., 341). A proper autopsy of the statement above would reveal that there is nothing positive about taking the African form of worship as "traditional," such a characterization of things creates a wrong impression about the African way of life. The term "traditional" is aligned with African worship, it denotes the lack of civilization. Christianity, Islam, Hinduism, Buddhism, and Confucianism (Yao 2000) are also traditional religions yet they have specific names and are not named as Traditional Religions. Due to the history of cultural imperialism and colonialism, it certainly carries serious offensive sentiments when referring to the way of life of the Africans and their experience as a "traditional religion." Then, therefore, it is warranted to use the notions of *sialala*, *vhurereli*, and *Urerela* as an appropriate way that captures the way the Vendas worship.

Conclusion

In the course of my explanatory task above, if *sialala* is a way of life and it has the properties of being a religion, then it would be warranted to speak the Vendas religion as *sialala*. Therefore, the Venda religion is *sialala*, not ATR.

Notes

1. These similarities are also expressed in the values that are shared amongst them, that is to say, Ubuntu and its values (Schoettler 1971).

References

Blacking, J. 1973. *How Musical is Man?* Washington, DC: University of Washington Press.
Blacking, J. 1971. "Deep and Surface Structures in Venda Music." In *Yearbook of the International Folk Music Council*. Vol. 3. Cambridge: Cambridge University Press, 91–108.
Blacking, J. 1995. *Music, Culture, and Experience: Selected Papers of John Blacking*. Chicago: University of Chicago Press.
Emberly, A. 2013. "Venda Children's Musical Culture in Limpopo, South Africa." In *The Oxford Handbook of Children's Musical Cultures*. Ed. Patricia Shehan Campbell and Trevor Wiggins. Oxford: Oxford University Press, 77–95.
Menkiti, I. A. 1984. "Person and Community in African Traditional Thought." In R. A. Wright (ed.), *African Philosophy: An Introduction*. Lanham: University Press of America, 171–181.
Molefe, Motsamai, and Mutshidzi Maraganedzha. 2022. "African Traditional Religion and Moral Philosophy." *Religious Studies*, 59 (2): 1–16.

Schoettler, G. S. 1971. "The Sotho, Shona, and Venda: A Study in Cultural Continuity." *African Historical Studies*, 4 (1): 1–18.

Ushe, Ushe Mike. 2018. "God, Divinities and Ancestors in African Traditional Religious Thought." In Ikechukwu Anthony Kanu, Ejikemeuwa J. O. Ndubisi, and Kanayo Nwadialor (eds.), *African Cultural Personalities in a World of Change: Monolithic Cultural Purity and the Emergence of New Values*. Bloomington: AuthorHouse, 298–340.

Shaw, Rosalind. 1990. "The Invention of 'African Traditional Religion.'" *Religion*, 20 (4): 339–353.

Wiredu, K. 1996. *Cultural Universals and Particulars: An African Perspective*. Bloomington: Indiana University Press.

Yao, Xinzhong, and Hsin-chung Yao. 2000. *An Introduction to Confucianism*. Cambridge: Cambridge University Press.

7

Embodying the Dao
Classical and Foundational Daoist Anthropological Views

Louis Komjathy

Chapter Outline

Comparative Reflections and Contextual Background	184
Informing Theological Views and Contemplative Practice	188
Daoist Contemplative Psychology	189
Primary Dimensions of Daoist Contemplative Psychology	195
Towards a Radical Daoist Anthropology and Beyond	197
7.1 Pneumatology	201
7.2 *Shēn* 身 (Body/Self)	205
7.3 Somatology	209

The present chapter examines classical and foundational Chinese Daoist anthropological views, with a specific emphasis on embodiment and psychology. It explores the "classical period" (*c.* 350–*c.* 90 BCE) of the Daoist tradition. This was the earliest Daoist religious community and the primary historical source-point of Daoism as an indigenous Chinese religious and cultural tradition. This period witnessed the emergence and development of some of the principal Daoist views of personhood, specifically as psychosomatic and energetic in nature. In the current contribution to our "Cross-Cultural Views of Self" project, I focus on indigenous Chinese Daoist concepts related to body/self, including *shēn* 身, *tǐ* 體, and *xíng* 形. I then move on to discuss what I refer to as "Daoist contemplative psychology," centering on *xīn* 心 (heart–mind) as the psychospiritual center of human personhood. This is a Daoist anthropological perspective informed by and informing contemplative practice-realization, with the ultimate goal of mystical embodiment of the Dao 道 (Tao/Way), the sacred and ultimate concern of Daoists. Here we rediscover the body-as-sacred.

Comparative Reflections and Contextual Background

What do we mean by "self"? What is the relationship between "self," "body," and "mind"? And what assumed view of personhood is employed in one's daily life and larger philosophical approach? We may begin with some potentially helpful comparative categories, which may assist in a cross-cultural investigation of human personhood. In my own work in Religious Studies, the interdisciplinary field dedicated to research and education on "religion, religions, and religious" (see, e.g., Smith 1998), I find the four categories listed below to be especially helpful. The asterisks indicate those advanced in my own work:[1]

> **Anthropology:** Discourse on, study of, and theories about personhood/self
> **Pneumatology*:** Discourse on, study of, and theories about *pneuma* ("breath/energy")
> **Psychology:** Discourse on, study of, and theories about *psychē* ("mind/soul/spirit")
> **Somatology*:** Discourse on, study of, and theories about the body and embodiment

Here we must emphasize that these are being used herein as *comparative categories*, in contrast to the social scientific disciplines and even professions of Anthropology and Psychology. As we will explore in the present chapter, each requires attention to culture-/tradition-specific technical terms like *pneuma* (Greek/Greece), *prāṇa* (Sanskrit/India), and *qì* 氣 (Chinese/China; Japanese: *ki*; Korean: *gi*) in the case of pneumatology. This is theory informed by exempla, and vice versa. It requires sophisticated knowledge of specific traditions as well as theory and method informed by and informing comparative and cross-cultural Religious Studies.

Along these lines, it may be helpful to consider some of the primary views of self. As developed in my own study, teaching, and thinking about personhood, especially with respect to dying, death, and associated funeral rites, there are five primary anthropologies:

> 1. Composite: a "self" comprised of disparate elements that usually separate upon death.

2. Docetic: Eternal/immortal soul, with post-mortem transcendence and survival as given.
3. Materialist: Biological organism destined to decompose. May include modern neurophysiological and digital views of identity.
4. Psychosomatic: Mind (soul)-body connection, integrity, and interdependence.
5. Spiritist: Transitory spirit (not soul), usually surviving for some (limited) duration after biological death.

As we will discover momentarily, classical and foundational Daoist views are primarily composite and psychosomatic, with some spiritist dimensions. Although apparently somewhat tangential to the present volume, one issue centers on the divinity/humanity/animality scale. How do views about human personhood relate to "non-human animals"? Do "non-human animals" have personhood?

Moving into the Daoist tradition, "classical Daoism" refers to the earliest moment in Daoist religious history, especially the late Warring States period to the middle of the Western Hàn dynasty (c. 350–c. 90 BCE).[2] "Classical Daoism" replaces the outdated and inaccurate construction of so-called "philosophical Daoism," which is rooted in colonialist, missionary, and Orientalist legacies. Use of so-called "philosophical Daoism" should be taken *ipso facto* as ignorance and misunderstanding concerning *the religious tradition which is Daoism*. Classical Daoism utilizes and develops traditional Chinese views of self as well as some distinctively Daoist approaches and perspectives. First, there is the question of the relationship between so-called "body" and so-called "mind." Daoism tends to be among the more body-affirming and world-affirming religious traditions with strong psychosomatic views. In the case of classical Daoism, I will later explain this view is better described as energetic. Here it is interesting that, like other classical Chinese movements and traditions, classical Daoism tends to give major attention to the "body" that Western readers associate with organic and physical existence. Along these lines, and perhaps surprisingly to some readers, there are three primary classical Chinese terms designating "body" (see Ames 1993; also Kohn 1991; Komjathy 2008, 2011, 2020a, 2023a):

shēn 身. Usually translated as "body/self." Probably a pictograph of the human physique. Used most frequently to refer to one's entire psychosomatic process. In passages where *shēn* as "person/self" refers to the physical body, it is one's "lived body" viewed from within rather than "body as corpse" viewed from without.

tǐ 體. Usually translated as "body." Related to "physical structure" said to be a "combination of twelve groups" or parts. Relates to the scalp, face, chin, shoulders, spine, abdomen, upper arms, lower arms, hands, thighs, legs, and feet.

xíng 形. Usually translated as "form" or "shape" (cf. *zhuàng* 狀). The three-dimensional disposition or configuration of the human process. Has a morphological rather than genetic or schematic nuance.

To these we may add *xiàng* 象 ("appearance") and *yán* 顏 ("countenance"; also *miàn* 面; *róng* 容), with both often indicating a given individual's physical features and qualities as perceived by others. The upshot of these preliminary points is not only that Chinese traditions have distinctive understandings of embodiment, including nuanced analysis expressed in specific Chinese characters that make for technical terms, but also that we need to be attentive to culture-specific and tradition-specific terms and views. These include the possibility that there is no such thing as "body," but rather different bodies/selves in different contexts and cultures. Although potentially beyond the confines of the present volume, we might, in turn, consider the full range of possibilities for embodiment, and thus of human being and becoming. In terms of *practice*, this includes a whole spectrum of training and activities such as exercise, martial arts, movement awareness, sports, and so forth.

The standard, traditional and thus foundational pre-modern Chinese anthropology centers on what is conventionally referred to as the so-called "two-soul model" (see Yü 1987; Komjathy 2013: 123–128). This centers on the *hún* 魂 and *pò* 魄, usually approximated in English as "ethereal soul" and "corporeal soul," respectively. As observant readers will note, both Chinese characters contain *guǐ* 鬼 (ghost), while *hún* also has *yún* 云 (cloud) and *pò* has *bái* 白 (white). Here "soul" (transcendent entity) is slightly problematic and misleading, as *guǐ*-ghost suggests an ephemeral apparition, and both are transitory in nature. *Hún* is thus better understood as the "*yang*-ghost," associated with heaven, and *pò* is better understood as the "yin-ghost," associated with earth. The *hún* is especially associated with dreaming, while the *pò* is especially associated with emotionality. In the standard Chinese account, upon physical death, the *hún* ascends into the celestial realms to become an ancestor (thus, cloud), while the *pò* descends into the earth to gradually dissipate with the flesh and bones (thus, white). Ancestors, thus the traditional importance of "ancestor veneration," are one's own direct biological and genealogical relatives, generally understood in terms of seven generations. Using our preceding comparative, interpretive framework, this is thus both a composite and spiritist model of human personhood. However, in the fully developed Chinese view, referred to as "correlative cosmology" and the "system of correspondences," there actually are five primary spiritual faculties, which are, in turn, located within the Five Phases (*wǔxíng* 五行; a.k.a. "Five Agents/Five Elements").

Table 7.1 The Five Phases with Associated Faculties

Associations	Wood	Fire	Earth	Metal	Water
Organ	Liver	Heart	Spleen	Lungs	Kidneys
Faculty	Ethereal Soul	Spirit	Thought	Corporeal Soul	Will
Sense Organ	Eyes	Tongue	Mouth	Nose	Ears
Tissue	Sinews	Vessels	Muscles	Sinews	Bones

Thus, human cognitive and psychological experience may be mapped according to these faculties, which we will explore more thoroughly below. For the moment, we may note the strong psychosomatic characteristics, including organ/faculty associations. One issue that emerges here, both within an indigenous context and from a comparative perspective, is the extent to which the faculties can function without the associated organ. For example, what happens to 'thought' if one does not have a spleen? What happens to 'will' if the kidneys are compromised? There are many other dimensions as well, but this provides a sufficient glimpse into the complexity and upshot. In terms of our current topic, it becomes clear that, at least theoretically, post-mortem continuation as *hún* must necessarily lack the other four faculties. So what type of awareness and presence does an ancestor have? Perhaps simply relational connection and influence.

Moving more deeply into classical Daoism, we find a strong composite view of self, centering on the universe as a transformative process (*huà* 化). This includes both the preceding *hún-pò* framework and a *qì*-based one, which we will explore in the next section. With respect to the former, the anonymous/pseudonymous *Zhuāngzǐ* 莊子 (*Chuāng-tzǔ*; *Book of Master Zhuang*; DZ 670; ZH 616; abbrev. ZZ), which contains historical and textual material dating from the fourth to second century BCE, explains,

> Human life between heaven and earth is like the passing of a white colt glimpsed through a crack in the wall—*whoosh!* and that's all. Overflowing, starting forth, there is nothing that does not come out; gliding away, slipping into silence, there is nothing that does not go back in. Having been transformed, one is alive; another transformation and one is dead. Living beings grieve over it, while humans mourn. But it is the untying of a heaven-lent bow-bag, the unloading of a heaven-lent satchel—disturbed, released, and the ethereal and corporeal souls are on their way, the body following after, on at last to the Great Return.
>
> (ZZ 22; adapted from Watson 1968: 240)

In addition to emphasizing dissolution and transformation, the reference to the "Great Return" (*dàguī* 大歸) is especially interesting. From a Daoist perspective, this is death as disappearance and return. Specifically, one returns to the sacred Source from which one emerged. Here we need to note that this is not some form of conscious post-mortem existence and survival; rather, one dissolves into the whole, with the latter including a cosmos that is understood as an impersonal, amoral process. This relates to what might be understood as "Daoist organicism," in which life is understood through a quasi-composting analogy:

> The seeds of things have mysterious workings (*jī* 機). In water they become Break Vine; on the edges of water, they become Frog's Robe. If they sprout on slopes, they become Hill Slippers. If Hill Slippers get rich soil, they turn into Crow's Feet. The roots of Crow's Feet turn into maggots and their leaves turn into butterflies…

Humans in time return again to the mysterious workings. So all beings come out of the mysterious workings and go back into it again.

(ZZ 18; adapted from Watson 1968: 195–196)

Composition, decomposition, recomposition. Thus, ultimately, we are part of a mutually enriching, interconnected and interrelated system. This is based on mutuality and reciprocity. The classical and foundational response is one of acceptance and attunement.

Informing Theological Views and Contemplative Practice

Before moving into Daoist contemplative psychology as such, specifically classical and foundational Daoist contemplative psychology, we need to familiarize ourselves with associated Daoist theological views and the associated Daoist contemplative practices. Here "theology" is again used in my publications as a comparative category referring to discourse on, study of, and theories about the "sacred," with the latter being another comparative category designating that which a given individual or community identifies as ultimately real. Daoism, as the "Tradition of the Dao," identifies the Dao as sacred; the Dao is the sacred and ultimate concern of Daoists, with the latter referring to adherents of the religious tradition which is Daoism. Pronounced something like *kə.lˤuʔ in Archaic/Old Chinese, *dào* 道 is, first and foremost, a Chinese character meaning something like "path" and "way." The Chinese character consists of *chuò* 辵/辶 (move/walk) and *shǒu* 首 ([human] head). It was adopted in classical Daoism as a theological category as "the Dao," the Way (reality) that encompasses all other lifeways (traditions). From a Daoist perspective, the Dao has four primary characteristics:

1. Source of everything (*yuán* 元/原)
2. Unnamable mystery (*xuán* 玄)
3. All-pervading sacred presence (*líng* 靈; also *qì* 氣)
4. Universe as transformative process (*huà* 化)

This is the cosmological and theological view informing Daoist contemplative practice and contemplative experience, and thus Daoist contemplative psychology by extension. From a comparative perspective, classical and foundational Daoist theology is apophatic, monistic, panentheistic, and panenhenic. Daoism is, in turn, one of the most world-affirming and body-affirming religious traditions. As we discovered in the opening section, it tends to be more strongly psychosomatic in terms of views of self.

Daoist contemplative psychology is informed by and informs Daoist contemplative practice. Among members of the inner cultivation lineages of classical Daoism, and as expressed in key classical Daoist texts like the *Lǎozǐ* 老子 (*Lǎo-tzǔ*; Book of Venerable Masters; a.k.a. *Dàodé jīng* 道德經 [*Tào-té chīng*; Scripture on the Dao and Inner Power]; DZ 664; ZH 553; abbrev. LZ) and above-mentioned *Book of Master Zhuang*, classical Daoists embraced and advocated apophatic and quietistic (emptiness-/stillness-based) meditation as their shared, assumed training regimen, almost to the point of quasi-orthopraxy.[3] The primary contemporaneous type of Daoist meditation, which is the earliest and becomes quasi-normative, basically involves sitting in silence. Here one issue centers on conceptions of silence (yes, conceptions of "silence"), which we will explore momentarily. For the moment, there are various classical Chinese Daoist technical terms used to designate the practice, which are instructive and provide important insights. The three most important and influential are probably *shǒuyī* 守一 (guarding the One), *xīnzhāi* 心齋 (fasting of the heart–mind), and *zuòwàng* 坐忘 (sitting-in-forgetfulness). These may be referred to as "Unified-Guarding," "Heart-Fasting," and "Seated-Forgetting" for short. The terms direct aspiring Daoist adepts to remain attentive, pure, and unconcerned. Here *yī* 一 refers to the sacred (One), the process (uniting), and the resultant experience (oneness/union). As we will discover, *xīn*-heart is understood as the psychospiritual center of human personhood, so here "fasting" refers to withholding sensory engagement and decreasing psychological habituation and reactivity. In addition to referring to the contemplative process, *wàng*-forgetting designates the resultant contemplative state (forgetfulness). In each and every case, one dissolves ordinary, apparently individual identity and disappears into the Dao. This is thus a "disappearance and return model" of contemplative practice. Classical Daoist apophatic and quietistic meditation is, in turn, contentless, non-conceptual, and non-dualistic. It utilizes what may be understood as "Daoist Quietism," which centers on *wúwéi* 無為 (non-action/effortlessness). One maintains open receptivity and abides in silence. Specifically, one trusts the Dao (*xìndào* 信道) as unfolding in/as/through one's own life. This relates to and clarifies one's fate (*mìng* 命), one's life-purpose and vocation. A radical consequence of such views is that human being, specifically human embodied and lived experience, is trustworthy. From a classical and foundational perspective, when rooted in clarity and stillness, when connected to the Dao-as-Source, one feels a greater sense of aliveness and purpose. There is a larger context and support for one's life.

Daoist Contemplative Psychology

Drawing upon the previous points about psychology as a comparative category related to consciousness and mind in a broad sense, "contemplative psychology" refers to psychological views informed by and informing contemplative practice and contemplative experience (see de Wit 1991; Komjathy 2015, 2018). Here we need to note that such psychological views tend to be period- and movement-specific, so we will focus on classical and foundational Daoist ones.

To begin, Daoist contemplative psychology, and thus Daoist anthropological views, identify the heart–mind (*xīn* 心) as the psychospiritual center of human personhood. Along these lines, the heart–mind often is referred to as the "center" (*zhōng* 中), with another technical term for classical Daoist apophatic meditation being *shǒuzhōng* 守中 (guarding the Center). Originally depicting the actual, physical heart (心), *xīn* may refer to the physical organ (*xīn* as heart) and to consciousness in a more abstract sense (*xīn* as mind). Thus, "heart–mind" is the most technically accurate translation, especially before the increasing influence of Buddhism on Daoism from around the fifth to the sixth centuries CE. Recalling the previous points about Chinese correlative cosmology centering on the Five Phases, some additional dimensions need to be kept in mind as we continue our current inquiry. Although possibly only nascent in classical Daoism, the heart–mind is the viscera (*zàng* 藏/臟; also "storehouse" and "yin-orb") associated with the Fire phase. From this traditional Chinese and thus Daoist perspective, it is psychosomatic in nature and part of a larger psychobiological network. Recall that it also is associated with spirit, the tongue, and the vessels. This partially explains the traditional Daoist practice of keeping the tip of the tongue touching the upper palate, which helps to settle the heart and stabilize spirit. Along these lines, utilizing a microcosmic view of the body as the country, the heart is often identified as the "ruler," with the other primary viscera (liver, spleen, lungs, kidneys) being "ministers." Thus, "heart" includes the entire spectrum of emotional and intellectual activity. Here we may note that all of the various associated Chinese characters include the *xīn* 心/忄 radical. These include *niàn* 念 (thought; also, memory), *qíng* 情 (emotions/feelings; also, disposition), *xiǎng* 想 (thought), *yì* 意 (thought; also, awareness and intention), *yù* 慾 (also 欲; desire), and *zhì* 志 (will; also, aspiration). This is not to mention the specific, assorted emotions, often identified as potential sources of disorientation, distraction, and dissipation in classical Daoist practice. Recall also that, in the fully developed system of correspondences, *yì*-thought is associated with Earth/spleen, while *zhì*-will is associated with Water/kidneys.

The inner cultivation lineages of classical Daoism developed their own unique conception and application of *xīn*-centered contemplative psychology. Interestingly, one of the umbrella names for classical Daoist religious training is *xīnshù* 心術 (techniques of the heart–mind), which also is translated as "arts of the heart" and may be referred to as "Heart-Work" for short. Recall that one of the technique-specific names is "Heart-Fasting," with another being "Mind-Nourishment" (*xīnyǎng* 心養; ZZ 11). Some of the most profound expressions of and insights into classical Daoist contemplative psychology, and associated contemplative practices, appear in the anonymous, probably mid-fourth century BCE *Nèiyè* 內業 (Inward Training; abbrev. NY). As received, this previously-lost classical Daoist text is preserved as Chapter forty-nine of the *Guǎnzǐ* 管子 (*Kuǎnzǐ*; Book of Master Guan) and is one of the so-called Xīnshù 心術 (Techniques of the Heart–Mind; abbrev. HMT/THM) chapters (Chapters 36–38, 49). Under my revisionist reading, it is the more technical sister-companion to the above-mentioned *Book of Venerable Masters* (see Komjathy 2023c, I.1; cf. Roth 1999). *Inward Training* may, in turn, be understood as the "inner text," while the *Book of Venerable Masters* may be understood as the "outer text" for general circulation. This view is supported by the parallel structure and semantic content of the two texts. Under a more radical reading, *Inward Training* was hidden by Daoists in the *Book of Master Guan* anthology in order to ensure its preservation and eventual rediscovery. In any case, as expressed in *Inward Training*, in which the advocated training centers on apophatic and quietistic meditation,

> Within the heart–mind, there is yet another heart–mind.
> That inner heart–mind is an awareness that precedes language.
>
> (NY 14)

Thus, we may make a distinction between the ordinary heart–mind/habituated consciousness and the original heart–mind/realized consciousness.[4] Through classical Daoist apophatic meditation, one deconditions and purifies consciousness. One comes to realize that the contents, expressions, and faculties of consciousness are not consciousness itself. In this way, classical Daoism appears to emphasize a contemplative and mystical state somewhat analogous to the Pure Consciousness Event (see Forman 1990; also Deikman 1982). The "outer heart–mind" of the above-passage in turn refers to consciousness characterized by agitation, habituation, reactivity, and the like, which are often misidentified as the heart–mind as such. However, there is an "inner heart–mind" that corresponds to pure awareness. This is the heart–mind as such. It is further viewed as a more complete, a less differentiated, expression of the Dao. According to *Inward Training*,

> Inwardly still and outwardly reverent,
> You can return to innate nature.
>
> (NY 22; cf. LZ 51)

This is the earliest extant classical Daoist reference to "innate nature" (*xìng* 性). The latter Chinese character consists of *xīn*-heart and *shēng* 生 (birth/life). It is the heart–mind with which one was born. From a Daoist perspective, innate nature is one's original and inherent connection to the Dao. Thus, it may be understood as the "inner heart–mind." As expressed in the second quotation, innate nature is characterized by internal stillness (*jìng* 靜) and external reverence (*jìng* 敬). This is extremely interesting for a variety of reasons. In addition to providing a "contemplative map," it suggests that such qualities are "contemplative marks" of spiritual fruition.

They reveal the degree to which a given individual is connected to and living through innate nature, and through the sacred (Dao) by extension. Moreover, it is not simply stillness that is a hallmark of Daoist meditation; reverence also is centrally important. One gains increased sensitivity to and recognition of the sacred infusing and manifesting through all things. World, place, animals, self, and so forth. This relates to the various dimensions of self-as-world and world-as-self, including one's very embodiment. Again, recall the psychosomatic qualities of Daoist practice-realization.

While *xìng*-innate nature does not appear in the earliest layers of other classical Daoist texts, it is contained in the later strata of the above-mentioned *Book of Master Zhuang*. Importantly and tellingly, one of the key discussions occurs in concert with an equine connection and equestrian distinction. This appears in "Mǎtí 馬蹄" (Horse Hooves), Chapter 9, which is associated with the Primitivist lineage:

> Horse hooves are for treading frost and snow, their coats for keeping out wind and cold. Munching grass, drinking from streams, lifting up their feet, and galloping—this is the authentic nature (*zhēnxìng* 真性) of horses.
>
> (Adapted from Watson 1968: 104)

The natural state of apparently wild horses is then contrasted with Bólè 伯樂 (Bó Lè; Count Amusement), with the latter being the honorific name of the legendary Sūn Yáng 孫陽, who was a horse tamer in Spring and Autumn period, supposed retainer of Duke Mù 穆 of Qín 秦 (r. 659–621 BCE), and a famous judge of horses. He also is traditionally identified as the inventor of equine physiognomy. According to the subsequent ZZ passage, Bólè's initial training method results in 20–30 percent deathrates, while his continued training results in 50 percent deathrates. Thus, at least three in four horses die. Here we find an implicit association of innate nature, whether equine, human, or other, with wildness, and of domestication with injury, violence, and ultimately death. We may, in turn, connect the first passage to a parallel one in "Qiūshuǐ 秋水" (Autumn Floods), Chapter 17, which is associated with the Zhuangist lineage.

> Oxen and horses have four feet—this is what I mean by the celestial (*tiān* 天). Putting a halter on a horse's head, piercing an ox's nose—this is what I mean by the human. So I say: Do not let what is human wipe out what is celestial; do not let what is purposeful wipe out what is fated; do not let desire for gain lead you after fame. Diligently guard it (*jǐnshǒu* 謹守) and do not lose it—this is what we mean by 'returning to the real' (*fǎn qí zhēn* 反其真).
>
> (Adapted from Watson 1968: 182–183)

Recall the classical Daoist technical usage of *shǒu*-guarding for "meditation." Again, wild beings are nourished by freedom, by open space and self-determination. However, this is disrupted by the ordinary human desire for control, domination, enslavement, and the like. In place of this, members of the inner cultivation lineages of classical Daoism imagined a world without cages, corrals, feedlots, nets, pens, prisons, slaughterhouses, snares, traps, and the like (see also ZZ 10). A world where all beings may be free and flourish. Here all beings have the opportunity to manifest innate nature and to flourish in their own unbridled movement. Returning to Daoist anthropology in general and contemplative psychology in particular, this means that biology, embodiment, organicism, and wildness are not only positive but also trustworthy. Here we also learn an emanationist and immanent view of sacrality: We are connected to and infused with the sacred as embodied beings alive in the world. In some sense, being human, at least as rooted in innate nature, is a hierophany, a manifestation of the sacred. From this perspective, physiology itself is a sacred presence, a view that challenges and potentially subverts secular materialism and neuroscientific reductionism.

Along these lines, innate nature may be further connected to "inner power" (*dé* 德), with the Chinese character also translated as "integrity," "potency," and "virtue." One interesting dimension of *dé* is that it is understood to be a natural expression of human innate nature, which is inherently virtuous or "good" in conventional terms. However, this is virtue in the Hellenistic sense of one's total character and conduct (see, e.g., Hadot 1995), rather than along moralistic lines. In fact, the classical and foundational Daoist view of *dé* involves a critique of Ruist (Confucian) morality as distortion pattern. Our current *dé* is the same character appearing in the title of the *Dàodé jīng*, the honorific title of the previously mentioned *Lǎozǐ*. The text may accordingly be understood as about "Reality and its human expression." The current character consists of *chì* 彳 ("step") and *zhí* 直 ("direct") above *xīn* 心 ("heart"). An aligned heart–mind expressed as embodied activity in the world. Here we note that both the original Chinese terms for *dào* and *dé* include "movement components," *chuò* 辵/辶 and *chì* 彳, respectively. This suggests process over substance and being, even becoming over knowing. Thus, in terms of both anthropology and somatology, we might consider and explore the ways in which religious traditions like Daoism become embodied *as distinctive movement patterns in the world*.

Like the "body turn" and "material turn" in Religious Studies, focusing on embodiment and material culture, respectively, we might challenge the overemphasis on "belief," "doctrine," and "thought" in the academic study of religion by focusing on *kinesthetics*. "Religious kinesiology." Also the "kinesthetic turn." In any case, from a classical and foundational Daoist perspective, inner power relates to the specific ways in which the Dao becomes expressed through human beings. Specifically, it assumes some type of actualization, cultivation, realization, and so forth, including in/as/through resultant states of temporary psychological shifts, and traits of enduring personality changes associated with Daoist apophatic and quietistic meditation. Understood contextually, it thus relates to not only various "beyond/non-states" (e.g., desirelessness, effortlessness, namelessness) but also associated Daoist commitments, principles, qualities, states, and values. We may, in turn, recognize (or not) the specific qualities and manifestations of Dao-infused being, that is, inner power. As expressed in Chapter 15 of the *Book of Venerable Masters*,

> Considering those in ancient times who were skilled as adepts,
>   They were subtle, wondrous, mysterious, and connected
>   They were so deep that they could not be recognized.
> It is only because they could not be recognized
> That we feel compelled to describe their qualities.
>   Cautious! As if crossing a river in winter.
>   Hesitant! As if fearing neighbors everywhere.
>   Impeccable! As if a guest.
>   Expanding! As if ice on the verge of melting.
>   Intact! As if unhewn simplicity.
>   Broad! As if a valley.
>   Murky! As if turbid water.

The latter may be understood as the Seven Qualities (*qīróng* 七容) (see Komjathy 2023c). Such are some of the qualities associated with realized Daoists, especially those transformed through Daoist contemplative practice. They represent a "spiritual signature" that enables Daoists to recognize each other, especially Daoist elders and those identified according to the classical Daoist ideal of the "sage" (*shèngrén* 聖人). Although generally anthropocentric, even though Daoism is one of the least anthropocentric religious traditions, there are some classical Daoist passages wherein *dé* is a capacity and quality associated with "non-human animals," specifically fish and roosters (see ZZ 17 and 19; Komjathy 2022b). Thus, and radically for our current line of inquiry, Daoist realized being suggests something like "shared animality." This includes understanding consciousness as experience beyond conventional human constructs, hierarchies, and rationalizations centering on "intelligence," "language-facility," and "rationality." There is sacred awareness and presence that is embedded, reciprocal, relational, shared, and so forth. When consciousness is purified, when innate nature is manifest, one finds a natural and subtle connection with other animals. This is the open field and expansive space of the Dao.

Thus far we have learned the intimate relationship between the heart–mind, specifically the "inner heart–mind," and innate nature, our original and inherent connection to the sacred. According to the *Book of Master Zhuang*, this is analogous to a wild horse in a wild territory. It is further connected to the reality of psychosomatic being, including as manifesting in/as/through embodied being-in-the-world. From a Daoist perspective, innate nature is literally housed in and manifesting through a physical organ (heart) in your chest, which further manifests as consciousness. An additional dimension of this heart/innate nature/inner power connection, albeit only nascent in classical Daoism, centers on "spirit" (*shén* 神; also, divine/divinity), which also was translated via Greek in earlier scholarship as "daemon" (cf. *qì* as pneuma). The Chinese character consists of *shì* 示/礻 (originally altar; also, manifest/omen/

reveal) and *shēn* 申 (originally lightning-bolt; also, extend). Spirit is a quasi-divine capacity to connect to hidden and unseen realms and realities. As discussed above, spirit is associated with Fire/heart in correlative cosmology. It is the spiritual faculty of the heart. From a comparative and cross-cultural perspective, one interesting issue here centers on the relationship between divinity, humanity, and animality. While we often encounter narratives about a hierarchal ordering, with divinity at the top and human beings aspiring upward, Daoist radical non-dualism, realized in/as/through apophatic and quietistic meditation, rather suggests interrelationality, integration, and even fusion. To be human, at least as such, is to be simultaneously animal and divine, to experience divinity within animality and animality within divinity. And ultimately beyond any and all such distinctions and dichotomies. Recall "guarding the One."

In the later Daoist tradition, the heart is associated with not only innate nature but also "original spirit" (*yuánshén* 元神). There are, in turn, various esoteric names for the heart region, including Cinnabar Prime (*dānyuán* 丹元), Scarlet Palace (*jiànggōng* 絳宮), and Square Inch (*fāngcùn* 方寸). In fully developed and systematized subtle somatology, which centers on actualizing and activating the "Daoist alchemical body" (see Komjathy 2011, 2020a, 2023a), the heart region is identified and engaged as the "middle elixir field" (*zhōng dāntián* 中丹田). It is so named because this is one of three somatic locations (head, heart, navel) associated with three somatic presences (spirit, *qi*, vital essence). Rooted in a Daoist alchemical view and approach, the "elixir" refers to a quasi-substance created through refinement and transmutation. We may thus map the fully developed Daoist contemplative psychology in terms of the following five primary dimensions:

Dào 道	**Xīn** 心	**Xìng** 性	**Shén** 神	**Dé** 德
Dao/Way	Heart–Mind	Inner Nature	Spirit	Inner Power

Primary Dimensions of Daoist Contemplative Psychology

While I have been emphasizing the psychosomatic (mind/body) characteristics of Daoist anthropology, it is, in fact, better characterized as energetic. Daoists and Daoist communities tend to emphasize what may be understood as an energetics of being and experiencing. This relates to the discussions of pneumatology and somatology above, which encompass more than conventional conceptions of psychology. In this way, it challenges mind-based and consciousness-centered approaches, systems, and traditions. Thus, it again brings attention to a specific form of human embodiment and a specific way of being human. In my comparative analysis, Daoism has one of the most developed "subtle somatologies," although certain Indian Tantric and Yogic traditions also are quite complex and sophisticated. While Daoist *qi*-based views are often associated with the later Daoist tradition, especially Daoist Yǎngshēng 養生 (Nourishing Life; health and longevity practice) and internal alchemy (*nèidān* 內丹), they are, in fact, present, advocated, and employed in the inner cultivation lineages of classical Daoism.

> The myriad beings carry *yin* and embrace *yang*.
> It is the empty *qi* (*chōngqì* 沖氣) that harmonizes these.
>
> (LZ 42; also Chapters 10 and 55)

~

> Listening stops with the ears, the heart–mind stops with joining, but *qi* is empty (*xū* 虛) and waits on all things. The Dao gathers in emptiness alone.
>
> (ZZ 4)

~

> If you can be aligned and still,
> Only then can you become settled.
> With a stabilized heart–mind at the center,
> With the ears and eyes acute and bright,
> And with the four limbs firm and stable,
> You can make a lodging place for vital essence.
> The vital essence is the essence of *qi*.
>
> (NY 8)

To begin, *qì* 氣, which is best left untranslated but which is approximated as "vital breath," "energy" and "pneuma," is the subtle quasi-substance (actually presence) animating and underlying everything in existence. The Chinese character consists of *qì* 气 (steam) and *mǐ* 米 (rice). It is thus analogous to vapor that appears from the cooking of rice. It may be understood as a subtle vapor, presence, and influence. Like *yin-yang*, it is part of the traditional Chinese worldview and of traditional Chinese cosmology in particular. Everything, including the so-called "body" and so-called "mind," may be mapped along a spectrum of *qi*, from the most substantial (rocks, for example) to the most rarified (primordial ethers, for example). While such an energetic view is pan-Chinese and eventually pan-East Asian, Daoists developed their own unique understanding and applications.

As expressed in the above passages, and as informed by and informing the previously discussed classical Daoist apophatic and quietistic meditation, Daoist practice centers on activating and strengthening energetic aliveness, sensitivity, and vitality. Specifically, it involves developing and increasing the ability of "listening to/ with *qi*" (*tīngqì* 聽氣). This is one of the more radical challenges of such approaches and perspectives: One listens to the deeper, underlying layer of being and experience, which is energetic. This helps to explain why Daoists tend to be less interested in, and in fact skeptical of, not only human beings, but specifically human cognition, conceptualization, linguistics, rhetoric, and so forth. As inherently limited, each has the potential to create confusion, and ultimately may lead to spiritual disorientation.

Interestingly, Daoists sometimes even utilize their own *qi*-referent character 炁, which is especially pronounced in the later Daoist tradition. This Chinese variant character consists of *jì* 旡 (amass/gather) and *huǒ* 火/灬 (fire). It may be understood as a subtle fire infusing the body. Under my "Daoist etymological reading" (Komjathy 2022a), *jì*-amass may be understood as *wú* 无 (無; non-being) and *yī* 一 (one). Realized Daoist practitioners are attuned and infused with the subtle presence of the Dao-as-One and the Dao-as-Nondifferentiation. There are, in turn, many types of *qi*, but perhaps not unsurprisingly Daoists are most interested in what becomes referred to as *dàoqì* 道炁, the "*qi* of the Dao" or "Way-Energy" for short. This is a more primordial and less differentiated form of *qi*. It is often understood as Source-Energy, an original presence beginning to manifest during the earliest moments of cosmogonic emanation and immanence. Recalling the third of the four primary characteristics of the Dao discussed above, it is a numinous sacred presence infusing everything. However, from a Daoist perspective, it may be more or less present, and Daoist practice-realization results in a greater density or concentration. Thus, this is one of the ways that realized Daoists recognize each other, and it may be further connected to Daoism as the "Teaching beyond/without Words"/"Wordless Teaching" (see LZ 2 and 43; ZZ 5 and 22).

The upshot is that so-called spiritual realization is not just in the mind, it is in the body. And more than that, it involves a felt energetic sense, a different mode of perceiving, being, and experiencing. This involves open receptivity and subtle listening. One issue that often arises among "non-Daoists" centers on *qi* as all-pervading and types of *qi*. If everything is the Dao and everything is *qi*, then why are there such distinctions. One explanation centers on the actual qualities and effects. Way-Energy is inherently beneficial and transformative, without accompanying distortion patterns or "aftertaste." As Chapter 35 of the *Lǎozǐ* tells us, "The Dao passing through the mouth—Bland! It is without any taste." So too with realized Daoists and associated Daoist expressions.

Towards a Radical Daoist Anthropology and Beyond

Classical and foundational Daoist anthropology is radical, even subversive. It offers major challenges to the assumptions and lifeways associated with domineering Western cultural and religious traditions. The Daoist views explored herein are rooted in Daoist contemplative practice, especially apophatic and quietistic meditation. These are psychosomatic and energetic. In this way, they represent an important glimpse into the embodied perspectives of somatology and pneumatology from a comparative and cross-cultural perspective. They express and utilize an emanationist and immanence cosmogony and theology in which both the world and the body are viewed as manifestations of the Dao. Thus, embodied being-in-the-world is not only positive but also trustworthy. It is theologically embedded, participatory, and relational. In this way, classical Daoism encourages us to consider unquestioned assumptions, informing views, and received narratives. Each of these has existential and ecological implications and repercussions.

From a Daoist perspective, this includes the ways in which specific human capacities and faculties are either emphasized or deemphasized, privileged or dismissed, developed or atrophied. Here one might reflect on the ways in which education and scholarship are rooted in political power and control. What are we allowed to think? What modes of perceiving and thinking are rewarded and why? From where do our thoughts originate? Perhaps most radically, classical and foundational Daoism emphasizes an energetic mode of being and experiencing. Beyond mere intellectualism, rhetoric, and rationality. So which faculties of consciousness are utilized in which systems? And what is consciousness according to community-, movement- and tradition-specific perspectives? And what about the body? From a Daoist perspective, it is possible to *embody the Dao*. The associated abilities, qualities, and sensitivities, perhaps akin to energetic intuition, are strengthened *through contemplative practice*. Thus, practice and experience, rather than doctrine, ideas, and thought, are more primary. We may, in turn, consider the ways in which specific views become embodied and enacted in the world, including in distinctive movement patterns. Such insights may help to explain why Daoists claim that Daoists tend to be largely unrecognized. Having dissolved the ordinary self and disappeared into the Dao, they are obscure. Perhaps invisible.

Notes

1. See the Bibliography for my work, from which I draw upon extensively in this chapter.
2. The present chapter utilizes traditional Chinese characters accompanied by Pinyin Romanization of modern "Mandarin" Chinese pronunciations. Numbers for Daoist textual collections follow Komjathy (2002, 2014), as well as my more recent online "Supplements to *Title Index to Daoist Collections*" (2020–2025). Unless otherwise indicated, all translations are my own.
3. This fact helps to explain the nearly systemic misinterpretation and misrepresentation of the tradition and the texts, in both academic and popular accounts (see Komjathy 2013: 205–211; 2023c: 61–87).

4. Although readers may hear (potentially anachronistic) Chán/Zen Buddhist influence here, the "influence line" actually moves in the opposite direction: Chán/Zen Buddhism may be understood as "Daocizied Buddhism." In addition to actual historical influences, one finds, for example, that the so-called "mind-mirror/mirror-mind analogy" originates in classical Daosim and in the *Book of Master Zhuang* in particular. See ZZ 5 and 7.

Bibliography

Ames, Roger. 1993. "The Meaning of Body in Classical Chinese Philosophy." In Thomas Kasulis (ed.), *Self as Body in Asian Theory and Practice*. Albany: SUNY Press, 157–177.

de Wit, Han. 1991. *Contemplative Psychology*. Pittsburgh: Duquesne University Press.

Deikman, Arthur J. 1982. *The Observing Self: Mysticism and Psychotherapy*. Boston: Beacon Press.

Despeux, Catherine. 1994. *Taoïsme et corps humain. Le Xiuzhen tu*. Paris: Guy Trédaniel.

Despeux, Catherine. 2018. *Taoism and Self Knowledge: The Chart for the Cultivation of Perfection (Xiuzhen tu)*. Trans. Jonathan Pettit. Leiden: Brill.

Feher, Michel, with Ramona Naddaff and Nadia Tazi, eds. 1989. *Fragments for a History of the Human Body*. 3 vols. New York: Zone Books.

Forman, Robert K.C., ed. 1990. *The Problem of Pure Consciousness*. Oxford and New York: Oxford University Press.

Hadot, Pierre. 1995. *Philosophy as a Way of Life: Spiritual Exercises from Socrates to Foucault*. Hoboken: Blackwell.

Huang, Susan Shih-shan. 2012. *Picturing the True Form: Daoist Visual Culture in Traditional China*. Cambridge: Harvard University Press.

Kohn, Livia. 1991. "Taoist Visions of the Body." *Journal of Chinese Philosophy*, 18: 227–252.

Komjathy, Louis. 2002. *Title Index to Daoist Collections*. Cambridge: Three Pines Press.

Komjathy, Louis. 2008. "Mapping the Daoist Body: Part I: The *Neijing tu* in History." *Journal of Daoist Studies*, 1: 6–92.

Komjathy, Louis. 2009. "Mapping the Daoist Body: Part II: The Text of the *Neijing tu*." *Journal of Daoist Studies*, 2: 64–108.

Komjathy, Louis. 2011. "The Daoist Mystical Body." In Thomas Cottai and June McDaniel (eds.), *Perceiving the Divine through the Human Body: Mystical Sensuality*. New York: Palgrave MacMillan, 67–103.

Komjathy, Louis. 2013. *The Daoist Tradition: An Introduction*. London and New York: Bloomsbury Academy.

Komjathy, Louis. 2014. "Title Index to the *Zhonghua daozang* 中華道藏 (Chinese Daoist Canon)." *Monumenta Serica*, 62: 213–260.

Komjathy, Louis, ed. 2015. *Contemplative Literature: A Comparative Sourcebook on Meditation and Contemplative Prayer*. Albany: SUNY Press.

Komjathy, Louis. 2017. *Taming the Wild Horse: An Annotated Translation and Study of the Daoist Horse Taming Pictures*. New York: Columbia University Press.

Komjathy, Louis. 2018. *Introducing Contemplative Studies*. West Sussex, England and Hoboken: Wiley-Blackwell.

Komjathy, Louis. 2020a. "Daoist Body-Maps and Meditative Praxis." In George Pati and Katherine Zubko (eds.), *Transformational Embodiment in Asian Religions: Subtle Bodies, Spatial Bodies*. London and New York: Routledge, 36–64.

Komjathy, Louis. 2020b. "Daoist Meditation." In Suzanne Newcombe and Karen O'Brien-Kop (eds.), *Routledge Handbook of Yoga and Meditation Studies*. London and New York: Routledge, 189–211.

Komjathy, Louis. 2021a. "Daoist Meditation: From 100 CE to the Present." In Miguel Farias, David Brazier, and Mansur Lalljee (eds.), *The Oxford Handbook of Meditation*. Oxford and New York: Oxford University Press, 310–331.

Komjathy, Louis. 2021b. "Review of Catherine Despeux's *Taoism and Self Knowledge: The Chart for the Cultivation of Perfection*." *Journal of the American Oriental Society*, 141 (1): 234–238.

Komjathy, Louis. 2022a. *Primer for Translating Daoist Literature*. Auckland: Purple Cloud Press.

Komjathy, Louis. 2022b. "Religion, Animals, and Contemplation." *Religions*, 13 (5): 457.

Komjathy, Louis. 2022c. "Towards a Daoist Comparative Theology." In Pim Valkenberg et al. (eds.), *Brill's Companion to Comparative Theology*. Leiden: Brill, 467–486.

Komjathy, Louis. 2023a. "Further Explorations of/in Daoist Embodiment." In Yudit Greenberg and George Pati (eds.), *Routledge Handbook of Religion and the Body*. London and New York: Routledge, 377–394.

Komjathy, Louis. 2023b. *Dàodé jīng* 道德經: *A Contextual, Contemplative, and Annotated Bilingual Translation*. Ravinia: Square Inch Press.

Komjathy, Louis. 2023c. *Handbooks for Daoist Practice*. Twentieth Anniversary Edition. 3 vols. Ravinia: Square Inch Press.

Komjathy, Louis. 2020–2025. "Supplements to *Title Index to Daoist Collections*" (STIDC). www.louiskomjathy.com/taoisme.

Roth, Harold. 1999. *Original Tao: Inward Training (Nei-yeh) and the Foundations of Taoist Mysticism*. New York: Columbia University Press.

Schipper, Kristofer. 1978. "The Taoist Body." *History of Religions*, 17 (3/4): 355–386.

Schipper, Kristofer. 1993. *The Taoist Body*. Trans. Karen Duval. Berkeley: University of California Press.

Smith, J. Z. 1998. "Religions, Religion, Religious." In Mark C. Taylor (ed.), *Critical Terms for Religious Studies*. Chicago: University of Chicago Press, 269–284.

Watson, Burton. 1968. *The Complete Works of Chuang Tzu*. New York: Columbia University Press.

Yü, Ying-shih. 1987. "O Soul, Come Back! A Study in the Changing Conceptions of the Soul and Afterlife in Pre-Buddhist China." *Harvard Journal of Asiatic Studies*, 47: 363–395.

Pneumatology
Chapter 7.1

Pneumatology refers to discourse on, study of, and theories about *pneuma*. The latter is a Greek term that may indicate "breath," "life," "soul," "spirit," "wind," and so forth. In this way, it has some overlap with *psukhḗ* (Latin: *psychē*), and psychology by extension. In a more technical sense, *pneuma* connects with *energeia* (Latin: *energia*; "activity") (see, e.g., Smil 2017). While "pneumatology" is often used in modern Christian theological contexts to refer the study of the Holy Spirit (see, e.g., Kärkkäinen 2002), here I want to propose employing it as a comparative and cross-cultural term for exploring culture-specific and tradition-specific terms and views related to vital breath and energy. Such a reframing extends the topic beyond Christocentric frameworks, although Christian views would be included. The comparative framework is particularly relevant for the study of Asian and Chinese philosophies/religions in general and Daoism in particular, although more recent cross-cultural encounters suggest wide application and relevance.

In terms of the Philosophy of Religion, especially as envisioned in its current "global-critical" trajectory, with an additional concern for embodiment, personhood, and subjectivity, pneumatology enables us to avoid certain common (Eurocentric/Christocentric) assumptions and to consider larger, tradition-specific and perhaps trans-cultural insights. Specifically, it inspires us to investigate dimensions of self beyond or within the more conventional "body," "mind," and/or "soul" frameworks. It raises the possibility of subtle, underlying, and perhaps mutually infusing influences and presences. While it is presumably uncontroversial to draw attention to "breath/breathing/respiration," and perhaps to bone, gesture, movement, skin, and the like, "subtle breath" and "subtle anatomy and physiology" are often taboo topics in mainstream academic discourse, perhaps invoking pre-modern and presumably "unscientific" ideas associated with "vitalism" (see Normandin and Wolfe 2016). So, while one might hear invocations of topics like "quantum physics" or "dark matter," such views are not necessarily extended to human identity and personhood. How does something like mass-energy equivalence ($E=mc^2$) or the so-called "observer effect" relate to subjectivity on a lived, phenomenological level? The possibility (actuality?) of energy moving in/as/through space and bodies inspires a variety of other questions, further investigation, and perhaps deeper or at least "alternative" modes of being and experiencing.

Pneuma was a central concept and concern among the ancient Hellenistic Stoics, for whom it generally designated the active, generative principle that organizes both the individual and the cosmos. In its highest form, *pneuma* constitutes *psychē* ("soul"). The latter, in turn, was regarded as a fragment of the *pneuma* that is the soul of the Divine (see Sellars 2006; also Hadot 1995). In this way, it may be further connected to *eudaimonía*, or flourishing in/as/through virtue. The Hellenistic concept in turn flowed into and influenced early Christianity, including in the form of Gnosticism, and specifically its Hellenized views regarding *khristós* as *logos* (cf. Hebrew: *messiah*) and accompanying *paráklētos* (cf. Hebrew: *ruach*; also *kavod*; *shekhinah*), usually taken to refer to the Holy Spirit. For present purposes, one area where *pneuma* enters into the comparative and cross-cultural study of religion is in the work of the Sinologist Edward Schafer (1913–1991) and his intellectual heirs. Like many scholars of his generation, Schafer drew on Classical Studies for his translation methodology, specifically choosing to translate the Chinese and Daoist concept of *qì* 氣 (*ch'i*; Japanese: *ki*; Korean: *gi*) as "pneuma" (see, e.g., Schafer 1966). This translation and interpretive trajectory influenced the current entry, although the presentation of *qi*-as-pneuma is problematic on multiple grounds (see Komjathy 2013). Briefly, it uses a foreign (Greek) concept to translate another foreign (Chinese) concept (*qi*), which obfuscates the matter. Like translating *shén* 神 as "daimon," it also invokes the accompanying ancient Hellenistic views and values to represent radically different ones. The term is thus better left untranslated as "*qi*," although it may refer to physical breath and a more subtle presence depending on context. If required, "subtle breath" or "vital breath" are perhaps most viable. Drawing upon the indigenous Chinese tradition, we may, in turn, think of "pneumatology" as *qìxué* 氣學 ("Qi Studies"), and vice versa.

As received, the character *qì* 氣 consists of *qì* 气 ("steam") over *mǐ* 米 ("rice"), thus suggesting that it is somewhat analogous to vapor. The esoteric Daoist variant 炁 consists of *jì* 旡 ("collect") and *huǒ* 火/灬 ("fire"), thus suggesting subtle warmth. Along within *yin-yang* 陰陽, *qi* is one of the key dimensions of traditional Chinese cosmology, including as utilized in both Chinese medicine and Daoism. Perhaps somewhat surprising to non-specialist readers, like the emphasis on ritual (*lǐ* 禮) as being human (*rén* 人), *qi* also has played a role in Ruist ("Confucian") views and practices. In any case, Daoism is particularly relevant for present purposes. As part of a classical and foundational Daoist worldview and lifeway, *qi* refers to a subtle, even numinous presence that underlies and infuses all of existence and every individual being, at times including "non-sentient" ones. While part of one's original and inherent constitution, *qi* may be more or less present, and one may be more or less sensitive to it. For Daoists, there are specific contemplative practices, including apophatic (emptiness-/stillness-based) meditation and internal alchemy (*nèidān* 內丹), that activate and strengthen this enlivening energetic presence. Qi, in turn, relates to other dimensions of human personhood from a Daoist perspective, including *xīn* 心 ("heart–mind") and "body" (*shēn* 身). Like everything in existence, these may be understood and mapped as manifestations of *qi*. From a Daoist alchemical perspective, *qi* also is located in an entire "theosomatics" centering on the "subtle body," which consists of subtle corporeal locations and energy channels (*mài* 脈). While *qi* flows throughout this network, the navel region, referred to as the

"Elixir Field" (*dāntián* 丹田) and "Ocean of Qi" (*qìhǎi* 氣海), is considered the primary storehouse of *qi* in the body. In addition, Daoists distinguish *different types of qi*. The most important is *dàoqì* 道炁, the "*qi* of the Dao" or "Way-Energy" for short, which also is referred to as *língqì* 靈氣 ("numinous *qi*"). This refers to a more primordial and less differentiated form of "energy," a sacred presence, associated with the Dao 道 (Tao/Way), the sacred and ultimate concern of Daoists, which Daoists attempt to connect with and live through. Such views and orientations further connect with Yǎngshēng 養生 (Nourishing Life) and modern Qìgōng 氣功 (Energy Work/Qi Exercise), which usually refer to health and longevity practice and which may or may not be Daoist (see Komjathy 2013).

As herein proposed, the Chinese and Daoist concept of *qi* thus represents a culture-specific and sometimes tradition-specific term related to "pneumatology." It may, in turn, be connected to parallel, cross-cultural terms like *àṣẹ* (Yoruba), *energeia* (Greece), *ki* 氣 (Japan), *mana* (Melanesia and Polynesia), *nilch'i* (Navajo), *pneuma* (Greece), and *prāṇa* (India), to name some.

The literature on pneumatology, broadly conceived, is vast, especially if one engages tradition-specific materials and studies. On the East Asian side, some works may have broader appeal as well as inspire deeper reflection and application. Yasuo Yuasa (1987, 1993) and Nagatomo Shigenori (1992) have attempted to advance a *ki*-centered theory and approach, with specific attention to the so-called (imagined/projected?) "mind-body problem." Shigehisa Kuriyama (1999) discusses issues of embodiment in Chinese and Greek medical traditions, including consideration of the central importance of *qi* in the former. Finally, Zhang Yu Huan and Ken Rose (2001) offer a "brief history of *qi*," with a specific focus on Chinese medicine.

Related Terms

anthropology, embodiment, energy, *mana* (Proto-Oceanic), *qì* 氣 (Chinese), *pneuma* (Greek), *prāṇa* (Sanskrit), psychology, *shēn* 身 ("body/self"; Chinese), somatology, *xīn* 心 ("heart–mind"; Chinese)

References

Hadot, Pierre. 1995. *Philosophy as a Way of Life: Spiritual Exercises from Socrates to Foucault*. Hoboken: Blackwell.

Kärkkäinen, Veli-Matti. 2002. *Pneumatology: The Holy Spirit in Ecumenical, International, and Contextual Perspective*. Grand Rapids: Baker Academic.

Komjathy, Louis. 2013. *The Daoist Tradition: An Introduction*. London and New York: Bloomsbury Academic.

Kuriyama, Shigehisa. 1999. *The Expressiveness of the Body and the Divergence of Greek and Chinese Medicine*. New York: Zone Books.

Nagatomo Shigenori. 1992. *Attunement through the Body*. Albany: SUNY Press.

Sebastian Normandin, and Charles Wolfe, eds. 2016. *Vitalism and the Scientific Image in Post-Enlightenment Life Science, 1800–2010*. New York: Springer.

Schafer, Edward. 1966. "Thoughts about a Students' Dictionary of Classical Chinese." *Monumenta Serica*, 25: 197–206.

Sellars, John. 2006. *Stoicism*. London and New York: Routledge.

Smil, Vaclav. 2017. *Energy and Civilization: A History*. Cambridge: MIT Press.

White, David. 1998. *The Alchemical Body: Siddha Traditions in Medieval India*. Chicago: University of Chicago Press.

Yuasa Yasuo. 1987. *The Body: Toward an Eastern Mind-Body Theory*. Trans. Nagatomo Shigenori and T. P. Kasulis. Albany: SUNY Press.

Yuasa Yasuo. 1993. *The Body, Self-Cultivation, and Ki-Energy*. Trans. Nagatomo Shigenori and Monte Hull. Albany: SUNY Press.

Zhang Yu Huan, and Ken Rose. 2001. *A Brief History of Qi*. Brookline: Paradigm Publications.

Shēn 身 (Body/Self)
Chapter 7.2

Shēn 身 is a Chinese character that may refer to "body," "person," and/or "self," depending on context. Etymologically speaking, the earliest forms (ᛐ/ᛑ) are pictographs, most likely depicting a pregnant woman. Under one reading, this suggests the capacity for birth and life as a biological organism in the world. As received, the character probably depicts the human torso viewed from the side. This is one's personal embodied personhood, and it in turn relates to a larger lexicon of Chinese and Daoist psychological and somatological terms.

In terms of the Philosophy of Religion, especially as envisioned in its current "global-critical" trajectory, with an additional concern for embodiment, personhood, and subjectivity, *shēn* brings our attention to culture-specific and tradition-specific technical terms related to embodiment, personhood, subjectivity, and the like. Such cultural, linguistic and philosophical sensitivity also encourages, and in fact requires, accompanying engagement with contextual meanings and applications. In addition, *shēn* inspires reflection on human being as embodied, enacted, and lived. We may inquire into the various dimensions of self from a comparative and cross-cultural perspective with attention associated indigenous terminology beyond Anglocentrism and Eurocentrism. Thus, terms like *shēn* may result in critical investigation of unquestioned assumptions and received views.

The Chinese character *shēn* 身 became a key religio-philosophical concept in the classical period of Chinese culture and literature, specifically from the Warring States period (480-222 BCE) to the Early Han dynasty (206 BCE–9 CE). However, it appears in earlier ancient literature, such as the *Shījīng* 詩經 (Classic of Poetry), as well. Again, we must be attentive to context-specific meaning. The character, in turn, relates to a larger repertoire of Chinese "body characters" and "self characters" (see Kohn 1991; Ames 1993; Komjathy 2011, 2013). Chinese and Daoist views of embodiment tend to be psychosomatic, with energetic and psychospiritual being equally important characterizations. There are three primary Chinese and Daoist terms related to "body," namely, *shēn* 身, *xíng* 形, and *tǐ* 體. First, *shēn*, probably a pictograph of the human physique, seems to be used most frequently to refer to one's entire psychosomatic process. In passages where *shēn* as "self" refers to the physical body, it is one's "lived body" seen from within rather than "body as corpse" seen from without. The second character relating to Chinese notions of "body" is *xíng*, which is the "form" or "shape," the three-dimensional disposition or configuration of the human process. *Xíng*-form has a morphological rather than genetic or schematic nuance. Finally, the third character designating "body" is *tǐ*, which relates to "physical structure" said to be a "combination of twelve groups" or parts. *Tǐ*-physical structure relates to the scalp, face, chin, shoulders, spine, abdomen, upper arms, lower arms, hands, thighs, legs, and feet. In addition to clarifying Chinese conceptions of body/self, these terms reveal that concern over "self" is not foreign to Chinese culture, contra to facile and conventional feminist or post-modern critiques. In addition, *shēn* may be used to refer to "person" and "self," so it may be further connected to other, related characters. These include *wǒ* 我/*wú* 吾 ("I-ness"), *jǐ* 己 ("self"), *míng* 名 ("name/fame"), and *zì* 自 ("self"). Here *míng* is particularly interesting, as it technically refers to one's given personal name, bestowed by one's parents. It thus has the added connotations of "fame" and "reputation," and social identity by extension. In any case, *shēn* brings our attention to the complexity of both indigenous terms and context-specific meaning. For example, Chapter 13 of the anonymous fourth-second century BCE *Dàodé jīng* 道德經 (Scripture on the Dao and Inner Power), a key classical Daoist text, contains the following line:「及吾無身，吾有何患？」. It has been mistranslated as "if I did not have a body, what calamities would I have?" when here *shēn* refers to a personal self, resulting in "if I did not have a self, what calamities would I have?" This relates to the Daoist aspiration to become "formless" (*wúxíng* 無形), "nameless" (*wúmíng* 無名), "selfless" (*wúsī* 無私), and the (un)like. Thus, we must be constantly attentive to not only contextual nuance, but also unrecognized assumptions and possible unintended consequences in translation work.

Daoist adherents and communities in turn developed some of the most sophisticated indigenous Chinese discussions of embodiment (see Schipper 1978, [1982] 1993; Kohn 1991; Despeux 1994; Komjathy 2008, 2009, 2011, 2020), which might be beneficially compared to the contemplative psychological cartographies utilized in Buddhist meditation systems. Daoist discussions include what may be referred to as the "Daoist body" and associated "Daoist body-maps" (*shēntú* 身圖). This is the human body actualized, cultivated, and explored in Daoist practice, and it may result in a different type of being-in-the-world. One noteworthy dimension of Daoist views centers on the *body as sacred*, the body itself as a manifestation of the Dao 道 (Tao/Way), the sacred and ultimate concern of Daoists. This emanationist and immanence "somatology" may challenge assumed mind-body dualism, or even calcified distinctions. While beyond the present entry, there are various, related technical terms, including *jīng* 精 ("vital essence"), *mìng* 命 ("life-destiny"), *qì* 氣 ("subtle breath/energy"), *shén* 神 ("spirit"), *xīn* 心 ("heart–mind"), and *xìng* 性 ("innate nature"). These may be further connected with what may be understood as the Daoist "alchemical body" and "mystical body" (see Komjathy 2011, 2020), which relates to the Daoist meditation practice of internal alchemy (*nèidān* 內丹). Specifically, the associated Daoist practitioners engage the "physical body" as containing a "subtle body," which consists of subtle corporeal locations and energy channels. The former are often designated with the technical term *dāntián* 丹田 ("elixir fields"), while the latter correspond to "meridians" (*mài* 脈). In more standardized accounts, the meridians include the twelve primary organ-meridians and the so-called Eight Extraordinary Channels, with the latter being especially important in Daoist practice.

A more general philosophical discussion of *shēn* and related terms in traditional Chinese culture has been published by Roger Ames (1993). Like Ames' work more generally, there are problematic categorizations centering on "philosophy," but the article nonetheless represents foundational reading. In terms of the "Daoist body," key scholars include Catherine Despeux, Livia Kohn, Louis Komjathy, Joseph Needham (1990–1995), and Kristofer Schipper (1934–2021). Komjathy's articles (2008, 2009, 2011, 2020) include summaries and critical analysis. This may be thought of as part of a larger "fragments for a history of the human body" (see Feher 1989; also Murphy 1992), a lived and living history that might include greater attentiveness to religion as manifesting *as embodied movement in the world*.

Related Terms

anthropology, body, embodiment, *míng* 名 ("name/fame"; Chinese), personhood, pneumatology, *qì* 氣 ("subtle breath/energy"; Chinese), somatology, *xīn* 心 ("heart-mind"; Chinese)

References

Ames, Roger. 1993. "The Meaning of Body in Classical Chinese Philosophy." In Thomas Kasulis (ed.), *Self as Body in Asian Theory and Practice*. Albany: SUNY Press, 157–177.

Despeux, Catherine. 1994. *Taoïsme et corps humain. Le Xiuzhen tu*. Paris: Guy Trédaniel.

Feher, Michel, with Ramona Naddaff and Nadia Tazi, eds. 1989. *Fragments for a History of the Human Body*. 3 vols. New York: Zone Books.

Kohn, Livia. 1991. "Taoist Visions of the Body." *Journal of Chinese Philosophy*, 18: 227–252.

Komjathy, Louis. 2008. "Mapping the Daoist Body: Part I: The *Neijing tu* in History." *Journal of Daoist Studies*, 1: 67–92.

Komjathy, Louis. 2009. "Mapping the Daoist Body: Part II: The Text of the *Neijing tu*." *Journal of Daoist Studies*, 2: 64–108.

Komjathy, Louis. 2011. "The Daoist Mystical Body." In Thomas Cottai and June McDaniel (eds.), *Perceiving the Divine through the Human Body: Mystical Sensuality*. New York: Palgrave Macmillan, 67–103.

Komjathy, Louis. 2013. *The Daoist Tradition: An Introduction*. London and New York: Bloomsbury Academic.

Komjathy, Louis. 2020. "Daoist Body-Maps and Meditative Praxis." In George Pati and Katherine Zubko (eds.), *Transformational Embodiment in Asian Religions: Subtle Bodies, Spatial Bodies*. London and New York: Routledge, 36–64.

Komjathy, Louis. 2023. "Further Explorations of/in Daoist Embodiment." In Yudit Greenberg and George Pati (eds.), *Routledge Handbook of Religion and the Body*. London and New York: Routledge, 377–394.

Murphy, Michael. 1992. *The Future of the Body: Explorations into the Further Evolution of Human Nature*. New York: Penguin Putnam Inc.

Schipper, Kristofer. 1978. "The Taoist Body." *History of Religions*, 17 (3/4): 355–386.

Schipper, Kristofer. [1982] 1993. *The Taoist Body*. Trans. Karen Duval. Berkeley: University of California Press.

Somatology
Chapter 7.3

Somatology refers to discourse on, study of, and theories about the (human) body. While more conventionally used to refer to a branch of anthropology (a.k.a. "physical anthropology") primarily concerned with the physical nature and characteristics of people or to a branch of biology concerned with the structure and function of the human body, the term may be used as a comparative and cross-cultural interpretive category. Etymologically speaking, "somatology" derives the Greek *sôma* ("body") and *lógos* ("study"). Thus, it may be applied to consider the embodied, enacted, and enfleshed dimensions of human being and experience, especially in terms of corporeality, embodiment, physicality, somatics, and the like. From an interdisciplinary perspective, some especially relevant, if under-consulted disciplines include body work, dance, disability studies, feminist studies, kinesthetics, movement studies, physical education, ritual studies, "sports science," theatre, and so forth.

In terms of the Philosophy of Religion, especially as envisioned in its current "global-critical" trajectory, with an additional concern for embodiment, personhood, and subjectivity, somatology inspires deeper exploration and reflection on "the body" as lived, phenomenological site of human being and experiencing. Here we must recognize that, while accepting certain shared, recurring morphological and structural features, there is no such thing as "the body," especially when we engage culture-specific views, "corporeal phenomenology," transformative body-techniques, and socio-political dimensions (see, e.g., Komjathy 2007). Thus, there is only my body and your body, and other bodies, both historical and contemporaneous. This is not to mention the assumptions often involved with categories like "*embodi*ment." Are consciousness and identity distinguishable from "the body"? We may consider the ways in which the mind is in the body, including the possibility of "philosophy in the flesh" (see, e.g., Lakoff and Johnson 1999) and perhaps an accompanying "philosophy of skin and touch" (see, e.g., Vasseleu 1998). Additional somatological trajectories include investigation of associated human (and "non-human") vulnerability and the centrality of pain in the human condition (see, e.g., Scarry 1985; Good et al. 1992). We may, in turn, think of this as the "somatic turn" in scholarship and perhaps in pedagogy, and it may open up more radical possibilities with respect to organic and ecological being-in-the-world.

As herein employed, that is, as a proposed comparative and cross-cultural category, there is no known "historical usage" of somatology, so here we will focus on intersection-points and additional possibilities. In addition to more straightforward investigation of culture- and tradition-specific views and enactments, including from comparative and cross-cultural perspectives (see References herein), somatology inspires consideration of the body as such. Here we may consider actual posture and movement patterns (see, e.g., Hewes 1955, 1957) as well as the anatomy of movement (see Calais-Germain 2007). One possible "thought-experiment" ("body-experiment"?) in this regard involves deeper reflection on and perhaps subversive interaction with the academic vogue of neuroimaging technology. While neuroimages are often presented as providing maps of consciousness (brain physiology), with accompanying legitimation narratives, once again mediated by technology (see, e.g., Heidegger 1977; also Komjathy 2015, 2018), a more direct engagement with human being and expression, here through the "lived/living body," is possible. One radical counterpoint centers on mapping *movement patterns*. For this, we may engage and potentially employ "movement notation systems," including Laban Movement Analysis (LMA). This includes consideration of the four dimensions of body, effort, shape, and space (see, e.g., Bradley 2008; also Komjathy 2018). Hypothetically, we can create notations of any activity or event that may become a historio-cultural record, including for potential future reconstructions (see, e.g., Goodman 1990).

Along these lines, somatology brings our attention to the ways in which human beings have transformed and can transform themselves/ourselves through "body-techniques" (see Mauss 1935, 1979; Martin et al. 1988; Murphy 1992; Hadot 1995; Komjathy 2007). While this occurs all of the time in various ways, including through cultural conditioning and architecture as mandated movement, there are intentional undertakings, whether through specific activities or larger training regimens, that result in specific, self-directed transformative effects. This may include latent and even anomalous capacities, including "paranormal" or "extraordinary" ones (e.g., extreme sports). While Philosophy and Religious Studies have tended to (over) emphasize "beliefs," "doctrine," and "thought," worldview is only one dimension of religious systems and traditions. A shift towards "experience" and even "embodiment" are welcome modifications, but these should ideally be combined with "practice" (see, e.g., Komjathy 2015, 2018). This involves attention to the technical specifics of said techniques and regimens, including transformative effects. In Contemplative Studies, the latter are often discussed in terms of "states" (temporary psychological shifts) and "traits" (permanent character changes).

Another noteworthy, related dimension of somatology involves the unique ways that lived, embodied experience may inform one's perspective and even writing. Here I am specifically thinking of *Écriture féminine* ("women's writing"), which is usually traced to the article "Le Rire de la Méduse"/"The Laugh of the Medusa" (1975) by the French feminist and literary theorist Hélène Cixous. This "movement," which involves writing in/as/through female embodiment and a more radical "femininity/feminism," also includes Luce Irigaray and Julia Kristeva as key members (see, e.g., Marks and de Courtivron 1981). Interestingly, and perhaps adding another layer of gender complexity, Cixous' writing is highly influenced by the German philosopher and culture critic Friedrich Nietzsche (1844–1900) and by her lifelong friendship with the French philosopher and post-structuralist Jacques Derrida (1930–2004). Comparatively speaking, one might consider *nǚshū* 女書 ("women's script"), which apparently was first developed between the thirteenth and fourteenth centuries, as a pre-modern Chinese precedent (see, e.g., Foster 2019). Like the late imperial Ruist ("Confucian") influence on the European enlightenment via Jesuit Catholic Latin translation, one also wonders about indirect influence on the modern French movement.

The scholarship on "the body" and "embodiment" is vast. Partially drawing upon Michel Foucault's (1926–1984) "archaeology of knowledge" via Nietzsche's "genealogy of morals," Michel Feher and his collaborators have published the three-volume *Fragments for a History of the Human Body* (1989). For individuals interested in "body-techniques" and associated "transformative practice" there are a number of relevant publications (see above; References herein). Summaries and syncretic theories appear in my various publications (2007, 2015, 2018). I also has advanced a theory of embodiment and transmission, wherein different communities and traditions become manifest as unique presences and movement patterns in the world. This relates to his larger theory of (religious) praxis, involving the interrelationship among views, methods, experiences, and goals. Finally, just as there is a need for deeper engagement with "neurodiversity" in Consciousness Studies and philosophy of mind, my proposed Somatic Studies needs to consider assumptions about and claims rooted in "able-bodiedness," especially in concert with perspectives from Disability Studies.

Related Terms

anthropology, embodiment, experience, personhood, pneumatology, psychology, *qì* 氣 ("subtle breath/energy"; Chinese), *shēn* 身 ("body/self"; Chinese), subjectivity, *xīn* 心 ("heart–mind"; Chinese)

References

Bermúdez, José Luis, Anthony Marcel, and Naomi Eilan, eds. 1998. *The Body and the Self*. Cambridge: MIT Press.
Bradley, Karen. 2008. *Rudolf Laban*. London and New York: Routledge.
Calais-Germain, Blandine. 2007. *Anatomy of Movement*. Rev. ed. Seattle: Eastland Press.
Coakley, Sarah, ed. 1997. *Religion and the Body*. Cambridge: Cambridge University Press.
Cottai, Thomas, and June McDaniel, eds. 2011. *Perceiving the Divine through the Human Body: Mystical Sensuality*. New York: Palgrave MacMillan.

Csordas, Thomas J., ed. 1994. *Embodiment and Experience: The Existential Ground of Culture and Self.* Cambridge: Cambridge University Press.

Feher, Michel, with Ramona Naddaff and Nadia Tazi, eds. 1989. *Fragments for a History of the Human Body*. 3 vols. New York: Zone Books.

Foster, Nicola. 2019. "Translating *Nüshu*: Drawing *Nüshu*, Dancing *Nüshu*." *Art in Translation*, 11 (4): 393–416.

Good, Mary-Jo, Paul Brodwin, Byron Good, and Arthur Kleinman, eds. 1992. *Pain as Human Experience: An Anthropological Perspective*. Berkeley: University of California Press.

Goodman, Felicitas. 1990. *Where the Spirits Ride the Wind: Trance Journeys and Other Ecstatic Experiences*. Bloomington: Indiana University Press.

Grosz, Elizabeth. 1994. *Volatile Bodies: Toward a Corporeal Feminism*. Bloomington and Indianapolis: Indiana University Press.

Hadot, Pierre. 1995. *Philosophy as a Way of Life: Spiritual Exercises from Socrates to Foucault*. Hoboken: Blackwell.

Heidegger, Martin. 1977. *The Question Concerning Technology, and Other Essays*. Trans. William Levitt. New York: Harper Torchbooks.

Hewes, Gordon. 1955. "World Distribution of Certain Postural Habits." *American Anthropologist*, 57: 231–244.

Hewes, Gordon. 1957. "The Anthropology of Posture." *Scientific American*, 196: 123–132.

Ingold, Tim. 2000. *The Perception of the Environment: Essays on Livelihood, Dwelling and Skill*. London and New York, Routledge.

Johnson, Don Hanlon. 1995. *Bone, Breath, and Gesture: Practices of Embodiment*. Berkeley: North Atlantic Books.

Komjathy, Louis, ed. 2015. *Contemplative Literature: A Comparative Sourcebook on Meditation and Contemplative Prayer*. Albany: SUNY Press.

Kasulis, Thomas P., with Roger T. Ames and Wimal Dissanayake, eds. 1993. *Self as Body in Asian Theory and Practice*. Albany: SUNY Press.

Komjathy, Louis. 2007. *Cultivating Perfection: Mysticism and Self-Transformation in Early Quanzhen Daoism*. Leiden: Brill.

Komjathy, Louis, ed. 2015. *Contemplative Literature: A Comparative Sourcebook on Meditation and Contemplative Prayer*. Albany: SUNY Press.

Komjathy, Louis. 2018. *Introducing Contemplative Studies*. West Sussex, England and Hoboken: Wiley-Blackwell.

Laing, R. D. 1967. *The Politics of Experience*. New York: Pantheon Books.

Lakoff, George, and Mark Johnson. 1999. *Philosophy in the Flesh: The Embodied Mind and Its Challenge to Western Thought*. New York: Basic Books.

Law, Jane Marie, ed. 1995. *Religious Reflections on the Human Body*. Bloomington: Indiana University Press.

Marks, Elaine, and Isabelle de Courtivron, eds. 1981. *New French Feminisms*. New York: Schocken.

Martin, Luther, Huck Gutman, and Patrick Hutton, eds. 1988. *Techniques of the Self: A Seminar with Michel Foucault*. Amherst: University of Massachusetts Press.

Mauss, Marcel. 1935. "Les techniques du corps." *Journal de Psychologie Normale et Pathologique*, 35: 271–293.

Mauss, Marcel. 1979. "Body Techniques." In *Sociology and Psychology*. Trans. Ben Brewster. London: Routledge and Kegan Paul, 95–123.

Murphy, Michael. 1992. *The Future of the Body: Explorations into the Further Evolution of Human Nature*. New York: Penguin Putnam Inc.

Scarry, Elaine. 1985. *The Body in Pain: The Making and Un-Making of the World*. Oxford and New York: Oxford University Press.

Vasseleu, Cathryn. 1998. *Textures of Light: Vision and Touch in Irigaray, Levinas and Merleau Ponty*. London and New York: Routledge.

8

The *Nguni* Conceptualization of *umina/ubumina* (the Self)

Analyzing *Impilo, Umoya* and *Ukufa* through Isintuism

Herbert Moyo

Chapter Outline

Introduction	215
Background to the Nguni Ways of Conceptualization	216
The *ubumina/umina* in Isintuism	220
Conclusion	225
8.1 *Impilo* (Life)	227
8.2 *Ukufa* (Death): A Cultural and Spiritual Perspective	230
8.3 Umoya/Imimoya	233

Introduction

In the Nguni Isintuism or Nguni ancestrology, who is the self (Moyo 2025: 285)? Who am I or who is me or what is me ("*Ngubani umina/buyini ubumina*")? *Iyini impilo* ("what is life")? How is *impilo* (life) conceptualized among the *Nguni* (Ownby 1981: 60–8)? *Yini ukufa* ("what is death")? How is *ukufa* (death) conceptualized among the *Nguni*? *uMoya*—I do not know how to render *uMoya* in English. The word may mean be any of the following: soul, the spirit, the breath, wind or air. What is *umoya* and how is it conceptualized among the peoples of the *Nguni* culture? To answer these questions, we must critically engage the *Nguni* cultures with a thorough understanding of Isintuism.[1] Isintuism is the sociocultural, religious, political and economic epistemological foundation of the Nguni culture.

This chapter seeks to explain the concept of umina/*ubumina* (the self) among the Nguni people of Southern Africa. The chapter will discuss *umina* through an explanation of the cosmology of the *Nguni* culture, which has four major languages: Zulu, Xhosa, Ndebele and Swati (Moyo 2023: 218). The people speaking these languages are mainly found in South Africa, Zimbabwe, Eswatini. There are also some traces of the *Nguni* in Botswana, Malawi, Zambia and Mozambique. The *Nguni* in the different geographical and political jurisdictions are not a culturally monolithic group (Maraganedzha 2025). They are now a diverse conglomeration of worldviews which impacts on their understanding of the *umina*, which is the word I will be using for "self."

Despite their contextual differences, the *Nguni* still espouse some aspects of Isintuism, which thereby creates some common understanding of the *umina* (Bailey 1995: 39–50). *Isintu* signifies the normative *Nguni* way of life. *Isintu* is the living out of one's life as a continuous practice of 'beliefs', customs and culture according to the *Nguni* normative lifestyle. The *Isintu* involves the economy, dressing, respect for the living and the dead, marriage, death, building homes, celebrations and food. The totality of being, religio-cultural realities, cosmology/worldviews and a Life lived through a variety of rituals, observances and behavioural patterns that can be referred to as customs, tradition, culture or religion. For *umina* to be said to be alive, everyday life must always be pleasing to the living and to the living dead. The *umina/umuntu* cannot be conceptualized outside of the Isintuism norms and values. The concept of *umina/ubumina* among the Nguni people of Southern Africa is complex and can be viewed from the broader Isintuism.

I engage the philosophy of *umina/ubumina* by analysing the *Nguni* praxis on *Impilo* (life), *ukufa* (death) and *Umoya* (Spirit). *umina/ubumina* as the spirit lives in perpetuity in *impilo, ukufa* and *umoya*. These different realms of *umina/ubumina* can be comprehended through the performance of appropriate rituals and rites of passage. The *Nguni* conception of *umina* is grounded on a cosmology that is beginningless and endless. Therefore, let me engage the foundations of the Nguni conceptualization of Isintuism as a foundation for understanding impilo, umoya, and ukufa.

Background to the Nguni Ways of Conceptualization

The Nguni People

I used the word "Isintuism" to explain the history and identity of the *Nguni*, the *Nguni* culture, *Nguni* cosmology and *Nguni* philosophy. Stan Schoeman confirms that the

Nguni are a group of *Bantu* (languages that use *ntu* as a root for a number of words) speaking people found across Southern Africa. "Like the Swazi, Zulu, Xhosa and even the distant *Ngoni* of Malawi, the Matabele of Zimbabwe and the Transvaal Ndebele belong to the same great *Nguni* branch of Bantu-speaking people" (Schoeman 1987: 192–198). The *Nguni* are found mainly in South Africa, Swaziland and Zimbabwe. There are also traces of the *Nguni* in Zambia, Mozambique, Botswana and Malawi. The major languages spoken by the Nguni are Zulu, Xhosa, Ndebele and Swati (Moyo 2023: 218). The *Nguni* ways of life, due to contact with other cultures around the world, has shifted some socioeconomic and traditional ritual practices. The *Nguni* originally come from what is currently known as South Africa mainly KwaZulu-Natal and the Eastern Cape. At the time there were no national borders between what is presently known as South Africa, Swaziland, Botswana, Malawi, Zambia, Mozambique and Zimbabwe. The *Nguni* simply belonged to different chiefdoms and Kingdoms. Through migrations in the nineteenth century the Nguni got scattered across many parts of Southern Arica. The first reason for scattering the *Nguni* was the tribal wars of the nineteenth century.

> The Nguni way of life changed greatly during the 19th century. One of the major factors was the Mfecane ("Crushing"), a period of wars and resettlement begun in the 1820s by Shaka, king of the Zulu. Shaka created an expansive Zulu state that waged war on neighbouring peoples, causing them to be incorporated into the Zulu state or to flee as refugees. These refugees, copying the new military discipline and the strategy developed by Shaka, were able to conquer other African peoples and to establish new states throughout southern and central Africa. These included the Ndebele state in south-western Zimbabwe, under Mzilikazi; the Gaza state in southern Mozambique, under Soshangane; the Swazi state in Swaziland, under the Dlamini family; and a cluster of Ngoni states in Tanzania, Zambia, and Malawi, under the successors of the *Ngoni* leader Zwangendaba.
>
> ("Nguni")

Colonialism and the entrenchment of European control over African resources led to the belittling of African customs and traditions. Industrialization, urbanization, monetarization, Christianization and Westernization have altered the essence of being *Nguni*. Colonialism divided Southern Africa into colonial nation states thereby consigning the *Nguni* to different countries. In the new countries the *Nguni* became neighbours to other tribal groupings in ways that affected their culture, in some cases even the *Nguni* language was affected. For example, in Zambia the *Nguni* are now called the *Ngoni*. The *Nguni* in different states across Southern Africa have been separated for over two centuries and their cultures have been drifting part such that presently the *Nguni* culture is as diverse as the number of groups in different countries (Maraganedzha 2025). Despite their contextual differences, the *Nguni* still refer to the ideal way of life as Isintu (Bailey 1995: 39–50). The *Nguni* are still united by several aspects of the philosophy of Isintuism (*Nguni* philosophy of life).

Isintu and Isintuism

Isintu is being a behavioural Nguni while Isintuism is the philosophy of life of the Nguni (Moyo 2021). The *Nguni* worldview is centred on the continuity of life as an endless cycle with no beginning and no ending. Isintuism may be understood by what has become known as African Traditional Religion (ATR) or African Indigenous Religion (AIR), which seem to imply that there is one religion for all Africans diverse as they are. Isintuism is the direct equivalent of ATR/AIR as it is the totality of the worldviews of the *Nguni*. Isintuism envelopes the knowledge systems, belief systems, practices, rites of passage, philosophies about life cycles, the economic and sociological aspects of the *Nguni* life. Isintuism is the foundation of *Nguni* norms and values in their communitarian lifestyles. Isintuism uses art, taboos and idioms to define principles and values that constitute philosophies underpinning acceptable human character or *Nguni* espoused ethical behaviour such as *Ubuntu* (being humane).

Communitarianism is a basic *Nguni* value in the construction of communities which is epitomized by the most popular *Nguni* idiom, "*Umuntu ngumuntu ngabantu*" (I am because we are/a person is a person because of other people/you cannot be a person alone). The deviation from *Isintu* can result in the loss of *Ubuntu*. *Ubuntu* is an ethical concept that shows adherence to *Isintu* which manifests itself through communitarianism, using the humanness of individuals who constitute a community (Moyo 2021: 125). *Isintu* is the living out of one's life as a *Nguni* who continuously practice *Nguni* values, traditions, customs and principle.

The knowledge, values, principles and being a *Nguni* is Isintuism. In the *Nguni* worldview there is no difference between culture, religion and Ubuntu, all these can be conceptualized as *Isintu*. Ubuntu is an expression of *Isintu*. *Isintu* requires other human beings, hence communalism. "*Ubuntu* is the ethic that drives the consciousness of the communally shared life-giving values such as relatedness, respect, communitarianism, hospitality and interdependency. These communal values are passed on through generations for the well-being of the individual, the wider community and the environment" (Moyo 2021: 125). *Isintu* is the practical aspect of the *Nguni* worldview which is manifested through visible operational acts called *ubuntu*. Mqhayi argues that *Ubuntu* is for the, "black people throughout Africa south of the Sahara" (Mqhayi 1931: 134). In everyday life if one does things according to the traditional way, then it is said "*Uyenza isiNtu* (practising *Isintu*)" (Moyo 2021: 125). Based on Mqhayi's understanding, *Isintu* is about the food eaten, dressing, mannerisms, kindness, language, economic activities, livelihoods and relationships with others and with the spirit world. The pinnacle of *isintu* is the relationship between people as individuals and as communities. Human life is lived in community hence the communitarian nature of Isintuism hence the saying, "*Umuntu ngumuntu ngabantu*" (a person is a person through persons). This is emphasized by Setiloane who says, "The whole African traditional life-style with its age-sets, rites of passage, several generations living together, is built on the principle that 'You cannot be human alone'.

"*Motho ke motho ka batho*" (Sotho for 'a person is a person through others'): Our humanity finds fulfilment only in community with others" Setiloane 1986: 13). In the communitarian *Nguni* way of life people learn to share almost everything. The *Nguni* people who do not espouse communitarianism do not have ubuntu because in Isintuism, humans become human in community ("*umuntu ngumuntu ngabantu*").

People who are anti-communitarianism are viewed as having negative spiritualties. In the community there are living people and the living dead who are spirits. In the spiritual realm of the community there are also communitarian spirits and anti-communitarian spirits. In other words, the Nguni believe that "The community is composed of both good and bad people, life-giving forces and life-denying forces; spirits (both good and bad), magicians, Sangomas, ancestors and witches are part of the community. Communalism extends beyond the visible to the invisible. Being in community may mean to say you appease human beings and spirits. You get protection from bad spirit using your good spirits" (Moyo 2021: 125). Every human being in flesh has a soul that is impacted spirits that are part of the community.

The Cosmology of the Nguni

In another project, I described the cosmology of the *Nguni*: "Cosmologically, the Ndebele believe that everything is cyclic, implying endlessness, continuity and perpetuity of cycles in nature including human life. People are born to grow and live life so that they can die and go back to where they came from. In this worldview, death is seen as a journey back to the ancestors or to the land of the living dead" (Moyo 2021). In the *Nguni* worldview the round shape or the circle is the primary original shape for almost everything. To understand the Isintuism there is need for an understanding of the *Nguni* epistemologies related to the circle. The circle is used to build things like houses, cattle corrals, homesteads, water wells, several other patterns of life such as dancing, singing and musical instruments. Pathisa Nyathi (2020) relates creation to the *Nguni* worldviews. Nyathi says that the moon, the sun, the stars and the earth are all rounds. The human body is also made up of several round shaped parts such as the eyes, mouth and nostrils. The human limbs are cylindrical in shape implying a pile of circles. The Nguni also create their own reality in circles in line with the created order. Moyo says "Systems such as seasons, months of the year, the days of the week, the sun, the moon dying and resurrecting systematically every month are all cyclic" (Moyo 2021: 125).

Nyathi and Chikomo say,

> A people's worldview and cosmology are a result of the interaction between nature and culture. Africans observed nature and got inspired by it ... The seasons of the year were repetitive, cyclical and characterised by birth, death and rebirth. Summer is symbolic of life; however, it is not a permanent phenomenon. Autumn follows and life wanes and declines. Winter follows autumn and is symbolic and an approximation of

death, a period of total rest in readiness for the next lively stage ... Spring is part of the cycle and holds promise for a new life. Trees develop buds and flowers blossom. This is the time when trees begin the all—important process of developing seeds, which give life to new trees; this is continuity of a species. For the Africans this marks the beginning of a new year—a nature—determined period that lies behind the process of fertility, continuity, perpetuity, immortality, endlessness and infinity.

(Nyathi 2016: 7).

The planets in nature are interdependent assuming the *Nguni* communitarianism. Phenomenon in nature does not live in isolation and the Nguni are imitating nature in their epistemologies of life hence the Isintuism. The *umina/ubumina* is located in the life cycles that have no beginning and no ending. The understanding of *Impilo, umoya and ukufa* through Isintuism is infirmed by the begginglessness and endlessness of life. This leads to the discussion on the concept of *ubumina/umina* in Isintuism.

The *ubumina/umina* in Isintuism

The *ubumina/umina* is a complex phenomenon. To have a Nguni understanding of the *umina/ubumina* there is a need to be knowledgeable of Isintuism as the foundation of the being of a *Nguni* person. The worldviews of the *Nguni* people are captured in Isintuism, and the understanding of the self *(Ubumina/umina)* is also located in Isintuism. Therefore, to make sense of the self, one should make sense of Isintuism which informs and forms the *Nguni* philosophies of life. One of the key characteristics of Isintuism is communitarianism. All things exist in communities, in groups and in families. The individual makes sense if understood in community. I am because we are which is captured in the proverb, "*Umuntu ngumuntu ngabantu*" (I am because we are/ a person is a person because of other persons). This applies to physical realties as well to abstract realities like *umoya* which cannot be understood on its own but in community with another phenomenon.

To understand the soul one should also understand the physical person and the spirit as well as the community that is defining such phenomenon. Isintuism uses art, taboos and idioms to define principles and values that constitute philosophies underpinning acceptable human character or behaviour such as the ethic of *Ubuntu* (Abubakre 2021). As already noted, communitarianism is a basic value in the construction of communities which can be epitomized by the idiom "*Umuntu ngumuntu ngabantu.*" In Isintuism spiritualties (religion), customs, traditions and culture are one and the same thing. *Isintu* is the living out one's life as a continuous practice of spiritualties, customs, ubuntu and culture (ibid.). In a way everyday life is the praxis of Isintuism. The understanding of the self, life and death is also hinged in the praxis of Isintuism.

Cycles in Isintuism

The *Ngu* see the concepts of the self, life and death as part of an endless cycle. Cosmologically the *Nguni* believe that everything is cyclic thereby implying endlessness, continuity and perpetuity in cycles of nature. The self is entangled in people that are born to grow and live life so that they can die and go back to where they came from. In this worldview, death is seen as journey back to the ancestors or to the land of the living dead.

In the *Nguni* worldview the circle is a basic shape for the house (the hut), the cattle corral, and the water well and the yard, just to mention a few. The *Nguni* looked up in the sky and saw that the created order is a circle. The moon, the sun, the stars and the earth are all circles. The human body is also made up of circles, the mouth the eyes, the nostrils, all the body openings are all circles. Since the Creator produced nature in the form of circles, the *Nguni* also create whatever they will be creating in the form of circles to fit the cyclic nature of creation. For example, seasons, the sun, the cycles of the moon showing dying and resurrection systematically every month. In fact, the moon is one central phenomenon that informs the *Nguni* worldview on the cycle of life. According to the *Nguni* understanding the moon is born, it grows to full moon then it starts to diminish and die. When it dies one knows that it will come back again renewed and young. Then it goes through the same cycle again. The cycle of the moon is likened to the menstrual cycle of a woman which is named after the moon: *usenyangeni* (she is in the moon). The cycles of the moon are used to understand life of the self and death and then life in the spirit of a human being the process of fertility, continuity, perpetuity, immortality, endlessness and infinity. The self, life, death, spirituality and the continuity of the self is inherent cyclical birth–death–rebirth that lies behind eternal life. Perpetual life or continuity is assured through this circle of life.

The philosophy of Isintuism is grounded on the *Nguni* worldview, cosmology and the repetitiveness of the natural cycles of seasons and cosmic bodies. The *Isintu* understands human reality as similar to that of natural cycles in nature. Now one can understand why almost everything is designed as a circle by the *Nguni* people. It is because philosophically life is a series of cycles of birth, death and rebirth. The philosophy of *Isintu* imitates the cosmos because of its ability to regenerate itself and live forever with no beginning and no end.

The self after birth and before death (the separation of the real self from the body) is the holistic individual comprising character, spirituality, mentality and consciousness. The self before birth and after death is a spiritual being, which is *umina*. *umina* names what is invisible outside of the body that nevertheless has influence and power over those who are still in the body.

To exist in actuality, the self requires socioeconomic, religious and political settings through either adaptation, rebellion, or both (as the case may be). The self-concept is influenced by the above contextual realities that affect the body and the mind which influences the heart. The conglomeration of these realities produces self as a theoretical entity. This conception of the self is learned rather than inherent. It is influenced by biological, environmental, and social factors. It develops through childhood and early adulthood. And, it can continue to evolve throughout life in the cycle of life and death. There is some level of reincarnation through the life cycle. The self comes back in other human beings in the family line through rebirth or through spirituality. In fact, *Ubumina/Umina* as reincarnation comes in two different forms: as a rebirth of someone who once lived and died, and, as being possessed by the spirit of a relative that lived and passed out of the body.

The publicly visible *ubumina/umina* is a complex reality that is incorporated to the physical visible body. The *ubumina/umina* in the public is composed of several other attributes that are visible to those who see and interact with me such as character made up of my thoughts and behaviour which are inseparable from the self. *umina* is understood to be able to be separable from the physical body and still exist outside of the body. The body is only able to be visible outside the body. The body is a carrier for the *ubumina/umina*, which is supposedly visible while it is in the body that carries it. It is visible as the life of the body. *ubumina/umina* is what sees, thinks, views, thinks, eats, drinks and talks. Some people think they have seen me by seeing the body that carries me. The *ubumina/umina* describes who I am and what I am (Beattie 1980). It is inclusive of the way I understand who/what I am and the communal understanding of who/what I am through the narrative of my life. The *ubumina/umina* is not tangible but dwells in the heart (or mind). The *ubumina/umina* is the sum of my experiences.

The *ubumina/umina* is neither coextensive nor identical with the physical body, even though it is difficult to imagine *ubumina/umina* without the body. The *ubumina/umina* can exist without the body through the narrative of my life by others even after death. The narrative helps others to create a mental model of my body which is directly linked to my behavioural and physical attributes. I may thereby live forever, in others. The forever aspect is linked to others' life spans as one exists in others while their self is still existing in the body, at least we have evidence for that in the level of memory of others whose self has departed from their bodies.

In Isintuism the concept of *ubumina/umina* is also viewed from a communitarian perspective. It is possible for traditionalists to avoid the *ubumina/umina* ("me") and prefer *thina* ("us"), since "me" can only be understood from the "us." The *umina* is not comprehensible without the *thina*. Hence sayings like, "*umuntu ngumuntu ngabantu*" (I am because we are/a person is a person because of other persons). Following this philosophy of identity one can tell that the *ubumina/umina* is inseparably intertwined with the *thina* (us). The *thina* is equally depended on *ubumina/umina* in community with others.

Ubumina/umina in Community

A communitarian conception of the self does not erase the individual. Amongst the Nguni the individual is visible and unique, despite being located in a group. The group makes the individual distinct. The *ubumina/umina* in a group helps to distinguish it through my experiences as opposed to, or, as similar to, the experiences of others. The *ubumina/umina* becomes prominent or clearly identifiable in the midst of others. The identity of the *ubumina/umina* is my life story, my narrative. If the narrative is taken away, then the *umina* ceases to exist. The *ubumina/umina* is a narrative made up of my principles, values and events of life that are linked to the community. The *ubumina/umina* in community is understood as identified based on the events of life performed by the body or through the body.

The *ubumina/umina* is located in my experiences creating what can be referred to as my personality. This Nguni view of *ubumina/umina* resonates with the ideas of Elinor Ochs and Lisa Capps who argue:

> Personal narrative simultaneously is born out of experience and gives shape to experience. In this sense, narrative and self are inseparable. Self is here broadly understood to be an unfolding reflective awareness of being-in-the world, including a sense of one's past and future. We come to know ourselves as we use narrative to apprehend experiences and navigate relationships with others. The inseparability of narrative and self is grounded in the phenomenological assumption that entities are given meaning through being experienced and the notion that narrative is an essential resource in the struggle to bring experiences to conscious awareness.
>
> (Ochs 1996: 20–21)

Ubumina/umina while locked in the body is not static but dynamic as it keeps transforming depending on experiences while in the body. The *ubumina/umina* narrative is dependent on past experiences which according to the *Nguni* are mainly located in the community. The narrative about the self makes the *Ubumina/umina* concrete in community as one cannot be understood as an individual but in community with other *ubumina/umina*.

The *ubumina/umina* viewed as *umuntu* (the person)

The *ubumina/umina* is used when I talk about myself. The *ubumina/umina* is a way of self-description where I point to my chest and narrate my life experiences. When others describe the *ubumina/umina* they will refer to it as the *umuntu* (the person). The ideal is that the others can also describe *umuntu* through a narrative that attaches communal principles and values of *ubuntu*. The *umuntu* can then be described as a good or a bad person depending on their life story. *Umuntu* is identified by the family they are born into, the date (period) of birth, life events, achievements, failure, and contributions or failure to contribute to the community and the date of death. If there is no story, then there is nothing to say and the *umuntu* ceases to exist.

The *umuntu* as a description of *ubumina/umina* by others depends on behavioral patterns as measured against whatever is normative in a given context. Amongst the *Nguni* the identity of *umuntu* can be viewed from words, actions and misdeeds. The *umuntu* is a given a name at birth and linked to a particular family, intertwining it into that family. If the *umuntu* is consistently behaving as expected in the norms and values of the family and community, then the *ubuntu* is affirmed. The *ubumina/umina* can cease to be *umuntu* if *ubumina/umina* does not espouse *ubuntu*. In the *Nguni* worldview *ubumina/umina* can struggle to exist without the communal *umuntu* aspect grounded in the norms of *ubuntu*. Hence the concept of "*umuntu ngumuntu ngabantu*" is described.

The nature of individuals and the community in the *Nguni* worldview is complex. As already noted above, it is untrue to claim the individual does not exist in the *Nguni* worldview but the individual is viewed through the community. The *Nguni* are aware that the individual exists and it is the individuals that make up the community. Without the individuals there is no community. At birth individuals are given individual names to exist as individuals but this individual gets tied to the family and or tribe by surname. Already at birth one is both an individual and a member of a community. This brings about the *ubumina/umina* (self) and the *umuntu* (person). The two terms *ubumina/umina* and *umuntu* complement each other to give identity to *ubumina/umina*. In fact, *ubumina/umina* develops from *umuntu*. When the *ubumina/umina* was young, chances are high that one could not give a narrative of the self. The narrative about the self is built partly from the narratives given to *ubumina/umina* by the family, such as the date of birth, the parents, and the siblings. The *ubumina/umina* is intricately and inseparably intertwined with the community as *umuntu*. Without the community around the *ubumina/umina* it may be difficult to conceive the self as the foundation of the self are the community (Beattie 1980).

The complexity of the *ubumina/umina* is that the narrative of the umina includes the past of the self and the past of the community. The narratives of the community get intertwined with the narrative of *ubumina/umina*. It is these community narratives that influence what becomes operational parameters called tradition, culture, religion and political imperatives such as race and social class constituting *ubumina/umina*. The *umina* is therefore becomes part of narratives that happened prior to *umina*'s birth. Such can actually influence the future development of the self. *ubumina/umina*'s activities mainly through or in the body is what is viewed as impilo.

Conclusion

This chapter has demonstrated that the concept of *umina/ubumina* (the self) among the Nguni is complex and can be viewed from the broader isintuism. The *ubumina/umina* is linked to the cosmology, culture, spirituality and languages of the Nguni. My key terms for this volume are useful for further understanding *ubumina/umina* through the *Nguni* praxis on *Impilo* (life), *ukufa* (death) and *Umoya* (Spirit/soul). I conclude that *umina/ubumina* as the spirit lives in perpetuity as *umina/ubumina* is present in *impilo, ukufa* and *umoya*. These different realms of *umina/ubumina* can be realized through the performance of appropriate rituals and rites of passage. The *Nguni* philosophy of *umina/ubumina* is grounded on the cosmological cycles of nature showing continuity, beggininglessness and endlessness.

Notes

1. The concepts that I am engaging such as *umina/ubumina* and Isintuism are issues that have existed in the oral traditions of the Nguni. There are no credible academic sources that have engaged these ideas. This is what makes my contribution. Most of the ideas fall under my experiential knowledge as an insider of the Nguni worldviews. Where others have engaged the concepts I will duly reference such academic pieces of work.

Bibliography

Abubakre, Mumin, Isam Faik, and Marcia Mkansi. 2021. "Digital Entrepreneurship and Indigenous Value Systems: An Ubuntu Perspective." *Information Systems Journal*, 31 (6): 838–862.

Bailey, Richard. 1995. "Sociolinguistic Evidence of Nguni, Sotho, Tsonga and Venda Origins." In R. Mesthrie (ed.), *Language and Social History: Studies in South African Sociolinguistics*. Johannesburg: David Philip, 39–50.

Beattie, John. 1980. "Representations of the Self in Traditional Africa." *Africa: Journal of the International African Institute*, 50 (3): 313–320.

Maraganedzha, Mutshidzi. 2025. "Poverty, Ubuntu, and Sustainable Development." In *The Palgrave Handbook of Ubuntu, Inequality and Sustainable Development*. Ed. Ezra Chitendo, Beatrice Okyere-Manu, Sophia Chirongoma, and Musa W. Dube. Cham: Springer Nature Switzerland, 521–535.

Mbiti, J. S. 1970. *African Religions and Philosophies*. New York: Anchor Books.

Moyo, Herbert. 2021. "The Death of Isintu in Contemporary Technological Era: The Ethics of Sex Robots among the Ndebele of Matabo." In Beatrice Dedaa Okyere-Manu (ed.), *African Values, Ethics, and Technology: Questions, Issues, and Approaches.* Cham: Springer International Publishing, 123–135.

Moyo, Herbert. 2023. "The Nguni Traditional 'Religious' Thoughts." In Nathan R. B. Loewen and Agnieszka Rostalska (eds.), *Diversifying Philosophy of Religion: Critiques, Methods and Case Studies.* London: Bloomsbury, 219–228.

Moyo, Herbert. 2025. "Isintuism: The Mother of Communalism among the Nguni of Southern Africa." In Gereon Kopf, Purushottama Bilimoria, and Nathan Loewen (eds.), *Engaging Philosophies of Religion: Thinking across Boundaries.* London: Bloomsbury, 285–300.

Mqhayi, S. E. K. 1931. *Ityala Lamawele.* Loved Ale: Loved Ale Press, 134.

"Nguni." *Encyclopedia Britannica.* www.britannica.com/topic/Nguni (accessed June 10, 2025).

Nyathi, P., and K. Chikomo. 2016. *Echoes from the Past: Interpreting Zimbabwe's Decorative Symbols.* Luveve: Amagugu Publishers.

Nyathi, Phathisa. 2020. Interview, March 1. Bulawayo, Zimbabwe.

Ochs, Elinor, and Lisa Capps. 1996. "Narrating the Self." *Annual Review of Anthropology*, 25 (1): 19–43.

Ownby, Carolan Postma. 1981. "Early Nguni History: Linguistic Suggestions." *South African Journal of African Languages*, 1 (1): 60–81.

Schoeman, Stan. 1987. "Settlement in South Africa: Early Migrants and the Nguni." *Africa Insight*, 17 (3): 192–198.

Setiloane, G. 1986. *Introduction to African Theology.* Johannesburg: Skotaville Publishers.

Impilo (Life)
Chapter 8.1

Impilo and *umoya* are inseparable as there is interdependency. *ubumina/umina* is tied to *umoya* for *ubumina/umina* to be active in the body. *ubumina/umina* is sustained in the body by *umoya*. There are times when the *umoya* is confused with *ubumina/umina*. *Impilo* is the continued intake of *umoya* by the body to sustain the relationship between *ubumina/umina* and the body. The sustained presence of the *ubumina/umina* in the body and in the place of the living dead after death is *impilo*. The *impilo* is important in all the stages of the cycle of *ubumina/umina*, before birth, in the body and as a spirit. *Ubumina/umina* lives in perpetuity though becomes visible at birth. Life means several things amongst the Nguni such as being connected to the spirit world, being communitarian as well as adherence to the norms and values of the community. *Impilo* also means that *ubumina/umina* is still in the physical body. Due to the influence of western religions, the Nguni now believe that *Impilo* (Life) comes from *umvelinqangi/Uthixo/Umdali/Unkulunkulu* (God/Gods[1]) through ancestors and one's parents.

In the *Nguni* worldview, people originated from *Emhlangeni* (reeds). The foundation of the *ubumina/umina* is a big river with reeds. This is why some Nguni groups have kept the annual Reed dance/festival celebrating the origins and continuity of life. In the annual reed dance festival young girls that have reached puberty are a demonstration of the ever-flowing river that can sustain the reeds for procreation. After the genesis of human life from the reeds, people now come from their ancestors. In fact, the ability to procreate is a key part of *Impilo*. Failure to procreate is tantamount to death. *Ubumina/umina* should procreate for multiplication and continuity. *ubumina/umina* understands that for multiplication and continuity there is need for others as this cannot happen at an individual level. This applies even in the reincarnation through possession of theirs spiritually, the individual needs others hence communitarianism.

Impilo in Nguni Cosmology

Impilo is cyclic and endless among the Nguni. In fact, in the Nguni cosmologically, everything is cyclic, implying endlessness, continuity and perpetuity of cycles in nature including human life. The circle is a basic shape for almost everything such as the house (the hut), cattle corral, water well and musical instruments. The circle by the Nguni imitates nature such as Planets, Solar system, phases of the moon, menstrual cycle of women and seasons. The human body, including limbs are cylindrical implying that the human body is a circle. In the Nguni worldview there are many actions in life that depict the cyclic worldview such as the sound of musical instruments that are repetitive, Nguni music, which is a repetition of the same phrase, playing games that set players into a circle or into cyclic actions, dancing for the Nguni usual cyclic, war formation, hunting formation are all cyclic.

Impilo in Communitarianism

Life is lived in community, hence the saying that "I am because you are," with the popular Nguni saying that "*Umuntu ngumuntu ngabantu*." This means that *umina* cannot be fully umuntu alone. This goes deeper into the concept of procreation. The *umina* cannot create the self. There is need for the community for the body of *umina/ubumina* to be created in the first place. The community of the living and the living dead brings about the birth of the *umina*.

The value of being communitarian is central in that even in our language we demonstrate being communitarian. For example, when greeting each other and asking about life we say "*Salibonani*" which is plural for "how are you." This Salibonani is said to individuals as they are believed not be individuals but beings in the community of spirits, family (both the living and the dead). In other words, individuals belong to the community of the living, the living dead and the yet to be born. They belong to the community of good spirits and bad spirits, the have and the have not.

Isintu is hinged around care for the other through sharing and communal respect responsibility. *Impilo* is the ability to participate in Ilima (coming together for farming projects to help individual/families as the case may be), *ukusisa* (lending animals especially cattle to those that do not have so that they can also have a kraal, milk and animal draught power for plowing) and *ukusiza* (offering help where necessary). Sadness, poverty, joy, challenges and celebrations are communal realities experienced and managed collectively. In general, life means interdependence. There is spirit of caring for one another especial the vulnerable such as the old, the young, travelers/foreigners and visitors. Such communitarianism is summarized in the ethic of *ubuntu* (being humane). *Ubuntu* of the *umina/ubumina* can be achieved through a life that shows that being of *umuntu* depends on others hence the proverb "*umuntu ngumuntu ngabantu*." Human beings cannot be human alone, they become human and alive through being communitarian.

Impilo in Summary

Impilo (Life) among the Nguni people is a concept deeply rooted in their cosmology and way of life, emphasizing interdependence, continuity, and community. The Nguni see life as sustained through a constant intake of *umoya* (breath or spirit), which maintains the vital force known as *ubumina/umina* within the body. This relationship is crucial for the existence of life at all stages, from birth to death and beyond. The Nguni worldview sees life as an endless cycle, reflected in the circular shapes of their dwellings, cattle kraals, and various cultural practices. *Impilo* is not just an individual experience but a communal one, where one's existence and well-being are intrinsically linked to the community as "Umuntu ngumuntu ngabantu." *Impilo* to be real must be sustained by adhering to the norms and values of the community, maintaining a connection to the ancestors, and ensuring the continuity of *ubumina/umina* through procreation. The failure to procreate is seen as a form of death, as it disrupts the cycle of life and the continuity of the community. In essence, *impilo* is a holistic and interconnected experience that transcends the *umina/ubumina*, encompassing the physical, spiritual, and communal aspects of existence. *Impilo* is ultimately linked to ukufa (death) as an aspect of the *umina/ubumina*'s life cycle.

Note

1. If the name of the Christian God is written in capital letter G, then the Nguni Gods from a Nguni perspective will also be a capital letter G. The Christian God is not superior to the Nguni Gods.

Ukufa (Death)
A Cultural and Spiritual Perspective
Chapter 8.2

The Nguni understand *Ukufa* as an inevitable eventuality in the life cycle of a human being. *Ukufa* is not viewed as the end of life but as a transition to another realm of existence with profound spiritual, social, and cultural ramifications. *Ubumina/Umina* is visible through the physical body. *Ubumina/Umina*'s human form is made possible by the physical material body in which the *ubumina/umina* dwells. The body and the ubumina/umina get intertwined to the point that there is no separation between the two. The communal *umina/ubumina* is enabled by *ubumina/Umina* being in the body. When ubumina/umina talks there is a sense of the separation between *ubumina/Umina* and the body. For example, *ubumina/Umina* seems to own the rest of the body in instances when it says, "my body, my arm my eye, my voice, my life, etc." When this that says "my" which the Nguni view as *umina/ubumina* departs from the body, *yikufa lokho* (the is death). The body without *umina/ubumina* decays and wastes away. It cannot even be able to inhale oxygen and exhale carbon dioxide. The Nguni will say X is no longer there or is gone while the body is still visible. In other words, *ukufa* is the departure of this controlling *umina/ubumina* that even speaks on behalf of the totality of the being. The power to control continues in the spiritual realm as *umina/ubumina* becomes an ancestor to control and influence the living.

The Language of *Ukufa*

The language used when *ukufa* occurs demonstrates that the understanding that ukufa is a transition from the physical to the spiritual realm, *ukufa* is not the end of life. Death is the biggest and most difficult life event among the Nguni in spite of their understanding that it is not the end but a transition to the spiritual realm (Msimang 1991: 448). Death as the separation between the spiritual *umina/ubumina* and the physical body "is the most respectful practice and a gateway to the ancestors" (Ngubane 2012). Death is the shift from the realm of the living to the living dead. It does not signal the end of life; it signals the departure of *umina/ubumina* from the physical body. According to Berglund (Berglund 1976), death is commonly known as *ukugoduka* (going back home), *ukushona* (to pass away), *ukudlula emhlabeni* (to move on leaving earthly life), or *ukuhamba emhlabeni* (to depart from the body) is usually understood and accepted by those who survive the deceased. *Ukugoduka* (to go home) is the death of elderly people who are believed to have gone back home to become ancestors. *Ukuphumula* (to rest) is death after a long illness or short very painful experience.

Sudden death, particularly for people that are young or at the prime of their life, is seen as tragedy and this where the work *ukufa* or *ukubhubha* are used. *Ukufa* and *ukubhubha* are not viewed as natural and may disturb the natural cycle and therefore are not acceptable compared to the other forms of death. A king does not die but *inkosi iyakhothama* (the king bows out). "Regardless of its course, death as perceived by many is a traumatic event" (Mbizana 2007). Specific death and burial rituals also show the inherent worldviews about *ukufa* (Zungu 2021). According to the Nguni death confers supernatural powers to the deceased. Those who have managed to get out of the body are more powerful than the living. The *umina/ubumina* outside the body in the spiritual realm after death has control over those who are still in the body. While in the spiritual realm after *ukufa ubumina/umina* could bless or to curse, and to give or to take life. This is why the living have an obligation to continuously appease and communicate with those in the spiritual realm to become good ancestors that bless and protect the family.

Funeral Rites and Rituals

Amongst the Nguni, *ukufa* is deeply intertwined with spiritualities and the belief in afterlife in the spirit world of the ancestors. Therefore death, as already noted, is seen as a passage to the ancestral world, where the spirits of the deceased continue to exist and influence the living. In other words, *umina/ubumina* continues to live and for this to happen in ways that benefit both the living and deceased, specific rites of passage and rituals must be performed correctly during and after the funeral. People are believed to come from their ancestors and therefore *ukufa* is a return to the ancestors. The dead have a possibility of coming back to the living through dreams, through reincarnation and rebirth.

Funeral rites must be performed correctly to honor the deceased, ensure their safe passage to the ancestral world, and provide comfort to the bereaved. The rituals are both communal and individual depending on the position and relationship to the deceased such as eldest child, parents and spouse. Some rituals are performed by direct family members while other rituals are performed by the community at large. These rites can vary significantly from one family to another, yet they share common elements of ritual, symbolism, and communal participation. The funeral rituals incorporate grieving, ancestral veneration, animal sacrifice, and the ritual cleansing of the home to protect the living from malevolent spirits. A specific family member can be a spokesperson for the family to instruct, advise and negotiate with the deceased *umina/ubumina*. The place of burial, the (*ithuna*) grave is venerated by the living. The body of the deceased is equally important, and the Nguni hardly imagine cremation as this takes away the body of the deceased. In fact, for traditional Nguni people, cremation is a big no.

Conclusion

Ukufa in the Nguni setting is a complex and multifaceted phenomenon that reflects the rich cultural, spiritual, and social fabric of the community. It is an event that transcends the mere cessation of life, embodying a transition to the ancestral realm and reinforcing the interconnectedness of the community between the living, the living dead and the yet to be born. Through elaborate funeral rites, communal mourning, and the veneration of ancestors, the Nguni honor the deceased and ensure the continuity of their cultural and spiritual heritage. Despite contemporary challenges and influences, the profound significance of death and the rituals surrounding it remain integral to the African way of life.

References

Berglund, A. 1976. *Zulu Thought Patterns and Symbolism*. Cape Town: David Philip.
Mbizana, Clifford. 2007. "Resilience in Bereaved Zulu Families." PhD diss., University of Zululand, Richards Bay.
Msimang, C. T. 1991. *Kusadliwa Ngoludala*. 2nd ed. Pietermaritzburg: Shuter and Shooter (Pty) Ltd. 448.
Ngubane S. 2012. "Death and Burial Practices in Contemporary Zulu Culture." *Mankind Q*, 53: 91–109.
Zungu, Evangeline Bonisiwe. 2021. "Juxtaposing Adherence to COVID-19 Regulations and Practising Proper Burial Rites: A Case Study of Zulu Traditional Religion." *Pharos Journal of Theology*, 102 (2).

Umoya/Imimoya
Chapter 8.3

Umina/Ubumina can also be understood from the *umoya/imimoya* perspective. As already noted, *umina/ubumina* is complexly intertwined with spiritualities extending from the yet to the born, the living and the living dead. *UMoya* (singular)/*Imimoya* (plural) is a central word in the Nguni isintuism. In English *umoya* translates to too many words, such as air, wind, soul, spirit.

The *umina/ubumina* that dwells in the body and has the ability to leave the body when it stops breathing is thought of as *umoya*. The problem is that the *umina/ubumina* at some point would say *umoya wami* (my *umoya*). In this case one views the *umoya* as the soul. But the *umina/ubumina* at times says, "my soul," which means *umina* is not the soul. At times when the *umina/ubumina* leaves the body, the Nguni will say "*umphefumulo suphumile*." This is difficult to translate, loosely this says, "breath has left." When breath leaves then the person is dead. May be *umina/ubumina* is the breath. *Umphefumulo* (breath) is *umoya* but in this case it means the oxygen that *umina/ubumina* needs to keep the body alive. *Ubumina/umina* is more than *umphefumulo*. Still, this is complex as in some instances *umina/ubumina* says *umphefumulo wami* (my breath). This still locates *umina/ubumina* beyond *umphefumulo* as *ubumina/umina* owns *umphefumulo*. *Umoya* belongs to *umina/ubumina*.

The understanding of *Umoya* is intricate when it comes to an attempt to translate it to English as the same word means several English words. *Umoya* is the word for spirit, breath and soul. However, all these English words that mean *Umoya* for the Nguni have something to do with the *umina/ubumina*. *Umoya* weaves together the essence of *umina/ubumina* as it connotes the soul, the being, the breath and the spirituality of the Nguni. The *umoya* is the essence of human existence in the physical, before birth and after death. The *umoya* with its different meanings means life in the different phases of the Nguni life cycle. *Umoya* highlights the intrinsic link of the material and spiritual realms as intertwined aspects of a larger, harmonious existence.

Umoya as Spirits in the Nguni Context of Imimoya

The Nguni context is full spirits (*Imimoya*). The *umina/ubumina* is continuously intertwined with *Imimoya*. The rites of passage and rituals are means for accurately locating the *umina/ubumina* in the context that has spirits (*Imimoya*). In the Nguni worldview the invisible world consists of *Imimoya* that are good and *Imimoya* that are evil. The Living Dead are also in the realm of *Imimoya*. Ancestors are also called *imimoya yabaphansi* (spirits of the deceased). *Imimoya* yabaphansi can be happy in the realm of the living dead depending on rites of passage performed correctly by the living. Alternatively, the *imimoya yabaphansi* can be troubled seeking for assistance from the living. In the Nguni worldview it is possible for *Imimoya yabaphansi* to torment the *ubumina/umina* in the physical realm. Life is premised around the fear, the love and the appeasement of *Imimoya yabaphansi*. *Umoya*, which is *ubumina/ umina* needs to appease *imimoya yabaphansi* while at the same time imimoya yabaphansi needs *umoya* to perform rituals for *imimoya* to be happy in the spiritual realm. *imimoya yabaphansi*. *There is interdependence between umoya and imimoya*.

The interaction between *umoya and Imimoya* are a key phenomenon in *Isintuism*. As already noted above, the Nguni context is filled with both good and evil spirits. *Imimoya emihle* (good spirits) are those that protect and prosper humans and nature. *Imimoya emihle* are mainly the spirits of happy ancestors. In the Nguni worldview, ancestors (*Imimoya emihle*) look after the wellbeing of their living relatives. Such ancestors (*amadlozi* or *abaphansi -imimoya emihle*) are happy spirits. The spirits communicate with the living through *Sangomas* (diviners), spirit mediums, dreams and other signs/symbols. The living performs *umsebenzi* to thank and appease *imimoya yabaphansi*. This relationship between the living and the living dead is perpetual through the relationship between umoya and *imimoya yabaphansi*. At times the living communicates with *imimoya yabaphansi* through Ukuthethela or *ukuthethwa kwedlozi* (Makhanya 1997). *Ukuthethela (ukuthetha)* is insulting (shouting) at *imimoya yabaphansi* for not properly looking after the umina/ubumina. This is a demonstration that the events in the *impilo* of *umina/ubumina* are intricately linked to the *imimoya yabaphansi*.

In the Nguni worldview *kulemimoya emibi* (bad spirits). These *imimoya emibi* are always bringing challenges, trauma, ill-luck, sickness, vulnerabilities and disasters to the *umina/ubumina* and the rest of creation. When the Nguni experience phenomenon such as sickness, poverty, lack of the normal, death, *inkanyamba* (storms), lightning strikes, droughts and floods they quickly think of the spirit world (*imimoya emibi noma imimoya yabaphansi engathokoziyo*). In general, all the undesirables come from imimoya emibi bad spirits against the *umoya*. Umina/ubumina while in the physical body need protection against *imimoya emibi*. Imimoya yabaphansi abangathokozile can also be part of *imimoya emibi* (Unhappy ancestral spirits can also be part of bad spirits against the *umina/ubumina*).

The Nguni believe that the umina/ubumina is vulnerable and hopeless when it comes to the ever-present spiritual attacks (*ukuhlaselwa yimimoya*). This is why it is important to keep imimoya emihle (good spirits) happy through *umsebenzi wabaphansi* (work for the ancestors). In the Nguni worldview there is a spiritual warfare between good and bad spirits over *ubumina/umina* and the rest of creation. Bad spirits can actual indirectly attack humanity through destroying part of the environment that is vital for human survival through such phenomenon as droughts or bringing locusts to destroy farm produce, floods, landslides, and storms. *Ubumina/Umina* cannot fight against spirits; *umina/ubumina* needs good spirits on their side to fight bad spirits on their behalf. There is always warfare between ancestors as happy good spirits against bad spirits. Happy imimoya yabaphansi (ancestors) fight to protect the wellbeing and interests of the *umina/ubumina*. There is an ever-present fear of witches who fall under the sphere of (*imimoya emibi*) bad spirits that fight against the welfare of the *umina/ubumina*. Since witches are in the spiritual realm the *umina/ubumina* needs *imimoya emihle* to fight and protect *ubumina/umina* against witches. The spiritual realm is more powerful than the physical realm, therefore, *umina/ubumina* in the physical realm cannot withstand witches (*imimoya emibi*), I need my own who are already in the spiritual realm to fight my wars in the spiritual realm.

Conclusion

In Nguni spirituality, *umoya* is understood as the vital life force that animates all human beings. It is the breath that sustains life and connects individuals to their ancestors, the natural world, and the transcended realms. The understanding of *umoya* is integral to various rituals and practices aimed at maintaining harmony and balance within the community of the living and living dead as well as with the universe. In Nguni traditional spirituality the *umoya* is linked to some rituals for recognition that *umoya* is central the Nguni existentialism. These rituals may include offerings to the ancestors, communal dances, and ceremonies that seek to honour and invoke the presence of *umoya* (ancestral spirits, *abaphansi* as *amadlozi*). In fact, in ancestral veneration the ancestors appear and interact with the living beings in the form of *umoya*.

References

Makhanya, Ntokozo Favourite. 1997. "*Isiko lokuthethwa kwedlozi*." PhD diss., University of Zululand, Richards Bay.

9

The Relative Self
Native American Conceptualizations of the Self

Fritz Detwiler

Chapter Outline

Autonomy and Relatedness	238
Self as Moral Agent	239
Self as Persons	240
Perspective	240
Native American Conceptions of the World	241
Conclusion	249
9.1 *Hózhǫ* and *Hóchxǫ* Walking in Beauty	252
9.2 *Mitákuye Oyásin*	257
9.3 Tlingit: *at.oow*	262

Honoring a tradition among Native American and First Nation peoples, I will begin with a story. Some years ago, I was living in the Ho-Chunk (previously known as the Winnebago) settlement near Black River Falls, Wisconsin, when a Ho-Chunk elder, George Funmaker, approached me. George was going to build some new playground equipment for the village's children. He asked me if I was willing to help him. I agreed to help even though I had no mechanical skills. On our walk to the playground, George asked me if I could tell Indians apart. The question surprised me, and I answered, "Yes, I think so." He replied, "That's interesting. I can't tell whites apart."

The conversation then went into the question of identity. I asked George, "What name do Native Americans prefer to be called: Native Americans, American Indians, Indians, or is there another name?" His response gave me a clear insight into Native American identity. George said, "Only 'eggheads' use 'Native Americans!'" Being an egghead who uses 'Native American,' his comment gave me pause to think.[1]

He continued,

> When whites refer to us, it's Indian. When we refer to each other from different tribes, it is the tribal name; when referring to our people, it is a clan name. When talking with a close relative, we use relational terms like "sister" and "mother's brother's daughter." We never use the person's name within the community for a name has power, and we do not want to strip them of their power.[2]

For Native Americans and First Nations people, what counts is to whom and how you are related. The "self" is related and autonomous, not isolated, as is common in North American white cultures.

One moral principle that children learn is that life-force connects every being in the universe. We are related to it all! This life-force enables people to do what they do but is morally neutral. Its moral value arises when the person makes choices for the detriment or benefit of the community. The "self" makes the life-force moral through the choices they make. If I act appropriately in my interactions with others, good life-force will flow from me to those I encounter. If I act inappropriately, then the reverse is true. We must be careful about the situations we place ourselves in because we want to be energized by good and avoid bad energies. Each human and nonhuman nation has guidelines for what is constructive to a moral universe and what is detrimental. Most nations, however, value some similar moral values. Among the most important are generosity, responsibility for others, courage, humility, and truthfulness.

These values are guidelines, not strict rules, and are left to the person to interpret for themselves within a somewhat limited range of acceptable ways of being. My economic circumstances may condition my generosity. Physical limitations may limit my courage. My responsibilities may be defined in terms of my encounters with other people or groups of people. For example, if my "friend" keeps stealing from me, I will not trust them, and my responsibilities to them might be reduced significantly. The good life is not something to achieve but a continuing process.

Autonomy and Relatedness

The concept of the "self" gets more complicated, however. Native peoples of North America believe that everything in our cosmos has life-force flowing in us. Each life-force is unique to every being. Life-force, known by different terms in each tradition, flows through the person and attaches to every other being with which they come in contact. I will illustrate this by asking what you had for breakfast this morning. Let's say you had cereal with milk and a banana. All those elements, the cereal, the milk, and the banana, have their life-force which you now have flowing in and through you. In other words, the "self" is a compendium of all the life-forces each person has acquired.

Further, this life-force connects every being in the universe. Life-force enables people to do what they do but is morally neutral. Its moral value arises when the person makes choices for the detriment or benefit of the community. The "self" makes the life-force moral through the choices they make. If I act appropriately in my interactions with others, good life-force will flow from me to those I encounter. If I act inappropriately, then the reverse is true. We must be careful about the situations we place ourselves in because we want to be energized by good and avoid bad energies. Each human and nonhuman nation has guidelines for what is constructive to a moral universe and what is detrimental.

Self as Moral Agent

Given that Native Americans, First Nation peoples, and other traditions outside North America are moral beings, we must explain what that entails. First, persons are autonomous. They are free to make their own decisions, but they have to accept responsibility for the consequences of their choices. Second, morality is not just one element of the self; it is the heart of the self. Third, in many traditions, the self is gifted with a moral guide. The moral guide is not an internal conscience but a gift to the self, often by spiritual beings. People are free to accept or reject their guidance. The spirit guide may withdraw their counsel if they reject the advice frequently.

Keith Basso tells the story of a girl ready to attend a community gathering. However, in a severe breach of protocol, her hair was in curlers. Her mother told her she should not go in curlers because to do so was disrespectful. She decided to ignore her mother and go with her hair in curlers. An elder approached her after some time had passed and told her a story about a particular location in a hill familiar to her. The story is about a similar type of transgression that occurred there. He said nothing about curlers. However, from that time forward, the spot reminded her of her error when the girl passed the location where the impropriety took place. She complained that the place was stalking her (Basso 1996: 61). Here, Basso describes the power of what Westerners call "nature" to give moral guidance.

Given the autonomy of the self, it would be unusual for anyone to confront the girl in curlers directly, as that would diminish her autonomy. People are left to make their own choices. Moral guidance primarily comes through story. It is up to the self to correct their behavior.

Self as Persons

My allusion above to the hill stalking the young woman brings us to a significant difference in Western and Native American/First Nation views of the self. Western and Native conceptions of the self accept the autonomy of the self. To the Western mind, the self is an autonomous individual who is on their own with rights and privileges rather than obligations and responsibilities. In part, this is due to living in a world of things. For Native Americans and First Nation people, this is a fiction. Natives extend the category of "person" to everything that is alive. To be "alive" means that the phenomenon has life-force and moral worth. It includes the hill that stalks the young girl and all other parts of nature, including solar phenomena and the earth itself. In many traditions, the sky is male life-force, and the earth female life-force.

Being related through life-force, all aspects of the universe have obligations and responsibilities. They have consciousness, decision-making ability, communication power, and moral worth. These are not attributes of the self; they are integrated with the self. The world beyond humans is one of obligations and responsibilities to each other and to humans. Reciprocally, humans have obligations and responsibilities to them, especially to honor their moral worth and respect their lifeways and interests.

Perspective

In another context the Indigenous Amazonian scholar Eduardo Viveiros de Castro has written on "relationality." He argues that each person has a single view of different worlds. We live in a multiverse. Our conceptualizations of the world and our interests drive our perspective (Viveiros de Castro 2015: 58). While conceptualizations about the world can be very similar among similar persons, each self within the shared group will have somewhat different conceptualizations and interests unique to themselves. These conceptualizations and interests are driven by the heart as much as the head. Among the most essential interests that all beings share are the need for food, shelter, and the continuation of the species, if not the self.

To illustrate, imagine four people standing at different corners of an intersection. One is a nurse, the other a lawyer, the third a police officer, and the fourth a person who is blind. They all witness a car crash. But do they all see the same thing? No, each perspective draws from the interests of each person. The nurse focuses on possible injuries, the lawyer sees liability, the police officers focus on potential breaches of traffic laws, and the blind person notices sounds. The four witness the same accident, but they see it differently. A canary on a building above the street corner will experience the same accident. However, it is nearly impossible to comprehend what the canary thinks or feels except as it wishes to communicate with others.

Viveiros de Castro says that beings of the same species recognize each other in ways different species cannot. In part, our physical structure and capabilities condition our perceptions. Dogs have much greater powers of smell, eagles have keener eyesight, and trees have greater strength (Viveiros de Castro 2015: 58).

Beings have species perception. Only humans see each other as humans. An exception to this is ceremony. In ritual settings, dancers can put on regalia that enables them to see the world through the perspective of the nonhuman person whose "clothing" they are wearing. The other factors that condition our viewpoints are physical and mental human and nonhuman environments. What kind of place do I come from?

The Tlingit of Southeastern Alaska gain their wisdom through the nonhuman beings with whom they share a rainforest, the sea, glaciers, and great mountains. The Southwest's Diné, or Navajo, gain knowledge from the desert, sky, and ever-present wind. The Haudenosaunee, or Iroquois, live in the Northeastern United States, Ontario, and Quebec forests. Their world is populated by great waterways, forest animals, and plants indigenous to that region. Finally, the Lakota environment consists of mountains, expansive sky, grasslands, rugged terrain, brutal winters, and scorching summers.

Native American Conceptions of the World

To understand and respect the Native peoples of North America, outsiders must seriously explore their perspectives. The choice of the plural "perspectives" refers to the fact that, while Native peoples share many conceptions of the world, each tradition and person in that tradition will have their differences. These differences are accepted as authoritative since each person bases their claims on personal experiences. Thus, within even small communities, various perspectives are present. Certain widespread conceptualizations of the world exist among Native peoples, however. Among these are a relational concept of the self, the expansion of the category of persons to nonhuman beings, emphasis on kinship, and the moral nature of the self.

When we accept the extension of personhood to nonhumans, including mountains, animals, waters, sky, earth, birds, and so forth, are alive, we must address what it means to "be alive to the world". Tim Ingold adds one concept that we have only touched on above. His primary concern "is the flow of life force among things, not between them" (Ingold 2013: 224). Life-force flows among things and intersubjectively connects all beings, however remote the connection may be. Those persons in closer proximity will be more intensively connected. Lawrence Gross's analysis of Anishinabe relational ontology illustrates this point. For the Anishinabe, a sock I am wearing is alive to me, but the moccasin into which the sock goes is not; the sock is related to the moccasin. Any life-force that comes to me from the moccasin flows through the sock (Gross 2016: 91–92).

Doug Ezzy adds the conception of ethics to the self. Ezzy writes, "It is impossible to be a person without always and already being enmeshed in ethical intersubjectivity" (Ezzy 2013: 182). Because of the flow of life-force among persons, we have moral responsibilities and obligations to them. Among these are respect for their moral worth, the continuation of their species, and awareness of their interests and ways of acting. The key ethical issue is how our actions affect other persons, human and nonhuman. The principle of reciprocity is central. If we are generous and compassionate toward others, they will reciprocate and help us. If we lack generosity and compassion toward them, they will withhold their life-force from us.

We now turn to three specific Native conceptualizations of the world to illustrate and concretize the above observations: the Tlingit, Diné, and Lakota.

Tlingit

The essential self for the Tlingit (pronounced (*Klingit*)) consists of several phenomena: a body that serves as a container for the inner self. The inner self seems to be connected to the bone structure. Bones are central to the Pacific Northwest Coast nations through formline art (Holm 1970) and ceremonies such as the First Salmon celebration (Crawford 2007: 54). The essential self is also a mixture of life-forces, unique to each being, which flows through every living thing, mainly through the ancestors. Names: names given to children at a young age may carry some of the essence of the ancestor's life-force. Each self has a brain and a heart. The brain is the seat of rational thought. The heart is the center of emotion. The self is associated with clan and house membership, which carries specific moral obligations and responsibilities. A guardian advisor and "ghosts" and spirits have strong connections with the self. Finally, the essential self is moral. The self lives in a cosmic moral matrix of intersubjective relations with other nonhuman persons.

The self's reputation and respect, or lack thereof, emerge through relationships with human and nonhuman persons with whom the Tlingit share their place. Like the two traditions discussed below, the Tlingit expands the notion of personhood to all living beings (Detwiler 2013: 169). A being is alive when it has life-force. This extension includes flora and fauna, trees, forests, ocean, sea and air creatures, mountains, and glaciers. As a unique aspect of the Tlingit, moral obligations and responsibilities relate to moral covenants that the ancestors formed with nonhuman persons in ancient times.

Tlingit originating stories help us understand how all of this comes together. The world pre-exists. It is dark because an old man captured Sun and put it in a box in his longhouse. Humans and nonhuman persons live together harmoniously in a subterranean room. They can communicate fully, knowing each other's interests and the protocols by which they prefer being treated. The Tlingit culture hero Raven stealthily steals Sun by impregnating the old man's daughter. The resulting child gives him access to the old man's house and the box where he keeps Sun. Raven carries Sun into the world outside the house, and light appears. Immediately, the various species see that they are different from each other and separate into their groups. The separation causes disharmony among the species, and they begin to see each other as food.

The separated species recognize they cannot live without each other. The Tlingit originating ancestors negotiate with nonhuman persons to bring order to the world. These negotiations create moral covenants in which beings' responsibilities and obligations toward other species are defined. The operative principle here is reciprocity. Humans and nonhumans share an understanding of the protocols and etiquette by which they want to be treated and how to respect the interests and needs of others. They agree to allow each other to provide food, ensuring their survival and well-being. If you break the covenant, you no longer have any obligations toward other parties and them to you. These moral covenants create the moral matrix central to Tlingit's worldview. With reciprocity as the cardinal principle, persons can expect respect and recognition of their interests. Failure to respect each other breaks the moral covenant, and the species must live without the help of the other (Swanton 1909).

According to Rosita Worl, the world "settled into an oppositional complementary structure in which various types of beings each had their interests but cooperated to maintain harmony and balance among all beings" (Detwiler 2013: 168). Complementary opposition exists in humans between males and females, brain and heart, humans and nonhuman persons, and species. Each recognizes its dependence on the others, and each ideally respects the interests, survival, and flourishing of the other.

The Tlingit represent the concept of moral covenants in their particular style of totem poles. Unlike most of the other peoples of the Pacific Northwest, for whom totem poles communicate the nonhuman origins of each clan, Tlingit totem poles represent the moral covenants belonging to each clan. It is a visual reminder of the covenants formed by each clan or house. Therefore, the "self" has inherent responsibilities and obligations specific to the clan or house. These covenants are with particular places and beings. It is *this* salmon in *this* place, *this* glacier in *this* place (Cruikshank 2005: 39). Each clan and house has places defined by the moral covenants made by the originating ancestors with all persons who share their specific environment. These covenants bind the self through the specific clan and house they are born into.

Due to the three-tiered hierarchical structure of Tlingit society, not all selves are equal. Aristocrats are at the top, then commoners, and finally, slaves. Aristocrats came from ranking members "of the matrilineal groups and their immediate matrikin" (Kan 1989: 25). Status required birth within a clan, achievement, acquired and inherited wealth, character, and accomplishments. By their positions, aristocrats had "access to supernatural power" (ibid., 86). Commoners were the junior matrikin of the aristocrats. Kan states that the two classes had a symbiotic relationship; the aristocrats provided ceremonial access to sacred knowledge while the commoners assisted in ceremonies and potlatches (Kan 1989: 95). The bottom rung on the hierarchy included illegitimate children and "dried-fish slaves," members of the community who depended on the largesse of others. "True slaves" were prisoners or those who were purchased from other nations. Slaves were not accorded full personhood (Kan 1989: 25).

From the above, it is clear that the clan and house ancestors play a vital role in Tlingit's life. The originating ancestors framed the moral covenants among human and nonhuman persons and shaped the world structure. The life-force of an ancestor continually moves through the relational matrix to succeeding generations. If a young child ceremonially receives a "name" related to a particular ancestor, the Tlingit believe that the ancestor's life-force is present in them. The child can physically resemble the ancestor and carry the ancestor's character with them. This inheritance creates serious obligations for the child as they grow into adulthood. The behaviors of the person receiving the name are transitive. They affect the ancestor and, by extension, those belonging to the clan or house. A good character enhances the status of the clan or house and the ancestor. A bad character denigrates the ancestor, clan, or house and reduces their status.

The Tlingit believe humans possess dual spirits and guardian spirits (Kan 1989: 53–54). They are essential parts of the self. At death, the Tlingit cremate the body. Tlingit bones are buried with the bones of their ancestors. After death, one spirit, Shadow, _kaa yakgwahéiyagu_, remains in the natural world at the burial site. The second spirit, Ghost, _kaa yahaayi_, travels to one of three distinct spirit lands. The naming ceremony calls the ancestors' spirits into the present and may be reborn in a child when given the name of an ancestor (Worl 1998: 86). The line of descent flows through the matrilineal ancestors.

The guardian spirit helps the person develop good moral character by advising them to act appropriately and fulfill their moral obligations and responsibilities. The guardian spirit can choose the person, or the person can seek it out. The relationship strengthens when the person accepts the guardian spirit's counsel. The ties can deteriorate by acting against protocols and ignoring their moral obligations and responsibilities. When a person continually disrespects the guardian spirit, the spirit may withdraw to the spirit world and allow the person to suffer the consequences of their disrespectful relations with other humans and their nonhuman neighbors.

Ghosts and souls also define the human person. Ghosts act like the Western concept of the "soul." Ghosts are buried with the body and remain with the body, eventually traveling to the land of the dead forever. There are two spirits in the self. At death, one remains at the burial site. The other goes to one of three spirit lands. This second spirit may be reborn into the dead person's clan. Ceremony calls the deceased spirits into the present (Worl 1998: 86).

Ancestors can transmit their spirit to their descendants. The spirit returns to the deceased's close matrilineal relatives to be born into another person (Detwiler 2013: 170). In ceremony, clan dancers and singers call on the spirits of the deceased to assist their living kin and to participate in ongoing ceremonial activities (Worl 1998: 86).

Diné or Navajo

Like the Tlingit, the Navajo or Diné extend the category of persons to all living beings. This extension includes mountains, Sky, Earth, baskets, hogans, looms, blankets, and prayers (Gill 1987: 187). The Diné self exists in a world in constant flux and dynamic change. Diné worldviews also describe beings existing in a synecdochic matrix. Maureen Schwarz describes "rules" pertaining to the "self" in this matrix. She writes,

> The 'law of similarities' maintains that 'like produces like' – if rain is needed, pouring water will produce it. The 'law of opposition' maintains that opposites work on opposites – rain counters dryness. The 'law of contagion' maintains that 'things that have once been in contact continue ever afterward to act on each other.' Holy People instituted these laws [Schwarz 1997: 607–610]. Holy People were (are) responsible for creating and sustaining the ordering principles of the world "in accordance with the design of the Creator."
>
> (Cajete 2000: 219–220)

The complex nature of the self comes out in Diné creation narratives. Initially, the cosmos exists in the mind of the Creator, who subsequently thinks the world into existence and enlivens it with breath or life-force and vibration. As a result of breath and vibration, Holy Wind appears in each of the four cardinal directions, creating clouds. First Man emerges from the cloud in the east, and First Woman from the cloud in the west. They appear as paired opposites. This pairing sets the ideal structure of the world.

First Man and First Woman are inner forms without outer physical shapes. Inner forms are the essence of being. Physical bodies are outer forms. Outer forms are containers for the inner form. They are unstable and always subject to change and can morph into other shapes. The inner form is unique to each person. It is a being's life-force and potentiality. Their spiritual power comes from Holy Wind. Holy Wind controls the way the brain functions. It provides humans with the ability to think ahead and communicate through language. Holy Wind gives life, thought, speech, and the power of motion to all living things and serves as the means of communication between all elements of the living world (McNeley 1981: 8). These abilities separate humans from other animals. Animals, according to Witherspoon, "only have calls and cries" (Witherspoon 1977: 30). Holy Wind enlivens everything.

Little Wind is the part of Holy Wind that dwells inside the person. In the case of humans, Little Wind enters the fetus when it develops human form. The fetus and newborn live in the spirit world until their first laugh. When that occurs, the child is now a person to the Diné, and the Diné recognizes the child as a full community member. Little Wind is unique for every person. It functions as a conscience and advises people how to act and to think. It functions as a spiritual and moral guide. Little Wind, also referred to as "small wind soul," governs the vegetative aspect of human beings. Humans, therefore, consist of an inner essence, Holy Wind, Little Wind, and outer forms or bodies.

Before the Diné appeared in the Earth-Surface World, the Holy Beings (*Diyin Diné'e*) and other creatures, such as Ant People, lived in three successive subterranean worlds. Each world existed in beauty until discord arose, usually around issues of sexuality, passion, jealousy, and anxiety. Those beings remaining faithful to the Creator's plan eventually move through these worlds and ultimately end up in the fourth and present world.

As the world develops, First Man finds a baby on Gobernador Knob, one of the four sacred mountains to the Diné. The baby quickly matures into Changing Woman. She is one of the most important of the Holy People. As she matures, First Man gives her his medicine bundle containing the plans of the Creator and the power and resources to fulfill the Creator's plan. She now has the responsibility to care for the Diné people. To prepare the world for the Diné, Changing Woman gives the outer forms of the present world inner forms. This act brings them life and personhood. She gives birth to twin sons, Monster Slayer and Born-to-Water. As the former son's name suggests, she directs Monster Slayer and his brother to clear the world of monsters who could affect a Diné's well-being. They were successful but decided to allow four monsters into the present world: Hunger, Poverty, Old Age, and Death. Their reasoning goes back to the concept of oppositional complementarity. Hunger cannot exist without abundance, Poverty without wealth, Old Age without children, and Death without life (Cajete 2000: 219–226).

Once Changing Woman prepares the world, she creates the Diné from her flesh, corn pollen, Earth, and precious stones (Schwarz 1997: 611–612). They are the "true people." The overarching task for the Diné is to seek harmony. Harmony has many components: beauty, walking in balance, long life, perfection, order, rejuvenation, happiness, reanimation, and wholeness. Harmony is not a "goal to be achieved." It is a pathway that needs continual attention. According to the concept of oppositional complementarity, harmony cannot exist without disharmony, beauty without ugliness, goodness without evil, and so forth. One does not rid oneself of these harmful elements. The Diné life pathway walks among beauty and ugliness with the idea of holding them in balance (Fixico 2013: 174).

Two other forces threaten the Diné: witches and Coyote, the trickster. The underground world remains a place of danger. There live ghosts of those who have died and have not lived a good life, as well as witches, also known as Skinwalkers. Farella notes that the ultimate source of witchcraft is the "witchcraft way." Witches are associated with spiritual imbalances surrounding Death. Clyde Kluckhohn notes that to enter the witchcraft way, one must kill a family member.[3] Farella identifies First Man and his associates as the source of witchcraft way. His associates include First Woman and the "primal Coyote" (Farella 1984: 33). While partially associated with witchcraft, Coyote, the trickster, sows disorder. In one form, Black God, trickster does not stand for teasing and has no sense of humor (Griffin-Pierce 1992: 159). Coyote is impulsive and "playful." Coyote will throw obstacles in peoples' ways to see how they react. In this form, without intention, Coyote tests people's character.

While the association of First Man, the Creator, with evil may surprise Westerners, it illustrates the Diné notion of oppositional complementarity. First Man and First Woman are Holy People. Holy People are Holy People because of the power and knowledge they possess. For the most part, they are amoral. They can use this power to create harmony and balance (*hózhó*) and disorder and disruption (*hochxo*). We will discuss these two terms in more depth in a subsequent chapter

The "self" then lives in a relational matrix full of beauty and ugliness. Selves consist of life-force, spirits, ghosts, and Little Wind's moral counsel. Life's process is to follow a pathway that continually balances both. In ceremony, the heart of Diné "religion," shamans who have direct access to the Holy People can restore a person to wholeness and balance. A subsequent chapter will expand on the Diné understanding of ceremony.

Lakota

The Lakota idea of themselves and their world begins with their creation narrative. D. M. Dooling's version sets creation into four different "times": creating sacred persons, emerging of the sacred persons' companions and descendants, populating the world, and setting the cardinal directions. Space only allows for a cursory account here. The first being to appear is Rock, *Iŋyaŋ*. Out of Rock's loneliness, he splits open and springs his blood and spirit from him. The first person to appear is Earth (*Makȟá*). She complains about being lonely, cold, hot, and dark at night. To appease her, Rock creates companions for her: Light, Sun, Day and Night, Wind, Thunder, Wisdom, disruptive forces Passion (*Unk*) and Crazy Buffalo (*Gnaški*), and the Feminine (*Wóȟpe*), each with their assigned places and roles.

Unk inherits Earth's passion and engages in incestual intercourse that produces perverse children (Walker 1917: 194–195). Wisdom and Passion force people to choose between Wisdom and Folly. Folly usually triumphs. The people preferred lightheartedness, entertainment, and recklessness rather than sober reflection

(Wisdom). Gradually, they forget the teachings of the Buffalo people. This leaves them vulnerable when they arrive in the world from Wind Cave and the Black Hills. Trickster (*Iktómi*), created as a disruptive force, takes advantage of their vulnerability. The Lakota find themselves in a bleak world during a raging winter storm. The people are starving. Feminine in the form of Wóȟpe appears to them as White Buffalo Calf Woman and gifts them knowledge, medicine, and seven rituals. These gifts enable the Lakota to restore their relationships with nonhuman persons and among themselves. Thereby gaining help from nonhuman people (Dooling 1992: 4–41).

These are the conditions of the present world. In another context, Doug Ezzy describes the world as a "primordial ethical enmeshment" (Ezzy 2013: 182). Ethical here does not mean that the world is inherently good. The term refers to the world condition and the necessity of making moral choices within a relational web or matrix. The overarching principles are the promotion of life, respect for the moral worthiness of all beings, and reciprocity. As we have seen, the moral world is also fraught with dangers, and the beings of the Lakota world will reciprocate when humans mistreat them.

The Lakota identify four different "souls" in humans. There is disagreement among scholars about precisely who they are. Here I am following Arthur Amiotte. Amiotte describes them as "spiritual counterparts". For Amiotte they are *niyá*, *nagí*, *šičuŋ*, and *naǧila*. Each plays a vital role in the Lakota self (Amiotte 2009: 328–329).

Niyá or Breath refers to the life-breath of a being. Working by itself, it has limited movement. Full movement occurs when Breath is in harmony with other souls. Proper eating habits and physical exercise can strengthen Breath. Sweat lodge ceremonies also expel evil powers in the person and create appropriate harmony with the rest of the Lakota cosmos. At death, Breath leaves the body. If the self is revived, Breath returns to the body. If not, it returns to the spirit world and connects with other.

Nagí is similar to the "ghost" concept, frequently found in Western religion and entertainment. Amiotte describes it as "a mirror image of the person's form" and carries with it the particularities of the self when it leaves the body (Amiotte 2009: 330). Illness and insanity can harm the person if Ghost should leave. A shaman can diagnose the cause of maladies and, using his medicine, restore the patient's Ghost. Ghost functions like a guardian spirit, noting one's character and advising the self. At death, Ghost reports to Sky or *Škáŋ*. Sky allows Ghost to enter the spirit world if the report is positive. If the report is negative, Ghost may hang around and threaten the community. Eventually, Ghost departs from the community and does not return. The Lakota leave the flesh and bones of the physical body on a scaffold as an offering of food for birds of prey or to naturally decompose.

Sičuŋ is the person's spirit or life-force. It is the potency unique to each being. Finger notes that it contains the power of the Holy Ones (Tedlock 1975: 212–214). Humans, therefore, have sacred power, but a minimal amount. The power the person does have allows them to communicate with sacred persons. Sky imparts life-force into a child when it is born. Any person can gift another person with their *šičuŋ*. Beings can also transfer life-force into any object. Such transfers are necessary to survive. Since humans are weak, they need Life-force from nonhuman persons. Most commonly, the transfer occurs through eating but also through prayer and ceremony. Aside from its physical properties, I am imbibing the life-force of the other when I eat a bowl of cereal. Shamans have particular abilities to receive a sacred person's life-force, giving them the power to diagnose illness and other maladies through maintaining close relationships with their sacred persons.

The fourth soul, *nağila*, is the energy of the cosmos that flows through persons, connects them to the entire matrix, and makes them relatives (Brown and Cousins 2001: 90). The Lakota express this universal relationality in the term *mitákuye oyásiŋ*, "all my relations." This universal connectedness is not with the universe in general. It is with all individual relatives with whom they share the Sacred Hoop.

Conclusion

This chapter lays the foundation for non-Native scholars to rethink Western conceptions of the "self." Five of the differences are: (1) Western concepts of the self focus on the individual as an autonomous competitive agent while Native Americans sees the community as the context in which the self exists as a related cooperative being; (2) Native Americans extend the category of "persons" much more broadly; (3) The universe is moral; and, (4) Morality is a way of life, not a goal; and, (5) Native Americans see their roles in terms of obligations and responsibilities, not rights. Finally, we have shown that Native American cultures and worldviews cannot be reduced to stereotypes given the diversity that exists among them.

Notes

1. George Funmaker, personal conversation, Winnebego Indian Settlement, Black River Falls, Wisconsin, 1973.
2. Ibid.
3. For an extensive discussion of Navajo witchcraft, see Kluckhohn (1962).

Bibliography

Amiotte, Arthur. 2009. "Our Other Selves: The Lakota Dream Experience." In Linda Hogan and Linda Hogan (eds.), *The Inner Journey: Views from Native Traditions*. Parabola Anthology Series. Sandpoint: Morning Light Press, 326–334.

Basso, Keith H. 1996. *Wisdom Sits in Places: Landscape and Language among the Western Apache*. Albuquerque: University of New Mexico Press.

Brown, Joseph Epes, and Emily Cousins. 2001. *Teaching Spirits: Understanding Native American Religious Traditions*. Oxford, [England: Oxford University Press.

Cajete, Gregory. 2000. *Native Science: Natural Laws of Interdependence*. Foreword by Leroy Little Bear. Santa Fe: Clear Light Publishers.

Crawford, Suzanne J. 2007. *Native American Religious Traditions*. Religions of the World. Upper Saddle River: Prentice Hall.

Cruikshank, Julie. 2005. *Do Glaciers Listen? Local Knowledge, Colonial Encounters and Social Imagination*. Seattle: University of Washington Press.

Detwiler, Fritz. 2013. "Moral Foundations of Tlingit Cosmology." In Graham Harvey (ed.), *The Handbook of Contemporary Animism*. Durham: Acumen Pub., 167–180.

Dooling, D. M., ed. 1992. *The Sons of the Wind: The Sacred Stories of the Lakota*. San Francisco: HarperSanFrancisco.

Ezzy, Douglas. 2013. "Embodied Morality and Performed Relationships." In Graham Harvey (ed.), *The Handbook of Contemporary Animism*. Durham: Acumen, 2013, 181–190.

Farella, John R. 1984. *The Main Stalk: A Synthesis of Navajo Philosophy*. Tucson: University of Arizona Press.

Fixico, Donald L. 2013. *The American Indian Mind in a Linear World: American Indian Studies and Traditional Knowledge*. New York: Routledge.

Funmaker, George. 1973. Personal conversation. Winnebego Indian Settlement, Black River Falls, Wisconsin.

Gill, Sam. 1987. *Native American Religious Action: A Performance Approach to Religion*. Studies in Comparative Religion. Columbia: University of South Carolina Press.

Griffin-Pierce, Trudy. 1992. *Earth is My Mother, Sky is My Father: Space, Time, and Astronomy in Navajo Sandpainting*. Foreword by N. Scott Momaday, illus. Trudy Griffin-Pierce. Albuquerque: University of New Mexico Press.

Gross, Lawrence W. 2016. *Anishinaabe Ways of Knowing and Being*. Vitality of Indigenous Religions. New York: Routledge.

Holm, Bill. 1970. *Northwest Coast Indian Art: An Analysis of Form*. Seattle: University of Washington Press.

Ingold, Tim. "Being Alive to a World Without Objects." In Graham Harvey (ed.), *The Handbook of Contemporary Animism*. Durham: Acumen, 213–225.

Kan, Sergei. 1989. *Symbolic Immortality: The Tlingit Potlatch of the Nineteenth Century*. Washington, DC: Smithsonian Institution Press.

Kluckhohn, Clyde. 1962. *Navaho Witchcraft*. Boston: Beacon Press.

McNeley, James Kale. 1981. *Holy Wind in Navajo Philosophy*. Tucson: University of Arizona Press.

Schwarz, Maureen Trudelle. 1997. *Molded in the Image of Changing Woman: Navajo Views on the Human Body and Personhood*. Tucson: University of Arizona Press.

Swanton, John. 1909. *Myths Recorded in English as Wrangle, Raven*. https://sacred-texts.com/nam/nw/tmt/tmt136.htm.

Tedlock, Dennis. 1975. *Teachings from the American Earth: Indian Religion and Philosophy*. Edited by Dennis Tedlock and Barbara Tedlock. New York: Liveright.

Viveiros de Castro, Eduardo. 2015. *The Relative Native: Essays on Indigenous Conceptual Worlds*. Special Collections in Ethnographic Theory. Chicago: Hau Books.

Walker, J. R. 1917. *The Sun Dance and Other Ceremonies of the Oglala Division of the Teton Dakota*. Anthropological Papers of the American Museum of Natural History. Vol. 16. New York: Published by order of the Trustees [of the American Museum of Natural History].

Witherspoon, Gary. 1977. *Language and Art in the Navajo Universe*. Ann Arbor: University of Michigan Press.

Worl, Rosita F. 1998. "Tlingit *at.Oow*: Taangible and Intangible Property." Unpublished diss. Harvard University, Cambridge.

Hózhǫ and *Hóchxǫ*
Walking in Beauty
Chapter 9.1

Hózhǫ is one of the most critical concepts for the Diné and has received much attention from scholars. It is often glossed as "beauty."[1] As we shall see below, there is no equivalent term in English, and "beauty" only scratches the surface of its depth. The other term, *hóchxǫ*, receives a lot less attention. "Ugliness" is how some scholars gloss the term (Gill 1981: 119). The lack of balanced attention to *hóchxǫ* term strikes me as curious given the principle of oppositional complementarity, or pairing central to Diné thought.

Perhaps some of that imbalance is due to the subtle tendency of Western scholars to frame the terms within the dualistic worldview of the West and Christianity, in associating *hózhǫ* with "good" and *hóchxǫ* with "evil." From this perspective, one's responsibility in life is not to balance good and evil but to use good to eradicate evil. Therefore, in the Western mind, *hózhǫ* is something that overcomes *hóchxǫ*.

From the Diné perspective, the two terms are complementary opposites or pairs. In this view, one cannot exist without its opposite. The goal of life, then, is not for one to overcome the other but to keep them in balance. John Farella uses the Diné term *alkéé naa'aashii*, or a universal process of opposition, to describe the pathway a Diné should walk during the course of their life (Farella 1984). In one of the Diné creation stories, the creation moves from non-existence to increasing complexity. As complexity increases, there is a corresponding increase in the presence of *hóchxǫ*. In other words, life becomes more dangerous.

Since, according to the principle of pairing, *hózhǫ* cannot exist without *hóchxǫ* danger or ugliness has been present in the universe since First Man and First Woman gave substance to the creation of the cosmos. Indeed, First Man and First Woman brought *hózhǫ* into existence. According to another key concept in Diné cosmology, the Diné live in a dynamic and fluid world. Nothing achieves a "state" of goodness, such as in John Wesley's concept of moving on to perfection or a "state" of evil. The struggle to maintain balance in life is ongoing and never entirely resolved.

"Pairing" refers to the idea that nothing is complete without its opposite. First Man and First Woman are paired together, as are the cardinal directions. A day needs both light and darkness to be complete; Earth needs Sky. Life needs death, and women and men need each other. Man needs woman to be complete and vice versa. In the creation narrative, the two sexes fight and separate from each other. Eventually, both the women and the men realized that their lives were incomplete without each other and reconciled.

The concepts *hózhǫ* and *hóchxǫ* are complex notions that cover a broad spectrum of meanings. *Hózhǫ* refers to anything beautiful, harmonious, orderly, and healthy, promote fecundity and well-being, incorporates aesthetic and moral qualities, is positive, and produces happy relations. *Hóchxǫ*, the paired opposite, refers to anything ugly, sows discord, promotes disease and illness, interferes with fecundity and well-being, works against moral qualities, is negative, and is disruptive of happiness.

Rejecting Western dualism, death is both *hózhǫ* and *hóchxǫ* and is accepted as necessary for life to continue. The ideal is to live to an old age but not too long. The ideal age to die is around ninety years. The death of people at younger ages due to illness or an accident can be an indication of imbalance in their lives. Death may also occur from chance or accidents.

Ceremony is at the heart of Diné life. Ceremony addresses all the dangers and imbalances present in the Diné world. It does so by bringing humans into contact with the Holy People and the creation process into their lives. The ceremonial complex has about fifty chantways, each addressing a specific problem confronting the Diné. Variations exist in each of these rites, many of which are regional due to personal preference or how the leader has been taught by his mentor. Each rite includes several songs, prayers, and extensive narratives addressing the nature of the Holy People who will be called upon and how they attain their power. The Diné cautioned that the rites must be performed with exact precision for them to be effective.

The primary concern of Diné ceremonies is to bring things back into balance and well-being through healing and pairing. Ceremony promotes *hózhǫ* and protects people from *hóchxǫ*. Ray Baldwin Lewis holds that the Diné ritual complex can be divided into two types: Blessingway, which promotes *hózhǫ*, and Enemyway, which counters *hóchxǫ* (Lewis n.d.). On the other hand, Gary Witherspoon believes there are three types of ceremonies: Blessingway, Evilway, another name for Lewis' Enemyway, and a third type called Holyway. Holyway "which deals with Holy People who are potentially malevolent" (Witherspoon 1977: 35).

Blessingway chants are the most common since they usually occur at the beginning of other ceremonies (Schwarz 2008: 66). John Farella writes, "*Hózhǫǫjí* [Blessingway] creates, reinforces, and celebrates the process of renewal. By means of it, other beings were created that take part in this cycle of reanimation" (Farella 1984: 100). The Blessingway complex is divided into rituals centered on healing and celebration. Healing rituals restore balance. Celebrations focus on rejoicing the goodness in life and in rites of passage. Examples of the celebratory rituals include *Kinaaldá*, marking a young woman's coming of age; the Wedding Ceremony that includes exchanging cornmeal to mark the couple's commitment to each other; the Baby Blessing Ceremony to welcome the new-born into the community; House Blessing; Harvest Blessing, and Protection and Purification (naa'ahóóhaiłbáhí 2023).

Blessingway healing rites create an environment that brings the appropriate Holy People into the process. The ceremony frequently involves sandpainting, creating a sacred environment representing the summoned Holy People. Once the patient positions themselves in the center of the painting, corn pollen is sprinkled on it. This action enlivens the sandpainting. Corn pollen is the power of life and growth. The healer prepares a medicine bundle as an offering to the Holy People (Gill 1981: 131–132). The offering compels the Holy People to bring their healing power. At the end of the rites, the sand, which contains healing power, is rubbed on the patient. If done correctly, *hózhǫ* is restored.

A personal story about Blessingway healing points out what *hózhǫ* restores. Many years ago, I invited the distinguished Navajo scholar Sam Gill to the campus of my small college to give a presentation on Navajo healing. He gifted me and those in attendance with still pictures taken from an authorized film of the Blessingway chant. As of that time, only two film copies had been made. One was sent to the Smithsonian for preservation. The second was sealed in a vault at the Navajo tribal headquarters. Sam's presentation was the first time still photos from the movie were publicly shown. After Gill completed his presentation, an audience member asked whether the rituals actually worked. From the student's perspective, by "worked," he asked whether the patient had healed. From a Diné perspective, Gill answered, "Yes, but sometimes the patient dies!" It worked in the larger function of restoring balance to the community and the cosmos.

Holyway rites locate and dispel the effects of malevolent Holy People and restore life-giving relationships (Gill 1981: 136). Holy People are neither good nor evil. They are both and can choose whether to be benevolent or malevolent. The Nightway chant addresses the malevolent actions of the Holy People. Its objective is to expel the malevolent forces and bring the patient into proper relations with them (ibid., 72).

Two other rituals confront *hóchxǫ* directly when someone has been contaminated through contact with someone or something in the community or a human who is foreign to the community. This contamination does not necessarily need direct contact. Through the transitive property, this contact can be remote, such as a sorcerer's attempt to harm someone, a biological physician dispensing drugs, or touching someone's possessions after their death. Evilway ceremonials combat injurious forces transmitted to the patient from inside the community. Examples include touching the dead or any personal belonging to the dead (Schwarz 2008: 22). Evilway acknowledges the reality of maleficent persons who wish to exact vengeance or want to capture wealth, or retaliation, or, in the case of witchcraft, [2]seek to harm or kill others.[3]

Enemyway counters contamination or malevolence from sources coming from outside the community. The Diné are concerned with anything foreign polluting their world, for they believe contamination is inherent in non-Diné persons or things that outside persons might use (Schwarz 2008: 128). Enemyway attends to soldiers who return from battle or have been associated with anything related to war. This might include a rifle or government-issued clothing.

The transitive theory of contamination also applies to things related to modern medical personnel and procedures. A Diné receiving a blood transfusion or an organ transplant requires a ceremonial purification. Again, noting the transitive nature of things, this would also extend to someone who consulted with or received treatment from a non-Diné person or place or touched the instruments attending the treatment. In some cases, the re-entering person might seek purification from a Sweat Lodge rite or, in more serious cases, a complete healing ritual. The specific healer or ceremony will be chosen based on the symptoms and situation and their reputation.

The Diné attribute disease and illness to bad behavior on the part of the person who is sick or to ghosts, sorcery, and malevolent humans and Holy People, among other sources. Thus, illness can come from touching something harmful or a sorcerer possessing something of a person's body, such as hair. The first step is diagnostic, determining the specific sources of the illness and gathering the appropriate antidotes. The next step is procuring a healer who can conduct the appropriate ritual and then conduct the ceremony.

While some Diné have serious reservations about modern medicine given the concept of contamination, Western medicine is not rejected out of hand. Like many other Native Americans, the Diné seek out power for living wherever they can find it. There is no question about the success of modern medicine; there is no question about the efficacy of Diné healing. They simply play different functions. Biomedical physicians treat the symptoms of an illness or disease while Diné medicine seeks the cause of it (Schwarz 2008: 78).

My concluding thoughts focus on the Diné phrase *są' naghái bik'e hózhǫ*, which, in its shorter version, refers to *hózhǫ*. It often is given the shorthand name SNBH. SNBH adds another level to *hózhǫ* in Diné cosmology. Farella maintains that SNBH means completeness or wholeness. He traces it to First Man's medicine bundle, which is "full of the reproductive fluids, flesh and life forces, that reanimate us" (Schwarz 2003: 23). Robert Drake adds to our understanding by noting that "*hózhǫ* is the sum of all of the parts of existence, and it is at the same time existence itself. It is also the sum of all the relationships between thought, speech, the gods, people, intentionality, noumenon and symbol, spiritual existence, phenomenal, or physical nature itself" (Drake 2004: 15). However, SBNH is not a static state or a complet*ed* state. Like the universe, it is always in process within a fluid and dynamic world. SBNH reminds the Diné to be vigilant and cautious at all times. In this sense, Farella notes that the Diné frequently use the phrase SBNH and, when said in the context of someone leaving, they will say, in translation, "may you walk or go about according to *hóchxǫ*" (Drake 2004: 15).

Notes

1. The author has left the keywords in the native language. While glosses are available, and a number of them appear in this chapter, the keywords are so complex the reader can unpack them as they progress through the chapter. For a Navajo–English translator visit Glosbe dictionary at *Glosbe Dictionary*, https://glosbe.com/nv/en. For pronunciation, www.native-languages.org/navajo_guide.htm.

2. For a detailed discussion of witchcraft, sorcery, wizardry, ghosts, and spirits see Kluckhohn, *Navaho Witchcraft* (1962).
3. For a detailed discussion of witches, sorcery, ghosts, and wizardry, see Kluckhohn, *Witchcraft* (1962).

References

Drake, Robert S. 2004. "*Hozho*: Dine' Concepts of Balance and Harmony." Graduate course paper, University of Arizona. www.robertsdrake.com/files/Hozho.htm. http://www.robertsdrafke.com/files/Hozho.htm.

Farella, John R. 1984. *The Main Stalk: A Synthesis of Navajo Philosophy*. Tucson: University of Arizona Press.

Gill, Sam D. 1981. *Sacred Words: A Study of Navajo Religion and Prayer*. Contributions in Intercultural and Comparative Studies, 4, 0147–1031. Westport: Greenwood Press.

Kluckhohn, Clyde. 1962. *Navaho Witchcraft*. Boston: Beacon Press.

Lewis, Ray Baldwin. N.d. "Navajo Culture: Walk in Beauty." https://discovernavajo.com/navajo-culture/.

naa'ahóóhaiłbáhí. 2023. "Traditional Navajo Ceremonies." September 1. https://peopleofonefire.com/traditional-navajo-ceremonies/.

Schwarz, Maureen Trudelle. 2003. *Blood and Voice: Navajo Women Ceremonial Practitioners*. Linguistic and cultural consultant Mae Ann Bekis and fieldwork assistant Amelda Sandoval Shay. Tucson: University of Arizona Press.

Schwarz, Maureen Trudelle. 2008. *"I Choose Life": Contemporary Medical and Religious Practices in the Navajo World*. New Directions in Native American Studies. Vol. 2. Norman: University of Oklahoma Press.

Witherspoon, Gary. 1977. *Language and Art in the Navajo Universe*. Ann Arbor: University of Michigan Press.

Mitákuye Oyásin
Chapter 9.2

Mitákuye oyásiŋ translates as "for all my relations" or "we are all related" (Heidenreich 2005: 708).[1] The purpose of this entry is to describe how Lakota relationships moved from inner to outer circles, eventually encompassing the entire cosmos or Sacred Hoop. The narrative lays out four different dimensions of relationality: Lakota social organization, *Haŋbléčheyapi* or Vision Quest, *oinikaǧe* or Sweat Lodge ceremony in which the individual comes into relationship with a *wakȟáŋ* or nonhuman person, and *wíwáŋyaŋg wačhipi*, the Sun Dance, in which Lakota relationality with the whole cosmos occurs. I will discuss these three levels sequentially, although they need not happen in this order. For example, an *oinikaǧe* rite is a pre-requirement for the Vision Quest, and young people will have experienced the Sun Dance before engaging with either of the other two. In this chapter, the focus is on *haŋbléčheya* as a rite of passage for a young man. In actual practice, any Lakota can seek a vision at any time in their adult life and do it more than once.

While *Mitákuye oyásiŋ* includes all persons in the universe, its most immediate meaning is more directly related to the practical problems, needs, and interests of the Lakota. The hoop extends from the local environment to the edges of their hunting grounds. The Lakota relate to their nonhuman relatives so that these relatives will continue to provide the Lakota with what they need. The situation demands reciprocity. In return for nonhuman persons helping the Lakota continue as a people, the Lakota accept the responsibility for ensuring their nonhuman neighbors' present and future well-being.

During the winter, the Lakota lived in small encampments with their immediate family called *thiwáhe*. Members of their extended family usually lived nearby and, together, constituted a *wičhóthi*. They would space their dwellings far enough from each other so that each *thiwáhe* would have enough nonhuman relatives to provide for them. During the summer, they gathered into fiercely independent larger encampments, *thióšpaye*, for social and sacred festivals and ceremonies. The quintessential *thióšpaye* occurred for the buffalo hunt in the early- to mid-summer. The greatest ceremony was the Sun Dance, which was held then. Thousands of Lakota would gather at an agreed-upon location. It was the year's most important social, ceremonial, and hunt (Powers n.d.: 1–20).

The Lakota gathered into fraternal and sororal societies to further extend formal social relations. Some of these were related to hunting and war for the males and childrearing and sewing for the females. In the warrior societies, members became blood brothers and swore to give their lives to protect the community. One kind of warrior society raided horses and secured food resources to supplement their diets from other tribes, such as the Crow and Pawnee. Since they were not part of the Seven Fireplaces, the Crow and Pawnee were not considered relatives, although the Lakota could adopt them. Mixed-gender societies also existed. Two other forms of relationship expanded Lakota relationality: *kóhlá* and *huŋká*. *Kóhlá* are best friends with no blood relationships. *Huŋká* ceremonies provided opportunities for older Lakota to adopt young people into the immediate family or to become relatives with non-Lakotas and to connect these new relatives with sacred and nonhuman persons (Blish 1967: 425).

The Lakota clearly defined gender roles—many roles related to hunting and war for men and domestic activities for women. While the roles were clear, men were free to become women and women to become men or *wiŋkte*. The former was more common than the latter. The only requirement was that the person fully commit to the gender role they have chosen. The Lakota held such persons in high regard and considered them sacred (Powers 1986: 188–189). The sacrality refers to the idea that, in most cases, nonhuman or wakȟáŋ persons chose the person with whom they desired a relationship.

Four other types of persons are known to the Lakota; *Wičhaša wakȟáŋ* and *Wíŋyaŋ wakȟáŋ* or holy men and women who established close relationships with *wakȟáŋ* or sacred persons and had ready access to them; *Pȟežúta wiŋyaŋ*, medicine women and *Pȟežúta wičháša* who diagnosed and treated physical symptoms; *heyókȟ* (Black Elk and Lyon 1990: 62) as or contraries who did things backwards such as dressing in winter clothes during the summer and vice versa; and *Iktómi* or tricksters who displayed bad behavior and tried to trick people by playing on their foolishness.

The Oglala elder Wallace Black Elk claims that the term "vision quest" is foreign to the Lakota. For the Lakota, the preferred term is *haŋbléčheya*, meaning being quiet during the night (ibid.). Among the Lakota, the initial quest typically is a puberty ritual or rite of passage for males. *Haŋbléčheya* is not limited to young men. Lakota can seek a vision anytime in their lives and can do it multiple times. Each experience potentially expands their knowledge and power.

Almost always, the *haŋbléčheya* rite is initiated by the quester (Deloria, Jr. 2006: xxi). The young man, under the instructions of a holy man, *wičhaša wakȟáŋ*, climbs to the top of a hill and, without food or water, totally naked or perhaps only with a blanket, fasts for four days and humbly asks for pity from nonhuman persons. During these four days, he takes stalk of himself and the life that lies before him and opens himself to any nonhuman or *wakȟáŋ* being will appear to him and gift him with their power, *šičuŋ*. This relationship should continue for the rest of his life.

If a dream comes to him, it will show him the basic lifeway and pathway the person who comes to him has given him power to follow. This general direction depends on the gifts of knowledge and *Šičuŋ* the nonhuman person chooses for him. His responsibility is to use that power for the benefit of the community.

After he completes the quest, the young man goes to his mentor, the *wičhaša wakȟáŋ*, and reports any dream that came to him. If *Wakiŋyaŋ*, or Thunder, appears to him his mentor will advise him to stop his efforts immediately (Walker 1917: 82). Thunder is disruptive and purifying, just as thunderstorms can destroy and cleanse. The power of *Wakiŋyaŋ* also can transform the individual into a *heyókȟa*, which means that from that point forward, the individual will have to act in a contrary way.

Next we move to *oinikaǧe* or the sweat lodge ritual. The ceremony centers on the physical and spiritual purification of the participants. For this reason, Pete Catches prefers the term Inipi, or "purification," to Sweat Lodge" (Catches 1999: 129). Suzanne Owen uses *Inikǧapi* for the rite and translates the term as "for making life/breath" (Owen 2022: 190).

The rite expands relationality in two ways. Although the capacity of the sweat lodge only permits a few people to participate in the rite, it expands the number of community people who form sacred bonds, in contrast to *haŋbléčheyapi*, which involves the questor and his mentor. The rite also opens the participants to a broader circle of sacred powers than *haŋbléčheyapi*.

Before the rite begins, invitees prepare for the sweat lodge by gathering wood and water and clearing their minds of thoughts that may distract them. When they gather at the lodge, they socialize and develop a sense of community before the rite begins (White Hat, Sr. 1999: 131).

The rite occurs in a small domed enclosure and requires a fire outside the lodge to superheat stones, a pit for the rocks at the center of the lodge, sage, and water. The lodge, which faces west, becomes dark when the leader closes the opening through which the participants, stones, and water passed. Darkness is the environment sacred persons prefer when communicating with holy men (Powers 1986: 25). West is the direction from which the creation unfolded, and, as such, it is the source of life (Rice 1991: 139). West is *Wakiŋyaŋ*'s domain from which he brings terrifying and purifying power. Here, Wakinyan's role is to purify.

As the rite begins, the leader places sage on the rocks inside the lodge to repel destructive spirits and protect those gathered. The fire, water, and kinnikinnick are how those present communicate with the sacred persons present in the lodge. All establish a sacred bond by gifting the sacred persons with the smoke. The rite continues as the leader sprinkles water on the stones, creating a superheated mist. When breathed in, it has a transformative effect on people as it focuses them on the life-sustaining power of breathing and strengthens their life power. The leader then lights a pipe filled with kinnikinnick, a tobacco favored by sacred persons. Each participant smokes the pipe in turn. The shared smoking creates a sacred bond among those present. Each person blows the smoke toward the sky as they smoke, thus gifting the sacred persons. The rite ends with a prayer, after which someone lifts the covering, allowing light to come in.

In an attitude of humility, the participants have opened themselves up to the life-giving power of sacred persons and become stronger to contribute their renewed strength to the community's well-being. They have also renewed and strengthened their relationship with sacred persons through prayers of thanksgiving, which are reciprocal actions of gift exchange honoring them.

Lakota maximum extension of relationality occurs during *wíwáŋyaŋg wačhipi*. The ceremony's common name is the Sun Dance. The term *wíwáŋyaŋg wačhipi* means "Gazing at the Sun, We Dance," and Lame Deer refers to it as the Vision Quest of the entire Lakota nation (Fire) Lame Deer and Erdoes 1972: 188). In his classic study of the Sun Dance, James R. Walker divides the ritual process into four stages: candidacy, local preparations, sending out invitations, the journey to the campsite, a four-day social camp, and the four-day sacred camp. The most well-known and spectacular events occur on the last day of the sacred camp when Lakota pierce their skin, and aides attach themselves to the Sun Pole, where they dance until they break free. During these four phases, the circle of relationality expands to include all persons, human and nonhuman, within the Lakota sacred hoop.

The first phase begins in the local settlement, a *wičhóthi* or *thióšpaye*, depending on the size of the camp or band. The band or camp needed to be of sufficient size to adequately contribute enough material and personnel support as required for the last two phases. During this time, the potential candidate consults with a holy man, *wičhaša wakȟáŋ*, to seek his approval and mentorship for the flesh sacrifice on the last day of the Sun Dance. The *wičhaša wakȟáŋ* would consult with his spirit relatives for their approval. Having given it, the *wičhaša wakȟáŋ* and the candidate began their preparations. The local encampment then sends out invitations to other encampments. If they accept, the invitees lend their support as well.

The second phase is a four-day journey to the Sun Dance campsite. Each day begins with a *wičhaša wakȟáŋ* offering prayers to Sun and Sky to ensure a blue or good travel day. Joy and anticipation marked the group's spirit in anticipation of seeing their friends and extended family.

The third phase, the social camp, was a time of gaiety. Young men and women might seek out life partners, and others would catch up on the latest news. The social-relational circle became larger. While all this occurs, the candidates continued their preparations and were isolated.

The final phase, the sacred circle, gradually expanded the relational circle to include all of the sacred persons of their cosmos. People would spend part of their time hunting and capturing the tree that will stand at the center of the circle, making meals, and constructing the sacred lodge. The sacred lodge becomes transformed into a microcosm of the universe. The camp council interviewed people for specific supporting roles. When the last day came, the candidates solemnly process into the center of the sacred lodge, offering their flesh sacrifice to the sacred persons. This act of thanksgiving revitalized their reciprocal relationships with the beings of the nonhuman world. The relational world was now complete.[2]

Notes

1. The author has left the keywords in the native language. While glosses are available, and a number of them appear in this chapter, the keywords are so complex the reader can unpack them as they progress through the chapter. For a Lakota–English translator: https://glosbe.com/en/lkt. For pronunciation: www.wolakotaproject.org/lakota-pronunciation-glossary/.
2. For a detailed interpretation of the Lakota Sun Dance see Detwiler, *Cosmology and Moral Community in the Lakota Sun Dance* (2022).

References

Black Elk, Wallace H., and William S. Lyon. 1990. *Black Elk: The Sacred Ways of a Lakota*. San Francisco: Harper & Row.
Blish, Helen H. 1967. Review of in *A Pictographic History of the Oglala Sioux*. Lincoln: University of Nebraska Press.
Catches, Pete S. 1999. *Sacred Fireplace (Oceti Wakan): Life and Teachings of a Lakota Medicine Man*. Ed. Peter V. Catches. Santa Fe: Clear Light Publishers.
Deloria, Vine, Jr. 2006. *The World We Used to Live in: Remembering the Powers of the Medicine Men*. Golden: Fulcrum Pub.
Detwiler, Fritz. 2022. *Cosmology and Moral Community in the Lakota Sun Dance: Reconceptualizing J. R. Walker's Account*. New York: Routledge.
Heidenreich, C. Adrian. 2005. "Oral Traditions, Western Plains." In *American Indian Religious Traditions an Encyclopedi. Vol. 2: J–P*. Ed. Suzanne J. Crawford and Dennis F. Kelley. Santa Barbara: ABC-CLIO, 707–716.
Lame Deer, John (Fire), and Richard Erdoes. 1972. *Lame Deer, Seeker of Visions, by John Fire*. New York: Simon and Schuster.
Owen, Suzanne. 2022. "What is a Sweat Lodge?" In eds. Molly H. Bassett and Natalie Avalos (eds.), *Indigenous Religious Traditions in 5 Minutes*. Sheffield: Equinox, 190–192.
Powers, William K. 1986. *Sacred Language: The Nature of Supernatural Discourse in Lakota*. Civilization of the American Indian Series. Norman: University of Oklahoma Press.
Powers, William K., ed. N.d. *Tiyospaye*. Kendall Park: Lakota Books.
Rice, Julian. 1991. *Black Elk's Story: Distinguishing Its Lakota Purpose*. Albuquerque: University of New Mexico Press.
Walker, J. R. 1917. *The Sun Dance and Other Ceremonies of the Oglala Division of the Teton Dakota*. Anthropological Papers of the American Museum of Natural History. Vol. 16. New York: Published by order of the Trustees [of the American Museum of Natural History].
White Hat, Albert, Sr. 1999. *Reading and Writing the Lakota Language*. Salt Lake City: The University of Utah Press.

Tlingit: *at.oow*
Chapter 9.3

At.oow is one of the most important concepts for the Tlingit because it grants hunting, fishing, and land privileges to those who possess it.[1] Typically, the privileges stem from sacrificial acts of ancestors who paid with their lives so that their descendants could live a better life on the northwest coast of Turtle Island. *At.oow* literally means "owned things" (Thornton 2008: 38). or "something you own" (Jonaitis 2006: 134). The Tlingit believe that *at.oow* can come in material and non-material forms. Materially, it appears in blankets, hats, crests, iconography, property, ceremonial regalia, and geographic sites such as "salmon streams, halibut banks, shellfish beds, fort sites, and prominent mountains." Non-material forms include names, stories, songs, and spirits (Thornton 2008: 38). In ceremony, *at.oow* connects the ancestors, future generations, and sacred places where an ancestor or someone in the past or present time had a qualifying experience.

At.oow are also marks of status within clans, house groups, or houses and, as such, are directly related to Tlingit social organization. Ownership passes through matrilineal clans, house groups, or houses and is part of the clan identity, heritage, and destiny. It proceeds through exogamous matrilineal lineage. The broadest category of identity are moieties. Among coastal Tlingit they are Eagle and Raven. Interior Tlingit are divided into Wolf and Crow (Cruikshank 2005: 32–33). Each moiety has many clans, further divided into house groups or houses, the smallest unit of Tlingit society. Each clan, house group, and house have a leader responsible for the status and well-being of his community. If the leader allows the status or well-being of those for whom he is responsible to decline or if factions begin to split the community, members are free to leave and find a better-status home. Those who remain are responsible for aiding the leader in performing his duties, including providing material support.

Identity, prerogatives and *at.oow* reflect Tlingit social organization. Not everyone in the clan has the same entitlement to the *at.oow*. The Tlingit society divides membership in the clan into three somewhat fluid classes and one non-Tlingit group: aristocrats, commoners, "dried-fish slaves," and slaves. Aristocrats, and those people to whom they give authority, are the only ones entitled to possess *at.oow*. Commoners aid the aristocrats and perform normal social duties. "Dried-fish slaves," those who depend on the largesse of others, include illegitimate children and outcasts whom their kin have abandoned. True Slaves are those who are from other societies and who have been captured in battle or sold by their kin (Kan 1989: 2).

The Tlingit trace clan identity through matrilineal descent. Clans typically divide into houses and subhouses depending on the size of the members of the house and function within a set geographical location. These units have a similar class structure. People belonging to one house are free to leave and join another clan house if they are not satisfied with their house leadership (Detwiler 2013: 171). The status of houses within a clan proceeds from the reputation of the house leader and is based on wealth and character.

Earned prerogatives through sacrificial actions help maintain order in Tlingit society as different clans, house groups, and houses compete for geographical places, food, and building resources. Susie James recalls such a heroic act by her Chookaneidi clan ancestor in the story of Glacier Bay. The story begins with a young woman going through her menstrual cycle. As was the custom for a woman her age, she was secluded in a hut outside her house. She gets bored and begins to taunt the nearby glacier by waving small pieces of meat at it, treating the glacier like a dog. The glacier becomes angry at the insult and begins to move toward the village. As it advances, the people of the village begin to worry. If it continues to come closer, they will have to abandon the place where they live. It continues, and the people prepare to get in boats and leave.

The villagers know that someone must pay for the insult with their life. The obvious choice would be the young girl who committed the offense. However, the grandmother volunteers to sacrifice her life. She reasons that the community's future lay not with her but with the young woman who would later bear children, thus contributing to the long-term continuation of the clan. The people escape, and the grandmother dies. She has paid the price. Satisfied, the glacier recedes, and the people are permitted to return (Cruikshank 2005: 39). By the grandmother's heroic act, Glacier Bay is now sacred to the Chookaneidi and is owned by them (Dauenhauer and Dauenhauer 1987: 409). It is now an *at.oow*, as is the grandmother, so long as someone in the clan continues to possess the *at.oow*. No other clan can lay claim to that land, nor can fish or hunt there without the clan's permission. Dauenhauer claims that the emphasis of the story is the grandmother's sacrifice and the Tlingit concept of "standing in" or "accepting responsibility not only for one's own actions but the actions of others as well" (Dauenhauer and Dauenhauer 1987: 408).

According to Tlingit elder Lydia George, sacred places have four components: "a name, a story, a song (typically accompanied by a dance), and a design (or crest) . . . Together, they constitute a cultural nexus of sacredness that endows places, and the people who possess them, with profound webs of significance" (Thornton 2008: 2) and connect them with the clan ancestors. Visual designs are not depictions of ancestral heroic deeds. They embody the "events, emotions, kin, places, and other themes that are fundamental to individual and social group identity" (ibid., 31).

In addition to Glacier Bay, as the grandmother is becoming an *at.oow* two other elements of the story are significant. The first is the moral dimension (ibid., 107). The story illustrates the consequences of inappropriate actions and the cost they may extract from the clan. It also demonstrates that decisions in paying the price are focused on the group, not the individual. If people act appropriately, then things will go well. Nora Dauenhauer notes, "Above all, humans must respect the world of the spirits – the spirits of animals and other forms of life and energy in the world. If these spirits are respected, the life in which they are embodied will continue to return to the people, sustaining human life" (Dauenhauer and Dauenhauer 1987: 407).

The second element is that *at.oow* has both an individual and collective dimension (Thornton 2008: 38). Two closely related Tlingit terms describe this. *Shagoon* refers to the collective destiny of the past and future. *Shuka* also connects to *shagoon* but adds an individual aspect to *at.oow*. In James' story, Glacier Bay and the grandmother are *at.oow*. The story's elements, including the glacier's sounds, the grandmother's and granddaughter's names, and the song and words compassed by a maternal uncle as they leave, are all part of *at.oow* (Worl 1998: 95). Names of ancestors follow the matrilineal line, and a person with such a name inherits some of the character of the ancestor for whom they are named, the *shuka* or destiny of that person, and the prerogatives of the ancestor (Kan 1989: 89). For this reason, no two people will have the same name in any generation.

Sergei Kan notes that Tlingit clan claims of ownership are expressed in story and song and through visual iconography (ibid., 193). The Tlingit commonly use crests as material and visual representations on coppers and ceremonial Chilkat blankets. Coppers are pieces of copper extracted from shipwrecks in Tlingit waters.

The process of making visual representations of *at.oow* involves both moieties and, at least for the Raven moiety, follows basic design patterns of the moiety's titular figure Emmons and de Laguna 1991: 32). As noted above, the coastal Tlingit would be either Eagle or Raven, while Wolf or Crow would adorn visual representations for the interior Tlingit. Variations of the visual representations within a moiety were common. Just as a given clan might have multiple sacred stories, crests vary in different clans or houses. Crests, therefore, were unique to *these* people or *this individual* who shared a geographical place and marked the prerogatives of the house or individual granted to them through the moral covenants that their ancestors established with nonhuman persons.

When a clan or house decides to convert a sacred event into an *at.oow*, they must enlist the services of the opposite moiety. Rosita Worl describes this arrangement as oppositional complementarity, a principle that governs the Tlingit universe. She notes that this principle allows the Tlingit to maintain social harmony (Worl 1998: 83). Worl describes turning a traditional Tlingit wooden hat into an *at.oow*. "The commission involved three separate tasks conducted by different individuals from an opposing clan. The first assignment involved securing raw materials that are used in the manufacture of the hat. The party went to a pre-selected site on land owned by the commissioning clan and selected an appropriate tree. The tree's spirit must be thanked for allowing itself to be used in the object, and a blanket is placed on the ground where they expect the tree to fall" (ibid., 104).

Another individual is retained to prepare and season the wood; finally, a third person, an artist, is commissioned to make the clan hat. The artist is given a suggestion about the design. An elder of the artist's clan must approve the design. Then, the person who commissioned the *at.oow* must accept the design (ibid., 104). A "high caste" crafter of the artist then makes the representation. After this work is finished, another clan elder of the artist reviews the object. If it meets Tlingit design standards, the object is sent to the clan, which has commissioned the transformation for their acceptance. If accepted, the authorizing clan hosts a ceremony, and the object is presented to the opposite clan to maintain social and spiritual harmony (ibid., 105).

The Tlingit potlatch ceremony embodies the principle of reciprocity and substantiates ownership of the *at.oow*. The potlatch has also attracted much attention for the enormous giveaways that are a major part of the ceremony. A house or clan leader sponsors a potlatch and gives away his entire wealth. Reciprocity requires those who have accepted the invitation to participate in the potlatch from other clans or moieties to sponsor a potlatch in the future. The size of the giveaway helps establish the status of the sponsoring house or clan. The sponsor usually brings an *at.oow* and presents it to the group. The leader's presentation is accompanied by songs and stories related to the *at.oow*. By their attendance, those outside the sponsor's clan or house accept the at.oow and the prerogatives accompanying it (Jonaitis 2006: 134). The ancestors arrive and are honored by reciting the history and singing the songs of the *at.oow*. In this way, *at.oow* helps maintain harmony and balance within the larger Tlingit community and distribute wealth, *at.oow* also helps maintain the past, present, and future destiny of the clan or house.

Notes

1. The author has left the keywords in the native language. While glosses are available, and a number of them appear in this chapter, the keywords are so complex the reader can unpack them as they progress through the chapter. For Tlingit-English translator visit https://glosbe.com/en/tli. For pronunciation: https://pronouncebee.com/tlingit/.

References

Cruikshank, Julie. 2005. *Do Glaciers Listen? Local Knowledge, Colonial Encounters and Social Imagination*. Seattle: University of Washington Press.

Dauenhauer, Richard, and Nora Dauenhauer, eds. 1987. Ha Shuká, *Our Ancestors: Tlingit Oral Narratives*. Seattle: University of Washington Press; Juneau Sealaska Heritage Foundation.

Detwiler, Fritz. 2013. "Moral Foundations of Tlingit Cosmology." In *The Handbook of Contemporary Animism*. Ed. Graham Harvey. Durham: Acumen Pub., 167–180.

Emmons, George Thornton, and Frederica de Laguna, eds. 1991. *The Tlingit Indians*. Seattle: University of Washington Press.

Jonaitis, Aldona. 2006. *Art of the Northwest Coast*. Seattle: University of Washington Press.

Kan, Sergei. 1989. *Symbolic Immortality: The Tlingit Potlatch of the Nineteenth Century*. Washington, DC: Smithsonian Institution Press.

Thornton, Thomas F. 2008. *Being and Place Among the Tlingit: Culture, Place, and Nature*. Seattle: University of Washington Press.

Worl, Rosita F. 1998. "Tlingit *At.oow*: Tangible and Intangible Property." Unpublished diss., Harvard University, Cambridge.hózǭǭhh

10

Iqbal and the Actualizing Self Gift or Task?

Abrahim H. Khan

Chapter Outline

Educational and Cultural Influences Contextualizing Iqbal's Construct of Selfhood	269
Constructing of *Khudi*/Self in Relation to *'Ishq*/Love and Immortality	273
Iqbal's Conception of Self as Khudi	273
Relevance of Iqbal's Construct of Khudi/Self in the Twenty-First Century	276
10.1 Immortality	280
10.2 *'Ishq*/Love	284

This chapter introduces the construct of the self (*khudi*), or personhood, according to the *Indo*-Muslim poet-philosopher Muhammad Iqbal (1887–1938). While the Iqbal's conception of khudi has affinities with the personalist tradition in western philosophy, and for that matter existentialist thought, it is not structured according to European philosophical thought. Iqbal draws on insights from the poetry and philosophy of the Persian thinker Rumi, the Muslim intellectual tradition, and the Quran. The discussion of *khudi* is developed in three sections following a contextualizing of his relevance with respect to his restructuring of the self and core texts for its discussion here. First is a discussion of the educational and cultural influence contextualizing his literary works as sources for his construct selfhood. The second section develops his construct of the self in relation to *'ishq*/love. The final section explains implications of Iqbal's construct in the twenty-first century, underscoring the centrality of being a person outside of a western/European *weltschaung*.

Iqbal by propensity is a poetic life-philosopher, and by career a jurist and socio-political reformer grappling with the challenges of modernity in the Indian subcontinent. He took to a reconceptualizing of the self through humanistic concepts and as having a telos to focus on its capacity for action and growth in becoming fully self-actualizing. His insights and knowledge for theorizing were occasioned by different factors and circumstances. They include primarily reflections on the sprit of the Quranic message, his rereading of Muslim intellectual history and his familiarity with developments in contemporary Western thought, psychology, and science vis-a-vis- the bondage of the self to British colonial logic or administration in India. In theorizing, a foremost question to his philosophical mindset was how the self is related to the universe and the conduct befitting the place that the self or individual occupies in the universe.[1]

Poetry and prose became the medium for the restructuring that Iqbal undertook. His 1915 Persian written philosophical epic *Asrár-i-Khudí* (*Secrets of the Self*) is a key text. Its English language translator, orientalist R. A. Nicholson at Cambridge University, noted that Iqbal "comes forward as an apostle, if not to his own age, then to posterity . . . 'as the voice of the poet of To-Morrow,'" and is said to be "a man of his age, a man in advance of his age; he is also a man in disagreement with his age."[2]

That poet's voice, awakening Muslims to regaining self-identity, was heard across and outside the Muslim world as having civic and political significances as well. Its concepts were adumbrating aspect of our shared humanity. That Iqbal belongs to all people is best expressed in the tribute by US Supreme Court Justice William O. Douglas paid standing at his tomb in Lahore. For Douglas, Iqbal's "concepts had a universal appeal. He spoke to the consciences of men of good will, whatever their tongue, whatever their creed."[3] Iqbal had bought forward new ideas to Muslim jurisprudence to meet the needs of social development in an independent India, in the emergence of Pakistan as a modern nation state, and expressive of a dimension of a Muslim *weltanschuuang*. A dynamic and reorienting thinker-writer, Iqbal is awakening Muslim communities from a self-negating, docile mindset. His poetic awakening call is to rise up for their freedom on the basis of qualities of being vitally human in accord with the call of the Quran, to break free from bondage of repeating the old ritualistic practices or values comprising tradition. to what is changeable (*Reconstruction*, 129). An ideological epistemology that accords with colonizing logic and social imaginary of British rule in the Indian subcontinent was largely responsible for a slumber self, for lacking the elasticity to becoming vitally human. Declining Muslim world politico-religious leadership precipitating the dissolution of the Ottoman caliphate and empire by the turn into the twentieth century also contributed to the loss of vitality for Muslim self-identity. Altogether, they form the backdrop against which Iqbal's philosophy of selfhood (*khudí*) is framed to engage constructively the materialistic emphasis and scientism of western modernism, the influx of modernist secular ideas associated with British colonial rule.

Two other texts augmenting *Asrár* on selfhood are a sequel poem *Rumuz-i-Bekhúdí* (*Mysteries of Selflessness*) in 1918, followed by *Reconstruction of Religious Thought in Islam* in 1930 published as a collection of English language university lectures in India, and in 1934 reissued with an additional essay. The preface to *Reconstruction* begins with this statement: "The Quran is a book which emphasizes deed rather than 'idea'" (*Reconstruction*, xlvi) suggesting that a self is not a diffused or quietist center but has a dynamism as well for creativity living or practical application. Its fourth essay on the human ego opens with what may well be summative of Iqbal's view of self: "The Qur'an in its simple, forceful manner emphasizes the individuality and uniqueness of man, and has, I think, a definite view of his destiny as a unity of life" (*Reconstruction*, 76). The titles mentioned above are the textual resources for three concepts to put in relief Iqbal's stance on self as an actualizing activity: *khudi*/ego, *'ishq*/love, and immortality.

Each of the three concepts has for Iqbal a core meaning or specific hermeneutical interpretation that may easily get overlooked. For they are represented by terms or words that have a universal appeal. The expository analysis proffered here has running through it an implicit argument: Iqbal's reconceptualizing of self is informed by intuitive sensitivity that accords with the Quran and aspects of *sufi* thought and hardly with a Cartesian "cogito ergo sum" or strands of modern western philosophical thought.[4] Accepting readily and uncritically western influences may hinder rather than aid in understanding his use of humanistic concepts to frame the self vis-à-vis the human condition experience shaped in his day largely by British colonial imperatives and education. The self to which he is awakening others is one of action and self-realization. It is one requiring continually striving to affirm and fully actualize itself within the worldly dimensions and by relating simultaneously and absolutely to the Ultimate. Such is the self canvased here for Iqbal, a self whose nature is to maintain itself as self (*Reconstruction*, 68), in contrast to a logically derived either Cartesian or Kantian self.

Educational and Cultural Influences Contextualizing Iqbal's Construct of Selfhood

Evidently global in perspective, Iqbal's stance on self has an affinity with strands of modern western philosophical thought. That affinity may be traced to his pre-1905 student years in the Punjab area of then British administered India. The impetus for his humanistic or vitalist thought process (intuitions and insights) about self came from at least three directions: (1) parental religious upbringing, (2) the Persian and

Arabic scholar Sayyid Mir Hasan tutoring, and the famous Urdu poet Daagh Dehlvi mentoring, and (3) his Lahore college professor Sir Thomas Arnold's inspirations and intellectual encouragement.

Through parental religious upbringing Iqbal became acquainted with Quran reading in the mosque and a Qadiryya stream of Muslim piety whose teachings included magnanimity and humanitarianism. The stream of Sufism, originating with the sermons of scholar preacher Abdul Qadi al-Jilani in the twelfth century, having no specific dress codes or requiring spiritual disciplining through meditation or exercises, stresses love for God. It held also to the idea of a unity of existence, meaning that creation and Creator were inseparable. Another was Mirian Mir (d. 1635) whose Urdu poetry emphasizing love inspired Iqbal's eulogizing of him in *Asrár-i-Khudí* as "a flute for the impassioned music of love."[5] This poetic-religious milieu nurtured his talent for poetry which he later direct to expressing political and patriotic yearnings and to awakening of Muslim community vitalism to decolonize and affirm their religio-cultural identity. He did so stressing love/*'ishq*, *one* of the three reframing concepts for his stance on self.

The two other directions to explain the affinity overlap to some extent. Iqbal 's familiarity with Western thought began with the meeting of two important scholars through Mir Hasan, his Urdu and Persian lyrics tutor and scholar. One is the Muslim social reformer and educationist Sayed Ahmed Khan, founder of the Anglo-Muslim College that is now Aligrah University. There, in 1892 Iqbal undertook liberal studies, gaining exposure to western thought and Muslim theological tradition. The other is the orientalist Thomas Arnold, teaching at that college and focussing his scholarship on combining modern western philosophical thought and Islamic culture. Iqbal came under his influence as an undergraduate majoring in Arabnic, English literature and philosophy while studying at the Government College in Lahore where Arnold had moved. Arnold, mentoring Iqbal as an undergraduate studying, Arabic, English literature, and philosophy at the Government College in Lahore where later he was appointed professor, recognized his academic and creative potential (see Durrani; and Mir 2006: 5, 6).

The mentorship influence deepening Iqbal's acquaintance with English literature and political thought continued through his graduate studies that ensued in a MA degree (1899) in philosophy followed by a teaching appointment in Lahore. Iqbal's recognition of the literary and philosophical training by his mentor is expressed in the dedication of his 1908 doctoral thesis to Arnold. Impetuses from parental upbringing, Muslim master poets, social-religious reformers, and orientalist scholars, comingled in late 19th century colonial India to form a matrix. Out of that matrix grew the stance on self Iqbal took publicly in 1915 in his Persian philosophical epic poem, *Asrár*.

Already an emerging scholar versed in Muslim theological tradition, Iqbal on Arnold's encouragement left India to widen his studies in Europe. In his three-year postgraduate studies in Europe (1905–1908), Iqbal had as teachers at Cambridge, the orientalist, Nicholson who would later translate *Asrár*, and philosophers such as Bradley, McTaggart, and Ward, while earning another MA in philosophy, followed by a PhD from Munich, and becoming qualified to practice as a barrister at law in London. The studies in Cambridge, Munich, and London intensified as well as broadened his engagement with modern western philosophical and socio-scientific thought, *strum und drang* writers, and the English romantic movement.

Hardly did studies in Europe deter his reading of Muslim philosophical thought. Instead, they sharpened his interest to look critically at similar lines in western thought with respect to his PhD thesis topic. The thesis, on the development of metaphysics in Persia, references names such as McTaggart, Bradley, Fichte, Hegel, Kant, Jacobi, Aquina, and Schleiermacher.[6] They made varying impact to his thought serving to support or differentiate what he has on subtopics or chapters. The names span from pre-Islamic and Greek dualisms, controversy with idealism and rationalism, Islamic occasionalism, Rumi on love, Al-Jili and three developmental stages of Pure Being, and to Mulla Sadr doctrines of the identity of subject and object, to that of the incorporeality of the imagination. The referencing range evidences his ability to relate two different intellectual traditions with respect to subjectivity, consciousness, and psychology. The topics taken up in the thesis are suggestive of insights, intuitions, critical directions, that would shape his reformulating of self. His inspiration to relate in a critical way the two intellectual traditions, European and Islamic, came from his Lahore teacher and guide, Professor Arnold.

Iqbal's stance on the self is shaped largely in the crucible of rereading of Muslim primary sources against the socio-cultural background of his day with priority given to scientism and secularization process. His 1908 PhD thesis for Munich University avers that modern western scholarship and discussions had not dampened his interest in the humanistic spirit of the Quran and aspects of Muslim intellectual thought for awakening Muslims society. That is, his discussions in Europe anticipate dispelling the illusion of European colonial imaginary as the sole reference point for becoming an authentically actualizing self.

He framed his thinking of self or *khudi* taking as his guide in Islamic thought names already mentioned. Insights of yet another, the school of the Suni scholastic scholar-theologian Al-Ash'ari are crucial for his ontological construction of *khudi* as self-actualizing. His awakening voice to Muslims is to seek knowledge, become self-conscious, and act for change, by bringing together the three. The theory of continuous creation in atomic time by thinkers of the Ash'arite school presuppose that nothing has a stable nature, meaning that reality is continuously occurring in atomic time by a Creator or Ultimate Ego or will of God. God's creative activity or divine energy being ceaseless makes all reality spiritual in varying degrees with respect to consciousness and self-actualizing (*Reconstruction*, 54, 57). The reality of the human self or personality is that with the highest degree of spirituality. In short, Iqbal's guidance in engaging modern western intellectual thought with respect to reality or what it manes to become a realizing self is by philosophical insights within strands of Islamic intellectual thought that are in keeping with the spirit of the Quran.

The philosophical-theological anthropology of Iqbal presupposes that the human is a physically as well as spiritually being that is a self-contained center, gifted to becoming fully a self-actualizing person. The goal or high point of self is to reflect through absorbing divinity attributes, thus divinizing itself and thereby attaining to a personal immortality in this life. Alternative put, for Iqbal a human is a tri-axial reality or ego-consciousness: body, mind and spirit/(Arabic *rūḥ*), the latter understood as issuing from God's command or as a transcendent reality.[7] Constitutive of *khudi* or self-actualizing, the physical-biological, psychological-passional, and spiritual-transcendent dimensions have to be willed freely by the individual to be related to one another for the self to regain its vitality or becoming fully what it is created to become, self-actualized. Thus, away from a Freudian ego or Unconscious, according to Iqbal's theory of selfhood everyone has the possibility to grasp or intuit reality not in a piecemeal way but as whole by relating the three dimensions to one another. The grasping or relating begins with the objectified self or human individual (body) thinking of itself inwardly (mind) in striving and becoming disciplined by love/*'ishq*, through a developing process that has three emerging levels. That is, self actualizing is from obedience to divine laws, to exercising moral self-control, and to becoming divine viceregency. Along the way, social-political realties can be stifling or arresting the impulses towards self-actualizing, whether the realties are conditioned by traditional religious thought, old ways, or debilitating aspects of modernity. In short, one can become lost easily to oneself or *khudi* as a gift through docility, negligence, diminishing faculties and capacities, or waning sensibilities and capabilities.

Iqbal is observant of developments and discourse defining modern western thought, engaging thinkers at points that are relevant for the self understood as both a gift and a task. Such thinkers include Descartes, Kant, Fichte, Badley, McTaggart, and Bergson to name a few. For Iqbal the self is given as a task that, according to the Quran (see Quran 33:22 and *Reconstruction*, xxii, 68, 70), is a divine trust, namely, freedom to choose between obedience and disobedience and be held accountable, a task that humankind accepted despite the declining of it by other created realms. The trust amounts to divinity taking a risk that humanity will excise its freedom to choose goodness over its opposite. For Iqbal that task translates as self-actualizing or *khudi*.[8] Thus, Iqbal disagrees with aspects of modernity, that is, the influx of secular modernist ideas that came with British colonialism, as well as aspects of the Muslim intellectual history and *Shariah* interpretations that are stifling to individuality or *khudi*. In his rereading of Muslim intellectual history, he is taking cues from the Quran as emphasizing deed rather than ideas, and from those thinkers in accord with the cues, such as Al-Jlili (1365–1424) and Rumi (1207–1273).

Constructing of *Khudi*/Self in Relation to *'Ishq*/Love and Immortality

Epistemologically pivotal to the anthropology in Iqbal's framing of self/*khudi* is that the human heart is an organ of insight as well. It is connecting with aspects of Reality not accessible by thought or logical thinking or sense-perception. Intuitive sensibilities give direct connection or appreciative encounter with those aspects of Reality and life, which thought veils or become symbolic in character when used for practical life functions (*Reconstruction*, 61f.). Away from classical Greek epistemological approach, evident also in Muslim intellectual history, the self or *khudi* is experientially existential, is direct apprehension of Reality attained inwardly though intuition. Conceptually *'ishq* and immortality are different stages, embodiment, or expressions of the experientially existential striving to self-actualise or immortalize. In short, immortalizing, or personal immortality, unlike speaking of the immortality of the soul (*nafs*) in the hereafter, is an existential activity to reflect divine attributes through absorption of them and thereby becoming a divine representative or viceregency on earth. Every human has the opportunity or gift for that: to express magnanimity, humility, and compassion in relation to others. Thus, that for which the self is striving—absorbing divine attributes is given as gift. It cannot fully actualize or immortalize without absorbing the divine attributes. It is always self-actualizing in serial time.

Iqbal's Conception of Self as Khudi

Iqbal uses a specialized term "*khudi*," a Persian–Urdu word in referencing what he means by self. The term, rendered in English as ego, person, or personhood is largely removed from accepted Freudian usage of ego. In Iqbal's usage *khudi* implies a complex construct innate to human nature, functioning as a center-point of subjective psychological purposive activity: affirming, expressing, and developing selfhood, or as acquiring fullness of personality compared to being haughty or egoistic. An individual may cultivate, resist or ignore its impulse to relate creatively by unifying. For self as *khudi* is a unifying agent of experience and passageway, comprised of all our mental activities and hence conscious of itself as I-am, in the sense of Descartes: *Cogito, ergo sum*.

His text, *Asrár*, expresses *khudi* or consciousness as "the luminous point,"[9] functioning not as a stream comprised of bits of mental activities hooked to one another. This glowing point, for Iqbal, rises, expands, and falls varying with our moods, impulses, tendencies, intentions, choices, expectations, and mistakes - all constitutive of our inner life. It is a state without "well-defined fringes; it shrinks and expands as the occasion demands" (*Reconstruction*, 33). Unlike William James' stream of consciousness, luminous point or consciousness is that of self having become conscious of itself as affirming, assimilating, developing, and having different levels such as missing the mark or opportunities to act, or having remorse, being sorrowful or regretting whether for omission or commission, or having anxiety as part of the process of becoming aware of oneself. That is, it is self-conscious of its own-self awareness and its expansion or directiveness, through a simultaneous double movement.

As the locus of consciousness or CenterPoint, *khudi* is holding together in a unity, dispersing experiences and activity in the direction of a constructive purpose (*Reconstruction*, 48). This it does by striving to ground itself in, by relating to, that which is absolute, namely Ultimate Ego without becoming lost or diffused in it. *Khudi*/self for Iqbal is very real and existent, its reality apprehensible through direct intuition rather than through conceptual relationship as Desecrates did. That is, it becomes disclosed as the center-point of all our activities and actions, including our subjectivity—hoping, desiring, wishing deciding, judging, resolving, and so on; and presupposes a telos. Iqbal expresses the psychologically purposive aspect poetically this way:

> Subject, object, means, and causes—
> All these are forms which it assumes for the purpose of action.
> The Self rises, kindles, falls, glows, breathes,
> Burns, shines, walks, and flies.
> The spaciousness of Time is its arena,
>
> (*Asrár*, 44f., lines 215-219)

This interior mental side, or consciousness describable in terms of psychologically purposive verbs, is self that is becoming awakened, is intuitively apprehensible as a self that is self-appreciative of itself.

Iqbal's self so far seems to bear a striking resemblance to familiar lines of thought in modern Western philosophy. However, unlike Cartesian *cogito ergo sum* dictum, Iqbal goes farther by holding two distinct claims: (1) self, that is self-appreciative consciousness or ego, is a reality that can be directly intuited. For Descartes the self is inferential, conceptual. It goes no further to tell anything about the nature of the self as purposive and unitive of internal experiences and activities associate with being in the world and is correlated to having a personality through relating to a telos. Another (2) is that the reality of the self is a differentiation of that to which it is striving towards, which is completely free, and thus has its own unique reality. The latter or telos is ultimate, designated as Absolute Ego, Independent Self or Highest Good. This may seem to be an echo of Iqbal's acquaintance with British Idealism through his Cambridge teachers, especially McTaggart, of the unreality of time and self, and immortality of self. But Iqbal is mindful to note that the self he is proposing is in a creative tension with the Independent Self or Absolute Ego and has to earn its immortality. As he puts it in a discourse, "Man is a candidate for immortal life which involves a ceaseless struggle in maintaining the tension of the ego" (Razzaqi 1979: 209). Personality or *khudi* correlates with being in and maintaining a state of tension with the Ultimate Ego, by removing through assimilation obstacles in serial or spatialized time to the tension. This includes modifying one's mindset to move forward by staying consciously related to what is ultimate and absolute. Hence, such modifying is the most valuable achievement of the human and a means towards one's immortality in an Iqbal's reframing of self.

Iqbal distinguishes spatialized time related to the material or sensual world, from real time which is in a flux or succession without change (Razzaqi 1979: 186). The ego in its environment is determined by several factors: activities related to biological needs, material requirements, sociocultural conditions, and physical surroundings, for example. The self may have come-and-go experiences associated with how it finds itself in society. But the experiences are not separate, standing alone. They are rather continuous without break, a succession without change, held together as in a chain of pearls, hence is a pure movement or duration without change as termed by Bergson (Enver 1944: 39, 46). It is in the moments of crucial life decisions to act that the ego directly apprehends itself to be free, self-determining, acting absolutely. Or ass Iqbal's lecture explains, to exist in pure duration, as opposed to serial time, is "to be able to be a self, and to be a self is to be able to say "I am" (*Reconstruction*, 45) in contrast to being not-self.

Ascribable to Iqbal is, evidently and by extension, a third claim that relates to the idea of divinizing or immortalizing and to the notion of freedom. We leave its treatment for later, moving on to another aspect to Iqbal's self. That is, its traversing of boundaries or stages in its assimilative movement to becoming immortal (*Asrár*, xx). By the movement it is approximating the uniqueness of the most Unique Individual or Ultimate Ego. It is a claim that has implication for Muslim ethical conduct, and thus differentiates Iqbal's stance of self from other stances in either Muslim thought or modern Western philosophy. That is, the self traverses three stages identified as obedience, moral self-control, and Divine Viceregency. The traversing is by its own impulse, becoming self-aware of the possibility of its own evolutionary direction and unity. The ego may fail in its struggle to complete the crossing of a stage as a result of indolence, weakness of will, distraction in its educative or schooling process, or simply debilitating mental faculties and diminishing sensibilities.

Iqbal in *Asrár*, Bk 1X, likens the ego to a camel whose traits are service and toil, but whose ways are patience and perseverance. The first stage "Obedience," correlates with the exercise of patience and perseverance with respect to duties and the Law, that is, with the religious customs that the Quran enjoins. For it is by obedience to Law one becomes worthy, that everything within oneself is stronger (*Asrár*, 73, 74).

Negligence results in lassitude and inactivity of the ego as a center-point. What is important is that the nature of self requires that it be educated or disciplined in reaching its full potential.

Having gone through that the self for Iqbal is self-assertive in relating itself to itself and in a forward thrust to the Absolute Ego, it may call to mind a strand of thought from the eighteenth-century, German philosopher Johann Gottlieb Fichte. Fichte claimed that the ego or I is at once a subject and object in its subjectivity—reflectivity or consciousness. Such is the starting point of Fichte's philosophy of knowing. Undoubtedly the similarity of the self or ego as self-referencing is striking: the ego is self positing, not a substance but act, and thus exist and is purposive in contrast to non-ego. But this self-positing feature has applicability to the Absolute Ego. The latter is Fichte's starting point or first principle in his philosophy. In contrast, Iqbal starts with the finite or human ego as self-positing or an act or revealing itself through mental states that are unified through a directive purpose in relation to the Absolute Ego. The emergence of self is within spatial time order and its purposive movement is based on it being a physical organism. Iqbal's inspiration for these ideas draw from the Quran 53, lines 39-41.[10]

Similarly, there is a seemingly familiar strand of the British idealist Francis Herbert Bradley in Iqbal's thinking of the self. It is that experience occurs in finite centers that gives it a finite-thisness and is inexplicable; the centers are sublated and united in an Absolute whereby they are no longer finite or distinctive. By contrast Iqbal's starting point is similar with a finite ego but the trajectory and process of the finite relation to the Absolute Ego is quite different. Iqbal has no sublation of the finite or loss of distinctiveness of the finite self in relating to the Absolute which for him is a personal God (*Asrár*, xvi–xvii; *Reconstruction*, 78f., 82f.). Finite self or ego is never dissolved but retains its uniqueness through struggling to maintain the tension for a directionally purposive movement. That is, the reality of my self or *khudi* lies, according to Iqbal, in my directive attitude; hence my personality is an activity of holding together a series of experiences in time (*Reconstruction*, 82f.). The experiences may include misunderstanding, misjudging, mistaking, inattention, forgetting—all leading to disappointment and anxiety, comingling with anticipation and expectation in relationships.

Relevance of Iqbal's Construct of Khudi/Self in the Twenty-First Century

Iqbal on self-actualizing is important not merely from the point of view of intellectual history, but more significantly for speaking to our present cultural situation with its global-political warp and woof. Characterization of that situation includes shifting demography associated with diaspora and/or refuge movements and hence religious pluralism, instant social medial access to information and disinformation, and IT developments such as AI powered chatbot and humanoid robots simulating human presence and interaction. Thus, the context includes having to deal with new social and relational uncertainties and mistrust, along with decolonizing and welcoming new voices of hope and serenity. That situation is making it imperative to redefine ourselves in relation to the other, to inquire critically about the other in order to gain insight about our self or inner cosmos, a step forward in realizing the divine trust. Iqbal is one such voice of hope and serenity in authentically self-actualizing.

A rereading of him as being relevant for our contemporary situation is well expressed by the Canadian philosopher Charles Taylor: "we also have shared reasons, Western, Muslim and Eastern merged together, in reading this remarkable man. Because our dialogues are troubled by a deep and mutual distrust. This distrust is partly derived from our own uncertainty regarding our identity, which sometimes gives us a feeling of insecurity under the gaze of others" (Taylor 2010: xii). In such seemingly global and social-cultural troubled milieu, Iqbal's awakening call is to rise up to the task of actualizing the gifted self by exercising virtues for approximating ideals of a shared humanity.

Notes

1. See the opening questions to his first lecture in Muhammad Iqbal, *Reconstruction of Religious Thought in Islam* (Oxford: Oxford University Press, 1934). Reissued and printed in 2013 by Stanford University Press. Hereafter cited as *Reconstruction*.
2. See Mohammed Iqbal, *Secrets of the Self* (*Asrár-i-Khudî*), trans. R. A. Nicholson (London: Macmillan and Company Limited, 1920), xxxi. Hereafter cited as *Asrár* (*Secrets*).
3. See the Forward by W. O. Douglas to *Iqbal: Poet-Philosopher of Pakistan*, ed. Hafez Malik (New York: Columbia University Press, 1971), ix.
4. To the implicit argument is the counterpoint stance that Iqbal's idea of self is a derivative of "modern, western understanding of the self going back to Descartes," taken by Hasam Azad (2014: 22). Another example is the claimed influence of James on Iqbal, by Mark J. Boone (2024). Contrastingly, the claim of Iqbal's dependency of Western thought is countered by, Abdul Khaliq in his preface to Nazir Qaiser, *Iqbal and the Western Philosophers* (2010); Kaliq, president of Pakistan Philosophical Association, contends that such critics commit the fallacy of "*Non Causa Pro Causa* i.e. what is not the cause is erroneously taken to be the cause*"* (viii). Qaiser holds that "Iqbal's concepts are qualitatively different from those of the Western philosophers," and provides a few examples of the differences (xiii–xix). Qaiser offers two main reasons for critics being misled in making a claim of influence. One is that the "critics themselves have neither sufficient knowledge of the Qur'an and Islamic

tenets nor of Muslim thought and sufi concepts." The other is that, "Iqbal's own discussion and appreciation of certain views of the above Western philosophers have not been understood in their true context by the critics of Iqbal" (xix, xx).
5. See Qadiryaa order or *tariqa* that spread to Punjab at: https://world-religions.info/qadiriyya-tariqa/; Buehler (1999: 1, 10, 11, 12); and *Asrár*, 118, lines 1340-1346.
6. The PhD thesis appeared in publication as a book. Muhammad Iqbal, *The Development of Metaphysis in Persia* (1908).
7. For a more extensive discussion on Iqbal's philosophy of self, see Schimmel (2024: 154–156).
8. *Reconstruction*, 68, where Iqbal states that the freedom to choose good implies the freedom to choose its opposite, and it is the nature of the self to maintain itself by seeking "knowledge, self-multiplication, and power."
9. *Asrár*, 28, line 323, where Iqbal refers to the luminous point as *khudi,* a self that is assimilative and affirming. Online at: https://archive.org/details/in.ernet.dli.2015.95990/page/n63/mode/2up?q=luminous.
10. A point note by Nazir Qaiser, *Iqbal and Western Philosophers* (2011: 7, 8).

Bibliography

Azad, Hasam. 2014. "Reconstructing the Muslim Self: Muhammad Iqbal, *Khudi,* and the Modern Self." *Islamophobia Studies Journal*, 2 (2).

Boone, Mark J. 2024. "William James and Allama Iqbal on Empirical Faith." PhilArchives (accessed January 20, 2024).

Buehler, Arthur. 1999. "The Indo-Pakistani Qadiriyya: An Overview." *Journal of the History of Sufism*, 1: 339–360.

Douglas, W. O. 1971. "Foreword." In Hafez Malik (ed.), *Iqbal: Poet-Philosopher of Pakistan*. New York: Columbia University Press, ix–x.

Durrani, Saeed A. "Sir Thomas Arnold and Iqbal." *Journal of the Iqbal Academy Pakistan*, 31, no. 1 (April): 11–25. www.allamaiqbal.com/publications/journals/review/apr91/5.htm.

Enver, Ishan Hasan. 1944. *The Metaphysics of Iqbal*. Lahore: Sh. Muhammad Ashraf.

Iqbal, Muhammad. 1908. *The Development of Metaphysis in Persia*. London: Luzac and Company. https://allamaiqbal.com/works/prose/english/development/development%20of%20metaphysics.pdf.

Iqbal, Muhammed. 1920. *Secrets of the Self* (*Asrár-i-Khudí*). Trans. R. A. Nicholson. London: Macmillan and Company Limited. Cited as *Asrár* (*Secrets*).

Iqbal, Muhammad. 1934. *Reconstruction of Religious Thought in Islam*. Oxford: Oxford University Press. Reissued and printed in 2013 by Stanford University Press. Cited as *Reconstruction*.

Lon, Ajaz Ahmad. 2012. "Allama Iqbal: A Psycho-philosophical Perspective on Man." *International Journal of Literary Studies*, 2 (2:): 109–114. www.academia.edu/23197390/Allama_Iqbal_A_Psycho_Philosophical_Perspective_on_Man.

Malik, Hafez ed. 1971. *Iqbal: Poet-Philosopher of Pakistan*. New York: Columbia University Press.

Mir, Mustansir. 2006. *Iqbal: Poet and Thinker*. Lahore: Iqbal Academy Pakistan. https://iqbalcyberlibrary.net/en/100007.html.

Qaiser, Nazir. 2010. *Iqbal and the Western Philosophers*. 2nd ed. Lahore: Iqbal Academy Pakistan.

Qaiser, Nazir. 2011. *Iqbal and Western Philosophers*. Lahore: Iqbal Academy Pakistan.

Razzaqi, Shahid Hussain, compiled and ed. 1979. *Discourses of Iqbal*. Lahore: Sh Gulam Ali & Sons.

Schimmel, Annemarie. 2024. "Muhammad Iqbal 1873–1938: The Ascension of a Poet." *Die Welt des Islams*, 3 (3–4): 145–157. www-jstor-org.myaccess.library.utoronto.ca/stable/1570162?seq=12.

Taylor, Charles. 2010. "Preface." In S. B. Diagne, *Islam and Open Society: Fidelity and Movement in the Philosophy of Muhammad Iqbal*. Dakar: Codesaria, xii.

Immortality
Chapter 10.1

The concept of immortality correlates with the idea of divine viceregency or representative (Arabic: *kalif*) or the third stage in the developmental process of *khudi*. The self, reaching its goal, is one that is fully self-actualizing, or in effect, self-immortalizing. As indicated earlier, *khudi* for Iqbal implies by extension a claim about immortality. That is, immortality is personal, related to being free to affirm oneself, I am-ness, in relation to ultimacy: Absolute Ego or God. It is in fact the beginning of the process by which the ego becomes aware of itself through intuitive sensibility and is disciplined by going through the developmental stages: obedience, then moral self-control. Immortalizing, the third stage, is the culmination of the assimilative movement that entails absorbing and expressing in one's life or action qualities that are divine, that correlated with becoming a divine viceregency or God's representative on earth, thereby actualizing the divine trust. Hence, *khudi* is aiding in the divinizing of itself or acting absolutely in gaining personal immortality.

Clearly then, immortality for Iqbal is an existential category related to the condition that *khudi* must act within the constraints of life while doing so absolutely. For the self, choosing how and when to act, has its freedom limited by its inner possibilities in affirming to realize its own immortality, to reflect the Absolute Ego. For immortality is not a given. It correlates with one's attitudinal orientation to maintain the ego tension with the telos. In Iqbal's view, this conception of immortality is quite different from that of either Nietzsche's associated eternal recurrence, which leads to fatalism, or Kantian postulation of immortality on the basis of the claims of justice (*Reconstruction*, 90–92). For Iqbal, a formal condition of thought to postulate an ontological substance is no guarantee that the postulated has a reality. Unlike Kant who denies metaphysical knowledge, and more in accord with Nietzsche who postulates an eternal recurrence, Iqbal relies on intuition understood as a direct mental apprehension of knowledge. That is, the intellect as capacity for acquiring knowledge has three stems: the sensible, the rational, and the intuitive knowing. The latter is related more to a Bergsonian understanding of the intellect and a specific comprehension of space and time (ibid., 2, 32, 38, 41, 42). Accordingly, time may refer to that which is durational without succession rather than serial, and space that which is in flux, thus allowing for the apprehension of Ultimate Reality or Absolute Ego. This intuitive apprehension of the self as I am-ness, for Iqbal, is direct, is through the heart that sees and feels as well (ibid.,13, 16, 17).

The self intuited as real, according to Iqbal, is by its very nature determining its own immortality through personal effort to deepen relating itself to what Quran enjoins (Sura 6:8 7:19).¹ This then would mean that every individual or self has the possibility of immortalising through their own effort or struggle, though some are likely to wither or fall short in their efforts. Or in Iqbal's words, "Personal immortality, then, is not ours as of right; it is to be achieved by personal effort. Man is only a candidate" (ibid., 95). He draws on the thirteenth-century Persian poet Rumi, who is consistent with the spirit of the Quran, that "the question of immortality is one of biological evolution, not decidable by metaphysical speculation," and that "the world of today needs a Rumi to bring an attitude of hope, rekindle the fire of enthusiasm for life" (ibid., 96, 97).

That is, Quranic values, understood as universally human, are to be realized in the forming, strengthening, or immortalizing of self. Though Iqbal employs no specialized usage of a Persian word, for immortalizing, he draws on two *sufi* terms. One represents the idea of the Perfect Man (*insan-ul-kamil*) according to the sufi saint Abd al-Karīm al-Jīlī. (1365–1424). For the idea of a perfected individual meshes with Quranic values that are universally human and to be realized in the immortalizing of self. Iqbal tells in poetic lines: "Love of God at last becomes wholly God/ Learn thou to love and seek to be loved" (*Asrár*, 29, lines 336, 337). Love for God requires relating mercifully to one's neighbour as well in the world by "both hand and tongue" (*Mysteries*, 47 [*Rúmuz*, pt. 18, vv. 25-27]). To recall some other lines, "Love makes peace and war in the World, The Fountain of Life is Love's flashing sword. The hardest rocks are shivered by Love's glance, . . . Seek an eye like Noah's, a heart like Job's!" (*Asrár*, 29, lines 9333, 335, 338).

Conceptually, self-actualizing is to be understood as involving sacrifice one's thirst or desire for material acquisitions in the service of causes greater than the self. The sacrifice is through '*ishq* or with respect to values associated with justice, mercy, and peace in the community—loving God. It is also connected with rehabilitating the self caught up in a quagmire of self negativity towards itself and the world. Simply put, self actualization involves getting the process started (obedience), keeping it going (moral self-control), and reaching the level of the Perfect Human or spiritually a divinely guided representative on earth (divine viceregency/*khalifa*) in accord with Quran 2:30 and 17:70. The immortalizing process is marked in part by human effort, struggle and striving, to actualize the qualities that are reflective of God's presence (telos), relating finitely to what is finite and temporal, and infinitely to what is Absolute or Ultimate. Such is the perfect human (*insan-ul-kamil*) or perfect believer (*Mard-e Mo'min*) of whom the spiritual Muhammad is the prototype (*Asrár*, 106f., lines 899–920). A key idea in the concept of self-actualizing is the struggling or striving to hold together body and mind with reference to Ultimate Ego or reflecting the divine attributes. For Iqbal immortality has to do with the single individual drawing nearest to God by assimilating divine attributes.² Such an individual is the most complete ego or person, actualizing goal of humanity, that of becoming God's representative on earth. Making oneself display maximally the divine attributes on earth and in heaven is the divine trust that humankind accepted from God (*Asrár*, 80, line 1077), and thus the goal of every human (Quran 33:70). Iqbal, in using either term (*insan-ul-kamil* or divine viceregency), is referencing a personal immortality, associated with self-actualizing maximally the divine attributes or Absolute Ego.

The struggle in self-actualizing is conceptually tied to Iqbal's anthropology, informed by Quran, and not by strands of modern western philosophy. For the default position of the human is a lack or incompleteness or fragility Iqbal expresses with lyrical lines: "Man, in whom clay is mixed with water, is fond of ease, / Devoted to wickedness and enamoured of evil" (*Asrár*, 76, lines 861, 862). Clearly a life of ease or relaxation or dwelling in wickedness or sin relaxes the state of tension necessary for the development of the self. That is, the tension established by the self or mind having a directional purpose, namely, to align itself with the highest good or Ultimate Ego. For the mind to become so aligned requires starting with obedience, willingness to act in accord with duties of the Quran as word of God. In short, that is, development through habitus, or *hexis* as character formation through inculcation of will attitudes, in the intellectualizing of the soul.

Altogether and summarily, the explicated three concepts above indicate the self or *khudi* for Iqbal is referencing a personal will attitude or orientation of oneself in the world. The will attitude is directly related to an ideal or telos that is absolute, thereby requiring one to relate absolutely to the telos, hence making *khudi* as ego or consciousness the center-point of one's life activity. As center-point, *khudi* is the psychological point of the individual that decides, chooses, judges, discerns, hopes, wishes, expects, with respect to remaining oriented or relating absolutely to the absolute. As a luminous or center point of experiences, *khudi* is characterized by an assimilative movement by which it regulates or overcomes habitus and dispositions and meets challenges that tended to come in between itself and the absolute ideal. The psychological inception of *khudi* is the awareness of an appreciative self apprehended by a direct illumination or intuition, a function of intellect that has also a cognitive side. And the actualizing of that self is a striving through heeding and realizing humanistic virtues to which the Quran beckons to heed.

Realizing the virtues requires heightening of consciousness or passional side of the individual, through *'ishq* or love. That is, *khudi* strives to remain absolutely aligned to the absolute, the Ultimate Ego or Highest good, going through developmental stages. First by obedience or putting into practice the values of the Quran: magnanimity, compassion, humility, and serenity. Next through an evolutionary like emergence to exercising moral self-control in life. Then, evolving further, by absorbing and reflecting divine attributes to becoming the perfect believer or self. Absorbing and reflecting divine attributes by self-actualizing, *khudi* is never annihilated in maximally relating to the Ultimate Ego. The entire process is an evolutionary one by which the self is self actualizing while a social-historical reality, self-immortalizing through the aid of transcendence in becoming God's representative on earth by absorbing and reflecting divine qualities or virtues that are valid in the here-now and here-after. Iqbal's awakening call is to become the self as described above, to take responsibility to exhibit the divine qualities that make for community and justice.

Notes

1. *Reconstruction*, 68, 92, 93. Iqbal notes that the nature of self is to maintain itself as self. That maintenance includes seeking knowledge, not just in the discursive sense of knowing (68).
2. *Asrár*, 17, which is part of Iqbal's introduction to the text. Also Surah 2:30, and 38:26 and Khalwati order and Floor (2003: 51–86 [sufism]).

References

Floor, Willem. 2003. "The Khalifeh al-kholafa of the Safavid Sufi Order." *Zeitschrift der Deutschen Morgenländischen Gesellschaft*, 153 (1): 51–86.

Iqbal, Muhammed. 1920. *Secrets of the Self (Asrár-i-Khudí)*. Trans. R. A. Nicholson. London: Macmillan and Company Limited. Cited as *Asrár (Secrets)*.

Iqbal, Muhammad. 1934. *Reconstruction of Religious Thought in Islam*. Oxford: Oxford University Press. Reissued and printed in 2013 by Stanford University Press. Cited as *Reconstruction*.

'Ishq/Love
Chapter 10.2

Iqbal uses the Arabic-Persian "*'ishq*," rendered by the English word "love," in a specialized way to assist in expressing what he means by *khudi*/self. No few words convey a complete picture of his concept *'ishq*. For the word, etymologically, suggests a passionate urge to cling, sharing the same root as the name of a species of ivy plant (*'ashaqat*) that twines on a tree. Not without resistance however, the word gained lexical acceptance in some quarters of the *sufi* (mystical) tradition and among some philosophical thinkers. They widened its sense complex to include a higher form of love, or essential desire, and applicable as a special attribute of Allah. Rúmí, from whom Iqbal takes guidance, widens its meaning to an evolutionary and assimilative action of the self or cosmic push while retaining the sense of ecstasy.

Iqbal, adoption of Rumi's sense-usage equates with *mahaba* an Arabic term used to denote the inner essence of *'ishq*, and uses it synonymously as did Rúzbihán Baqli,[1] a disciple of the mystic al-Hallaj (850–922), claiming that *'ishq* is the perfection of *mahabba* which is an attribute of the Real. Iqbal uses both terms in *Asrár* which introduces the luminous point as the center of self formation or consciousness:

> The Luminous point whose name is the Self, Is the life spark beneath our dust.
> By Love [*mahabbat*] it is made more lasting, more glowing.
> Love ['*ishq*] instructs it to illumine the world.
> Love of God at last becomes wholly God . . . .
>
> (*Asrár*, 54f., lines 322–336)

Iqbal continues his imaginative and bold description in the fourteen-line stanza, conveying that *'ishq* is a dynamic cosmic energy, or life spark. That is, it regenerates and strengthens the self, in its conscious participation of the ego. That is, the self first must take the initiative to ground itself in the Ultimate Ego or God though seeking love and thereby gain dominion of the outward and inwards forces of the universe. In the sequel poem *Rúmuz-i-Bekhúdí*, he refers to *'ishq* as a marvellous power capable of making all things possible. as form of intellect, as transformative, eternal, and infinite in that the process by which the finite self is becoming divinized, gaining its immortality.[2]

Here is a consideration with respect to Iqbal's claim about love: how is the finite ego or self to seek love? An answer would be that for Iqbal *'ishq* and desire are identical at a basic level, that the human heart has within it a push or desire to seek its grounding. The self then, in this push or desire, becomes aware of itself, is self-conscious and intuitively posits itself, as with F. H. Bradley[3] who claims that the self is finite and real nevertheless, and is not space-bound as the body. However, unlike Bradley, Iqbal thinks that the self/ego having become conscious of itself desires to ground itself to that which is steadfast, limitless, infinite, and absolute, namely

Ultimate Ego. That is, desire is a phenomenon of *'ishq* or cosmic energy that gives every being its push, tug, urge to grasp as in taking hold, to remake or recreate. It is clearly an impulse to move forward in an evolutionary process. In life-forms the push is to another emerging level. With the human ego as self/*khudi*, the urge is to make things better than they are, including deepening one's own grasping elation to the Ultimate ego or chief good, becoming immortalized, unlimited, and completely free. Hence, it is solidifying one's personality in the sense of becoming fully a person.

Iqbal's conceptual linkage between *khudi* and *'ishq* follows that by Rumi (1207–1273), his spiritual mentor. True knowledge for Rumi is tied to whole being or the personality which is strengthened by *'ishq*. That is, *'ishq* is a specific mode of knowing or experiencing the living reality, unlike reason or a principle of moral behaviour (Kamali 1971: 238f.). A passion, or metaphysical principle, *'ishq* is an impulse, a creative urge or push of life, unfolding itself in the world through the self relating itself to others, compared with reason whose limited function is separating and uniting. By loving the seeker/ego, according to Rumi, develops or absorb the attributes of the beloved. Thus, love brings "to open relief the real bonds that connects individuals" (ibid.), and forms communities in its assimilating rush that is a forward movement as in growth or evolution. That is, it seeks kinship and justice, namely, love for neighbour. With Iqbal the movement occasioned by the pulse of *'ishq*, carries the ego/self through three stages in becoming immortalized: obedience, moral self-control, and viceregency. It is this evolutionary-like outlook by Rumi that Iqbal carries forward in his stance on the self to which he is awakening Muslims.

The three developmental or emergent stages of self as *khudi* have to be considered as functioning against the backdrop of what Iqbal has to say about *'ishq*/love. That is, it means "the desire to assimilate and to absorb," and that its "highest form is the creation of values and ideals and the endeavour to realize them."[4] Obedience as the first stage is to Divine Law or duties of the Muslim. His use of the camel as a metaphor for the qualities that correlate with each stage is instructive.

In the sequel poem on selflessness Iqbal ties conceptually God's mercy, love for God, and faith. Love for God is not abstract but is understood as membership in a sacred community that is bounded by God's laws. Iqbal expresses the idea in verse this way:

The nature of the Muslim through and through
Is lovingkindness in both hand and tongue
He strives to be a mercy in the world
As he whose fingers split the moon in twain
Embraces in his mercy all mankind
Noble was he, in every attribute;
Thou art no member of our community
If from his station thou departest far.

(*Mysteries*, 47 [*Rúmuz*, pt. 18, vv. 25-27])

Summarily, in at least three ways *'ishq* conceptually relates to *khudi* fore Iqbal. It is a desire or cosmic energy by which the self is disciplining itself, thereby deepening its directional relation to Ultimate ego. Another is that it is a means by which the self is creatively realizing values for itself as a member of the community or social fabric. And a third way is that the values are ones in accord with the duties or responsibilities divinely ordained, hence universally shared, are cosmic and requiring creativity and ingenuity in realizing them. Communities are historically, culturally, politically, and environmentally conditioned, thus requiring ingenuity and creativity for realizing what is basic to *khudi*. For *'ishq*, according to Iqbal "makes precious all that exists," and "renovates old ways of life" when developed fully by assimilating through *'ishq* the qualities by which the Ultimate Ego is known (*Asrár*, 82, lines 930, 932). The self then is no metaphysical being or substance but a deed-oriented activity in which body and mind (deciding and acting) are in harmony.

Notes

1. See n. 17 in Khan(2009: 937). See also, Al-Hallaj's idea of *'ishq*/love as dynamics, "an active and creative force," that "tries to draw man nearer to God," and Iqbal's attitude to al-Hallaj, in 1908 and 1922, by Annemarie Schimmel (1971: 314, 317–324).
2. See for a full description "A Hint of *Rahmat* in Iqbal's *'ishq*,'" 929.
3. According to Iqbal, mystical intuition for Bradley is also a curse of Knowledge. See Iqbal's 4th Lecture, "Human Ego – His Freedom and Immortality," *Reconstruction*, 78f., and its footnote 6, and 13 off that chapter.
4. See his remarks cited by Nicholson in *Asrár*, 21. Iqbal is commenting on Chapter 3, lines 323ff.

References

Iqbal, Muhammed. 1920. *Secrets of the Self* (*Asrár-i-Khudí*). Trans. R. A. Nicholson. London: Macmillan and Company Limited. Cited as *Asrár* (*Secrets*).
Kamali, A. H. 1971. "The Heritage of Islamic Thought." In Hafez Malik (ed.), *Iqbal: Poet-Philosopher of Pakistan*. New York: Columbia University Press, 211–242.
Khan, Abraham. 2009. "A Hint of *Rahmat* in Iqbal's *'ishq*.'" *Man in India*, 89 (4): 923–939.
Malik, Hafez, ed. 1971. *Iqbal: Poet-Philosopher of Pakistan*. New York: Columbia University Press.
Schimmel, Annemarie. 1971. "Mystic Impact of Hallaj." In Hafez Malik (ed.), *Iqbal: Poet-Philosopher of Pakistan*. New York: Columbia University Press, 317–324.

11

A Plural Conception of Self Reading Jacques Derrida

Nathan R. B. Loewen

Chapter Outline

Introduction	287
Who is Jacques Derrida?	288
Situating the Topic	289
Speech and Phenomena (1973)	291
Circumfession	294
Monolingualism of the Other, or, Prosthesis of Origin (1998)	296
Conclusion	298
11.1 Ipseity	301
11.2 Secrecy	305
11.3 Sovereignty	310

Introduction

In this chapter, I am going to present you with a plural conception of self. I develop this conception by a selective reading of texts written by the French philosopher Jacques Derrida (1930–2004). The sense of "plural" in this chapter will be "always more than one." My inspiration for the chapter is that Derrida's critical writing on Western philosophy provides ideas about what logical conditions are required to have the common notion of "self" in Western societies. That is to say the proposals in this chapter likely lose their sensibility from other cultural perspectives. I should also say that my proposal of a plural self is quite possibly limited to my reading of three texts. All three are short essays. Derrida wrote over 40 books and published hundreds of essays. My decision to focus on three essays is, of course, contestable. Hopefully the plural conception of self that I work out below aligns well with Derrida's other writings. The first essay is an early writing that shows Derrida's unique method of closely analyzing language in particular to upset philosophy in general: "Speech and Phenomena: Introduction to the Problem of Signs in Husserl's Phenomenology" (1973). Second will be a quirky intervention Derrida called "Circumfession" (1991), where personal anecdotes are used to defeat a friend's attempt to create a computer program called Derridabase. The final essay draws together the topics of the first two. "Monolingualism of the Other; or, the Prosthesis of Origin" (1998) explains how the particularities of language create upsetting conditions for philosophy. By the time of the conclusion, I hope to have explained a conception of self that insists on there always being more than one self. In French I would write, "*il y a toujours plus d'un.*" That phrase requires a double translation: "there is always more than one/there is always no more than one." Perhaps this will make sense at the end of the chapter!

Who is Jacques Derrida?

Derrida passed away on October 9, 2004. He was born to a Jewish family near El-Biar, Algeria when it was a colony of France. He originally wished to be a footballer ("soccer" in the U.S.), since he skipped school to play footy with the Italian prisoners of war. On the one hand, Derrida's intellectual career could be portrayed as a failure: he failed university entrance exams, he failed state exams to qualify for advanced university positions, and his French peers actively resisted granting his doctorate for twenty years. These details are found in the short biography that accompanies the first essay discussed in this chapter. On the other hand, "Derrida" is impossible to avoid in any account of twentieth-century thought.

Derrida is both infamous and famous because he wrote texts aimed specifically at challenging the most basic assumptions of Western philosophy. But, critique does not have to include pessimism or accusation. Derrida's texts exhibit an optimism that philosophers can decide to do better philosophy by paying close attention to others. The texts are typically written in the first-person singular, "I," and the texts often include forms of second person address to some "you." I usually presume that "you" is singular, too. When Derrida's texts use the first-person plural, the "we" is specified. That is, Derrida's texts do not take any community for granted. Unless, that is, the discussion is about an "inoperable community" whose membership is unknown and boundaries are undecidable. This is the "community of the question." Unlike France's state exams, which Derrida failed to pass on several occasions, nobody can prevent anyone else from joining inoperable communities that pop up whenever and wherever people are open to sharing their questions.

"Deconstruction" is a term now seen in pop culture (e.g., baking and cooking) that may be traced to Derrida's writings. Many philosophers view the word with disfavor. In fact, philosophers' concerns about "deconstruction" led to a movement aimed at preventing Cambridge University from awarding Derrida an honorary degree in 1992. Why? Concerns about "Derrida" usually have to do with politics as much as specific contents. For example, Derrida published three books in 1967–1968. The year 1968 was one of political upheaval around civil rights in the United States, as well as a year a student revolutions against authoritarianism in France. *Of Grammatology* is likely best-known of these early publications, since it is where people go to understand what "deconstruction" means. Most basically speaking, the point of these books was to show how the discourses of philosophy mask the instability of their meanings. Close attention to history and literature shows the political contingency of boundaries and centers. While they may be real and have life-or-death consequences, the fact that they may be thought otherwise suggests investigating their conditions. Asking questions may be revolutionary acts. *Of Grammatology* represents Derrida's works well, because its exhaustive analyses make great demands upon any reader's attention. These texts are demanding precisely because they do not draw any lines in the sand, they explain the sandy, shifty, unstable foundations of concepts such as the human, race, immigration, rights, and violence. Never presuming any "we," Derrida's texts press readers to arrive at their own conclusions. In fact, one remarkable feature of these books and essays is how Derrida regularly foregrounds the voice of the first person singular. Derrida writes "I" to ensure readers know they are being presented with a particular, situated position.

Situating the Topic

"Doubt all things" is what Rene Descartes commands in the *Meditations on First Philosophy*, first published in 1641. *Cogito ergo sum* is that book's most well-known Latin phrase. One outcome of "I think therefore I am" is to foreground the first-person "I" for philosophical reflection. Another outcome is the term "cogito" situates a common topic in the theory of knowledge (epistemology): where does thinking and awareness happen? In Western philosophy, even prior to Descartes, the term "cogito" names a key element of the self, according to the history of Western philosophy. A certain sort of thinking is presented as a requirement for being a certain kind of self. When I read for a concept of self, I see these Cartesian legacies being invoked by Derrida's texts: doubt all things, especially *cogito*, but only "I" can do this.

Descartes promised a method of removing anything uncertain to reveal a stable source of certainty: the interior monologue of speaking to yourself. *Cogito* seems like a technical word in contrast to "self," which seems like a common folk term. That changes in the moment of asking who the folk are and what is presumed to be held in common. To use another Latin term, the *habitus* of academic philosophy carries along a certain folk conception of self. The general social arrangements of academia involve customs such as citing texts by using the last name of an author and postulating other thinking minds to form a "we" of general inquiry. The thinking subject named by *cogito* is the result of a thought experiment that Derrida finds highly audacious (Derrida 1978: 31–63). The phrase *cogito ergo sum* proposes a zero point of hypothetical self-possession that reduces existence to an inner world. To conceive "self" as a thinking subject located within an ultra-interior space is strange to people outside of contemporary, Western societies. Even more strange, compared to other cultures, is a concept of self that takes place in the form of a monologue whose "speech" requires a living, human body on the one hand, but will never be registered by any body's senses on the other. The texts below show how Derrida used reason and logic to doubt all things, including whether a singular self is invented through unspoken speech.

One objection to the above is that Descartes' proposal about the cogito was the invention of the subject and not the self. French philosophers were indeed focused on questions of subjectivity, and not the self, during the twentieth century. I am not certain that Derrida's construal of the subject is likely equivocal to the self. Research and writing on phenomenology and existentialism focused respectively on the epistemological and ethical development of European philosophical ideas since Descartes. In the late 1980s, Jean-Luc Nancy invited twenty French philosophers to make contributions to a volume entitled *Who Comes After the Subject?* Nineteen responded. Derrida did not. Nancy then had Derrida agree to publish an interview, "'Eating Well,' or the Calculation of the Subject: An Interview with Jacques Derrida" (1991), which included a statement from Derrida that summarizes this chapter's approach to the self: "The singularity of the 'who' is not the individuality of a thing that would be identical with itself, it is not an atom. It is a singularity that dislocates or divides itself in gathering itself together to answer to the other, whose call somehow precedes its own identification with itself, whose call I can *only* answer" (Derrida 1991: 100–101). Written otherwise, I read this quote as saying that subjectivity, the possibility of an "I," is always and only a singular response to a "self" that is already something other than the "I." What's more, every instantiation of I-answering is not identical to all others. If that seems like a dense argument, I hope this chapter is able to unpack it by presenting a plural conception of self. The work of this chapter is to extend Derrida's texts to a proposal about the self, rather than make a definitive declaration about "the self" according to Jacques Derrida, born in 1930 and deceased in 2004.

Another objection is that rugged individualism is a straw doll that is easily composed by a hasty reading of John Locke's conception of the possessive individual or the *unum quid* that unites Descartes' cogito with the human body. While there is a common sense in Western society about individuality of ownership, agency, and responsibility that parallels a largely Christian religious inheritance, the history of ideas about "persons" are more ontically abstract than theological postulations of soul as an eternal substance. But much of contemporary and modern philosophy does make an egological postulation the thinking individual as a requirement for experience. That is what allows Miri Albahari to argue that the self is an illusion of the habitual assumption that there is a conscious subject who is a unified, unbrokenly persisting, ontologically distinct, bounded, 'me' that owns experiences, thoughts, and agency (2006: 2). Thus, Derrida's interview with Nancy includes the statement that the idea of the subject is, "conventional fiction" (1991: 102). Not that fictions cannot exist. "I" is a useful fiction that is regularly encountered in Derrida's texts. But recall the quote above. I want to show why and how Derrida understands self as a singularity whose logical conditions are necessarily plural, and, whose actual conditions belie the habitual assumptions and conventional fictions of modern, Western societies.

Speech and Phenomena (1973)

There is a poem by the children's book author, Theodor Geisel, who is better known as Dr. Seuss. "Too Many Daves" is a poem about a mother who names all her twenty-three children Dave (Geisel 1961). The mother realizes the error each time she calls out, "Dave!" All twenty-three children come running! The poem goes on to suggest various other possible names for each child, such as Hoos-Foos, Shadrack, Putt-Putt, and Sneepy.

"Too Many Daves" makes a simple point about proper names that Derrida argues in *Speech and Phenomena*. A proper name is unlike an ordinary noun, since a proper name is supposed to be "proper" to only one entity. "Dave" ceases to function as "proper" in the poem. I can imagine how the problem in the poem could work on a grander scale. It would be possible to have a "Dave convention" with hundreds of people named Dave.[1] I can reflect further and decide that the problem in the poem is not ultimately solved by renaming the Daves. Take Hoos-Foos, for example. "Hoos-Foos" only functions as a proper name so long as Hoos-Foos is not repeated within the network of proper names. But "Hoos-Foos" betrays itself as a proper name the moment I conceive of it as a common noun ("Would you please pass the hoos-foos? Thank-you."). All other possible names – the poem offers Shadrack, Putt-Putt, Sneepy, and so on – only work as such within a system by which they could just as easily function as common nouns. There's no absolute origin point for any name. Each depends on exerting the force of propriety, what is "proper" only to one entity, against other meanings through reiteration. "Too Many Daves" shows how any proper name betrays itself in the instant of its utterance.

For the sake of argument, let's say that the poem involved only one child. "Dave" still requires repetition to be meaningful. "Dave" still needs to name each instance of that entity, whether it is unborn, living, or dead. For "Dave" to work as a proper name, there must be the possibility of repetition. But each instant of "Dave" is not identical to any other instant in space or time. More specifically, the proper name logically requires there to be "too many Daves" for the word to name the that "Dave" in each instant. The name simply won't do the work proper names are supposed to do if there is one, absolutely singular "Dave."

Proper names and nouns are linguistic signs which, according to Derrida, are "always caught up in an indicative system. Caught up is the same as contaminated" (1973: 20). The claim could be disproven if and only if there were a situation in which some sign is no longer entangled, or contaminated, by relations to any other sign. Such an absolutely individual sign would need to be unworldly, however, which means it would be unknowable to humans. The "empirically interwoven" (ibid., 27) linguistic situation of any sign is not the result of some 1:1 direct correlation of language to the furniture of the world. That is disproven quickly enough by the empirical fact that the world has more than one language, and, there is more than one word for any one thing named by those languages. Otherwise, the name Hoos-Foos would not be an alternate name for some child. "The totality of speech is caught up in an indicative web" (ibid., 31).

Likewise, suppose that someone named Dave were to conduct an interior monologue that imagines someone who is uniquely "Dave." The conditions of repetition necessary for Dave to meaningfully put "I am Dave my self" into language requires more than one, single instant of time. Dave's realization of "Dave-self" cannot be an instantaneous experience to be actual. Dave's realization can only be that of an uncertain trace of Dave that are connected, by the force of reiteration, to other traces of Dave. There must be too many Daves for there to be any Dave. Furthermore, there is the fact that the specific instant of these actions is not originary. There is no "first Dave" to make the name proper. The logical conditions for propriety that might allow some Dave to be singled out by a proper name is for Dave to be plural. Looping back to Descartes' phrase, these conditions apply even when Daves think to themselves, "Dave thinks, therefore Dave is." The same goes for your name!

I think of "Too Many Daves" when reading the following phrase in *Speech and Phenomena*, "nonpresence and otherness are internal to presence" (Derrida 1973: 66).[2] Derrida's argument is that, at least for Western philosophy, it is impossible to make claims for a simple self-identity (ibid., 68). The term "auto-affection" is introduced to explain how the impossibility of absolute identity is the basic condition for identity. The idea of self is a conventional fiction that is made possible by auto-affection, which masks the working of difference in order to seem as if there are conditions of immediacy that might allow for claims such as "Dave," *cogito*, and self. From the perspective of that essay, I conclude that Derrida's text conceives of self as one among many fictions working in everyday society that invents forms of continuity to mask differences.

But Derrida's essay was not based on a children's book. *Speech and Phenomena* focuses on Edmund Husserl's (1859–1938) writings, where is found an interesting dependence on the idea of an internal voice by which someone might speak to themselves. Husserl uses this culturally-specific idea developed in Western European literature and philosophy to propose an absolutely self-present consciousness. For Husserl, an interior monologue is a space of pure ideality. It could be the location for truth (see Derrida 1973: 54 n. 4) precisely because of its separation from the materiality of any exterior. Derrida's critique is based on the implications of Husserl's imposition of this interior space: were it possible to have an inward, interior monologue as the sphere of absolute certainty and absolute existence, then such speech is absolutely separated from the actual world. Derrida's essay therefore locates a point in Western philosophy where the stakes are high. For example, the Christian concept of God makes sense if there is such a space of pure ideality and truth. Derrida's analysis of proper names, however, also applies to the conditions for any presence. If speech requires the actual world's empirical conditions of time, then Husserl has not identified a space of pure ideality and truth. Absolute ideality is absolute nonsense.[3] The essay not only undoes Husserl's claims, it also undoes Western assumptions about presence. To get the possibility of any concept's meaningfulness up and running, there must be an unstable network of others that bears non-identical traces of the concept across time. The "ideal space" for any concept is created by exerting force to retain meaning amid and across these differences.[4] So long as though requires language, no concept exists as absolute presence. Every concept, even the idea of God, requires constant doubling and redoubling to be a sustained across time and space.

Derrida's ultimate point is that thinking can only be performed in some particular here and now. And if meaning requires finitude, then humans have no access to ideas that have the quality of infinity. The argument about proper names applies to every noun, such that all humans have is language. Humans have no access to some meta-language that operates outside all finitude as a set. The proof arrives in the experience of repetition.

When I say "I am," even to myself, the phrase is meaningful only as a repetition. I need to say it at least twice in order to divide time such that "I" functions in the absence of its object. Derrida puts it bluntly: "The statement "I am alive" is accompanied by my being dead, and its possibility requires the possibility that I be dead; and conversely" (Derrida 1973: 96–97).

In conclusion, *Speech and Phenomena* may explain Derrida's plural concept of self. The "I" of an absolutely interior monologue would be recognizable exclusively to itself only in a singular instant, since it has no relations to anything. One name for such conditions is silence. Derrida's argument is that absolute presence has no phenomena. Speech requires phenomena. I suggest that the possibility of self depends on entanglement with plurality. A phenomenal "self" is not singular. There always must be a web of many for there to be one.

Circumfession

Derrida's writings regularly tested the limits of what could be done with a book. The most infamous example may be *Glas* (1986), but "Circumfession" is by far more accessible. The essay "Circumfession" appears across the bottom third of the pages in Geoffrey Bennington's book *Jacques Derrida* (1993). To learn what is going on, I read the preface, which states, "the guiding idea of the exposition comes from computers: G.B. would have liked to systematize J.D.'s thought to the point of turning it into an interactive program which, in spite of its difficulty, would in principle be accessible to any user" (Bennington 1993: 1). The preface's next sentence explains what is important for what I wish to explain: "As what is at stake in J.D.'s work is to show how any such system must remain essentially open, this undertaking was doomed to failure from the start, and the interest it may have consists in the test, and the proof, of that failure" (ibid.). I will read Derrida's essay to claim that "self" is an essentially open system.

In one sense, my very attempt to explain Derrida's concept of self is a rehearsal of both Bennington and Derrida's objectives. This chapter can only succeed by failing to absolutely fulfill its objective. Since the logical conditions for writing entail meaning cannot be communicated absolutely, I embraced failure in order to write the chapter. I read "Circumfession" as Derrida's effort to show how failure is necessary. The text aims to, "succeed in surprising him [Bennington] and his surprising his reader," (Derrida 1993: 32) in order to create an improbable event that is, "some perjury that his programming machine couldn't providentially account for" (ibid., 34). An absolutely perfect explanation for "Derrida's plural concept of self," if such a thing existed, would be impossible for anyone else to understand (see n. 5).

"Circumfession" is an intervention that Bennington's "program" cannot "debug." The essay frames the issue in religious terms familiar to Western audiences. If Bennington's program successfully reproduced "Derrida," then it would be something analogous to the Christian conception of God. The essay argues that Bennington's program would have to know everything about "Derrida" in order to replicate Derrida's thought such that anyone could access Derrida anywhere at any time. The bugs introduced by the essay are, "singular events that can dismantle G.'s theologic program" (Derrida 1993: 305). In fact, the essay claims, "it's enough to recount the "present" to throw G.'s theologic program off course" (ibid., 311). How might that be the case?

The core strategy of "Circumfession" is to philosophically question whether and how any self is knowable. Derrida returns to the French translation of St. Augustin's *Confessions* he first read (Robert Arnauld d'Andilly, 1649), where the title of Chapter 1, book 9 is, "Why We Confess to God, When He Knows (Everything about Us)?" That question suggests that if God is all-knowing, then it is plausible to claim that there is a single set of data that could, in sum, be called a self. If an infinite being such as God knows all, then must God know everything about any finite being's entire existence. Furthermore, there must be a sum total set of phenomena that encapsulate everything God knows about any single self. But this assumption leads to several philosophical entailments whose hypothetical conditions need to proving. For example, issues of free will and determinism arise for living humans who, in their singularity, are absolutely known by God. Dead humans are less of an issue to reconcile an all-knowing God's absolute knowledge with the phenomena of time. "Circumfession" asks whether Geoffrey Bennington's project, to create a program of Derrida's thought, "capable of the absolute knowledge of a nonfinite series of events" (ibid., 30). Derrida calls it a "theologic program elaborated by Geoff who remains very close to God, for he knows everything about the 'logic' of what I might have written in the past but also of what I might think or write in the future, on any subject at all" (ibid., 16). Derrida can defeat Bennington's program if the essay shows what resists theologization.

The essay undermines theologic programming, similar to *Speech and Phenomena*, by considering the problem of origins. If a project encapsulating "Derrida" were to take place, it would have to begin somewhere at some time. Derrida's text self-reflexively notes how it is being written by someone who, at the time of writing in 1989, is alive somewhere in the world. The program for "Derrida" would be required to interact with finite phenomena such as the fact that Derrida's mother had a stroke during the time of writing,[5] or Derrida's childhood and adult experiences of anti-Semitism.[6] How could a theologic program account for these examples? Such interaction means the programming has to start somewhere determinate, which suggests that even the program needs repeated exposure to contingency. The problem highlighted by "Circumfession" is that such contingencies would ultimately need removal so that the program could hypothetically begin at any other time. That is, any point of contact between the program and its dataset would have to work back through all possible counterfactuals. It would have to reiterate, or loop, all of its processing. The program would have to come back around (L., *circum*) to offer a "confession" of Derrida's thought to any one of the program's end-users. The surprise noted by the text is that such confessions, as repetitions, must take place in instants existing in different times. Doing so triggers new looped iterations to the point of absurdity. The very operation of Bennington's program itself undoes the possibility of an exhaustive dataset related to "Derrida." Just as with God in St. Augustine's *Confessions*, one condition for absolute knowledge is that it cannot exist in any relation to time.[7] As far as finite beings are concerned, a God with such an attribute must be silent. So, too, a successful version of Bennington's program must have outputs that are less than null.

I take a simple lesson about self from "Circumfession": producing self is a task that can never be completed. The contingency of the task does not mean there is no self, but rather that whatever happens to be included is the result of starting somewhere. There is no absolute beginning and there is no absolute end. According to my reading of "Circumfession," an absolute signification pointing towards a complete set called "self" is impossible. The idea of "self" is a useful, but not necessary, fiction. Those humans who do inherit the idea cannot easily do without it. As the final essay considered in this chapter shows, concepts of self depend upon specific historical and political structures.

Monolingualism of the Other, or, Prosthesis of Origin (1998)

The last essay considered in this chapter presents something of a dialogue. But it is unclear who the dialogue is with. Unlike the preface of Bennington's book where "Circumfession" appears, there is no indication of two different contributors. The text of "Monolingualism of the Other, or, Prosthesis of Origin" at first seems to engage readers with something of a conversation. The essay begins: "– Picture this, imagine someone who would cultivate the French language" (Derrida 1998, 1), and then:

"I have only one language; it is not mine."
Or rather, and better still:
I am monolingual.

(Ibid.)[8]

Readers of the essay could easily assume they are being imaginatively engaged by some inventive textual strategy. The problem with this reading is the appearance of the second person on the next page: "– You speak the impossible. Your speech does not hold water. It will always remain incoherent, "inconsistent," as one would say in English" (ibid., 2).[9] At this point, a reader may wonder what to think about the essay's use of imagined conversations, autobiographical notes, events in world history, and references to a speech given in 1992 at Louisiana State University. For this chapter, I wish to focus on what the text does with paradoxical phrases such as: I am monolingual, I have only one language; it is not mine, and, my language is the language of the other. As with the other essays discussed in this chapter, Derrida's texts often highlight and amplify impossibilities to understand conditions for possibility in the actual world. Since the essay discusses topics of ownership and agency, it is a good candidate for making claims for a plural conception of self.

"Monolingualism of the Other" continues the pressing Derrida's arguments against the possibility of an absolute metalanguage. Just as with *Speech and Phenomena* and "Circumfession," the essay uses literary tools and logical argumentation to demonstrate how, "this experience of monolingual solipsism is never one of belonging, property, power of mastery, pure "ipseity" of whichever kind" (Derrida 1998: 22–23). I have already shown examples of various conversations and textual arrangements presented by the text. They suggest various ways that the forms of interior speech proposed by Descartes and Husserl are better imagined as conversations. Derrida suggests these conversations typically take place in one language. But the language used is borrowed, not invented. The essay argues that "inalienable alienation" is the condition of language (ibid., 25). The monolingualism of these conversations comes from some other. Indicating how interior speech uses actual language restates the argument that the empirical facts of finitude strike out the possibility that philosophy is able to postulate, much less operate within, some idealized truth-space.

My aim is to read this essay in support of the proposal for a plural concept of self by extending the argument about language and ownership to the earlier discussions about interior speech. The phrase "I only have one language, yet it is not mine" is expanded in the essay to two propositions:

1. We only ever speak one language.
2. We never speak only one language.

(Ibid., 7)

On the next page, these propositions are offered as a "double law":

1. We only ever speak one language—or rather one idiom only.
2. We never speak only one language—or rather there is no pure idiom.

(Ibid., 8)

Aside from the grammatical shift from first-person singular to first-person plural, there is a rationale developed in the transitions from paradoxical phrase to proposition to double law. The essay starts with the fact that no human completely invents whatever language is spoken. The discussion of *Speech and Phenomena* involved Derrida's argument that any instance of speech is, "always caught up in an indicative system" (1973: 20). Likewise, the discussion of "Circumfession" included the argument that any program aiming to comprehend finite conditions "must remain essentially open" (1993 1). "Monolingualism of the Other" applies these insights to considerations of language and identity. All languages must remain essentially open. What that entails, however, is that every use-case scenario of language is incomplete. If the imperfection of each use-case is what makes language possible, then there is no perfect speech. There is only idiom.

The stated interest of Derrida's essay is to press the point that identity is not self-determined. If any instance of language is idiom, then that puts the lie to various political agendas that establish conditions for identity or membership. While the original text was delivered to a conference about francophone issues outside of France, Derrida's examples point back to his relationship with French citizenship laws as someone born in Algeria to Jewish parents. As in "Circumfession," this essay recounts how within the lifetime of Derrida's parents, French citizenship was granted to Algerian Jews with the Cremieux Decree of 1870, revoked in 1940, and then later restored after the end of World War II. Derrida shows how identity lies outside propriety. Social and political circumstances inform whatever "self" may be. The languages used to create these fictions is not owned by anyone, but that does not make their effects any less real.

To close this section, what I wish to do is analogically rework the arguments in this essay towards a plural conception of self. The idea of "self" proposed here should be understood as a useful fiction. The idea involves acting as if self is something singular that is proper to someone. The conditions for acting as if that is the case, however, are that the tools used to do so rely on plurality. The notion of a singular self is a phantom master who can never come into existence absolutely. As a result, every fictitious instance of self is an unfulfilled promise of propriety that cannot ever arrive. The idea of the self is always a promise to some other self that ultimately comes from the other. That is to say, each self is always already divided by its own projection into time. The Derridean notion of self is calculable, but not in the form of a closed program or system. The self is always already $N+1$.

Conclusion

I promised you a chapter about Derrida's conception of self, which the French phrase "*il y a toujours plus d'un*" makes sense. A plural concept of self is attractive to me, primarily because it supports a critical perspective. Social and political debates about identity mask ideological disputes that are often based upon metaphysical desires which are, more often than not, based on a totalitarian fever-dream where the finite, actual world is forced to conform to something terrifyingly unreal. To agree with my proposal, or with Derrida's arguments, is not a descent into relativism where anything goes. Quite the opposite. The alternative proposed by a plural conception of self is to practice charitable hospitality to all others, especially to our selves!

Notes

1. To help imagine this, search for "These Are the Daves I Know," performed by the sketch comedy group The Kids in the Hall (Season 1, episode 4, 1989).

2. Dan Zahavi's analysis, which speaks more directly to phenomenology, is that, "Rather than being a simple, undivided unity, self-awareness is consequently characterized by an original complexity, by a historical heritage. The present can only appear to itself as present due to the retentional modification. Presence is differentiation; it exists only in its intertwining with absence" (2005: 69).
3. Here is where I will mention Derrida's term "deconstruction," whose idea is nicely proven by the fact that the term is regularly used by scholars without any attention to Derrida's use of the term. Derrida's deconstructions are literary demonstrations that there is no pure, simple, or absolute origin for any specific sign in particular, or for language in general. Many of Derrida's writings demonstrate "deconstruction" by testing concepts meanings when idealized under absolute conditions. For example, several texts attempt to work out the idea of an absolute gift. Does a pure gift allow the giver and receiver know each other? How would anyone know they've received an absolute gift? May a pure gift be exchanged for anything else? At the end of it all, can an ideal gift be anything other than never present? These philosophical questions are based on the attempt to investigate with the least bias and presupposition. But all the while, Derrida's writings demonstrate these questions cannot be asked without engaging the actual world in all its contingency. Derrida has to start somewhere, and so his texts study others' writings for the absolute conditions of their concepts.
4. "This is why hearing oneself speak experienced as an absolutely pure auto-affection, occurring in a self-proximity that would in fact be the absolute reduction of space in general" (Derrida 1973: 79) The problem is that hearing oneself speak depends upon time. The concept of time requires differentiation between instants. As such, "temporalization is at once the very power and limit of phenomenological reduction" (ibid., 86).
5. "I am writing here at the moment when my mother no longer recognizes me" (Derrida 1993: 22).
6. As a child, Derrida experienced the anti-Semitism historically characteristic to Western Europe, "when the French Algeria in its Governor-General, without the intervention of any Nazi, had expelled me from school and withdrawn my French citizenship, the undertaking of the Decremieux thus being annulled, a decree less old than my grandfathers" (ibid., 288–289).
7. G. W. F. Hegel's project was to prove quite the opposite, where the differences of time and space are constitutive of absolute knowledge. Perhaps the best place to begin exploring Derrida's arguments with Hegel are in the essay, "From Restricted to General Economy: A Hegelianism without Reserve," in *Writing and Difference* (1982a). Thanks to Craig Martin, who very helpfully pointed out the need for this important note.
8. Advanced readers would note the allusion to Martin Heidegger in the next sentence of Derrida's essay. The present chapter will not discuss the intricate relationship of Derrida's texts with Heidegger's thought.
9. The decision to not discuss Heidegger continues, along with the decision to not discuss this likely allusion to engagements with English philosophers such as John R. Searle.

Bibliography

Albahari, Miri. 2006. *Analytical Buddhism: The Two-Tiered Illusion of Self*. New York: Palgrave Macmillan.

Bennington, Geoffrey, and Jacques Derrida. 1993. *Jacques Derrida*. Chicago: University of Chicago Press.

Derrida, Jacques. 1973. *Speech and Phenomena: And Other Essays on Husserl's Theory of Signs*. Trans. David B. Allison and Leonard Lawlor. Evanston: Northwestern University Press.

Derrida, Jacques. 1976. *Of Grammatology*. Baltimore: Johns Hopkins University Press.

Derrida, Jacques. 1978. "Cogito and the History of Madness." In *Writing and Difference*. Trans. Alan Bass. Chicago: University of Chicago Press, 31–63.

Derrida, Jacques. 1982a. "From Restricted to General Economy: A Hegelianism without Reserve." In *Writing and Difference*. Trans. Alan Bass. New York: Routledge, 251–285.

Derrida, Jacques. 1982b. *Writing and Difference*. Trans. Alan Bass. New York: Routledge.

Derrida, Jacques. 1986. *Glas*. Trans. John P. Leavy Jr. and Richard Rand. Lincoln: University of Nebraska Press.

Derrida, Jacques. 1991. "'Eating Well,' or the Calculation of the Subject: An interview with Jacques Derrida." In E. Cadava, P. Connor, and J.-L. Nancy (eds.), *Who Comes After the Subject?* New York: Routledge, 96–119.

Derrida, Jacques. 1998. *Monolingualism of the Other, or, Prosthesis of Origin*. Trans. Patrick Mensah. Stanford: Stanford University Press.

Geisel, Theodor. 1961. *The Sneetches and Other Stories*. New York: Random House, 36–41.

Zahavi, Dan. 2005. *Subjectivity and Selfhood: Investigating the First-Person Perspective*. Cambridge: MIT Press.

Ipseity
Chapter 11.1

Danger

The concern with self in Jacques Derrida's oeuvre may be read as a message he worried nobody seemed to be getting. The texts presuppose Western and European audiences who would relate philosophical thought to their historical contexts: past, present, and future. As an Algerian Jew of the twentieth-century, Derrida's historical contexts included experiences of exclusion due to French colonialism, white racism, European antisemitism, and academic elitism. As a philosopher, Derrida's experiences included widespread acclaim and opprobrium. I think Derrida's writings reflect an ongoing concern to continue sending out the message: self-talk is always dangerous because self-talk is always self-defeating; there is no protection from that danger; realizing the unavoidable defeat of self-talk is the only chance for salvation. I am sure Derrida never wrote or said it this way, but I do think almost all his texts repeat this message.[1]

The dangerous thing in Derrida's texts is "self." These texts explain how philosophical discourses participate in various forms of social and political exclusion. European philosophy, particularly leading into the Colonial era through the Enlightenment period, aims to define and locate some "itself" that might make possible the original condition for self. The itself would be some kind of grounding origin that makes possible claims about identity, propriety, and presence. In short: self claims. These provide grounds to legitimate borders that justify exclusion. Self-talk involves the auto-justification of egodicy,[2] even when that talk aims to develop whatever "itself" creates the *a priori* conditions for self.

Émmanuel Levinas

The term "ipseity" does not occur regularly in Derrida's writings. It appears in the context of reading Émmanuel Levinas' critiques of Western philosophy. Levinas argued that the violence of the twentieth century was a feature, not a bug, of Western thought's focus on freedom and universality.[3] Levinas' book *Totality and Infinity* argues, "Western philosophy has most often been an ontology: a reduction of the other to the same by interposition of a middle and neutral term that ensures the comprehension of being" (Levinas 1969: 42). Levinas confronts metaphysics, where "[t]otality absorbs the multiplicity of beings" (ibid., 222), with the phenomenology of the "face," a primordial "subject insoluble into objectivity, and to which exteriority would be opposed" (ibid., 290). Derrida's 1964 essay, "Violence and Metaphysics" notes that Levinas' phenomenology of "face" distinguishes between identity and ipseity (1978: 109). The former prioritizes totalization through sameness (universality) and the latter non-violence through singularity. Levinas' project was to confront universality with something more originary, an "itself" that forces a non-violent relationship because it is prior to the objectification of language. Ipseity would interrupt egodicy. However, Derrida's essay cautiously criticizes Levinas for presupposing all that he seeks to put into question (1978: 133).

Ipseity

Ipseity is a term used to indicate something more originary than first or second persons references such as I, you and us. This is how Derrida explains his translation of Heidegger's concept of *Selbstheit* (Derrida 2021, in Brewer and Mendoza-Jesús 2021: 272). Ipseity is also identified by Derrida as the foundation for Husserl's "irreducibly egoic essence of experience" (1978: 131). Derrida goes so far as to declare in his essay on Levinas' thought: "No philosophy responsible for its language can renounce ipseity in general, and the philosophy or eschatology of separation may do so less than any other" (ibid., 131). Self is only possible on the conditions of ipseity.

According to Derrida, the idea of ipseity does not offer salvation from danger. Violence is unavoidable: "[a] speech produced without the least violence would determine nothing" (Derrida 1978: 147). If absolute non-violence is more total than the sameness imposed by metaphysics, then Derrida proposes some minimal, transcendental violence is needed to make the differences that create the space and time for responsibility to others. Derrida's alternative to Levinas is to risk the worst by choosing, "the least violence by a philosophy which takes history, that is, finitude, seriously; a philosophy aware of itself as *historical* in each of its aspects (in a sense which tolerates neither finite totality, nor positive infinity) . . . as *economy*" (ibid., 117). On my reading, this is Derrida's repeated message. The known dangers of self-talk require "vigilance" (ibid.)

Derrida's vigilance is an attention to the language of ipseity. More precisely, the matter is Derrida's argument that ipseity, if there is such a thing, requires speech. And furthermore, Derrida argues that wherever there is speech there, too, is space and time. These claims form the basis for how Derrida addresses danger.

Phenomenology

These arguments are presented in Derrida's 1967 essay, "Speech and Phenomena," which is a critique of Edmund Husserl's *Logical Investigations*. Levinas' work builds upon Husserl's phenomenology, which includes an explanation for the fundamental conditions of knowledge. Husserl aimed to understand these fundamental conditions by stripping away (Western) metaphysical presuppositions and biases. Derrida notices how Husserl's inheritance of the *cogito* remain. Husserl postulated a knower whose perception of self-consciousness is supposed to be immediate. That should entail that self-perception is unlike any other kind of perception (which Descartes also claimed). This claim postulates an interior perception that purportedly differs from all other, external perceptions. The latter would involve the representation of knowledge in time and space through the mediation of some natural language. The former, for Husserl, would involve an interior monologue. All this piques Derrida's curiosity about Husserl's explanation of self-relation. Derrida's essay focuses on the idea of speaking to oneself. Whatever is said, the saying takes the form of some natural language. A babbling, incoherent monologue cannot perform the operation of representation required for Husserl's explanation of consciousness (Derrida 1967: 99). And if so, natural language uses repeatable, phonic forms which are only meaningful because they are indefinitely repeatable. Interior speech may perhaps be faster than musing aloud, but that does not make it immediate.

These conditions for consciousness that discount the possibility of pure presence of oneself to itself. Ispeity, the itself of self, may be postulated but never experienced if the retentional and representational phases of consciousness require the repeatable, phonic forms of some language. These forms require consciousness to involve non-presence, since they may be repeated at some indeterminate future space and time where their exact indication is unpredictable. Language introduces the experience of otherness that Levinas indicated with the term face.

Salvation

On my reading, "ipseity" is proposed to usefully name the experience of spacing for self. It is a dangerous experience because, all too often, there is an urge to secure the self as something singular. The desire, or urge, is for some itself that might exercise sovereignty such that it prevails against time and space. I think Derrida has in mind the vitalist sentimentality of populist movements that proclaim universal freedom for themselves at the expense of all others. According to my reading of Derrida, there is a point of convergence between the (Western) metaphysical universality and Levinas's singularity in experiences that seem absolute, but ultimately cannot because consciousness requires language.[4] Derrida's texts repeat this message, perhaps because the indications expressed through the ongoing history of (Western) philosophy repeatedly resist being aware of themselves as historical.

Notes

1. Leonard Lawlor puts it this way: "it is possible to say without exaggeration that every deconstruction Derrida has ever written targets auto-affection. Deconstruction aims to show that all auto-affection, however it is conceived, is really and fundamentally hetero-affection" (Lawlor 2014: 130).
2. See Chapter 3 of *Gift of Death* (Derrida 1995), which amplifies Kierkegaard's confrontation of absolute responsibility with the generality of ethics, "egodicy" (62), to consider how "*every other (one) is every (bit) other*," such that "the concepts of responsibility, of decision, or of duty are condemned a priori to paradox, scandal, and aporia" (68).
3. See Levinas' 1934 essay, "Reflections on the Philosophy of Hitlerism" (1990), and the introduction to *Totality and Infinity*, where he asks after Hitler's demise whether the West continues to be "duped by morality" (Levinas 1969: 21).
4. On the topic of religion, Derrida writes, "'the thing' tends thus to drop out of sigh as soon as one believes oneself able to master it under the title of a discipline, a knowledge or a philosophy" (1998: 39)

References

Brewer, Benjamin, and Ronald Mendoza-de Jesús. 2021. "The Hidden Law of Selfhood: Reading Heidegger's Ipseity after Derrida's Hospitality." *Oxford Literary Review*, 43 (2): 268–289.

Derrida, Jacques. 1973. *Speech and Phenomena: And Other Essays on Husserl's Theory of Signs*. Trans. David B. Allison. Evanston: Northwestern University Press.

Derrida, Jacques. 1978. "Violence and Metaphysics." In *Writing and Difference*. Trans. Alan Bass. Chicago: University of Chicago Press, 79–153.

Derrida, Jacques. 1995. *Gift of Death*. Trans. David Wills. Chicago: University of Chicago Press.

Derrida, Jacques. 1998. "Faith and Knowledge: The Two Sources of 'Religion' at the Limits of Reason Alone." Trans. Samuel Weber. In *Religion*. Ed. Gianni Vattimo and Jacques Derrida. Stanford: Stanford University Press, 1–78.

Lawlor, Leonard. 2014. "Auto-Affection." In Claire Colebrook (ed.), *Jacques Derrida: Key Concepts*. London: Routledge, 130–138.

Levinas, Emmanuel. 1969. *Totality and Infinity: An Essay on Exteriority*. Trans. Alfonso Lingis. Boston: Mirtinus Nijhoff Publishers.

Levinas, Emmanuel. 1990. "Reflections on the Philosophy of Hitlerism." Trans. Seán Hand. *Critical Inquiry*, 17 (1): 62–71.

Secrecy
Chapter 11.2

Singular Problems

If there is "self," then how might such a thing be studied? Most conceptions of self include something to do with human beings and their experiences. The ideas for these conceptions typically include claims that self is an important part of how humans experience. The practice of experiencing, in these explanations, involves self. And self is usually presented not only in the singular, but also as singular. *A* self is who experiences. One problem for studying self is how such a thing may be studied. How may the object of a study also be the subject of study? Won't such studies be somehow biased or self-confirming? A possible answer is that humans conduct all sorts of studies where some aspect of human being is also the object. Medical sciences and management are good examples. Such studies are empirical. They study bodies and the data produced by measurements of bodies. Humans experiencing self is difficult to measure empirically. For example, by what measure is a human's recognition of a face in a mirror an example of self? Perhaps that recognition is merely neurological response to physical stimulus processed through a series of biological organs, where those processes are neither causal nor necessary for experiencing self.

Singular Methods

In the history of Western philosophy, studying self is often an important method for determining foundational issues of truth and certainty. If there is no certainty about self, how then can there be certainty about anything else? The general idea is that if there is some ultimate bedrock for thinking, then other certainties may be built out from that foundation. Rene Descartes proposed a method of subjecting all claims to doubt, precisely in order to arrive at certainty about what cannot be doubted. Descartes argued that whatever it is that does the doubting cannot doubt itself. The doubting thing is not the brain. Do all animals with brains demonstrate the exercise of doubt? Humans have a foundational experience of self as a thinking entity, *cogito*, when they reflect on doubting, to briefly summarize Descartes' ideas. Edmund Husserl pursued questions of certainty by asking how a *cogito* may re-present experiences, such that reflection on doubting, for example, is actually knowing. Martin Heidegger criticized the idea that practicing doubt is an adequately foundational human experience of self. Heidegger argued that all humans undoubtedly experience anxiety about their deaths.

Death presents humans with an impenetrable silence whose certainty produces anxiety about the closure of the future. Briefly put, Heidegger proposed the German word *Dasein* (roughly translated as "being-there") to replace *cogito* as the baseline for experiencing self. Heidegger's book, *Being and Time* (1962), could be understood to mark a shift in how Western philosophy studies self. The idea of self remains, however, a singular locus of experiencing.

Singular Death

If there is self, must it be something observed as alive? Human deaths may be empirically observed. Death is commonly understood as the total absence of life. The common assumption is that dead humans cannot experience self. Some approach to persistence presents ways around the problems death presents to the idea of self. Most approaches of persistence involve something that continues experiencing after the death of the human body. Less common approaches involve dividing lived, human experiences into separate selves that might not have contact with each other. Self continues to be presented in the singular, except *a* self who experiences is not necessarily contiguous with any other self. These selves may have shared a living, organic body as among the sufficient causes for their experiences. But that is no different from the shared need of all biological basics. Despite sharing a body, these multiple selves might as well be dead to each other. The others need not necessarily be living for another's self-experience. With this approach to persistence, the experiences of Cartesian doubt and Heideggerian anxiety are those of distinct selves. Whatever each self may or may not know is a secret to others.

Religious Secrecy

All of the above is prefatory to discussing Jacques Derrida's short book, *The Gift of Death* (1995), whose discussions run across the history of Western philosophy from Plato on through to Heidegger. The text proposes that philosophy is, "a *thinking* that "repeats" the possibility of religion without religion" (Derrida 1995: 49). The thinking in question that purportedly repeats religion is that line of thought that supposes truths are not immediately graspable. Instead, the surface-level appearances of the world in human experience need to be either somehow circumscribed or circumvented in order to access foundational knowledge with certainty. Derrida explains how Western philosophers draw upon Jewish and Christian religious narratives about sacrifice to do this, such that texts such as Heidegger's, which profess atheism, are clearly religious.

The religiosity in question is the outcome of thinking that conceptualizes the self as a singular entity that comes into being through the experience of responsibility. The experience of responsibility is how the self becomes capable of understanding the "I" of "Here I am." Derrida's book studies how the account of Abraham's near-sacrifice of Isaac, found in Genesis 22 of the Hebrew Bible, is understood by the nineteenth-century philosopher Søren Kierkegaard, who wrote that Abraham's willingness to sacrifice Isaac on Mount Moriah exemplifies a paradox, "that the single individual as the particular stands in an absolute relation to the absolute, or Abraham is done for" (1985: 144). According to the Genesis narrative, Abraham kept God's command a secret such that Isaac only realized what was to happen at the very moment when the sacrifice was interrupted on the altar at Moriah. Derrida compares Abraham's secrecy to Jesus' teaching in Matthew 6:6 of the Christian Bible, "But whenever you pray, go into your room and shut the door and pray to your Father who is in secret; and your Father who sees in secret will reward you." Derrida notes Kierkegaard's emphasis on secrecy as essential to responsibility, where both Abraham and Jesus announce a form of religiosity that is a secret, absolute duty to a transcendent other that likewise remains secret and unseen. Were Abraham's sacrifice or Jesus' command to pray in private announced to others and explained, according to Kierkegaard, then they are no longer exceptional examples of authentic singularity. There is no self without secrecy.

General Secrecy

Derrida's text argues, however, that what Kierkegaard exalts as exemplary is in fact a general demand of responsibility. The secrecy that seems exclusive to the divine being of a religion who confronts humans as absolutely unknowable, is presented by the contemporary human awareness of the globalized world. It is as impossible to know everyone in the world as it is impossible to know God. Furthermore, writes Derrida, each decision enacted in the twenty-first-century world involves sacrificing others: "Let us not look for examples, there would be too many of them, at every step we took ... I am sacrificing and betraying at every moment all my other obligations: my obligations to the other others whom I know or don't know, the billions of my fellows (without mentioning the animals that are even more other others than my fellows), my fellows who are dying of starvation or sickness ... in this land of Moriah that is our habitat every second of every day" (Derrida 1995: 69). Each decision is riven with secrecy, which is, "the paradoxical truth of our responsibility and of our relation to the *gift of death* of each instant" (ibid., 79). Rather than Cartesian doubt or Heideggerian anxiety as the approach to experiencing self, it is the experience of responsibility for the deaths of unknown others that founds certainty of self.

The Gift of Death concludes by making several further moves to demonstrate the possibility of religion without religion. "Wholly other" is one way to describe the absolute alterity attributed to YHWH/God/Allah of Judaism, Christianity and Islam. These religions propose their divinity knows all things, where humans experience limitations. Humans cannot expect to access the secrecy of divine truths. The final chapter of Derrida's book hinges on the French phrase, "*tout autre est tout autre*," which translates as "every other (one) is every (bit) other" (Ibid., 82), which is used to argue that the infinite alterity is not only the religious relationship to the divine but also each human's experience of everyone else. One reading of this chapter is to find Derrida taking issue with the selfishness of Western philosophers who propose various turns inward. The self-confirming biases of these approaches produce their own problems for studying self. Experiencing the secrecy of each other, as an other who is as worthy of responsibility as any divinity, is proposed as a form of religiosity without religion.

Secret Selves

But there is another direction that Derrida's text considers the French phrase above. Having proposed that the absolute secrecy of the divine espoused by so many religions fittingly characterizes the nature of everyday human experience in a globalized world, Derrida aims to highlight something distinctive about the singularity experienced by a human who realizes the enormous responsibility exercised in a decision. That experience, itself, never happens again. The singularity means, for Derrida, that whomever made that decision is wholly other than whoever makes the next. If every other (one) is every (bit) other, then, the "I" who once said "Here I am" is wholly other, too. Whomever made a decision in this body yesterday, last year, or a decade ago is other to the "I" who is making a decision right now. Derrida writes, "I can have a secret relationship with myself and not tell everything, once there is secrecy and secret witnessing within me, then what I call God exists, (there is) what I call God in me … God is in me, he is the absolute "me" or "self" (ibid., 109).

Derrida's text does not suggest that humans begin worshipping themselves. It is not arguing that each person is their own religion. What can be read from this text is a unique approach to the problems of studying self by means of thinking about persistence differently than most religions, and yet doing so by drawing on trajectories of thought that are typically understood to be religious. Divine commands are sometimes used to sanction actions that would otherwise not be permitted, on the grounds that a god's absolute alterity demands human obeisance. Wars and sacrifices of living things, for example, may be thereby seen as religious exercises of responsibility to a divinity whose reasons are shrouded in secrecy. Secrecy, according to Derrida, is a general condition that obtains through the experience of responsibility for others. If mirrors produce an experience of self, it is because they present an experience of absolute responsibility for an other who is wholly other.

References

Derrida, Jacques. 1995. *Gift of Death*. Trans. David Wills. Chicago: University of Chicago Press.

Heidegger, Martin. 1962. *Being and Time*. Trans. John Macquarrie and Edward Robinson. New York: Harper Collins.

Kierkegaard, Søren. 1985. *Fear and Trembling*. Trans. Alastair Hannay. New York: Penguin Books.

Sovereignty
Chapter 11.3

Who's the Boss

I once saw a t-shirt that said, "You're not the boss of me." The point is likely familiar to most readers: individuals in contemporary Western society are understood to be masters of themselves. Basic social and moral norms are activated by such shared understandings of self-propriety. Most versions of feminism, for example, draw upon these resources to establish the status of women and their bodies as autonomous individuals. Men do not, and should not, have authority over women and their bodies. This key word chapter does not contest those arguments or positions. The ideas behind this t-shirt point towards the topic of "sovereignty" in the works of Jacques Derrida.

The idea of sovereignty is usually reserved for political discussions about the locations of borders of land, airspace, and territorial waters. These borders demarcate a zone for within which a constitution establishes the basis for legislation and policy that is meant to govern whatever goes on within the borders, and, to govern whatever may be allowed to pass through the borders. The same constitution will establish conditions for the leadership, including the head of state, who will represent the legislation and policies both within and beyond the borders. The head and its offices are typically located at a capital. These arrangements map nicely onto Western imaginations of the self as a sovereign, whose bodily borders are governed by its *caput*. Nobody else is boss of a sovereign.

Rogue States

Derrida's last lecture of his life in 2002 was entitled *Voyous*, which was translated into English as *Rogues* (2005). There, Derrida connects some earlier thoughts on the politics of sovereignty. *L'autre Cap* (1991) was published as *The Other Heading* (1992), which continues a line of political questioning from *The Politics of Friendship* (1997). Prior to these, a 1978 essay on the thought of twentieth-century philosopher Georges Bataille discusses "sovereignty" as what confronts philosophy with nonlogic (Derrida 1978: 267). Derrida's foreword to *Without Alibi* (2002b) remarks how the editor, Peggy Kamuf, identified sovereignty as the essential trait of the essays collected in that volume. Derrida's argument in *Rogues* is that, ultimately, every sovereign state is a rogue entity. This is both good and bad news, since it means whatever form a state may take is never final or absolute. The task of philosophers, according to Derrida, is to remind people of this. This chapter find those ideas useful for thinking about the topic of self, too.

Absolute Conditions

One common strategy of Derrida's writing is to take a concept and work out its absolute conditions. That strategy is meant to demonstrate the limits of the concept. Where are its borders? What does the concept contain? What does the concept govern? And, most important for Derrida's texts: what are the conditions where borders and governance break down? In other words, Derrida's strategy asks: when is a concept not the boss of itself? From this perspective, perhaps "sovereignty" is a theme running across all Derrida's works! Derrida's discussion of sovereignty is useful to understand what Derrida may have to say on the topic of "self." When considered on absolute terms, the conditions that make claims for sovereignty possible are the same conditions that make sovereignty impossible. Absolute sovereignty is the dissolution of sovereignty. Therefore, the grounding legitimacy of any claim to sovereignty in the actual world is a fiction not far removed from a declaration printed on a t-shirt. No self is ever the boss of anyone else, much less themselves.

Thinking through a concept on absolute or ultimate terms is a practice well-known to philosophers of religion. While conceptualizing "God" lends itself nicely to the practice, all other concepts may be analyzed in this manner, too. Reflecting on a concept requires a philosopher to imagine 'stepping back' from an idea so that it may considered 'as if' it were absolute. Philosophers of religion do this with classical theism. "God" is conceptualized as an *omni*-X entity, where "X" is some attribute such as power, goodness, knowledge, etc. These omni-X's position the God of theism as an ultimate entity whose attributes are absolute. We can see how "sovereignty" lends itself well to God-thoughts, and how the idea is closely related to the theological inheritance of the Western metaphysical traditions.[1] To practice stepping back, however, is a necessarily atheistic move that does not copy the form or content of debates about God's existence. For Derrida's practice of philosophical analysis, atheism names an orientation towards theological prejudices (Derrida 1993: 155). Derrida argued that theological prejudices inflect all Western philosophy that avoids testing the absolute conditions of its concepts (including so-called atheism[2]). To think about the concept of "self," according to this philosophical practice, requires stepping back from theological prejudices about the idea to consider what absolute and ultimate conditions are necessary in order for these to be "self."

Absolute Sovereignty

As previously noted, the conceptual axiomatics of sovereignty are propriety and dominion. Dominion requires borders, within which there is an indivisible domain under sovereign control. The conditions of absolute sovereignty, on the one hand, require that the sovereign domain be undetermined and untouched by whatever is beyond its borders. On the other hand, total sovereignty entails that the sovereign is unaffected by whatever takes place within its proper domain. At this level of consideration, the exception from both external and internal relationality is foundational to the concept of sovereignty. In his essay on Bataille, we read, "Sovereignty is absolute when it is absolved of every relationship, and keeps itself in the night of the secret" (Derrida 1978: 266; refer to "Secret" in this volume). Derrida later writes in *Rogues*, "A pure sovereignty is indivisible, or it is not at all" (Derrida 2005: 101). Some may find this analysis of a concept on its absolute terms absurd. The sheer idiosyncrasy required for ultimate sovereignty requires ontological isolation in conditions where relationality is impossible. We might say that absolute sovereignty is omni-idios, where the Greek "ἴδιος" indicates a condition of ultimate privacy. Or, as Derrida once wrote, sovereignty is, "the *idiot* itself (the innocent, the proper, the virgin, the originary, the native, the naïve, the great beginning: just as great, as erect, and as autonomous as, *submissive*, etc.; Derrida 1995: 260)." The omni-idios exists without relationship to anything. This quick analysis aims to set aside the theological prejudice that absolute sovereignty may be actualized in any possible world. Furthermore, it seems actual sovereignty is always compromised in some way or another.

Perhaps there's something amiss about taking a common idea to be tested as an absolute concept. That sense of impropriety may be important for understanding Derrida's writings. When Derrida was interviewed about the 2001 terrorist attacks in the United States, he noted, "A 'philosopher' ... would be someone who analyzes and then draws the practical and effective consequences of the relationship between our philosophical heritage and the structure of the still dominant juridico-political system that is so clearly undergoing mutation" (Derrida 2003: 106). Philosophy involves balancing 'as if' imagination with similarly imaginative projections of practical affairs in some possible world. Of course, absolute sovereignty cannot be actualized because any actual form of sovereignty entails relations with other entities. The content of the concept is limited by the demands of actual form.

The Political

Sovereignty is one of many ideas that may teach this lesson. "Religion" is another. When Derrida was asked to contribute an essay on religion, he wrote: "The fundamental concepts that often permit us to isolate or *pretend* to isolate the *political*—restricting ourselves to this particular circumscription – remain religious or in any case theologico-political" (Derrida 1998: 25). Derrida's writings show how terms like sovereignty and religion ask philosophers to do the difficult work of connecting abstractions to the relational conditions of actual, possible worlds. The practice of thinking concepts in their absolute terms, as if they are unbounded by conditions, is a theologico-political practice that requires Derrida's certain kind of atheism. Politics, as the organization of actual beings within a realm or the world, is the particular outworking of the possibility of the political. The political establishes the circumstances within which sovereignty may be conceptually imagined, because sovereignty is always and already compromised in any actual world of relationships among entities. There is a difference between thinking about the general conditions that make possible political entities and their relations versus politics, which encapsulates the set of considerations about the structuring of already-existing relations and their relevant entities. Thinking about "the political" allows for metaphysical considerations that foreground politics. The distinction helps us understand what kind of thinking bridges common, folk conceptions and philosophical analysis.

Sovereign Fictions

What Derrida found interesting about sovereignty is that deploying the concept in actual politics requires the fictive, as-if thinking of the political. The conditions for actual sovereignty requires a plurality of agreement on the part of many others to pretend as if a sovereignty is real. For example, sovereignty relates tenuously to law because if the former involves the capability to determine laws, then it must be somehow outside those laws. Giorgio Agamben calls this the paradox of sovereignty (Agamben 1998: 15). Carl Schmitt identifies it as the state of exception (Schmitt 1985: 5). The paradox is that the actualization of sovereignty requires perjury. The sovereign is simultaneously and contemporaneously inside and outside a juridical order of its own making. The sovereign authorizes the order, but as such does so from outside that order. Sovereignty is its own alibi against any law. To be *alius ibi* literally means to be in some other place; providing an alibi defends one before an allegation of the law. In other words, an alibi removes one from the position of having to be before the law. Sovereignty, according to Derrida, establishes itself as a theological phantasm: "*the phantasm - thus a certain fable and a certain 'as if'- of the political onto-theology of sovereignty*" (Derrida 2002b: xix). Sovereignty is expected to act as if transcendent of all conditions, and yet produce effects within finitude. This requirement for fictive thinking towards transcendence is what Derrida describes as a "theological phantasm" (ibid., 244). The implication is that if thinking about sovereignty demands thinking paradoxes such as these, then Derrida's version of atheism may be the best perspective for thinking about sovereignty.

The Impossible Problem

Derrida's final lecture, *Rogues*, explores the paradox that forms the problem of sovereignty:

> As soon as there is sovereignty, there is abuse of power and a rogue state. Abuse is the law of use; it is the law itself, the 'logic' of a sovereignty that can reign only by not sharing. More precisely, since it never succeeds in doing this except in a critical, precarious, and unstable fashion, sovereignty can only *tend*, for a limited time, to reign without sharing. It can only tend toward imperial hegemony.
>
> (Derrida 2005: 102)

The legitimacy of sovereignty is a function of having an alibi for any law. Derrida construes the core conception of sovereignty as the capacity to exist, and thereby act, without giving reasons (Derrida 2005: 100). But that also means the recognition of sovereignty is madness. The madness required to sustain the fiction of sovereignty is a certain kind of madness called "faith," since sovereignty requires others to ignore the conditions that makes it possible. The concept of sovereignty also demonstrates the fiction of the secular-sacred distinction. According to Derrida, the concept of sovereignty has "the heritage of a barely secularized theology" (Derrida 2002b: 207).

Derrida's writings thereby show how impossibility forms the conditions for sovereignty, and pretending otherwise is the faith that sustains it in politics. As with Derrida's writings on law, this is not bad news. "One may even find in this the political chance of all historical progress" (Derrida 2002a: 242). The impossibility of sovereignty means there are always alternatives to absolute rule. For philosophers of religion, perhaps in particular, Derrida's thought has much to offer: "In speaking of an ontotheology of sovereignty, I am referring here, under the name of God, this One and Only God, to the determination of a sovereign, and thus indivisible, omnipotence. For wherever the name of God would allow us to think something else, for example a vulnerable nonsovereignty, one that suffers and is divisible, one that is mortal even, capable of contradicting itself or of repenting (a thought that is neither impossible nor without example), it would be a completely different story, perhaps even the story of a god who deconstructs himself in his ipseity" (Derrida 2005: 157–158). A mortal, vulnerable, divisible nonsovereignty capable of making mistakes and repenting is perhaps a worthwhile basis for a philosophy of self.

Notes

1. "In speaking of an ontotheology of sovereignty, I am referring here, under the name of God, this One and Only God, to the determination of a sovereign, and thus indivisible, omnipotence" (Derrida 2005: 157).
2.
    Here I do not mean those 'theological prejudices' which, at an identifiable time and place, inflected or repressed the theory of the written sign . . . These prejudices are nothing but the most clearsighted and best circumscribed, historically determined manifestation of a constitutive and permanent presupposition essential to the history of the West, therefore to metaphysics in its entirety, even when it professes to be atheist. (Derrida 1974, 323 n. 3)

References

Agamben, Giorgio. 1998. *Homo Sacer*. Trans. David Heller-Roazen. Stanford: Stanford University Press.
Derrida, Jacques. 1974. *Of Grammatology*. Trans. G. Spivak. Baltimore: Johns Hopkins University Press.
Derrida, Jacques. 1978. "From Restricted to General Economy: A Hegelianism without Reserve." In *Writing and Difference*. Trans. Alan Bass. Chicago: University of Chicago Press, 251–277.
Derrida, Jacques. 1992. *The Other Heading*. Trans. Pascal-Anne Brault and Michael B. Naas. Bloomington: Indiana University Press.
Derrida, Jacques. 1993. "Circumfession." Trans. Geoffrey Bennington. In *Jacques Derrida*. Chicago: University of Chicago Press.
Derrida, Jacques. 1995. *On the Name*. Trans. Thomas Dutoit. Stanford: Stanford University Press.
Derrida, Jacques. 1997. *The Politics of Friendship*. Trans. George Collins. London: Verso.
Derrida, Jacques. 1998. "Faith and Knowledge: The Two Sources of 'Religion' at the Limits of Reason Alone." Trans. Samuel Weber. In *Religion*. Ed. Gianni Vattimo and Jacques Derrida. Stanford: Stanford University Press, 1–78.
Derrida, Jacques. 2002a. "Force of Law: The "Mystical Foundation of Authority."" In *Acts of Religion*. Trans. and ed. Gil Anidjar. London: Routledge, 230–298.
Derrida, Jacques. 2002b. *Without Alibi*. Trans. and ed. Peggy Kamuf. Stanford: Stanford University Press.
Derrida, Jacques. 2003. "Autoimmunity: Real and Symbolic Suicides." Trans. Pascal-Anne Brault and Michael B. Naas. In *Philosophy in a Time of Terror*. Ed. Giovanna Borradori. Chicago: University of Chicago Press, 85–136.
Derrida, Jacques. 2005. *Rogues*. Trans. Pascal-Anne Brault and Michael B. Naas. Stanford: Stanford University Press.
Schmitt, Carl. 1985. *Political Theology: Four Chapters on the Concept of Sovereignty*. Trans. George Schwab. Cambridge: Cambridge University Press.

Epilogue
Comparative Philosophical Conclusions

Timothy D. Knepper

Chapter Outline

Who Am I?	318
Where Do I Come From?	319
Where Am I Going?	321
How Do I Get There?	322
What Obstacles Are in My Way?	323
Evaluation	325

As suggested, I will use this conclusion as an opportunity to apply the methodology of my 2022 (undergraduate) textbook *Philosophies of Religion: A Global and Critical Introduction* to the essays of this collection, using them as religio-philosophical content about which to philosophize cross-culturally, especially as this relates to teaching philosophy of religion globally and critically in the (undergraduate) classroom.[1] Although this method is three-stepped—thick description, formal comparison, and critical (multidimensional) evaluation—it is the latter two that are especially germane here, as the chapters themselves constitute our "thick descriptions," each of which addresses at least two of my "four corners" of description: logical form, conceptual meaning, contextual setting, and political use.

Turning, then, to comparison (and later evaluation), we are immediately confronted with a couple of difficulties. First, what exactly is it that we are comparing? Selves, yes—but selves in what respect(s)?[2] Second, what exactly is meant by "self," and what makes it a fruitful category for cross-cultural comparison, one that does not bias too much toward those sign-systems in which "self" serves as an established sign-function?

To start with the latter, I deploy here the minimalistic understanding of "self" used in my textbook—the locus of human awareness, control, and identity—in hopes that it "leaves open" religio-philosophical issues regarding in what sense this self even exists, let alone whether it can be identified with a substance-soul, is separable from the body, persists after death, and so forth. (I also encourage religio-philosophical comparativists to try out other relevant comparative terms, including *person* in the case of English and any of the many "self" terms from non-western religio-philosophies.[3]) In the case of the former difficulty above, given that this volume was designed as a companion to my textbook, I will focus my comparisons through the five "self" questions raised in my textbook, all of which are derived from the component parts of the journey metaphor: (1) Who am I? (2) Where do I come from? (3) Where am I going? (4) How do I get there? (5) What obstacles are in my way?

In each case, I will primarily compare, noting what I take to be interesting and important similarities and differences amongst the content of this volume. Not until the end, will I make some brief remarks about how we might cross-culturally evaluate these ideas and arguments. Given space restrictions, this will all be a bit sketchy. Still, I hope it will be useful in (undergraduate) teaching contexts.

Who Am I?

My book focused this question on whether religio-philosophical "selves" were primarily conceived of (and argumentatively defended) as individual substances, relational roles, or compositional processes. Of course, these are ideal types—no "self" is not individual, relational, and compositional in some sense. Nevertheless, religious and other philosophers usually assume, articulate, and defend "selves" that lean in one of these directions. Indeed, this is the case for most of the contributors.

In the case of the Venda, *murunzi* is said to possess both individualist/ontological and relational/communitarian dimensions. For the Nguni, by contrast, it is the communitarian aspects of *uMina/ubumina* that are stressed, especially with respect to *ubuntu*—that I am because we are. For Candomblé, the compositional aspects of self are showcased, with the *ori* constituting just one part of the self and *orixá* possession serving as the means through which "a more or less undifferentiated individual becomes a structured person and a generic *orixá* is actualized into an individual saint." In the case of Native American peoples, especially the Tlingit, Diné (Navajo), and Lakota, the self is fundamentally relational (and moral), as captured by the Lakota phrase "All My Relations." For Derrida, the plurality of self is emphasized (even though we are always both one and more than one); here, the task of producing the self is "never ending." In Confucianism, there is "broad, but not uniform, agreement on the social and relational nature of Confucian subject." Daoism, likewise, as well as by contrast, thinks of the self in largely as psychosomatic (mind-body connection) and composite (disparate elements that separate at death). For Shinto, there is no solid self; rather, self emerges in interaction with others and world, ever-changing through these interactions. The self (*ātman*) of Nyāya (Udayana) and Jainism (Haribhadra) are eternal substance-souls. And for Iqbal, the self is also a substance-soul, albeit one that continually strives to actualize itself in relationship with the ultimate.

How might we compare over these heterogenous selves, especially with respect to whether the self ought to be understood as an individual substance-soul, a web of relations and roles, or an underlying flux of processes. Well, since comparison is just to offer interesting and important differences and similarities, we can start by pointing out that these differences sure are interesting! In the very least, this should bring a measure of humility and caution for anyone tempted to insist that one's own view of self is the only correct one. Not only are these differences interesting; they are also important, as the nature of self is in each case crucial to it reaching its end. (As corollary, we might say that Jain selves can't meet Confucian ends; Venda selves, Buddhist ends; Sufi selves, Lakota ends, and so forth.) For me, this point cannot be underscored enough. No matter how dense and detailed these "self" conceptions and arguments are (usually as the result of contention by rival religio-philosophies), they are (deemed) crucial to the "self" achieving its (ultimate) destination, even a destination as worldly as Derrida's "Monolingualism of the other." If there is an interesting and important similarity amongst this content, it is just this (perhaps also that no matter how far a "self" leans toward one of the three directions above—substantial, relational, compositional—it would seem in need of some measure of balance, lest it open itself up to commonsense and culturally bound objections from rival philosophies).

Where Do I Come From?

With this second question my textbook homed in on the original condition of the "self," as this has been a more widespread and contentious issue in religio-philosophical traditions and contexts over time and space (in comparison to the question of from what or whom "self" originates). This encompasses debates about the original goodness (or badness) of the self in East Asia, about the original enlightenment (or nescience) of the self in South Asia (and East Asia), about the original freedom (or pre-determinism/pre-destiny) of the self in the Mediterranean and West Africa, and about the original sacredness of the self among the Lakota of North America.

Now, the "original condition" of "self" was not the focus of the essays in this volume. Nevertheless, we get plenty of glimpses about what this condition is for these selves.

For the Venda, the self possesses a "profound spiritual dimension" by means of which it communes with ancestors. This is true as well for the Nguni "self," though in both cases we should note that "self" is prone to sickness and misfortune, the sources of which must be ascertained (through divination) and addressed (through healing rituals and medicaments). So too for Candomblé, where each "self" has a destiny that is revealed at birth through one's *odu*, governed throughout life by specific *orixás*, and interacted with by means of divination, possession, and sacrifice. In the case of Native American peoples (especially the Tlingit, Diné, and Lakota), morality is the heart of the "self," which is gifted with a moral guide by spiritual beings (at least in many traditions). For Derrida, we might say that the human condition is to be never quite one and always more than one, ever aiming to realize a presence that can never be (of meaning, identity, immediacy, etc.). For Confucians, the "self" came to be seen as originally and inherently good, perhaps through the influence of Daoism, where the "self" is also naturally in connection with the sacred. In Shinto, a balance of good and evil is stressed. In many South Asian religio-philosophies, here Nyāya (Udayana) and Jainism (Haribhadra), the embodied "self" carries karmic allotment of some sort and therefore is ignorant to some degree. And in the case of Iqbal, the "self" seems originally incomplete, needing to actualize itself in relationship to the divine.

How might we compare these original conditions of these selves? Two things strike me most of all: first, that certain regions of religio-philosophy have been preoccupied with certain original conditions and not others; second, that all religio-philosophies must contend with the fact that most of us are *not* (perfectly) good, free, enlightened, healthy, successful, or sacred, even if we are putatively conditioned originally as such. This first observation is one about difference: why should East Asia be traditionally concerned with the original goodness of humans; South Asia, with original knowledge (ignorance); the Abrahamic faiths (especially certain Christianity-s and Islam-s), with free will; sub-Saharan Africa, with health and fortune; and so forth? By contrast, my second observation is one about similarity: how do religio-philosophies explain the fact that things are usually (always?) not the way they are "originally" said to be, especially if this original condition is one of (perfect) goodness, knowledge, freedom, etc.? Although I will not attempt answers to these questions here (in the spirit of this volume serving pedagogical purposes in [undergraduate] classrooms), I will suggest that one might appeal to a common set of factors concerning natural environment, social organization, and political rule (possibly also divinity theology) in the former case, but to particular religio-philosophical arguments in the latter case. Paradoxically, then, a similar set of factors might be able to explain these important and interesting differences, whereas religio-philosophical particularities would need to be consulted to explain this important and interesting similarity.

Where Am I Going?

For this third question, my book focused on whether the "self" survives death and, if so, how. This is the question of persistence—or at least one of the questions of persistence—examined by the essays of this book. Nevertheless, answers to these questions are not always clear and are sometimes complex.

We do not learn much here about Venda views of afterlife, though for the neighboring Nguni we are told that the "self" comes back in other human beings in the family line, whether through rebirth or "spirituality," also "living forever" in others through narrative. Nor do we learn much here about the specifics of Candomblé views of afterlife, though for their West African progenitors the "self" had multiple postmortem destinations, some involving passing on to the realm of the ancestors, others, reincarnation. The same is often true with Native America peoples, here the Lakota, whose multi-parted "self" remains, reincarnates, and moves on to the spirit/ancestor realm. Of course, there's not much here (or elsewhere) about Derridean views of afterlife. And afterlife never seemed to be of much concern for East Asian religio-philosophers, whether Confucian, Daoist, or Shinto (though we do learn here about the Chinese notion of *hún/yang*-souls/ghosts, which rise to the heavens/sky upon death, and *pò/yin*-souls/ghosts, which descend into the earth, as well as about the Daoist view that we simply return to and dissolve in the Dao/whole upon death). By contrast, release from rebirth was of preeminent concern for South Asian religio-philosophers, with a variety of theories about whether final release involved some sort of individuated heavenly existence, individuated non-conscious existence, amalgamated non-conscious existence, or simply non-existence. For Iqbal, finally, there is not much here, though we would suspect that postmortem existence involves the paradise of Islam, perhaps with a mystical/Sufi tinge of unification with Allah.

How might we compare over these postmortem destinations of the "self"? Again, what strikes me most is that only certain types of souls can go to certain types of postmortem destinations and, relatedly, that it matters to what degree "duality" or "individuality" is seen as a problem to be overcome. The substance-souls of the Abrahamic traditions generally go to heavenly realms where they remain individuated and conscious, since duality is usually not a "problem" for them, save in certain mystical sub-traditions where afterlife scenarios can involve absorption into some god. By contrast, the substance-souls of South Asia, where duality typically is a "problem," usually lose consciousness (of duality) upon death, even if they remain in individuated states (rather than being absorbed into some god or ultimate reality). In certain East Asian traditions, especially Daoism and Buddhism, duality/individuality is also a problem to be overcome and therefore postmortem destinations ultimately involve the loss of individuality, whether as absorption into the Dao/whole or the "blowing out" of nirvana. Again by contrast, duality and individuality do not seem to be ultimate problems for the indigenous traditions of sub-Saharan Africa and the Americas (where the self itself is often multi-parted); rather, ultimate norms and goals usually involve right relationship with ancestors, to the realm of which one goes upon death (if one lives in right relationship with them and others during life).

How Do I Get There?

Of all the "self" questions of my book, this one felt most unruly due to an overabundance of content. Most basically, this question asks how some religion is practiced; answers to it could fill books. Also, matters of practice do not appear to be philosophical issues per se, since questions of truth and value do not arise for them as such—except in the case of the question of whether one's particular practice is "true" in the sense of leading to its destination. This, then, was the way my book focused this question, especially as filtered through the western-Christian problem of religious pluralism: Do all religious paths lead to their destination, or only one, or none at all? In other words, can all religions be true (or valuable or useful), or only some, one, or none?

For starters, let us recognize that postmortem destinations are not the only destinations that matter in religious traditions. Even a religion that is as seemingly "heaven-focused" as Christianity conceives of salvation *not* as entering heaven (after death) but as being saved from sin (in this world). The same is true for most religions, viz., that they have both postmortem and this-worldly "destinations." In fact, some religions are really only concerned with this-worldly destinations or do not have postmortem destinations at all. All of this is to say that in asking whether the practice of some religion successfully reaches some destination, we are asking as much about, if not more than, whether it achieves some this-worldly destination as some postmortem destination.

As for the content of this book, the chapters on the Venda and Nguni stress the importance of maintaining harmonious ancestral and communal relations through the correct practice of one's ritual responsibilities. This too is the case both in Candomblé, where rituals are itemized as initiation, possession, and sacrifice, and in many Native American traditions, where "all my relations" includes natural objects and organisms, ancestors and spiritual beings, even human-made objects. Although Derrida-ism is of course not a religion, plenty of postmodern theologians see a "religion beyond religion" in his works, one that practices hospitality toward the other and openness to the future. For Confucianism, correct practice of "ritual" is all-important, as is moral self-cultivation. In Daoism, meditative techniques are more frequent, as are yogic, dietary, and other practices. (Although, as the saying goes, every Chinese person, traditionally, was not only both Confucian and Daoist but also

Buddhist as well.) For Shinto, we learn about the importance of cleansing impurities, maintaining purity, observing societal norms, and cultivating personal conduct. In the case of Nyāya it is the practice of philosophy and attainment of knowledge that is most important (though of course one's dharmic responsibilities are also be crucially important). The fourteen-sage path of Jainism is structured into the "Three Jewels" of deep faith, pure conduct, and right knowledge, with the chapter on Haribhadra emphasizing the ascetic practice of *bhava-tapas*. And Islam of course follows the "Five Pillars," though the chapter on Iqbal stresses self-actualization and the discipline of love (*'ishq*).

Do all these practices successfully reach their destinations? For starters, especially with respect to this-worldly destinations, we can say, "of course so," or at least "it seems so," since these techniques have been practiced for centuries (in most cases) and therefore must successfully lead to some related destination or produce some related goal, be that salvation, obedience, submission, generation of good karma (or removal of [bad] karma), balance, harmony, purification, healing, proper relationality, or other. But are all these religions "true," you might nevertheless ask? Well, for one answer to this question, the *ultimate* postmortem question, we will just have to wait and see. But for now, not only can we say, to repeat, that each of these sets of practices sure seems to "work" for its practitioners, but we can also observe that each of these sets of practices seems tailored for its practitioners. This is yet another case in which we see that only certain kinds of selves with certain kinds of original conditions reach certain kinds of destinations *by means of certain kinds of practices*. If you want to live in alignment with the Dao, you engage in Daoist meditative, yogic, and dietary techniques; you do not undertake Shinto rituals of purification, master Indian logic and metaphysics, sacrifice a cow to your ancestors, or ask forgiveness of your sins.

What Obstacles Are in My Way?

Our fifth and final question about the self asks about the obstacles in the way of the "self" reaching its destination(s). As I wrote in my textbook, answers to this question involve everything from our "original conditions" (of sinfulness, ignorance, imbalance, etc.), to our "bad actions" (that are sinful, ignorant, unharmonious etc.), to the "bad actions" of evil beings (like malevolent gods, demons, witches, etc.), to our individuated existence itself (in which we are separated from what is really real), to other human beings, especially the unjust and oppressive social environments and institutions that humans create and perpetuate (here mentioning slavery and racism, patriarchy and sexism, even capitalism and classism in cases where they serve unjust and oppressive ends). But the focus of the corresponding chapter of my book, as well as this conclusion, is religion itself, since notable religio-philosophers have found religion to be one of the biggest impediments to the "self" reaching its destination, especially when religious paths (beliefs, practices, moralities) get confused as the end rather than the means.

This said, there is really only one case in this volume in which we see hints of going "beyond religion" or "against religion" for the sake of being "truly religious"—Daoism. I will address that in time. For all the others, I will speak more generally about the obstacles that stand in the way of the destinations for the "selves" of these "religions." To begin with the Venda and Nguni, obstacles include failing to meet one's communal and ancestral duties, falling into misrelation with ancestors, and suffering sickness and misfortune (at the hands of the ancestors or malevolent beings). Similarly, in Candomblé, it is a neglect of ritual obligations (in this case with regards to the *orixá* and ancestors) that causes a misbalance of *axé*, resulting in sickness or misfortune. In many Native American traditions, at least the ones featured in this volume, the greatest obstacle is failure to heed one's moral guide, which causes relations to be strained with spiritual beings, human beings, and all living things. For Derrida, we might say that the chief obstacle is the "dream of presence," our seemingly irrepressible desire to convey meaning without loss, to be immediately and intuitively self-present, to have met the moral law without exception, to have fulfilled our responsibilities and obligations to every other, and so forth. In the case of Confucianism, improper moral education and insufficient ritual-ethical cultivation are the usual suspects, at least in classical Confucianism. As for classical Daoism, obstacles encompass all the ways in which we get misaligned with the natural, spontaneous, effortless way of the Dao. Here, Confucians were sometimes a target, as their efforts to "cut, file, and polish" the "self" through moral self-cultivation were accused of making unnaturally bad that which was naturally good. Thus, the anti-moralistic, even anti-social, aspects of classical Daoism, which sometimes flaunted (at least in text) the social conventions, moral norms, and cultivation techniques of Confucianism. (It is not for nothing, then, that Daoism is referred to in this volume as "radical, even subversive.") Moving on to Shinto, impurity is the obvious obstacle. In the case of South Asia generally, ignorance is one crucial obstacle, especially as caused by and causing (bad) karma, which keeps us bound to the wheel of rebirth. Finally, in the case of Iqbal the greatest obstacle seems to be the failure to self-actualize through docility, negligence, diminishing faculties and capacities, and waning sensibilities and capabilities.

At the risk of repetition, this comparison again shows that the obstacles "selves" encounter are particular to the paths they are on, which are particular to the destinations they seek, which are particular to their original conditions, which are particular to the kinds of selves they are. If I know who I am (in some religio-philosophical tradition), then I know my original condition, the destination I must reach, the path I must walk to reach that destination, and the obstacles I will encounter along the way. This said, when religion itself becomes an obstacle on the path I must walk to the destination I must reach, then things are a bit, well, out of the ordinary.

Given that religions are institutions that must codify beliefs, routinize practices, stipulate moralities, and organize social power, they obviously cannot hold these beliefs, practices, moralities, and polities as obstacles to be overcome. Why then do some religio-philosophers come to see their very religion (or aspects thereof) as an obstacle to be overcome? (Here, I am thinking of some of the examples I showcased in my textbook, especially ones that come from Christian mysticism, Islamic mysticism, and Zen Buddhism.) Attempts to answer to this question might take us a bit afield of the central focus of the present volume; nevertheless, I will at least observe that, if religion concerns matters of "ultimate concern," whereas religious institutions are concerned with doctrines, rituals, moralities, and polities that, at least in some sense, have temporal origins and histories, then it is not such a stretch to see how the latter could come to be viewed by some as an obstacle to the former (especially in contexts where religious and political power coincide or intermingle).

Evaluation

Finally, let us ask what it would mean to evaluate these selves, their conditions, destinations, paths, and obstacles. Readers of my textbook will know that I think of evaluation primarily as a personal activity, one that is intimately related to how I choose to live my live. (Of course, it is dialogical too, insofar as I engage in discussion and debate with others—but this too is quite personal for me.) Readers of my textbook will also know that I reject both the claim that evaluation can't be done, for lack of "tools," and the view that evaluation shouldn't be done, for fear of offending the "other." With regards to the former, I forward five tools for evaluation in my textbook: argument analysis, theory assessment, probability calculation, experiential intuition and interpretive insight, and authority clarification. (More on some of these soon.) With regards to the latter, I argued that we respect the other—and ourselves—in taking "seriously" their ideas about what is real, true, and good, asking whether these ideas could be real, true, and good for us (rather than setting them aside as interesting curiosities). This is not for the sake of appropriation or denigration; rather, it is to respect the other, as well as myself (as one who also cares about what is real, true, and good).

As for the tools that I find especially relevant for the evaluation of the "selves" contained in this volume, I will focus on two: theory assessment, and experiential intuition and interpretive insight. (Generally speaking, these are the ones that I find most useful to my students and myself.)

Theory assessment looks at how some theory—here, of "self"—fares with respect criteria that generally get employed in ascertaining the truth of some theory, empirical adequacy, external coherence, and practical usefulness most of all (though also internal consistency, theoretical simplicity, and explanatory scope). Is there empirical evidence relevant to the truth of these theories? Do these theories cohere or fit with other widely accepted practices, values, and ideas? Are they useful to how we live our lives, whether individually or socially? Note that what counts as relevant empirical evidence will vary, as will the relevant practices, values, and ideas with which fit should be achieved, also of course what is useful to some individual and their society. Nevertheless, these criteria give us questions to begin asking about our own and other theories of "self," ones that allow us to get some critical perspective on what is otherwise merely assumed, ones that might even lead us to modify or replace our own personally held view of "self" (as indeed has happened for me over the years).

Experiential intuition and interpretive insight are even more "personal." With the former, I have in mind a rudimentary phenomenology that attends to the "lived experience" or "life world" of others and oneself. Doing so for others—here, the religio-philosophers and religio-philosophies featured in this book—helps us understand and appreciate why they see the world (and "self") the way they do. Doing so for oneself—here, one's own views about "self"—helps us understand and appreciate why we see the world (and "self") the way we do. Interpretive insight takes this a step further, opening up one's own life-world to the other. Here, I have in mind a rudimentary (Gadamerian) hermeneutics in which the act of interpretation "fuses" the "horizons" of the other (often a text in the case of Gadamer) and oneself (often a reader in the case of Gadamer). This is not to say that other/text and self/reader become mystically unified; rather, that the self/reader not only comes to awareness of the "prejudices" (pre-judgments) brought to the "interpretation" of the other/text but also makes those "prejudices" vulnerable to correction by the other/text. Might any of the ideas in this book, any of these theories of "self," come to challenge your own worldview, your own theories of "self"?

This, for me, is the personal aspect of (global) philosophy of religion, which requires a healthy dose of humility and fallibility, not to mention a goodly measure of contextual sensitivity.

You will recall that one comparative observation above was that (traditional) theories of "self" align with their conditions, destinations, paths, and obstacles. Nguni selves have Nguni conditions, destinations, paths, and obstacles; Shinto, Shinto ones; Jain, Jain ones. This is true enough, especially traditionally. But things are not so traditional anymore. The world has become much "smaller," to be sure. The institutionalized religio-philosophical traditions are not what they once were. Multiple-belonging is more common, as are innovated, hybridized, individualized religious paths. As I tell my students, one of the boons of studying religion critically is that it makes possible the seeing and doing of new modalities of religiosity, ones that need not fit into the cookie-cutter shapes of institutionalized religion.

So, contextual sensitivity, yes—by all means. And with that, deep humility—there are so many other ways of seeing the world, of understanding who we are, where we are going, how we get there, and what obstacles are in our way. But with those, a fallibility that is open to "thinking differently," understanding that this need not mean (and usually doesn't mean) swapping out one whole system/religion for another. Rather, thinking differently can simply involve enriching one's current understanding of oneself with others' views of self.

We have things to learn from one another. Indeed, I have learned much from all the authors of this book—about the importance of ancestors, destiny, relationality, plurality, cultivation, balance, purity, knowledge, non-violence, self-actualization. No doubt my view of self has been enriched and therefore changed. I hope yours has been as well.

Notes

1. Knepper (2022).
2. See the third paragraph of Lambert, Chapter 5, in this volume for some of these possible respects, especially as they pattern Western philosophy.
3. Here, I note some of the many non-Western "self" terms present in this book: *murunzi* (lit., "shadow") for the Venda; *uMina/ubumina* (with meanings that range from soul, to spirit, to breath, to wind or air) for the Nguniu; *ori* (literally "head"), which is just one of many dimensions of "self" in Candomblé; *niyá* (breath), *nagí* (ghost), *sičun* (spirit), and *nağila* (energy) for the Lakota; *shēn* (body/self), *tǐ* (body), *xíng* (form or shape), and *xīn* (psycho-spiritual center of human personhood) for Daoists in particular and the Chinese in general; *ātman* and *jiva* in South Asia (especially for Udayana and Haribhadra); and *khudi* in the case of Iqbal.

Bibliography

Knepper, Timothy D. 2022. *Philosophies of Religion: A Global and Critical Introduction.* London: Bloomsbury.

Index

A Treatise of Human Nature, 72. *See* Hume.
absence, 75, 79, 168, 172, 293, 299 n. 2, 306
Absolute, 49, 63, 116, 274–6, 280–2, 284–5, 293, 307
Absolute Ego, 274–6, 280–5
absolute conditions, 299 n. 3, 311
absolute responsibility, 304 n. 2, 309
absolute sovereignty, 311–12
absorbing, 157, 272–3, 280, 282–3
act, 48–50, 112–13, 130, 246, 262–3, 276, 314
action, 21, 32–3, 36, 45, 63, 76–9, 89, 94–5, 108, 135, 180, 224, 227–8, 239, 242, 253–4, 259–60, 263–4, 268–9, 273–5, 280, 284, 286, 298, 325
actualizing, 51–2, 246, 267–9, 272–3, 277, 280–2, 327
Advaita Vedānta, 17–19, 31, 34 n. 1
Africa, 2, 6, 8, 27 n. 1, 42-3, 160, 164, 179–80, 216–18, 321
African Indigenous Knowledge Systems, 180, 218, 321–2
African spiritualties, 219–20
Afro-Atlantic self, 42
Afro-Brazilian religions, 61–2, 67, 69
Afro-Catholic syncretism, 44, 61–2
afterlife, 25, 38, 89, 231, 321
Agamben, Giorgio, 313
agent, 24–5, 27 n. 12, 64, 68, 129, 180, 186–7, 239, 249, 273
ahanachi (畔放), 108
ahiṃsā, 32, 37, 84, 327. *See* non-violence
aiê (earthly realm), 43–4, 55
akaki/mei (明), brightness, 108
Akan Thought, 165–71
Ancestral Connection, 171–2, 177
Al – Jilani, Abdul Qadi, 270

Al-Ash'ari, 271
Albahari, Miri, 291
alchemy, 195–5, 202, 206
Algeria, 10, 288, 298, 299 n. 6, 301
alkéé naa'aashii, a universal process of opposition, 252
Amaterasu, Amaterasu Oomikami, (天照大神), 94, 97, 101, 111, 116
amatsutsumi (天つ罪), 108, 112–13 n. 1
Ames, Roger, 128, 131, 133, 138 n. 14, 207
Amiotte, Arthur, 248
Analects of Confucius, 128, 130, 132, 135–6, 137 n. 4, 6, 138 n. 9, 144
ancestor, 9, 43, 57, 94, 101, 148, 150, 152–3, 157, 172, 177, 186–7, 219, 221, 227, 229–32, 235, 242–5, 262–5, 320–4, 327
ancestrology, 215
Angola, 43
Anishinabe, 241–2
anthropology, 66, 152, 184, 186, 193, 195, 197, 203, 207, 209, 211, 272–3, 282
apophatic meditation, 7, 188–9, 190–1, 193, 195–8, 202
apprehension, 22, 25, 273, 280
Aquinas, Thomas, 3, 17
arahitogami (現人神), 96
aramitama (raging fierce *tama*, 荒魂), 98, 104, 121
argumentation, 16–17, 26, 297
aristocrats, 243–4, 262
Aristotle, 4, 72–3
Arnold, Sir Thomas, 270–1
ascesis, 76
Ashiharanonakatsu (葦原中国), 111
Asrár, 268–70, 273, 275, 277 n. 2, 278 n. 9, 284, 286 n. 4

assentamento (settlement), 47, 58–9, 61–2, 64, 66, 69
assento (seat), 47, 61–2, 64, 66, 69
assimilating, 274, 281, 285–6
at.oow, 262–5
atheism, 306, 311, 313–14
ātman, self, 3, 16, 19–22, 25, 27 n. 10
Ātmatattvaviveka (Investigation of the Reality of the Self), 16, 18, 26, 31. *See* Udayana
attributes, 33, 72, 87, 222, 240, 272–3, 281–2, 285, 311
Augras, Monique, 44, 49, 51, 58, 62–3
Augustine, 4, 295
authority, 42, 137, 146, 154–6, 163, 325
auto-affection, 292–3, 299 n. 4, 304 n. 1
autonomous, 19, 32–3, 58, 128–9, 133–4, 238–40, 248, 310, 312
awakening, 268–71, 277, 283, 285
awareness, 4, 11, 18, 31–3, 38, 44, 77–9, 83, 126–8, 130, 133, 153, 156, 186–7, 190, 223, 242, 274, 282, 289, 299 n. 2, 307, 318, 326
axé (spiritual life force), 44–5, 48–50
ayamachi (過), 108

balance, 44–5, 52, 100, 103, 123, 131, 144–5, 149, 163, 235, 243, 246–7, 252–4, 265, 319–20, 323–4, 327
Bantu, 43, 52 n. 1, 59 n. 1, 61, 161–2, 164, 217
Barysan, 102, 106 n. 9
basic monism, 50
Basso, Keith, 239
Bastide, Roger, 46–7, 50–1
Bataille, Georges, 310–12
batsu (punishment, 罰), 123
batuque (religious tradition), 42–3
becoming, 101, 122, 128, 133–4, 138 n. 14, 146, 150, 170, 186, 193, 263, 268, 271–5, 281–5
beggininglessness, 220, 225
behavioral patterns, 224
being, 32, 42, 44, 47, 62, 68, 73, 76, 90, 93–4, 103, 161, 165, 176–7, 179–81, 198, 201, 206, 223, 230, 233, 239, 241–9, 271, 286, 295
Being (Ontology of), 167–8, 176

Being and Time, 304
belief, 56, 93–7, 103–4, 108, 114, 117–18, 122, 129, 133, 146, 153, 164, 166, 168, 179–80, 193, 216, 218, 231, 324–5
Bell, Daniel, 137
benevolence, benevolent, 37, 122, 143, 146
Benin, 43
Bennington, Georffrey, 294–6
Benzaiten (弁財天), 97
Bhāsarvajña, 17
Bilimoria, Purushottama, v, 27 n. 10, 28 n. 18, 26, 32–4, 36, 39 n. 2
birth, born, 18, 20–1, 25, 28 n. 3, 33, 45, 47, 49–50, 56, 62, 89, 108, 111–12, 130, 164, 167, 180, 191, 205, 219, 221–4, 227–9, 232–3, 244–6, 248–9, 253, 288, 292, 320
Blessingway, 253–4
bliss, *ānanda*, 19, 21, 33, 38, 90
blood sacrifice, 45, 48–9, 69
Book of Changes [*Yijing* 易經], 131, 139
Book of Master Zhuang, 155, 187, 189, 192, 194, 199 n. 4. *See* Zhuāngzǐ
Book of Rites [*Liji* 禮記] 139 n. 19
Book of Songs (Shijing), 144
Book of Venerable Masters, 189, 191, 194
borders, 217, 301, 310–12. *See* Lǎozǐ
bori (head-feeding ceremony), 48, 57–9
Born-to-Water, 246
Bosatsu (菩薩), 97
Bradley, Francis 10, 270–1, 276, 286 n. 3, 284–5
Brazil, 42–4, 55, 61
British, 9, 268–9, 272, 274, 276
Buddhism, 18–19, 34 n. 2, 90, 95–7, 99, 103, 105 n. 4, 181, 190, 199, 321, 325
    Mādhyamika, 18
    Mahāyāna, 18
    Sautrāntika, 18
    Vaibhāṣika, 18
    Yogācāra, 18–19
    Zen, Chan, 199 n. 4, 325
Buddhist, 3–5, 11, 16, 18–20, 22–6, 27 n. 8, 28 n. 21, 31–3, 78, 83, 86, 89–91, 97, 103, 105 n. 4, 116, 199 n. 4, 206, 319, 323
    Buddhist philosophers: Dharmakīrti 18, 78, Jñānaśrīmitra 18, 27 n. 8
búzios (cowrie shells) 45, 57

cabeça (head), 45, 55, 58, 60
Cambridge, 9, 268, 271, 274–5, 289
Candomblé, 2–4, 41–53, 55–9, 61- 4, 66–9, 318–22, 324, 327 n. 3
Candomblé Angola, 43, 52 n. 1, 53 n. 3
Candomblé Jêje, 43, 52 n. 1
Candomblé Nagô, 43–4, 52 n. 1
capaciousness, 143
Capps, Lisa, 223
carrego (load), 45–7, 51, 58–9
carrego de santo (saint-load), 45–6, 58
Cārvāka, Lokāyata (Materialists), 3, 16, 18–20, 22, 26, 31–3, 34 n. 3
caste, 265
categories, 3–4, 7, 11, 23, 27 n. 6, 32, 48, 72, 74, 108, 122, 127, 131, 138 n. 12, 161–2, 165, 173, 184, 188–90, 207, 209, 240–1, 245, 249, 262, 280, 317
Categories, 72. *See* Aristotle
Catholic, 42–4, 61–2, 211
causality, causation, 3, 5, 18, 24, 31–3, 38, 49, 78, 83, 95, 98, 116–17, 122, 131, 217, 243, 248, 305
cause, 5, 20, 32–3, 38, 78, 83, 255, 274, 277 n. 4, 281, 306, 324
cavalo de santo (saint's horse), 49
Chadha, Monima, 16, 28 n. 15
Chakrabarti, Arindam, 16, 28 n. 15
Chakrabarti, Kisor Kumar, 16, 22, 24, 28 n. 15
Changing Woman, 246
chantways, 253
Chewa Culture / Language, 160–4
character, 122, 128, 135, 138 n. 13, 143–5, 149, 156, 173, 193, 210, 218, 221–2, 244, 247–8, 263–4, 282
Chilkat blankets, 264
chimaki, 110
Christianity, 96, 103, 116, 155, 180–1, 202, 252, 308, 320, 322
Circumfession, 288, 294–8
clan hat, 265
Classical Indian Philosophy of Mind, 16
cleansing, 48, 98, 104, 109–12, 116, 231, 323
clothing, 241, 254
cogito, 162–3, 269, 273–4, 289–91, 293, 303, 305–6. *See* Descartes, Rene

cognition, 3, 18, 20, 22–6, 31–4, 36–7, 78–9, 197
colonial, colonialism, 3, 44, 61, 179, 181, 185, 217, 268–72, 301
commoners, 177, 243–4, 262
communal principles, 223–4
Communalism / Communitarianism, 6, 8, 160–5, 172–3, 180, 218–20, 222–4, 227–9, 230, 232, 235, 318, 322, 324
communicability, 116
Community and Personhood, 159–66, 180–1
community, 6, 8–9, 45, 58–9, 103, 108, 128, 130, 132–4, 137, 145–6, 153, 157, 162–4, 166, 172, 177, 183, 188, 195, 198, 206, 211, 219–20, 222–4, 227–9, 232, 235, 238–9, 242, 244, 246, 248–9, 253–4, 257–60, 262–3, 265, 268, 270, 281, 283, 285–6, 288–9, 320
comparative categories, 7, 184, 188–90, 201, 209–11
comparative philosophy, 2, 17, 186–7, 195, 198, 201, 205, 209–11, 317–27
comparative religion, 202
complementary opposition, 243, 252
concept, conception, 1–13, 15–26, 31–4, 36–9, 42–3, 45, 55, 87, 89, 94, 96–105, 108–9, 114–29, 132–7, 143–6, 153, 160–73, 176, 179–80, 183–4, 189–90, 195–7, 201–6, 215–29, 237–49, 252, 255, 262–3, 267–70, 273–4, 277–8, 280–6, 287–303, 305–7, 311–14, 317, 319
conduct, 90, 100, 127, 130–3, 143, 145–6, 148–51, 153–7, 193, 268, 275, 323
Confucian, Confucianism, 6, 96, 99, 127–37, 138, 143–81, 193, 202, 211, 318–24
Confucius, 128, 130, 132, 136, 138 n. 9, 143–6, 148–51, 155–6
Congo, 43
conscious, 20, 33, 41, 63, 76, 79, 187, 223, 284, 291, 321
consciousness, 9–10, 18–20, 23–4, 32–4, 44, 59, 63, 78–9, 86, 90, 100, 116–18, 170–1, 189–90, 191, 194–5, 198, 209–11, 218, 221, 240, 271–6, 282, 284, 293, 303, 321

contemplative practice, 7, 184, 188–90, 194, 197–8, 202
contemplative psychology, 184, 188–90, 193, 195, 206, 210
continuity, 21, 24, 33, 91, 116, 218–21, 225, 227–9, 232, 293
coppers, 264
correlate, 79, 274–6, 280, 285
cosmic, 6, 52, 77, 132, 190, 221, 242, 284–6
cosmological cycles, 89, 219, 221, 225–7
cosmology, 55, 103, 126, 131–2, 134, 138 n. 11, 12, 179, 186, 188, 190, 195–6, 202, 216, 219, 221, 225, 227–9, 252, 255
cosmos, 6, 67, 131–2, 138 n. 12, 187, 201, 221, 238, 245, 248–9, 252, 254, 257, 260, 277
cosmos (*tian*), 131–2, 138 n. 12
counterfactual, (though experiment) 13, 15–17, 38, 168, 295
Coyote, 247
crest, 262–4
Cremieux Decree, 298
Critique of Pure Reason, 74
cross-cultural philosophy, 1–2, 4–5, 7, 10, 15–17, 27 n. 1, 2, 183–4, 195, 198, 201–3, 205, 209–10, 317–18
crossroads of forces, 42, 44
Cuban Lucumí, 43
cultivation, 37, 55, 58, 69, 94, 296
culture, 1, 3, 6, 8, 11, 67, 95–6, 100, 102, 108, 110, 129, 145, 149, 157, 160–2, 164, 166–8, 171–2, 176–80, 184, 186, 193, 201, 203, 205–7, 209–10, 215–20, 224–5, 238, 243, 249, 270, 289–90

Daagh Dehlvi, 270
Daikokten (大黒天), 97
Dao (Tao, path or way), 6–7, 127–8, 130–2, 138 n. 7, 144, 149–51, 154, 184, 188–9, 191–8, 203, 206, 321, 324
Daoism, 128, 155, 183–5, 187–98, 198 n. 2, 199 n. 4, 201–3, 205–7, 318–21, 324, 327 n. 3
Dasein, 304
Dasti, Matthew, 28 n. 28, 33–34, 36–7
Daya, Krishna, 36

Dazaifu (大宰府), 98
Dé 德 (virtue, power or influence), 193
debates, 3–4, 6–7, 11, 13, 16–19, 21–2, 26, 27 n. 2, 31, 36, 38, 148, 150, 154–5, 163, 172, 173 n. 4, 298, 311, 319, 325
decolonial, decolonize, 9–10, 270, 277
deconstruction, 289, 299 n. 3, 304 n. 1
deep-sleep, 26, 37
Deleuze, Gilles, 50
demerit, 20, 24, 34, 38
Derrida, Jacques, 10, 210–11, 287–98, 299 n. 3–8, 301–3, 304 n. 1, 2, 4, 306–8, 310–14, 315 n. 1–2, 318–20, 322, 324
Descartes, Rene, 128, 162–3, 272–4, 277, 289–92, 297, 303, 305. *See cogito*.
desire, 7, 20–21, 24, 26, 28 n. 17, 33, 37, 76, 89, 90–1, 104, 127–8, 130, 133, 135, 149, 153, 190, 192–3, 258, 281, 284–6, 298, 303, 324
destiny, 26, 37, 45, 55–8, 168, 206, 262, 264–5, 269, 319–20, 327
determinate, 82, 295, 303
Detwiler, Fritz, 8–9, 237–66
developmental, 135, 153, 271, 280, 282, 285
dialogue, 17, 64, 89, 277, 296
Diné, 9, 241–2, 246–7, 252–5, 318, 320
disposition, 7, 18, 20, 25, 28, 31, 36, 38, 135, 143–6, 148–9, 185, 190, 205, 282
diversity, 83, 211, 249
divination, 45–6, 320
divine, 4–5, 43, 46, 51, 55, 58–9, 68, 94–5, 97, 100–4, 110, 116, 120–1, 123, 194–5, 201–2, 271–3, 275, 277, 280–3, 285–6, 307–8, 320
doctrine, 19, 28 n. 21, 76, 82, 85, 129, 164, 193, 198, 210, 271, 325
Doctrine of the Mean, 156–7
Dominican Vudú, 43
Dooling, D. M., 247–8
dualistic, 50, 121, 189, 252
Dzobo, N. K., 162

Earth-Surface World, 246
ebó (offering), 48, 58
ecological, ecology, 8, 67–8, 198, 209
effortlessness, 189, 193, 324

ego, 86, 138 n. 7, 174, 269, 271–6, 280–6
egodicy, 301–2, 304 n . 2
egoism, 99, 128
egum (soul of the dead), *egum de santo* (saint-egum), 46
f dos Santos, Juana, 43, 57, 59 n. 1
eledá (true soul), 46, 57
Elinor Ochs, 223
Eloff, Aragorn, 11
embodied freedom, 102–3
embodiment, embodied, 20–1, 26, 33, 37, 44, 68, 90, 101, 127, 136, 145, 157, 189, 198, 205, 207, 209–10, 264, 320
emergence, 4, 6, 18, 20, 31–3, 58, 132, 245, 247, 272, 276, 282, 285, 319
emi (soul), 46
emotions, 7, 21, 25, 33, 52, 68, 86, 104, 114, 117–18, 121, 126, 131, 148–50, 157, 168–9, 172, 186, 190, 242, 263
Emperor Daigo (醍醐, r. 897–930), 108
Engishiki (延喜式, 905), 95, 108
English, 4, 9, 12, 36, 72, 126, 148, 186, 215, 233, 252, 271, 273, 284, 299 318
English language, 1–2, 168, 268–70
Eno, Robert, 137 n. 5
enredo (storyline/plot), *enredo de santo* (saint's storyline), 47, 51–2, 58–9
epistemology, epistemic, 2–3, 7, 11, 15–16, 36, 78, 83–4, 163, 166, 171, 216, 219–20, 268, 273, 289–90
equiprimordial (equally original or co-original; *gleichursprünglichkeit*), 118
erê (childlike quality of orixá), 46
ethical maturity / moral achievement, 164, 180–1
European, 5, 8–10, 12–13, 16, 129, 211, 217, 267, 271, 290, 293, 301
ever-changing dynamism, 98, 121, 319
evolutionary, 275, 282, 284–5, 289
Ewe, 43, 52
existence, 2–5, 7–8, 16–26, 31–4, 37–9, 42–44, 47, 50, 55, 73–74, 76, 83, 86–7, 94, 97–8, 115, 123, 132–3, 162, 169–72, 185–7, 196, 202, 229–30, 233, 245, 252, 255, 270, 290, 293, 295, 298, 311, 321, 323

existential, 5, 9, 97, 173, 198, 235, 267, 273, 280, 290
experience, 9, 19–22, 25, 28, 32, 35, 44, 48–51, 63, 67–9, 75, 77, 91, 133, 136, 138 n. 7, 156, 163, 168, 171–2, 179, 181, 187–90, 194–8, 209–11, 222–3, 228–30, 234, 240–1, 257–8, 262, 269, 273–6, 282, 291–3, 295, 297, 299 n. 4, 6, 301–3, 305–9, 326
Ezzy, Doug, 242, 248

fazer o santo (making the saint), 47, 62
feelings, 20, 33, 116–18, 133, 149, 190
feitura (making/initiation), 47–52, 58–9, 62–3
feminine, 100, 102, 247–8
feminism, 206, 209–10, 310
ferramentas (iron tools), 47, 64, 66
Fichte, Johann G. 10, 271–2, 276
fiction, 209, 292–3, 296, 298, 240, 311, 313–14
Fingarette, Herbert, 5–6, 127–8, 134, 138, 143, 151
First Man / First Woman, 245–7, 252
Five Elements and Five Phases, 186–7, 190
Flaksman, Clara, 45, 47, 51, 53
Flanagan, Owen, 34 n. 2, 129, 135, 137 n. 2, 138 n. 7
focus-field self, 131–2, 135, 138 n. 14
Fon, 43, 52 n. 1
Force Thesis (Tempels), 161–3
form, 21, 43, 44, 46–50, 55, 57, 62–3, 66, 68, 72–4, 77, 82, 90, 93–4, 97, 102, 130–2, 135, 137, 138 n. 18, 145, 147, 151–3, 167, 179–80, 185, 195–6, 201, 203, 205–6, 221–2, 230, 245–8, 258, 262, 264, 274, 284–5, 297, 301, 303
formline art, 242
fractal self, 42
France, 10, 288–9, 298
freedom, 21, 25, 28 n. 25, 36, 38, 39 n. 3, 89, 96, 102–3, 121, 192, 268, 272, 275, 278 n. 8, 280, 286 n. 3, 301, 303, 319–20
Fujiwara no Seika (1561–1619, 藤原惺窩)
fujō, 不浄, 99
fundamentos (foundations), 47
Funmaker, George, 237, 249 n. 1

*God, 2–3, 16, 33–4, 37
Gadamer, Hans-Georg 326
Ganeri, Jonardon, 12, 34 n. 2, 84
Gautama, Akṣapāda, 17, 27 n. 5, 28 n. 25, 36–7, 39 n. 3
Geisel, Theodor, 291
genius loci, 102
Ghana, 43
Gift of Death, 304 n. 2
Glacier Bay story, 263–4
Glas, 294
Gnaški, Crazy Buffalo, 247
gnoseological, gnoseology, 79, 88, 90
goal, 34, 36, 38, 46, 76–9, 82, 126, 184, 211, 246, 249, 252, 272, 280–2, 322–3
God, 17, 43, 115, 163, 165, 227, 229, 270–2, 276, 280–5, 286 n. 1, 307–8, 311, 314, 315 n. 1, 321, 323
God, Christian, 116, 229 n. 1, 293–5, 308
gods, 32, 51, 68, 94–5, 97–8, 111, 229, 247, 255
Goddess, Sun Goddess Amaterasu, 94–5, 97, 101, 111, 116
Goldman, Marcio, 45–7, 49–51, 53 n. 3, 62–3
goodness, 98, 143, 155–6, 246, 252–3, 272, 311, 319–20
gosekku (五節供, five season festivals), 110
Great Learning [*Daxue* 大學], 6, 132–3, 146
Gross, Lawrence, 241–2
Guisso, Richard, 134
Guǎnzǐ 管子 (*Kuǎnzǐ*; Book of Master Guan) 191
gyoku (玉), 120

habitus, 282, 290
Haitian Vodou, 43
Halloy, Arnaud, 48, 68
Han Feizi, 155
haŋbléčheyapi (Vision Quest), 257, 259
happiness, 21, 34, 36, 38, 115–16, 122, 246, 253
harae (祓), 96, 98, 108–10, 112, 123
haraenokotoba (祓詞), 116
Haribhadrasūri, Haribhadra, 4, 32, 71–80, 83, 87, 319–20, 323, 327 n. 3

harmony / harmonious, 9, 100, 103, 115, 120–1, 132, 148–9, 151, 160, 235, 243, 246–8, 264–5, 286, 323
hashira (柱, pillar), 120
Haudenosaunee, 241
Hayao Miyazaki (宮崎駿), 102, 106 n. 6
Hayashi Razan (1583–1657, 林羅山), 99
heart, 56, 139 n. 19, 146, 164, 186, 195, 222, 240, 242–3, 280, 284, 373
heart-mind, (*xīn* 心), 7, 135–6, 138 n. 9, 184, 189–91, 193–6, 202–3, 206–7, 211, 327 n. 3
heart-mind (*kokoro*, 心), 99, 116–17
Hegel, George W. F., 127, 137, 271, 299 n. 7
Heian (平安), 98, 100–1, 103
Heidegger, Martin, 210, 299 n. 8, 302, 305–7
Herskovits, Melville J., 42
heyókȟa (contraries), 258–9
himorogi, (神籬), 120
hinahachi (樋放), 108
Hinamatsuri, 110
Hinduism, Hindu, Hindus, 16–18, 27, 86, 91, 97, 181
Hirata Atsutane (1776–1834, 平田篤胤), 5, 99
Ho-Chunk, 237
hochxọ, 247
Holy People, 245–7, 253–5
Holy Wind, 245–6
Holyway, 253–4
honji-suijaku (本地垂迹), 96–7, 105 n. 4
hózhọ, 247, 252–5
human, humanistic, humanity, 3–5, 8–10, 12–13, 19, 26, 33, 42, 45, 47, 49–51, 55–6, 59, 61–64, 67, 72, 76–7, 79, 93–5, 98–102, 104, 108–9, 115–18, 120–23, 125–34, 138 n. 9, 12, 14, 143–6, 148–51, 156, 160–1, 164–5, 167–73, 174 n. 5, 180, 184–98, 201, 205–7, 209–11, 218–22, 228, 230, 233, 235, 238–9
humanness (*ren*), 143–8, 154, 202
Hume, David, 72
huŋká, 258
Husserl, Edmund, 288, 293, 297, 302–3, 306

'ishq, 269–73, 281–6, 323
iaô (new initiate), 49
ibá (shrine), 47, 69
ichirei-shikon (一霊四魂, one-soul-four-spirits), 122
ideality, 293
identity, 4, 6, 8–9, 11, 20–1, 24, 33, 35, 38, 44, 52, 57–9, 62, 68–9, 71–80, 83, 86–91, 126, 128–35, 138 n. 9, 152, 157, 163–73, 185 n. 3, 189, 201, 206, 209, 216, 222, 238, 262, 270–1, 277, 292, 297–8, 301
   identity of *umuntu*, 216, 218–24, 228–9
iktómi, trickster, 248, 258
Ikuenobe, Polycarp, 165–6, 173
imagination, 271, 310, 312
imimoya emihle (good spirits, ancestors), 233–5
immortality, immortalize, immortalizing, 10, 220–1, 269, 272–3, 275, 280–2, 284–5, 286 n. 3
imperceptibility, 21–2, 28 n. 17, 33
impilo (life), 8, 215–16, 220, 224–5, 227–9, 234
incorporation, 44, 46–7, 49–50, 61–2, 64
indeterminate perception, 22–3, 26, 37
India, 17, 26, 32–3, 184, 203, 268–70
Indian philosophy, 3, 15–16, 18–19, 25, 27 n. 10, 31, 33–4, 36, 73–4, 77, 83, 86, 89, 196, 203, 323
Indian, American Indian, 237–8
individual, 4, 6, 8, 10, 20, 22, 24, 27 n. 12, 31, 33–4, 42–53, 55–8, 59 n. 1, 61–3, 66, 68, 73–7, 80, 87–8, 90, 98, 104, 110, 126–8, 130–7, 138 n. 9, 150–1, 157, 160, 162–7, 169, 172–3, 174 n. 6, 176–7, 180, 186, 188–9, 192, 201–2, 211, 218, 220–1, 223–4, 227–9, 231, 235, 257, 259, 263–5, 268–9, 272–3, 275, 281–2, 285, 290–2, 307, 310, 318–19, 321, 326
individuality and identity, 164–6, 172
inference, 21–2, 28, 33
Ingold, Tim, 241
Inipi (Sweat Lodge), 259
initiation, 4, 42, 44, 46–52, 57–8, 62, 66, 68, 322

inner forms, 245–6
inner *kami* (*uchinaru kami*, 内なる神), 102–3
inquices (Bantu deities), 52 n. 1
insan-ul-kadim, the Perfect man, 281–2
insight, 38, 271–3, 277, 325
intellect, 23–4, 86, 280, 282, 284
intellectual, 2, 9, 17–19, 21–2, 36–7, 84, 99, 102, 126, 190, 202, 267–72, 276, 288
intentionality, 4, 77–80, 89, 210, 255
interaction, 6, 10, 67, 105, 131–3, 150–1, 156, 172–3, 210, 219, 234, 238–9, 277, 282, 295, 319–20
interdependency, 120, 127, 131, 185, 218, 220, 227–8, 234
intersubjectivity, 241–2
Introduction to Logic (*Nyāyavatāra*), 83
intuition, 91, 198, 269, 271, 274, 280, 282, 286 n. 3, 325–6
intuitive, 136, 269, 273–4, 280, 284, 324
Investigation of Authorities (*Āptamīmāṃsā*), 83
invisible, 62, 67, 93–4, 97, 103, 114–15, 117, 120–1, 132, 198, 219, 221, 233–4
invisibleness, 114, 120–1
Iŋyaŋ, Rock, 247
ipseity, 297, 301–3
Iqbal, 9–10, 267–77, 277–8 n. 4, 278 n. 5, 6, 7, 8, 9, 10
Irohajiruishō (1144–1165, 色葉字類抄), 101
Isintuism, Isintu, 8, 215–25, 228, 233–4
Islamic, Islam, 9, 181, 269–72, 277 n. 1, 277–8 n. 4, 308, 320–1, 323, 325
iwakura (磐座), 101
iwasaka (磐境), 101
Izanagi (伊弉諾尊), 104, 108, 111–12
Izanami, 111

Jacques Derrida, 294
Jainism, 2–4, 16, 18, 28 n. 21, 31–2, 34 n. 4, 71–80, 82–4, 86–91, 319–20, 323, 326
jigoku (地獄), 103
Jina Mahāvīra, 82–3
jinja (神社), 95–6, 99
jinkaku (人格, personhood), 121

Jñānaśrīmitra, 18, 27 n. 8
jō (情), clarity, 108, 114, 117
jōmeishōchoku (浄明正直), 108–9, 114–15
Jōshi (上巳), 110
juka-shinto (儒家神道), 99
juso (呪詛), 116
justice, 108, 137, 280–3, 285

ḳaa yakgwahéiyagu (shadow), 244
Kagame, Alexis – Shadow Thesis, 164–5
Kaphagawani, Didier N.,159–65, 173
Kinship Relations (Akan), 165
ḳaa yahaayi, Ghost, 244
kagami (鏡, mirror), 120
kagura (神楽), 96
Kagutsuchi, 111
Kaikō (1764, 歌意考), 99
Kakimoto no Hitomaro (柿本野人麻呂), 115
Kamata, Toji, 115–16, 121
kami (神), 4–5, 93–104, 105 n. 4, 114–16, 120–3
Kamo no Mabuchi (1697–1769, 賀茂真淵), 99–100
Kamuf, Peggy, 310
Kan, Sergei, 244, 262, 264
kan'nushi (神主), 96
Kanda shrine (神田明神), 100
Kang, Nam-Soon, 134
Kant, Imanuel, 4, 74, 138 n. 7, 269, 271–2, 280
kara-gokoro (漢意), 99
kāraṇa, 20
karma, 3–4, 24–5, 32, 34, 38, 76, 79, 89–90, 323–4
Karube, Tadashi (苅部, 直), 99
Kasulis, Thomas, 94–6, 116
kegare (穢), 94, 96, 108–12, 123
kessai (潔斎), 96
Khan, Abraham H., 9–10, 267–86
Khaṇḍanakhaṇḍakhādya, 17
khudi, 9, 267–86, 327 n. 3
Kierkegaard, Søren, 304 n. 2, 307
Kinaaldá, 253
kinship, 165, 241, 285
Kita-no-tenmangu (北野天満宮), 98
kiyoki/ jō (浄), purity and clarity, 108, 114
Kluckhohn, Clyde, 247, 249 n. 3, 256 n. 2

Knepper, Tim, xiv, 11, 13 n. 1, 317–27
knowledge, 4, 11, 19–22, 25–6, 28 n. 23, 25, 32, 34, 36–8, 39 n. 3, 77, 79, 83, 89–91, 94, 126, 139 n. 19, 145, 156, 163–4, 179, 184, 218, 220, 241, 244, 247–8, 258, 268, 271, 278 n. 8, 280, 283 n. 1, 285, 286 n. 3, 289, 295, 299 n. 7, 303, 304 n. 4, 306, 311, 320, 323, 327
kóhlá, 258
Kojiki (古事記), 94–5, 99–101, 106 n. 7, 108, 111–12, 114–17, 120–1, 123
Kojiki-den (古事記伝), 95
Kokinwakashū (古今和歌集), 100
kokoro (心), 99, 116–17
kokugaku (国学), 95–7, 99, 105 n. 4, 108, 116, 122–3
Komjathy, Louis, 4, 7, 27 n. 2, 183–213
Konohanasakuyahime (木花之佐久夜毘売), 97
koto (kotoba, words, 言葉), 114–15, 117
koto-no-ha (言の葉), 114
koto (事), 104, 114, 118
kotoage-seji (言挙げせじ), 115
kotoba, 114–16
kotodama (言霊), 4–5, 94, 103–6, 114–18
kuchiyose (口寄せ), 116
Kumamon, 102, 106 n. 9
Kundakunda, 90
kuni umi (国生み), 95
kunitsutsumi (国つ罪), 108
kusaki-koto-tou (草木言問), 115
kusamochi, 110
kushimitma (奇魂), 104, 121
Kuzuhana (くず花), 99

Lakota, 9, 241–2, 247–9, 257–8, 260, 261 n. 1, 2, 318–21, 327 n. 3
Lambert, Andrew, 4–6, 125–57, 327 n. 2
Lǎozǐ 子, *Book of Venerable Masters*, (also: Dàodé jīng 道德經, *Scripture on the Dao and Inner Power*), 189, 191, 193, 196–7
law of opposition, 245
Lawlor, Leonard, 304 n. 1
Levinas, Emmanuel, 301–3, 304 n. 3
Lewis, Mark, 138 n. 11

Lewis, Ray Baldwin, 253
Li, Jin, 137 n. 1, 2
Li, Ling 李零, 138 n. 11
liberation, release, *mokṣa*, 4, 19, 21, 24–6, 32–4, 36–8, 76–80, 83, 87–91
life, 8, 10, 20, 25–6, 27 n. 4, 28 n. 23, 32–3, 37–8, 43–5, 47–8, 55, 57–8, 62, 68–9, 76–9, 89, 96, 98, 103–4, 110, 116, 126–36, 143, 145, 148–52, 160, 162, 179–81, 184, 187, 189, 191, 196, 201–3, 205–6, 210, 215–25, 227–35, 238–49, 252–5, 257–60, 262–4, 268–9, 272–5, 280–2, 284–6, 289, 306, 320–2, 326
life-force, 8, 240–2, 244–5, 247–9
literature, 4, 25, 34 n. 2, 4, 42, 59, 91, 98, 154, 176, 179, 203, 205, 270, 289, 293
Little Wind, 246–7
Locke, John, 128, 291
Loewen, Nathan, 10, 28 n. 18, 287–315
logic, 3, 16–18, 36, 166, 269, 287, 290, 291–2, 294, 297, 317, 323
Logical Investigations, 302
longevity practice, 196, 203
love, 135, 143, 145, 234, 267, 269–3, 281–5, 286 n. 1, 323
luminous, 273–4, 278 n. 9, 282, 284

Magakoto (まがこと, 禍事), 133 n. 3
Magatsuhi (禍津日), 111–12
Majeed, Hasskei Mohammed (Critique of Quasi-physicalism), 169–71
Makhá, Earth, 169–70
makoto (真), 98
makoto-no-kokoro (真の心), 99, 117
malevolent, 122, 231, 253–5, 323–4
Manyōshū (万葉集), 99–100
Maraganedzha, Mutshidzi, 6–7, 159–82
Martin, Craig, 299 n. 7
masuraoburi (益荒男振り), 99–100
materialism, 3, 16, 18–20, 22, 26, 31–4, 185, 193, 268. See Cārvāka, Lokāyata
Matilal, Bimal K., 16, 17, 27 n. 5, 28 n. 15, 73–4, 84
Matolino, Bernard, 6, 160, 162–5, 173
Matory, J. Lorand, 41–2

matrilineal groups, 165, 243–5, 262–4
matrix, 242–5, 247–9, 270
matsuri (rituals, 祭, 祀), 96, 122–3
matsuri-goto (politics, 政), 96
Mbiti, John (Communal Thesis), 6, 160, 162–3
McTaggart, 271–2, 274–5
medicine, 202–3, 255, 258
medicine bundle, 246, 253–5
meditation, 37, 131, 164, 189–93, 195–8, 202, 206, 270, 322–3
Meditations on First Philosophy, 289
Meiji Restoration, 5, 95–6
memory, 7, 20, 24–5, 28 n. 20, 23, 44, 190, 222
Mencius, 125, 151, 153, 155–6
Mengzi 孟子 (text), 125, 131–2, 137 n. 6, 138 n. 8, 143, 146, 150–1, 153, 155–6
Menkiti, Ifeanyi (Normative Personhood) 6, 159–60, 163, 173 n. 2, 180
mental states, 21, 24, 38, 63, 76, 136, 191, 276
mercy, 281, 285
mergence, mergeable, 26, 37, 67, 97, 172
merit, 20, 24, 34, 38
metaphysics, 11, 36, 72–3, 83, 86, 89, 165, 301, 315 n. 2
Metaphysics, 72. See Aristotle
miko (巫女), 116
Milgram, Stanley, 135, 139 n. 20
Mill, John S., 127, 157
Milla Sadr, 271
Mīmāṃsā, 18
mind, 20, 33, 36–7, 78, 94, 99, 117, 126, 131, 133, 135, 138 n. 6, 172, 184–5, 189–91, 196, 203, 222, 272, 281–2, 319
Mir Hasan, 270
Mirian Mir, 270
misogi (禊), 94, 98, 103–4, 109–12
Mitákuye oyásiŋ, 249, 257
mitamashiro (御霊代), 120
Mithilā, 17
mizoume (溝埋), 108
Mizuhonokuni (瑞穂の国), 116
modernity, 90, 105, 137, 268, 272
mokṣa (liberation), 19, 21, 25–6, 32–4, 89. See persistence
Molefe, Motsamai, 167, 173, 181

momentariness theory, 18–19, 24, 78, 86
mononoke (もののけ), 97
Monolingualism of the Other; or, the Prosthesis of Origin, 288, 296–8, 303
Monster Slayer, 246
moral personhood / normative conception,159–66, 172–3, 181
Motoori Norinaga (本居宣長), 5, 95, 97, 99–100
Moyo, Herbert, 5, 8, 27 n. 2, 215–35
Mozambique, 43
multi-layered-ness, 118, 172
multiplicity, 42, 51, 73, 82
Munich, 9, 271
Mundra, Anil, 4, 27 n. 14, 38 n. 1, 71–91
Munro, Donald, 127, 137
Murunzi (Shadow / Essence of Being), 160, 167–73, 176–7
Muslim, 2, 9–10, 267–8, 270–3, 275, 277, 277–8 n. 4, 285
Mt. Fuji, 97
Muthu (Venda term for "person"), 167, 180–1

nafs (soul), 273
nagashibina, 110
nagí, Ghost, 248, 327 n. 3
nağila, cosmic energy, 327 n. 3
names, 51, 181, 190, 224, 242, 262, 264, 289, 271, 291–3
nanakusa gayu, 110
Nancy, Jean-Luc, 290
naobi/ naobinotama (直毘霊), 100, 116–17, 121, 123
naoki, or *choku* (直), 108, 114
narrative, 8, 42–4, 58–9, 61, 78, 95, 117, 138 n. 14, 195, 198, 210, 222–4, 252, 247, 253, 257, 306–7, 321
Nation and Sacrifice, 250. See Takahashi
nature, 5, 8, 12, 32, 44–5, 50, 52, 61, 63, 93–4, 96–7, 99–105, 110–12, 115, 117–18, 120–3, 131, 138 n. 12, 148, 163, 191–5, 206, 219–21, 225, 227, 231, 234–5, 239, 240–1, 244, 248, 320, 322, 324
Néiyé 內業 (Inward Training, NY), 191, 196
Needham, Joseph, 138 n. 11

networked self, 42
neurology, 305
neuroscience, 193
neutrality, 5, 109, 114, 116–17
newborn, 21, 25, 28 n. 23, 32, 246
Nguni worldview, 218–19, 221, 224, 227, 229, 234
Nigeria, 43
nigimitama (和魂), 104, 121
Nihonshoki (日本書紀), 94–5, 99, 100–1, 115–16, 120, 212, 123
niḥśreyasa, 26, 34, 36–7
Niniginomikoto (the ancestor of the emperor, 瓊瓊杵尊), 101
Nisbett, Richard, 135
niyá, Breath, 248, 327 n. 3
no-self theory (*anātman*), 22, 31, 34 n. 2
non-one-sidedness, theory of (*anekāntavāda*), 71, 73, 82–4, 87
non-violence, 32, 37, 83–4, 302, 327
nonpresence, 292
Norinaga, Motoori (本居宣長), 95, 97, 99–100
norito (祝詞), 95, 108, 109, 116
normative (vs. ontological) personhood, 160–6, 172–3
Nyāya, 15–36, 19–22, 83, 319, 320, 323
Nyāya-vārttika-tātparya-ṭīkā-pariśuddhi (Correctness of the Notes on the Meaning of the Gloss on the Commentary on Nyāya), 17, 27 n. 5
Nyāyabhāṣya, 34, 36
Nyāyakusumāñjali (A Handful of Flowers of Logic), 16, 18
Nyāyasūtra, 17, 27 n. 6

obedience, 154–6, 272, 275, 281–2, 285
obligations and responsibilities, 44, 46, 156, 160, 165, 240, 242, 244, 307, 324
obrigações (obligations), 46
odu (life path/destiny), 45, 57, 320
Of Grammatology, 289
oinikağe (Sweat Lodge ceremony), 257, 259
okra/ōkra (Akan Soul / Life-principle), 165, 169–70
olori (owner of the head), 45

omniscience, 79, 90–1
Ōmori Shōzō (1921–1997, 大森荘蔵), 117–18
onmyōdō (onmyō style, 陰陽道), 103
onmyōji (陰陽師), 103
Ontology, 79, 89, 160–72, 173 n.3, 176, 241, 301
Ooharae (大祓, purification ceremony), 110
Oomiwa (大三輪), 109–11, 122
Oomononushi (大物主神), 122
Oonamuchi (大穴牟遅神), 122
oonusa (大麻, 大幣), 109–10
Ootonohogai norito (大殿祭祝詞), 108
oppositional complementarity, 243, 246–7, 252, 264
organisms, 20, 33, 185, 205, 276, 322
organ, organs, 18, 20, 28 n. 23, 31–2, 36, 48, 68–9, 186–7, 190, 194, 207, 254–5, 273, 305–6
ori (head), 42, 45, 55–9, 318, 327 n. 3
orientalism, 1–2, 185
orixás (deities), 43–7, 66–9, 320
orum (spiritual realm), 43, 57
otás (stones), 47, 64, 66

pain, 20–1, 24–5, 28 n. 23, 25, 33, 38, 39 n. 3, 89, 209, 230
pairing, 131, 245, 252–3
parental, parent, 105, 108, 130, 149–50, 153–5, 206, 224, 227, 231, 269–70
Penelhum, Terence, 12
Penfield, Wilder, 117
perception, 19, 21–4, 26, 27 n. 12, 28 n. 16, 32, 68, 75, 136, 241, 273, 303
perfection, 246, 252, 284, 320
performance, 17, 49, 57, 96, 104, 110–12, 115, 137 n. 5, 149–52, 167, 173, 223, 225, 231, 234, 253, 293, 296, 303
Persian, 9, 267–70, 281
persistence, 36–38
personal cultivation, 126–8, 131–7, 139 n. 19, 143–4, 146–7, 156, 189–93, 196, 206, 273, 322–4, 327
personal identity, 76, 126, 131, 138 n. 9, 157, 162
personal narrative, 223

personality, 4, 20, 33, 45, 50, 55, 57, 63, 90, 105, 121–2, 128, 145, 162, 164–5, 193, 223, 271–5, 276, 285
personhood, person, 6–8, 34, 41–2, 45–6, 55, 58–9, 69, 96–7, 100–3, 105, 112, 121, 159–68, 171–2, 176, 180, 183–6, 189–90, 201–2, 205, 207, 209, 211, 241, 244, 267, 273, 325
  in African Philosophy, 159–66, 172–3, 180
  in Candoblé, 45–6, 55–6, 58–9, 69
  in Confucianism, 126–31, 136, 137 n. 1
  in Daoism, 183–6, 189–90, 201–2, 205
  in Indian thought, 20, 22–24, 31, 33–4, 36, 38
  in Islamic thought, 267, 273
  in Jainism, 76–9, 86
  in modern continental thought, 302, 308
  in Native Americans, 241–2, 244, 246
  in Shinto, 96–7, 100–3, 105, 112, 121
phenomenology, 4, 299 n. 2, 303
Phillips, Stephen, 34, 36–7
philosophy of mind, 78, 211
philosophy of religion, 2, 11–13, 27 n. 1, 26, 86, 201, 205, 209–10, 317, 326
philosophy, 1–3, 10, 16, 42, 207, 210, 267, 282, 287, 290–3, 297, 301–2, 303, 305, 310–12, 327 n. 2
physicalism, 4, 170
pleasure, 20–1, 24–6, 33, 36–8, 151
plurality, 10, 294, 298, 318, 327
pneumatology, 184, 195, 201–4
poetry, 9–10, 98, 114–15, 267–70
Porcher, José E., 3–4, 41–69
potlatch ceremony, 244, 265
power, 90, 97, 114–17, 122, 126, 131, 133, 146, 150–1, 155, 157, 189, 193–5, 198, 206, 221, 231, 238, 244, 245–9, 253–5, 258–9, 278 n. 8, 284, 297, 311, 314, 325
Prabhācandra, 83
practice, 1, 4–5, 7, 37, 42, 44, 46, 48, 57–8, 61–2, 66–9, 76, 91, 95, 103, 111, 125–6, 128–9, 131–2, 136, 137 n. 5, 145, 148–51, 177, 179–80, 184, 186, 188–90, 192, 197–8, 202, 207, 211, 216–18, 229–30, 235, 257, 280, 311–13, 322–6
Prakrit, 73, 82–3

Prandi, Reginaldo, 44, 55–7, 59 n. 1
praxis, 88, 211, 216, 220, 225
prerogatives, 262–5
Prior Analytics, 72
process cosmology, 131, 134
proclamation of the Great Doctrine (Taikyō senpu, 大教宣布), 105 n. 5
proper name, 291–2
psychology, 67, 135, 154, 184, 188–90, 195, 201, 268, 271
purification, 37, 48, 100, 104, 108, 109–11, 123, 253, 254, 259, 323
purity, 122–3
push, 284–5

Qadiryya, 270
Qi (energy or psycho-physical force), 109–10, 112, 131, 184, 187–8, 192–7, 202–3
qì 氣, 131, 184, 188, 202, 206–7, 211
qi-departure (気離れ), 109. See kegare
qi-exhaustion (気枯れ), 109. See kegare
qualities, 53 n. 4, 67, 73–6, 87, 133, 144, 186, 192, 194
Quasi-physicalism 169–72
Quran, 268–9, 272, 276, 281–2

Rabelo, Miriam, 47, 58, 67
Ram-Prasad, Chakravarti, 18, 21, 27 n. 11, 38
Raphals, Lisa, 137 n. 1
rationality, rational, 12, 16, 19, 36, 117, 126, 128, 133, 136, 169, 194, 198, 242, 271, 280
Raven, 243, 262
reality, 24, 31, 82, 114, 138 n.12, 166, 171, 188, 193, 271–3, 280, 321
reason, 83, 99, 150, 285, 290
rebirth, 19, 21, 32–4, 36–8, 231, 321, 324
reciprocity, 242, 265
recollection, 25, 28 n. 20
Reconstruction/ Reconstruction of Religious Thought in Islam, 268–9, 271, 272–6, 277 n. 1, 278 n. 8, 280, 283 n. 1, 286 n. 3
Reflections on the Philosophy of Hitlerism, 304 n. 3
Regla de Ocha, 43

rei (霊), 121–2
relationality, 98, 103, 105, 117–21, 163, 195, 240, 257, 259, 312, 323
renunciation, 90
repetition, 227–8, 292–3, 295, 324
Ṛg Veda, 89
Rio de Janeiro, 42
rites, 46–8, 62, 148, 184–5, 216, 218, 225, 231–4, 253–4
ritual, 5, 42–6, 48, 50–2, 55, 58, 61, 67–9, 88–9, 95–6, 98, 104, 108–12, 116, 122–3, 125–6, 128–33, 136, 137 n. 5, 138 n. 18, 143, 145, 147–52, 177, 179, 202, 209, 216–17, 225, 231–2, 234–5, 241, 248, 253–5, 258–60, 268, 322–5
Rogues, 310
roles (social), 105, 125–6, 128–3, 135, 143, 147–9, 152, 154–5, 157, 258
Rosemont, Henry, 128–30, 138 n.14
Rostalska, Agnieszka, 2–4, 15–26, 33–4, 36, 77
Rumi, 272, 281, 284–5

są' naghái bik'e hózhǫ (SNBH), 225
sacrifice, 42, 44, 49, 57–8, 127, 148, 232, 260, 281, 306–7, 322–3
sage, sagehood, 21,132, 138 n.7, 15, 194, 323
Salvador, 42, 43
Samantabhadra, 83–4
Sāṃkhya, 18, 32, 34 n. 5
saṃsāra, 31–2
Sanmatitarka, 73-4
Sansi-Roca, Roger, 48
Sanskrit, 12, 23, 34, 36, 71, 76, 81–3, 86, 89, 184, 203
santería, 43
santo (saint), 46, 61–65
Sato, Hiroo (佐藤 弘夫), 102
Sato, Maki, 4–5, 27 n. 2, 93–124
Sayed Ahmad Khan, 270
Schmidt, Bettina E., 44–5
Schmitt, Carl, 313
Schwarz, Maureen, 245–6, 253–5
Searle, John R., 299 n. 9
secret, secrecy, 48, 117, 268, 306–8, 312
secularization, 271, 314

Segato, Rita Laura, 44, 48–9
self (*ātman*), 19, 21, 25, 27 n. 10, 31–4, 71, 76, 82, 319, 327 n. 3
self and Persistence (Venda concept), 166–8
self-actualization, self-actualizing, 268–72, 281, 324
self-control, 135–6, 272, 275, 280–2, 285
self-discipline, 96–9, 103
self-immortalizing, 273, 275, 280, 282–4
selfhood, 6, 9–10, 123, 125–7, 129, 132–6, 137 n. 2, 267–9, 272–3
Seligman, Rebecca, 44
sensei (潜性), 100
settlement, 47–9, 58, 61–2, 66–8, 237, 260
Shadow (as Spiritual Double), 168–72, 176
Shagoon (collective identity), 264
shēn 身, 138 n. 18, 183, 185, 191, 194–5, 202, 205–7, 327 n. 3
shinboku (神木), 101
shinbutsu-shūgō (神仏習合), 96
shinchoku (entrusted words, 神勅), 116
Shinobu Origuchi (折口信夫, 1887–1953), 112 n. 1
shinsen （神饌）, 96
shintai (神体), 101
Shinto (神道), 94–6, 98–9, 106 n. 6, 319, 323
Shintōdenju (神道伝授), 99
Shoemaker, Sydney, 4, 71–2, 75–6
shōjiki (正直), 103
Shuka (individual identity), 264
Shun, Kwong-Loi, 135, 138 n. 9, 15
Shuowen Jiezi, 143
Shusterman, Richard, 138 n. 17
Sialala (Venda Philosophy of Life), 179–82
šičuŋ, Spirit or life-force, 28, 249, 258
Siddhasena, 73–4, 83–4, 87
Silva, Vagner Gonçalves, 45, 52
singularity, 73, 290, 303, 308
Sivin, Nathan, 138 n. 17
slaves, 243–3, 262
smṛti, 20
social organization, 262, 320
society, 98, 105, 108, 121–3, 127–8, 135, 149–51, 162–3, 275, 291, 293, 310, 326
somatology, 184, 195, 198, 205–6, 209–10
Sommer, Deborah, 126, 132, 138 n. 17, 18

sorcery, 66, 255
sovereignty, 310–15
Speech and Phenomena, 291–4, 288, 292, 297, 302
speech, interior, 292, 297
spirit possession, 42, 44
spiritual, spirituality, 4, 8, 20, 25–6, 33, 37, 43, 45, 47–8, 50, 55, 57, 66–7, 69, 76, 101, 103–4, 109, 114, 116, 121, 169, 172, 189, 195, 229, 230, 235, 320, 322, 324
Śrīharṣa, 17
Śrīhīra, 17
stage, 55, 66, 227, 229, 260, 273, 275–6, 280, 282, 285
State Shinto (国家神道), 96, 99, 105 n. 5
Strawson, Galen, 11–12
striving, 269, 272–4, 282, 319
struggle, 164, 223–4, 252, 281–2
Studio Ghibli, 102
subjectivity, 129, 201, 205, 242, 271, 274, 276, 290
substance, 19–20, 27 n. 6, 28 n.17, 32–3, 72–5, 87, 89, 193, 195–6, 252, 276
subtlety, subtle, 7, 22, 100, 194–7, 201–2, 206–7, 211, 252
sufi, 269–70, 277 n. 4, 281, 284, 319, 321
Sugawara no Michizane (菅原道真) 97-8, 100
Susanoo, the son of Izanagi, 108, 111, 116
suzu-bell (鈴), 115
Swanton, John, 243
Swinburne, Richard, 12
syncretic, 17, 97–8
syncretism, 44, 61, 62, 84

Tachibana Tadakane (橘忠兼), 101
Tachikawa, 18, 27 n. 4
tadashiki, or *shō* (正), 108, 114
Tajiri, Yuichiro (田尻, 祐一郎), 99
Takamimusumi (高御産巣日神), 116
takusen (託宣, revelation), 116
tama-furi (魂振), 123
tama-shizume (鎮魂), 123
tama （魂、霊）, 94, 97, 99, 101, 103, 114–18
Tambor de Mina, 43

tanka (short poems, 短歌), 99, 114–15
Tao. *See* Dao
Taoism. *See* Taoism
taoyameburi (手弱女振り), 100
tatarigami (cursing god, 祟り神), 98
Tattvārthasūtra (That Which Is), 73-4, 83, 86, 90
Taylor, Charles, 129, 277
telos, 268, 274, 280, 281–2
Tempels, Placide, Force and Communal Thesis, 160–4
temporal, 26, 37, 72–4, 76, 78, 98, 120, 280, 299 n. 4, 325
Tenjin (天神), 97
Tenjōmukyū (天壌無窮), 116
tension, 275–6, 282
terreiro (temple), 43, 45, 47–9, 51, 53 n. 3, 63, 67, 69
testimony
The Essay on the Dialectic of Right Thinking (Sanmatitarkaprakaraṇa), 83, 87
The Other Heading, 310
The Politics of Friendship, 310
theism, 311, 313
theology, 7, 42, 188, 198, 314, 320
Thevhula (Sacrificial Ritual), 177–8
thióšpaye, 257, 260
thiwáhe, 257
thought experiment, 16, 210, 290
ti (body), 132, 157, 183, 185, 205, 327 n. 3
time, 24, 37, 50, 72, 76, 83, 90, 138 n. 12, 151, 168, 273, 275, 280, 292, 293, 299 n. 4, 5, 302, 319
Tlingit, 241–4, 262–5, 265 n. 1, 318, 320
tochi-gami (土地神), 102
toga (mistakes, 咎/科), 108–9, 123
Togo, 43
Too Many Daves, 291–2
toraijin (渡来人), 96
Torii gate, 111
Totality and Infinity, 304 n. 3
Totem poles, 243
traits, 34, 36, 44–5, 63, 75–6, 79, 128, 135, 164, 193, 210
trance, 37, 41, 44–5, 48, 51, 61
transatlantic slave trade, 43

transformation, 32, 44, 51, 57–58, 62–4, 68, 74, 98, 112, 114, 132–5, 137, 143, 149, 157, 162, 187–8, 194, 197, 209–11, 223, 259–60, 265, 284
tsukumo-gami (付喪神), 101–2
Tsukuyomi, 111
tsumi (罪, sins), 108–9, 112 n. 1, 123
tsurugi (剣, sword), 120
tsutsushimi (verb. *tsutsushimu*, 慎む), 112 n. 1

Ubuntu, 167, 177, 181
Udayana, 15–36, 319, 320, 327 n. 3
ujō (有情), 117
Ukufa, 225, 230–3
ultimate, 31, 34, 170, 188, 203, 247, 269, 305, 311–12, 319, 321–2, 325
Ultimate Ego, 271, 274–5, 280–2, 284
Umāsvāti/Umāsvāmi, 73–4, 83, 86, 90
umina/ubumina, 216, 220, 225 n.1, 318, 327 n. 3
umoya, 216, 220, 225, 227, 229, 233–5
umuntu ngumuntu ngabantu, 218–20, 222, 224, 228–9
umuntu, 216, 218–20, 222–4, 228
United States of America, 42, 241, 289, 312
unk, Passion, 247
*Upaniṣad*s, 86
Urdu, 270, 273
Urerela / Vhurereli (worship / religion), 180–1
uttarapakṣa, 17

value-neutrality, 114
value, 67, 76, 78–9, 83, 93–4, 98, 114, 116–18, 128–30, 145, 151–7, 172–3, 177, 180, 181 n. 1, 193, 202, 216, 218, 220, 223–4, 227–9, 238, 268, 281–2, 285–6, 322, 326
Vedas, 21, 86
Venda Culture and Personhood, 166–72, 176–82
vessel-based model (of self), 42
Victory-Flag of Non-One-Sidedness (Anekāntajayapatākā), 83, 87
violence, 32, 37, 83, 84, 192, 289, 301–2, 327

virtual/actual distinction, 50
voduns (*Fon/Ewe* deities), 52 n. 1
Viveiros de Castro, Eduardo, 240–1
viceregency (Divine Viceregency), representative, *khalifa*, 270–3, 275, 280–3
virtue, 6, 37, 58, 103, 108, 114, 129, 133, 143–6, 154–5, 180, 192–3, 202, 277, 282–3
Vaiśeṣika, 17, 22, 27 n. 6
vāda, 17, 27 n. 6

Wafer, Jim, 51
Wang, Aihe, 138 n. 11, 12
wellbeing, well-being, 234–5, 253, 262
White Buffalo Calf Woman, 248
Who Comes After the Subject?, 290
Wičháša wakȟáŋ (Holy Men)
Wilder Penfield, 117
William James, 117, 274
wiŋkte, 258
Wíŋyaŋ wakȟáŋ (Holy Women), 258
Wiredu, Kwasi, 165, 169–70, 180–1
witches, 177, 219, 235, 247, 256 n. 3, 323
Without Alibi, 310
wíwáŋyaŋ wačhipi (Gazing at Sun Dance), 257, 260
Wóȟpe, the Feminine, 247–8
Wolf, Margery, 134
Wong, David, 133, 135–6, 137 n. 1
Worl, Rosita, 243, 264
world, 1, 3, 5, 7, 9, 10, 13, 24–5, 31, 43–6, 50–1, 55–6, 66–9, 89–90, 94–5, 97–101, 103–5, 111, 114, 116, 120, 123, 127, 131–4, 138 n. 12, 139 n. 19, 151–2, 157, 169–71, 173, 185, 188, 192–4, 198, 205–7, 209, 211, 217–18, 223, 227, 235, 240–8, 252–5, 260, 264, 268–9, 274–5, 281–2, 284–5, 290, 292–3, 295–6, 298, 299 n. 3, 306–8, 311–13, 319, 322–3, 326–7

worldviews, 2, 8, 32, 38, 45, 129, 131, 134–5, 179, 196, 202, 210, 216–21, 224–5, 227–9, 231, 233–4, 249, 252

Xangô (Pernambuco tradition), 43–4, 48, 61, 63, 64 n. 1, 66, 68
xin, *xīn* (mind/heart-mind), 135, 138 n. 9, 145, 184, 189–91, 193, 202, 206, 327 n. 3
xíng (form or shape), 183, 185, 191–2, 195, 205–6, 327 n. 3
xing (human nature), 134, 138 n. 18, 183, 185, 191–2, 195, 205–6, 327 n. 3
xue (learning), 130
Xunzi [荀子] (*Xunzi* text), 125, 131, 138 n. 18, 143, 145, 148–9, 155

yadoru (宿る), 120
Yagokoro-omoikane (八意思兼神, eight consciousness and thoughts), 116
yaku-barai (厄払, to prevent misfortune), 110
Yamanoue no Okura (山上憶良), 115
Yamato, 大和, 115
Yamazaki Ansai (1619–1682, 山崎闇斎), 99
yaorozu no kami (八百万の神), 95
yashiro (社), 95
yin-yang, 103, 131, 196, 202, 321
yogoto (寿詞), 116
yōkai (妖怪), 97
yomi (黄泉国, hades), 111
yorishiro (依代), 101, 110, 117, 120
Yoruba-Atlantic model, 42
Yoruba, 42–3, 45, 52 n.1, 55–57, 59 n.1, 61
Yoshida Shinto (吉田神道), 96
yuru-kyara (ゆるキャラ), 102

Zahavi, Dan, 299 n. 2
Zhongyong [中庸], 138 n. 8
Zhuāngzǐ, Zhunagzi, 莊子, 155, 187, 189, 192, 194, 199 n. 4. See *Book of Master Zhuang*
Zuozhuan [左傳], 138 n. 8